Ineffective Assistance of Counsel: Overcoming the Inevitable

Kelly Patrick Riggs

Freebird Publishers
www.FreebirdPublishers.com

Freebird Publishers

221 Pearl St., Ste. 541, North Dighton, MA 02764
Info@FreebirdPublishers.com
www.FreebirdPublishers.com

Copyright © 2019
Ineffective Assistance of Counsel: Overcoming the Inevitable
By Kelly Patrick Riggs

All Freebird Publishers titles, imprints and distributed lines are available at special
quantity discounts for bulk purchases for sales promotions, premiums,
fundraising educational or institutional use.

ISBN-13: 978-1-7332826-3-5

Printed in the United States of America

confirm all available citations for accuracy before quoting in briefs and/or motions. Some words have been added or omitted to enhance the clarity for the layman of law.

FOREWORD

My name is Thomas Robert Rodella, and I am a federal prisoner at the Federal Correctional Institution in Seagoville, Texas. I am not a professional spokesperson, nor am I being paid to write this foreword. In reality I was surprised when Kelly Patrick Riggs asked me to share my experiences with others who could benefit. At first, I was emotional, but I also felt honored that Kelly asked me to share my thoughts with the world.

My nightmare started shortly after I was elected Sheriff of Rio Arriba County in Northern New Mexico. I ran for office on the platform that I would fight the federal authority of the Forest Rangers who were victimizing our citizens. I had vowed to discontinue the previous standard of "Commissioning the Forest Rangers," which would stop them from having authority to enforce federal laws on County and State highways in Rio Arriba County. I was the first county sheriff in the state of New Mexico to take a stand against the Forest Rangers. Not long after I announced my plans, the United States Attorney, Damon Martinez, promised that he would prosecute me on "federal charges" if I interfered with the Forest Rangers being deputized.

On March 11, 2014, Damon Martinez would finally get his chance to prosecute me as promised. My son and I were driving home when a reckless driver entered onto the roadway without stopping or yielding to oncoming traffic. The driver skidded to a stop after two near collisions. We pulled over to be present in the event the driver required medical assistance.

As I approached his car on foot, I believed the driver to be dazed as he waved for me to come closer to his car. To my surprise, the driver sped away, nearly striking me with his car. Years later, new evidence would reveal that the driver had a gun. After a short pursuit, the driver again attempted to run me over. Although he was unsuccessful, he did strike me with his car. During my attempt to end the dangerous situation, the driver attempted to strip me of my firearm. I have no doubt that had he been successful, he would have used it against me. He was later arrested, a process that involved three other deputies. Although I didn't know it at the time, the deputies mishandled or concealed evidence, thus withholding important additional elements of probable cause. With help from deputies who were willing to mishandle and conceal evidence and lie under oath, U.S. Attorney Damon Martinez was able to fulfill his threat to prosecute me.

In preparation for trial, I hired Robert Gorence, a Federal Attorney who I believed knew the system well. I discovered, after paying him a large detainer, which he failed to investigate any aspect of my case outside of the evidence offered by the prosecution, he failed to request the "Jencks material" after the government's witness testified, and he refused to allow me to testify in court and defend myself as the first defense witness. I was ultimately convicted, followed by a swift denial of my appeal.

Soon after, the Supreme Court refused to hear my case.

I was transferred to Seagoville Federal Correctional Institution, and I began to prepare to make a federal post-conviction claim, which is reserved for federal prisoners. At that time, I had the good fortune of meeting two knowledgeable inmates who provided me with assistance in reviewing and gathering thousands of documents in preparation for filing my motion under § 2255. When the time came to reduce all our efforts to writing, God smiled upon me once again.

In January of 2019, I heard about a new arrival to the prison who, other prisoners claimed, had written some legal self-help books. I had trouble believing this, of course, but he was happy to show me. When I asked him, Kelly loaned me one of his books to read over the weekend. By the next week I realized that I needed Kelly on my team. I had heard about his technique of focusing on only the legal procedures that mattered, and his irritating habit of dismissing everything else. One of his favorite statements is, "You wanna go home, or do you wanna complain? You can't do both."

When I asked Kelly to help with filing my motion, his attention changed. It was like someone flipped a switch in his head, his conversation all but ended. Instead, he started to analyze my every word. It seemed that he was listening for something in particular. I had asked him to read my thousands of pages of material, but he always declined. I later learned what he was listening for – it was something that the court didn't already know. He had a level of concentration I had never seen before, like a puzzle master looking for the missing piece.

The first thing we did was write out the events from the beginning. I again nearly demanded that he read my pages; I had no idea that he was searching for my memories. One day about two weeks later, something I said clicked in his head. His change was almost audible. He told me something that I didn't realize; the key that separated my guilt or innocence was the "probable cause" to make an arrest. Once Kelly found his key, he started to demand that I bring him particular pages that he heard me talk about. Kelly had not yet read a single page out of my many boxes of papers, but it was like he already knew which ones he wanted, and he knew they were in there.

When we started to write my § 2255 motion, I wanted to argue about the evidence given at my trial. Again, Kelly dismissed my thoughts immediately. He said, "Don't give them what they already have, give them something *new* to consider."

We wrote out all of the important events from the beginning. Once we were finished Kelly said, "Now let's prove it. We don't just make a claim; we show them that we are correct by offering evidence."

Kelly and I engaged in many conversations about what I thought needed to be raised. He often didn't agree, nonetheless he showed a great deal of patience as we constructed my grounds for relief. He explained the need to present the facts that are not known to the court. When we were done, he set out to predict how the court would respond at each stage. As difficult as it was for me to believe, he was almost always right.

When we were finished writing my § 2255 motion, I read for the first time my own story in vivid detail. I couldn't help but think that the way it was presented was as clear as any modern novel. Kelly has a method of turning the facts of a case into a complete and informative narrative that tells the whole story. The most extraordinary aspect of my § 2255 motion is that it was filed 17 months after the statutory limitations of 28 U.S.C. § 2255 had expired. But Kelly showed me the procedure that allowed the motion to be filed, and in his latest book – that you now hold – he shows everyone else how to do it too!

Thomas R. Rodella

ACKNOWLEDGEMENT

As with most year-long projects there are many people to thank. I'm grateful to those prisoners who trusted me enough to allow me to assist them in their fight for relief. Without them I wouldn't have had the drive to learn so many different aspects of federal criminal law. I would like to give a special thanks to former attorney Michael Billings for his past and future guidance.

Most importantly, I would like to thank Diane Schindelwig, the CEO of Freebird Publishers, for believing in me and giving me my big chance to become a published author. She, of course, still spurs me on today. I encourage all my readers to give Diane a call if you're serious about writing a book.

SCOPE AND PURPOSE

My goal, as I write this book, is to provide an understanding of what ineffective assistance of counsel is, rather than simply show examples. This goal can only be accomplished by exposing you, the reader, to what is considered to be the *effective* assistance of counsel. What you are about to see is the standard of the effective assistance of counsel that is prescribed by The American Bar Association, along with the standards as viewed by the Supreme Court of the United States, thereby taking you beyond mere examples of the opposite, ineffective assistance of counsel. This book will provide the reader a clear and comprehensive view of what the courts view as the prevailing professional norms of defense counsels' performance in state and federal criminal courts.

This book is written in simple-to-understand terms. It is presented in the same format I have previously used in other books I have written about the post-conviction relief process. My goal is to present what are reasonable expectations about the legal profession in a language that the layman can understand and show you that anything your lawyer did – or did not do – that prevented you from presenting your case is Ineffective Assistance of Counsel.

TABLE OF CONTENTS

INTRODUCTION

All good books start with a good idea, the discipline to finish, and great passion for a subject. Although I have the passion and discipline to finish, the idea was not entirely my own. The idea for this book came from my publisher – yes, my very own heart and soul when it comes to writing. Also, it wasn't until I traced back over my years of study and research – coupled with my own experiences with the legal profession – that I realized the need for a more modern reference that defines ineffective assistance of counsel. Needless to say, had I known years ago what I know now, things in my life would be much different.

For those of you who have read my collection of books on post-conviction relief, you know that I have touched on this subject before. But, at no time before now have I illustrated such a clear view of what reasonable expectations you should have, under the law, when you are represented by counsel in a criminal proceeding. What's most important, however, is that these expectations are hardly ever met. I have also discovered that many practicing attorneys themselves have no idea what level of duty or service the client is actually entitled to.

In my seven-year study of advanced *habeas corpus* procedure, I have discovered that the ineffective assistance of counsel is the normal rather than the exception. In most cases I have studied, and in nearly all cases I have assisted in the litigation of, counsel failure was a common cause of judicial failure. It occurs so often that it no longer shocks the senses of any court but is defended in every court. The ineffective assistance of counsel is in fact a national epidemic that is at the root of the mass incarceration problem in America. As we can see with The First Step Act, which was passed into law on December 21, 2018, the U.S. Congress is attempting to correct the harms that lawyers have laid upon the backs of the American people. One very specific example is that of interpreting 18 U.S.C. 924 (c)(1)(C)(i), which refers to a "second or subsequent conviction." I am truly amazed at the years lost and the pain caused because of lawyers who refuse to provide their honest service. These four words clearly mean that it was passed to punish conduct that followed a previously finalized conviction, yet judges and attorneys refuse to implement a lawful reading of the statute. This is an example of ineffective assistance of counsel at its best. Read also *Welch v. United States*, 136 S. Ct. 1257 (2016) concerning retroactivity.

This plague, however, doesn't stop effecting only the reputations of lawyers; it goes on to erode the trust we can have in the integrity of our courts, and it undermines the freedom of America as a whole. It is for this reason that I have written this book for the layman and the ethical lawyers who represent them.

PART ONE
CHAPTER ONE

THE RIGHT TO COUNSEL

I have said many times before that you can't repair what you are unable to identify as broken. With that in mind try to imagine how you can possibly identify attorney conduct as ineffective if you are unfamiliar with what is expected, under reasonable professional standards. Unfortunately, specific guidelines that set bright line limitation on the prevailing norms of practice do not exist. The American Bar Association standards, and other standards that are similar, provide guides to determining what is reasonable, but they are nothing more than guides.

The effective assistance of counsel is defined as: "A conscientious, meaningful legal representation, whereby the defendant is advised of all rights and the lawyer performs all required tasks reasonably according to the prevailing professional standards in criminal cases," see Fed. R. Crim. P. 44; and 18 U.S.C.A. §3006A.

> "The law is in flux on precisely what constitutes the 'effective' assistance of counsel. The Supreme Court has yet to set forth a definitive standard, and lower courts have adopted differing ones. Prior to the 1970's the most common standard was the 'mockery of justice' standard, under which counsel's assistance was 'ineffective' only when it was so inadequate that it reduced the trial 'to a farce' or rendered it a 'mockery of justice.' Since that time, most courts have abandoned this formulation in favor of more stringent requirements, stipulating, for example, that 'counsel must exercise [the] normal skill and knowledge which normally prevails at the time and place' (Moore v. United States, 432 F.2d 730 (3rd Cir. 1970)), that counsel must render the 'reasonably competent assistance of an attorney acting as his diligent advocate' (United States v. Decoster, 487 F.2d 1197 (D.C. Cir. 1973)), or that counsel's representation must be 'within the range of competence demanded of attorneys in criminal cases' (Marzullo v. Maryland, 561 F.2d 540 (4th Cir. 1977)). All of these new standards beg the question of what traditional level of practice is to be regarded as 'customary,' 'diligent,' or 'reasonable.' Thus, little has been definitively resolved by the new, higher standard," Arval A. Morris, "Right to Counsel," in Encyclopedia of Crime and Justice 278, 283 (Sanford H. Kadish Ed., 1983)." – Blacks Law Dictionary Tenth Edition (Bryan A. Garner, Editor in Chief).

As you can see, in this not-so-simple definition, the meaning of "effective assistance" of counsel has never been established clearly. That's why, in my opinion, many of the books in print, and all the decisions by the Supreme Court of the United States, stop short of giving a clear and absolute definition. In the alternative, most sources provide only examples of what the effective assistance of counsel is or is not. This lack of definition ordinarily leaves the defendant, in the average case, without guidance as to whether his own counsel was or was not ineffective. Therefore, in the event the average defendant suffers from the effect of a less-than-diligent lawyer, he or she is left without relief unless counsel's deficiencies are identical to that of the deficient performance provided in a case previously decided.

Generally speaking, the effective assistance of counsel is a product of rights established by the Constitution of the United States and the laws of the United States, which shall be made in pursuance thereof. In America, any person accused of a serious offense has an absolute right to the assistance of counsel for his or her defense. More recently, the courts have decided that defense counsel must be provided to a criminal defendant who is unable to retain counsel on their own. That, of course, is at the government's expense. The right to counsel also means more than having an attorney by your side in court. Simply having an attorney physically present at the defendant's side during a criminal proceeding is insufficient to protect a defendant's rights. Thus, the right to counsel is understood as implying a right to the effective assistance of counsel, who is capable of actively advocating for the rights of his client.

THE SIXTH AMENDMENT

The fundamental right to the assistance of counsel in all criminal prosecutions is provided by the Sixth Amendment to the Constitution of the United States. Don't misunderstand; the Sixth Amendment prescribes a number of additional rights that a criminal defendant may enjoy that are not discussed here. For those who wish to possess a more thorough understanding of the rights provided by the Sixth Amendment, see Post-conviction *Relief: Advancing Your Claim*, available from Freebird Publishers.

Author's *Note: In my endeavor to assist the layman, pro se litigants, and their families; I am hesitant to present the amendments listed in this book, in part. Thus, I listed the amendments in full, italicizing the pertinent parts for clarity.*

The Sixth Amendment states that:

In all criminal prosecutions, the accused shall enjoy the right to a speedy and public trial, by an impartial jury of the state and district wherein the crime shall have been committed, which district shall have been previously ascertained by law, and to be informed of the nature and cause of the accusation; to be confronted with the witnesses against him; to have compulsory process for obtaining witnesses in his favor, and to have-the assistance of counsel for his defense."

Although this fundamental right is straight forward for all to understand; it has been continuously eroded by court decisions, one after another, for the last 228 years.

Understand also that the Sixth Amendment to the U.S. Constitution is a federal right. Thus, it absolutely pertains to federal prosecutions. The Supreme Court of the United States recognized the Sixth Amendment as to require that "counsel must be provided in federal courts for defendants unable to employ counsel, unless the right to counsel is competently and intelligently waived," see *Johnson v. Zerbst*, (1938) 304 U.S. 458, 82 L.Ed. 1461, 58 S. Ct. 1019.

THE FOURTEENTH AMENDMENT

The bill of rights, which was ratified in 1791, provided the right to the assistance of counsel in the Sixth Amendment. The ratification of the Fourteenth Amendment, in 1868, however, was the cause of the right to counsel being bestowed upon defendants in state prosecutions as well. It is a general implication from the Sixth Amendment, being applied through the due process clause of the Fourteenth, that brought equality among the federal and the state right to counsel in criminal prosecutions. The courts, however, have perverted congress's intent over the years to deny defendants in the state preceding the right to counsel. One Supreme Court decision in particular held that the due process clause of the Fourteenth Amendment does not confer on an indigent person charged with [a] crime in a state court an absolute right, independent of the circumstances, to have counsel appointed for him, see *Betts v. Brady*, 316 U.S. 455, 86 L. Ed. 1595, 62 S. Ct. 1252 (1942). The high court went on to say that "The Sixth Amendment of the national Constitution applies only to trials in federal courts. The due process clause of the Fourteenth Amendment does not incorporate, as such, the specific guarantee found in the Sixth Amendment," 316 U.S. 461 id.

The Fourteenth Amendment states:

Section 1 [Citizens of the United States]

All persons born or naturalized in the United States, and subject to the jurisdiction thereof, are citizens of the United States and of the State Wherein they reside. No State shall make or enforce any law which shall abridge the privileges or immunities of citizens of the United States; nor shall any

State deprive any person of life, liberty, or property, without due process of law; nor deny to any person within its jurisdiction the equal protection of the laws.

Section 2 [Representatives – Power to reduce apportionment.]

Representatives shall be apportioned among the several States according to their respective numbers, counting the Whole number of persons in each State, excluding Indians not taxed. But When the right to vote at any election for the choice of electors for President and Vice-President of the United States, Representatives in Congress, the Executive and Judicial officers of a State, or the members of the Legislature thereof, is denied to any of the male inhabitants of such State, being twenty-one years of age, and citizens of the United States, or in any way abridged, except for participation in rebellion, or other crime, the basis or representation therein shall be reduced in the proportion which the number of such male citizens shall bear to the whole number of male citizens twenty-one years of age in such State.

Section 3 [Disqualification to hold office.]

No person shall be a Senator or Representative in Congress, or elector of President and Vice-President, or hold any office, civil or military, under the United States, or under any State, Who, having previously taken an oath, as a member of Congress, or as an officer of the United States, or as a member of any State legislature, or as an executive or judicial officer of any State, to support the Constitution of the United States, shall have engaged in insurrection or rebellion against the same, or given aid or comfort to the enemies thereof but congress may by a vote of two-thirds of each House, remove such disability.

Section 4 [Public debt not to be questioned – Debts of the Confederacy and claims not to be paid.]

The validity of the public debt of the United States, authorized by law, including debts incurred for payment of pensions and bounties for services in suppressing insurrection or rebellion, shall not be questioned. But neither the United States nor any State shall assume or pay any debt or obligation incurred in aid of insurrection or rebellion against the United States, or any claim for the loss or emancipation of any slave; but all such debts, obligations and claims shall be held illegal and void.

Section 5 [Power to enforce amendment.]

The Congress shall have the power to enforce, by appropriate legislation, the provisions of this article.

GIDEON V. WAINWRIGHT

The Supreme Court of the United States, only 21 years after deciding *Betts v. Brady*, did a complete 180 degree turn away from its controlling precedent concerning state defendants. In *Gideon v. Wainwright*, 372 U.S. 335, 9 L. Ed. 2d 799, 83 S. Ct. 792 (1963), the defendant, who stood trial in a Florida State court for the charge of burglary – having broken and entered a poolroom with intent to commit a misdemeanor – was denied appointed counsel by the trial court on the ground that under the laws of Florida, only a defendant charged with a capital offense was entitled to such an appointment. After his conviction, the defendant filed in the Supreme Court of Florida the present *habeas corpus* petition, attacking his conviction on the ground that his federal Constitutional rights were violated by the trial court's failure to appoint counsel. The court denied relief.

On petition for *certiorari*, the Supreme Court of the United States reversed, in doing so it overruled it's previous holding in *Betts v. Brady*, 316 U.S. 455, wherein it had been decided that the due process of law did not require that in every case, regardless of circumstance, an indigent defendant must be provided counsel by the State.

In the opinion by Justice Black, it was held that the Sixth Amendment's provision that in all criminal prosecutions the "accused shall enjoy the right to have the assistance of counsel for his defense" was made obligatory upon the States by the Fourteenth Amendment.

18 U.S.C. §3006A

As you can see by these few illustrations, the Constitutional term "assistance of counsel for his defense" has been evolving for many years. It's obvious that depending on the courts to settle on a unanimous understanding of its meaning is a lost cause. Thus, the United States Congress took a shot at it as well. Congress addressed the meaning of the Sixth Amendment right to "the assistance of counsel for his defense," as a form of damage control in the aftermath of *Gideon v. Wainwright*. The right was codified in 18 U.S.C. §3006A in 1964, the year following the court's decision.

> *Author's Note: Notice also that Congress changed the wording of the right in an attempt to be clear that the act was not in any way an attempt to amend the amendment. In the new law, Congress established an independent right, "adequate representation," as opposed to "the right to the assistance of counsel for his defense." In my opinion, this is where ineffective assistance of counsel was born.*

The *assistance of counsel* and *representation* are two different things: assistance of counsel means that you have a right to have someone studied in law with you in a criminal proceeding to help you present your case, to protect your due process right that allows you to be heard. Representation, on the other hand, is a condition where someone acts on someone else's behalf, pretending to be the person represented, in persona. In most cases the representative meets with the client, quickly gleans through the facts, and decides for the client what should be heard. Unfortunately for most, the representative demands a large retainer then seeks to determine the quickest resolution to the case. This is done to minimize the cost of time spent, thus maximizing his profits.

18 U.S.C. §3006A is a long statute that is procedural in nature. Its purpose is to direct judicial districts concerning how to compensate representatives more so than confer rights on American citizens. Again, I'm including the full text of the statute only to be thorough, the pertinent points are italicized.

18 U.S.C. §3006A states the following:

§ 3006A. Adequate representation of defendants

(a) Choice of plan. Each United States district court, with the approval of the judicial council of the circuit, shall place in operation through the district a plan for furnishing representation for any person financially unable to obtain adequate representation in accordance with this section. Representation under each plan shall include counsel and investigative, expert, and other services necessary for adequate representation. Each plan shall provide the following:

(1) Representation shall be provided for any financially eligible person who –

(A) is charged with a felony or a Class A misdemeanor;

(B) is a juvenile alleged to have committed an act of juvenile delinquency as defined in section 5031 of this title [18 USCS §5031];

(C) is charged with a violation of probation;

(D) is under arrest, when such representation is required by law;

(E) is charged with a violation of supervised release or faces modification, reduction, or enlargement of a condition, or extension or revocation of a term of supervised release;

(F) is subject to a mental condition hearing under chapter 313 of this title [18 USCS § 4241 *et seq.*];

(G) is in custody as a material witness;

(H) is entitled to appointment of counsel under the sixth amendment to the Constitution;

(I) faces loss of liberty in a case, and Federal law requires the appointment of counsel; or

(J) is entitled to the appointment of counsel under section 4109 of this title [18 USCS §4109].

(2) Whenever the United States magistrate [United States magistrate judge] or the court determines that the interests of justice so require, representation may be provided for any financially eligible person who –

(A) is charged with a Class B or C misdemeanor, or an infraction for which a sentence to confinement is authorized; or

(B) is seeking relief under section 2241, 2254, or 2255 of title 28.

(3) Private attorneys shall be appointed in a substantial proportion of the cases. Each plan may include, in addition to the provisions for private attorneys, either of the following or both:

(A) Attorneys furnished by a bar association or a legal aid agency.

(B) Attorneys furnished by a defender organization established in accordance with the provisions of subsection (g). Prior to approving the plan for a district, the judicial council of the circuit shall supplement the plan with provisions for representation on appeal. The district court may modify the plan at any time with the approval of the judicial council of the circuit. It shall modify the plan when directed by the judicial council of the circuit. The district court shall notify the Administrative Office of the United States Courts of any modification of its plan.

(b) Appointment of counsel. Counsel furnishing representation under the plan shall be selected from a panel of attorneys designated or approved by the court, or from a bar association, legal aid agency, or defender organization furnishing representation pursuant to the plan. In every case in which a person entitled to representation under a plan approved under subsection 9(a) and appears without counsel, the United States magistrate [United States magistrate judge] or the court shall advise the person that he has the right to be represented by counsel and that counsel will be appointed to represent him if he is financially unable to obtain counsel. Unless the person waives representation by counsel, the United States magistrate [United States magistrate judge] or the court, if satisfied after appropriate inquiry that the person is financially unable to obtain counsel, shall appoint counsel to represent him. Such an appointment may be made retroactive to include any representation furnished pursuant to the plan prior to appointment. The United States magistrate [United States magistrate judge] or the court shall appoint separate counsel for persons having interests that cannot properly be represented by the same counsel, or when other good cause is shown.

(c) Duration and substitution of appointments. A person for whom counsel is appointed shall be represented at every stage of the proceedings from his initial appearance before the United States magistrate [United States magistrate judge] or the court through appeal, including ancillary matters appropriate to the proceedings. If at any time after the appointment of counsel the United States magistrate [United States magistrate judge] or the court finds that the person is financially able to obtain counsel, or to make partial payment for the representation, it may terminate the appointment of counsel or authorize payment as provided in subsection (f), as the interests of justice may dictate. If at any stage of the proceedings, including an appeal, the United States magistrate [United States magistrate judge] or the court finds that the person is financially unable to pay counsel whom he had retained, it may appoint counsel as provided in subsection (b) and authorize payment as provided in subsection (d), as the interests of justice may dictate. The United States magistrate [United States magistrate judge] or the court may, in the interests of justice, substitute one appointed counsel for another at any stage of the proceedings.

(d) Payment for representation.

(1) Hourly rate. Any attorney appointed pursuant to this section or a bar association or legal aid agency or community defender organization, which has provided the appointed attorney shall, at the conclusion of the representation or any segment thereof, be compensated at a rate not exceeding $60 per hour for time expended in court or before a United States magistrate [United States magistrate judge] and $40 per hour for time reasonably expended out of court, unless the Judicial Conference determines that a higher rate of not in excess of $75 per hour is justified for a circuit or for particular districts within a circuit, for time expended in court or before a United States magistrate [judge] and for time expended out of court. The Judicial Conference shall develop guidelines for determining the maximum hourly rates for each circuit in accordance with the preceding sentence, with variations by district, where appropriate, taking into account such factors as the minimum range of the prevailing hourly rates for qualified attorneys in the district in which the representation is provided and the recommendations of the judicial councils of the circuits. Not less than 3 years after the effective date of the Criminal Justice Act Revision of 1986, the Judicial Conference is authorized to raise the maximum hourly rates specified in this paragraph up to the aggregate of the overall average percentages of the adjustments in the rates of pay under the General Schedule made pursuant to section 5305 of title 5 on or after such effective date. After the rates are raised under the preceding sentence, such maximum hourly rates may be raised at intervals of not less than 1 year each, up to the aggregate of the overall average percentages of such adjustments made since the last raise was made under this paragraph. Attorneys may be reimbursed for expenses reasonably incurred, including the costs of transcripts authorize by the United States magistrate [United States magistrate judge] or the court, and the costs of defending actions alleging malpractice of counsel in furnishing representational services under this section. No reimbursement for expenses in defending against malpractice claims shall be made if a judgment of malpractice is rendered against the counsel furnishing representational services under this section. The United States magistrate or the court shall make determinations relating to reimbursement of expenses under this paragraph.

(2) Maximum amounts. For representation of a defendant before the United States magistrate [United States magistrate judge] or the district court, or both, the compensation to be paid to an attorney or to a bar association or legal aid agency or community defender organization shall not exceed $7,000 for each attorney in a case in which one or more felonies are charged, and $2,000 for each attorney in a case in which only misdemeanors are charged. For representation of a defendant in an appellate court, the compensation to be paid to an attorney or to a bar association or legal aid agency or community defender organization shall not exceed $5,000 for each attorney in each court. For representation of a petitioner in a non-capital *habeas corpus* proceeding, the compensation for each attorney shall not exceed the amount applicable to a felony in this paragraph for representation of a defendant before a judicial officer of the district court. For representation of such petitioner in an appellate court, the compensation for each attorney shall not exceed the amount applicable for representation of a defendant in an appellate court. For representation of an offender before the United States Parole Commission in a proceeding under section 4106A of this title [18 USCS §4106A], the compensation shall not exceed $1,500 for each attorney in each proceeding; for representation of an offender in an appeal from a determination of such Commission under such section, the compensation shall not exceed $5,000 for each attorney in each court. For any other representation required or authorized by this section, the compensation shall not exceed $1,500 for

each attorney in each proceeding. the compensation maximum amounts provided in this paragraph shall increase simultaneously by the same percentage, rounded to the nearest multiple of $100, as the aggregate percentage increases in the maximum hourly compensation rate paid pursuant to paragraph (1) for time expended since the case maximum amounts were last adjusted.

(3) Waiving maximum amounts. Payment in excess of any maximum amount provided in paragraph (2) of this subsection may be made for extended or complex representation whenever the court in which the representation was rendered, or the United States magistrate [United States magistrate judge] if the representation was furnished exclusively before him, certifies that the amount of the excess payment is necessary to provide fair compensation and the payment is approved by the chief judge of the circuit. The chief judge of the circuit may delegate such approval authority to an active or senior circuit judge.

(4) Disclosure of fees.

    (A) In general. Subject to subparagraphs (B) through (E), the amounts paid under this subsection for services in any case shall be made available to the public by the court upon the court's approval of the payment.

    (B) Pre-trial or trial in progress. If a trial is in pre-trial status or still in progress and after considering the defendant's interests as set forth in subparagraph (D), the court shall –

        (i) redact any detailed information on the payment voucher provided by defense counsel to justify the expenses to the court; and

        (ii) make public only the amounts approved for payment to defense counsel by dividing those amounts into the following categories:

            (I) Arraignment and or plea.

            (II) Bail and detention hearings.

            (III) Motions.

            (IV) Hearings.

            (V) Interviews and conferences.

            (VI) Obtaining and reviewing records.

            (VII) Legal research and brief writing.

            (VIII) Travel time.

            (IX) Investigative work.

            (X) Experts.

            (XI) Trail and appeals

            (XII) Other

    (C) Trial completed.

        (i) In general. If a request for payment is not submitted until after the completion of the trial and subject to consideration of the defendant's interests as set forth in subparagraph (D), the court shall make available to the public an un-redacted copy of the expense voucher.

        (ii) Protection of the rights of the defendant. If the court determines that defendant's interests as set forth in subparagraph (C) require a limited disclosure, the court shall dis- close amounts as provided in subparagraph (B).

(D) Considerations. The interests referred to in subparagraphs (B) and (C) are –

(i) to protect any person's 5th amendment right against self-incrimination;

(ii) to protect the defendant's 6th amendment rights to effective assistance of counsel;

(iii) the defendant's attorney-client privilege;

(iv) the work product privilege of the defendant's counsel;

(v) the safety of any person; and

(vi) any other interest that justice may require, except that the amount of the fees shall not be considered a reason justify any limited disclosure under section 3006A(d)(4) of title 18, United States Code [18 USCS 3006A (d)(4)].

(E) Notice. The court shall provide reasonable notice of disclosure to the counsel of the defendant prior to the approval of the payments in order to allow the counsel to request redaction based on the considerations set forth in subparagraph (D). Upon completion of the trial, the court shall release un-redacted copies of the vouchers provided by defense counsel to justify the expenses to the court. If there is an appeal, the court shall not release un-redacted copies of the vouchers provided by defense counsel to justify the expenses to the court until such time as the appeals process is completed, unless the court determines that none of the defendant's interest set forth in subparagraph (D) will be compromised.

(F) Effective date. The amendment made by paragraph (4) shall become effective 60 days after enactment of this Act [enacted Nov. 26, 1997], will apply only to cases filed on or after the effective date, and shall be in effect for no longer than 24 months after the effective date.

(5) Filing claims. A separate claim for compensation and reimbursement shall be made to the district court for representation before the United States magistrate [United States magistrate judge] and the court, and to each appellate court before which the attorney provided representation to the person involved. Each claim shall be supported by a sworn written statement specifying the time expended, services rendered, and expenses incurred while the case was pending before the United States magistrate [United States magistrate judge] and the court, and the compensation and reimbursement applied for or received in the same case from any other source. The court shall fix the compensation and reimbursement to be paid to the attorney or to the bar association or legal aid agency or community defender organization which provided the appointed attorney. In cases where representation is furnished exclusively before a United States magistrate [United States magistrate judge], the claim shall be submitted to him and he shall fix the compensation and reimbursement to be pa*id*. In cases where representation is furnished other than before the United States magistrate [United States magistrate judge], the district court, or an appellate court, claims shall be submitted to the district court which shall fix the compensation and reimbursement to be paid.

(6) New trials. For purposes of compensation and other payments authorized by this section, an order by a court granting a new trial shall be deemed to initiate a new case.

(7) Proceedings before appellate courts. If a person for whom counsel is appointed under this section appeals to an appellate court or petitions for a writ of *certiorari*, he may do so without prepayment of fees and costs or security therefor and without filing the affidavit required by section 1915(a) of title 28.

(e) Services other than counsel.

(1) Upon request. Counsel for a person who is financially unable to obtain investigative, expert, or other services necessary for adequate representation may request them in an ex parte application. Upon finding, after appropriate inquiry ill an ex parte proceeding, that the services are necessary and that the person is financially unable to obtain them, the court, or the United States magistrate [United States magistrate judge] if the services are required in connection with a matter over which he had jurisdiction, shall authorize counsel to obtain the services.

(2) Without prior request.

(A) Counsel appointed under this section may obtain, subject to later review, investigative, expert, and other services without prior authorization, if necessary, for adequate representation. Except as provided in subparagraph (B) of this paragraph, the total cost of services obtained without prior authorization may not exceed $800 and expenses reasonably incurred.

(B) The court, or the United States magistrate [United States magistrate judge] (if the services were rendered in a case disposed of entirely before the United States magistrate [United States magistrate judge]), may, in the interest of justice, and upon the finding that timely procurement of necessary services could not await prior authorization, approve payment for such services after they have been obtained, even if the cost of such services exceeds $800.

(3) Maximum amounts. Compensation to be paid to a person for services rendered by him to a person under this subsection, or to be paid to an organization for services rendered by an employee thereof, shall not exceed $2,400, exclusive of reimbursement for expenses reasonably occurred, unless payment in excess of that limit is certified by the court, or by the United States magistrate [United States magistrate judge] if the services were rendered in connection with a case disposed of entirely before him, as necessary to provide fair compensation for services of an unusual character or duration, and the amount of the excess payment is approved by the chief judge of the circuit. The chief judge of the circuit may delegate such approval authority to an active or senior circuit judge.

(4) Disclosure of fees. The amounts paid under this subsection for services in any case shall be made available to the public.

(5) The dollar amounts provided in paragraphs (2) and (3) shall be adjusted simultaneously by an amount, rounded to the nearest multiple of $100, equal to the percentage of the cumulative adjustments taking effect under section 5303 of title 5 [5 USCS §5303] in the rates of pay under the General Schedule since the date the dollar amounts provided in paragraphs (2) and (3), respectively, were last enacted or adjusted by statute.

(f) Receipt of other payments. Whenever the United States magistrate [United States magistrate judge] or the court finds that funds are available for payment from or on behalf of a person furnished representation, it may authorize or direct that such funds be paid to the appointed attorney, to the bar association or legal aid agency or community defender organization which provided the appointed attorney, to any person or organization authorized pursuant to subsection (e) to render investigative, expert, or other services, or to the court for deposit in the Treasury as a reimbursement to the appropriation, current at the time of payment, to carry out the provisions of this section. Except as so authorized or directed, no such person or organization may request or accept any payment or promise of payment to represent a defendant.

(g) Defender organization.

(1) Qualifications. A district or part of a district in which at least two hundred persons annually require the appointment of counsel may establish a defender organization as provided for either under

subparagraphs (A) or (B) of paragraph (2) of this subsection or both. Two adjacent districts or parts of districts may aggregate the number of persons required to be represented to establish eligibility for a defender organization to serve both areas. In the event that adjacent districts or parts of districts are located in different circuits, the plan for furnishing representation shall be approved by the judicial council of each circuit.

(2) Types of defender organizations.

(A) Federal Public Defender Organization. A Federal Public Defender Organization shall consist of one or more full-time salaried attorneys. An organization for a district or part of a district or two adjacent districts or parts of districts shall be supervised by a Federal Public Defender appointed by the court of appeals of the circuit, without regard to the provisions of title 5 governing appointments in the competitive service, after considering recommendations from the district court or courts to be served. Nothing contained herein shall be deemed to authorize more than one Federal Public Defender within. a single judicial district. The Federal Public Defender shall be appointed for a term of four years, unless sooner removed by the court of appeals of the circuit for incompetency, misconduct in office, or neglect of duty. Upon the expiration of his term, a Federal Public Defender may, by a majority vote of the judges of the court of appeals, continue to perform the duties of his office until his successor is appointed, or until one year after the expiration of such Defender's term, whichever is earlier. The compensation of the Federal Public Defender shall be fixed by the court of appeals of the circuit at a rate not to exceed the compensation received by the United States Attorney for the District where representation is furnished or, if two districts or parts of districts are involved, the compensation of the higher paid United States attorney of the districts. The Federal Public Defender may appoint, without regard to the provisions of title 5 governing appointments in the competitive service, full-time attorneys in such number as may be approved by the court of appeals of the circuit and other personnel in such number as may be approved by the Director of the Administrative Office of the United States Courts. Compensation paid to such attorneys and other personnel of the organization shall be fixed by the Federal Public Defender at a rate not to exceed that paid to attorneys and other personnel of similar qualifications and experience in the Office of the United States attorney in the district where representation is furnished or, if two districts or parts of districts are involved, the higher compensation paid to persons of similar qualifications and experience in the districts. Neither the Federal Public Defender nor any attorney so appointed by him may engage in the private practice of law. Each organization shall submit to the Director of the Administrative Office of the United States Courts, at the time and in the form prescribed by him, reports of its activities and financial position and its proposed budget. The Director of the Administrative Office shall submit, in accordance with section 605 of title 28, a budget for each organization for each fiscal year and shall out of the appropriations therefore make payments to and on behalf of each organization. Payments under this subparagraph to an organization shall be in lieu of payments under subsection (d) or (e).

(B) Community Defender Organization. A Community Defender Organization shall be a nonprofit defense counsel service established and administered by any group authorized by the plan to provide representation. The organization shall be eligible to furnish attorneys and receive payments under this section if its bylaws are set forth in the plan of the district or districts in which it will serve. Each organization shall submit to the Judicial Conference of the United States an annual report setting forth its activities and financial position and the anticipated caseload and expenses for the next fiscal year. Upon application an organization may, to the extent approved by the Judicial Conference of the United States:

(i) receive an initial grant for expenses necessary to establish the organization; and

(ii) in lieu of payments under subsection (d) or (e), receive periodic sustaining grants to provide representation and other expenses pursuant to this section.

(3) Malpractice and negligence suits. The Director of the Administrative Office of the United States Courts shall, to the extent the Director considers appropriate, provide representation for and hold harmless, or provide liability insurance for, any person who is an office or employee of a Federal Public Defender Organization established under this subsection which is receiving periodic sustaining grants, for money damages for injury, loss of liberty, loss of property, or personal injury or death arising from malpractice or negligence of any such officer or employee in furnishing representational services under this section while acting within the scope of that person's office or employment.

(h) Rules and reports. Each district court and court of appeals of a circuit shall submit a report on the appointment of counsel within its jurisdiction to the Administrative Office of the United States Courts in such form and at such times as the Judicial Conference of the United States may specify. The Judicial Conference of the Unites States may, from time to time, issue rules and regulations governing the operation of plans formulated under this section.

(i) Appropriations. There are authorized to be appropriated to the United States courts, out of any money in the Treasury not otherwise appropriated, sums necessary to carry out the provisions of this section, including funds for the continuing education and training of persons providing representational services under this section. When so specified in appropriation acts, such appropriations shall remain available until expended. Payments from such appropriations shall be made under the supervision of the Director of the Administrative Office of the United States Courts.

(j) Districts included. As used in this section, the term "district court" means each district court of the United States created by chapter 5 of title 28 [28 USCS §§81 *et seq.*], the District Court of the Virgin Islands, the District Court for the Northern Mariana Islands, and the District Court of Guam.

(k) Applicability in the District of Columbia. The provisions of this section shall apply in the United States District Court for the District of Columbia and the United States Court of Appeals for the District of Columbia Circuit. The provisions of this section shall not apply to the Superior Court of the District of Columbia and the District of Columbia Court of Appeals.

UNITED STATES V. CRONIC

Thanks in large part to the passing of 18 U.S.C. §3006A, criminal defendants started to take a long hard look at what "adequate representation" was, and more importantly what it was not. Of course, the right to representation is not Constitutional, as is the right to have "the assistance of counsel for his defense." Thus, those who realized the difference – and how even the Supreme Court of the United States preys on Americans by playing word games – began making Constitutional claims of "ineffective assistance of counsel." The most monumental claim of our modern time is that of *United States v. Cronic*, 466 U.S. 648, 80 L. Ed. 2d 657, 104 S. Ct. 2039. The Supreme Court made a significant attempt at clarifying the meaning of the sixth amendment. Although, previously addressed by courts around the country; *Cronic* was one of the first cases where the Supreme Court attempted to establish a bright line standard of the "effective assistance of counsel."

On July 17, 1980, Mr. Cronic was convicted in a United States district court. He was later sentenced on August 28, 1980. His counsel perfected a timely appeal, which was entered into record on September 11, 1980. Mr. Cronic made a claim challenging the competence of his trial counsel. The court of appeal denied his claim and appointed new counsel for his appeal instead. On April 19, 1982, the court of appeals for the 10th Cir. reversed his conviction. The U.S. Attorney's Office filed for a petition writ of *certiorari* in the Supreme Court. The Supreme Court ruled against Mr. Cronic on May 14, 1984.

The court held that the principle that a defendant had the right to counsel; was in fact the right to have effective assistance of counsel. The court in *Cronic* made an attempt to show that the text of the sixth amendment suggested that the right to the effective assistance of counsel has always existed. The *Cronic* court noted that the sixth amendment requires not only that counsel be provided to criminal defendants, but that the "assistance" of counsel "for his defense" be provided. Therefore, the court held that the purpose of the sixth amendment's counsel guaranty is to assure that the defendant has that "assistance" at trial, when the defendant is confronted with both standards of law he doesn't understand and the tenacity of a professional public prosecutor; the Constitutional guaranty of, "the assistance of counsel for his defense," is violated when no actual assistance is provided.

The high court, in *Cronic*, determined that the adversarial process, protected by the sixth amendment, requires that counsel act as an advocate for the defendant. This determination established that the right to service the effective assistance of counsel is the right to require that the government's case be able to service meaningful adversarial testing. When a true adversarial trial in a criminal court has been conducted, the right to the effective assistance of counsel has been satisfied even if defense counsel may have made mistakes that can be proven, and regardless of the defendant's satisfaction or dissatisfaction with counsel's performance.

Bottom line, a defendant has a due process right to be heard in both state and federal courts, established by the fifth and fourteenth amendments to the Constitution of the United States. A criminal defendant has a right to the "effective assistance of counsel" to ensure that the due process right is fulfilled.

CHAPTER TWO

DEFINING INEFFECTIVE ASSISTANCE OF COUNSEL

In an effort to dismiss opinions that tend to split hairs concerning the application of the "effective" assistance of counsel standard set forth in *Cronic*; let me remind you that the Supreme Court has applied the standard upon all who represent another in criminal court. The Supreme Court has routinely rejected any arguments claiming that; the conduct of retained counsel should be treated differently because the State and or the government had no part in counsel's employment. The Court has held that the right to the effective assistance of counsel applies equally to counsel who is hired privately by the defendant. Needless to say, the Circuit court decision in *Cronic* caused a rush to the courthouse. In April of 1982, just like now, there are no shortages of legitimate Constitutional claims concerning ineffective assistance of counsel. The *Cronic* case was so pivotal that defendants, both state and federal, were drafting similar claims even before the U.S. Attorney's office was granted *certiorari*.

> *Author's Note: Keep in mind that Cronic had won his appeal in the Tenth Circuit court of appeals on April 19, 1982. It was based on that appeal that others were basing their claims. Mr. Cronic ultimately lost in the Supreme Court but not without defining the sixth amendment right to counsel.*

One of those cases was *Strickland v. Washington*, 466 U.S. 668, 80 L.Ed. 2d 674; 104 S.Ct. 2052. In the *Strickland* case, Mr. Washington had filed a motion for post-conviction relief in a Florida U.S. District Court, wherein he was denied relief. Mr. Washington filed for appeal in what was then the Fifth Circuit Court of Appeals. Mr. Washington won his appeal; the Warden of the Florida prison filed a petition for a writ of *certiorari* which was granted.

It's unclear if Mr. Washington specifically made a significant claim based on *Cronic*'s appeal in his initial brief; but it is clear that the Supreme Court of the United States intended to address its previous view of the right to counsel. The Court in *Cronic* established that the right to have "The assistance of Counsel," means - the right to the "effective" assistance of counsel. The high court, recognizing the possible outcome of the *Cronic* decision, along with the number of possible claims it was likely to produce, decided to hear the *Strickland* case on the very same day.

Mr. Cronic won his appeal in the Tenth Circuit on April 19, 1982. Mr. Washington won his appeal in the Fifth Circuit, now the Eleventh Circuit, on December 23, 1982. Both the Warden in *Strickland* and the U.S. Attorney in *Cronic* filed a timely petition for writs of *certiorari*. The Supreme Court had recognized an opportunity to address the issues of the growing ineffective assistance of counsel epidemic. This, however, could only be done by hearing both cases on the same day. January 10, 1984. Additionally, both were decided on the same day as well, May 14, 1984.

The Supreme Court had finally established a bright dividing line that separated claims that warranted relief from those who wished to take advantage of any possible technicality. The court had set out that if counsel's performance failed to live up to reasonable professional standards, at any critical stage of the criminal proceeding, then the defendant may have grounds for relief from his conviction and/or sentence. To limit this broad right to relief, established by *Cronic*, the court specified the conditions under which the relief may be granted.

STRICKLAND V. WASHINGTON

The Supreme Courts view in *Strickland v. Washington*, 466 U.S. 668, 80 L.Ed. 2d 674, 104 S.Ct. 2052, is the standard upon which all claims of ineffective assistance of counsel are decided. In evaluating if a defendant's right to the effective assistance of counsel have been violated, to a degree that entitles them to relief, all courts consider two main factors, known as the Two Prong *Strickland* Test:

- Prong One – Whether a lawyer's performance was below professional standards; and
- Prong Two – Whether the lawyer's client was prejudiced by that deficiency.

To decide on the first prong, whether the lawyer's performance was in fact deficient, courts look to whether the assistance provided by the lawyer was reasonably effective under prevailing professional norms, taking a wide variety of circumstances into consideration. Courts have repeatedly stated that such judicial scrutiny of counsel's performance must be highly deferential avoiding hindsight and evaluating counsel's alleged misconduct from counsel's perspective at the time it occurred. In other words, the court must protect the lawyer's reputation whenever possible, without basing its decision on the resulting harm to the client or the obviously erroneous assistance that caused an adverse outcome in the proceeding. It has been held that counsel's performance will be presumed to fall within the wide range of reasonable professional assistance and that a defendant raising a claim of ineffective assistance of counsel bears the heavy burden of proving the contrary.

As you can see the language used by the court is ambiguous at best. This places virtually all claims of ineffective assistance out of reach to the layman of law. Ever since 1984 the courts have decided ineffective assistance of counsel claims without any regularity in the outcome of the many proceedings.

Once you have reason to believe that your criminal defense lawyer provided unconstitutionally ineffective assistance of counsel, you must also consider how such a claim can be presented. In the Supreme Court's decision in *Massaro v. United States*, 538 U.S. 500 (2003), the court determined that a failure to raise an ineffectiveness claim on direct appeal could not serve as a bar against a prisoner who raised an ineffectiveness claim in a first-tier collateral proceeding. Although, the *Massaro* ruling seemingly favored prisoners; it also had a negative impact. The Thirteen Circuits of the U.S. Court of Appeals has since determined that all claims of ineffectiveness must be reserved for a collateral proceeding (2255). Thus, not only is the claim required to face the *Strickland* crucible; but now a prisoner must present the claim without the benefit of appointed counsel.

Taking a closer look at the *Strickland* standard also shows that the standard is actually a different process, in collateral proceedings as opposed to in direct appeal. The Supreme Court's decision, in *Strickland*, sets a standard to judge ineffective assistance of counsel claims. The stringent standard that *Strickland* presented was difficult for attorneys to particularize in the direct appeal process. After the *Massaro* decision an ineffectiveness claim became nearly impossible for a layman to define without the benefit of counsel to perfect the claim.

The *Strickland* standard took on a new level of scrutiny when applied to the collateral process as opposed to the direct appeal process. Because of the court's decision in *Massaro*, all claims of ineffective assistance of counsel, raised in a federal court, must be raised under 28 U.S.C. §2254, for state prisoners, or §2255 for federal prisoners. This raised a particularly troublesome problem for federal prisoners because, unlike the state prisoner, a federal prisoner has never had the benefit of counsel while evaluating for an ineffectiveness claim. In a §2255 proceeding all claims other than ineffectiveness claims are procedurally defaulted for not having been raised on direct appeal. Thus, every claim in a §2255 must be presented under the umbrella of an ineffective assistance of counsel claim.

What's most important for all prisoners and post-conviction lawyers to realize is that the *Strickland* standard sets a presumption; that all criminal defense lawyers have provided effective assistance. This is like starting a football game giving one team fifty points before they begin to play. Setting a presumption that one side of a litigation has already won, is not the standard in any other civil litigation. In all civil litigations, except collateral proceedings under §2254 and §2255, the parties start equally, with no presumptions; wherein one party, or the other, must demonstrate their side of the case by a simple preponderance of the evidence, or 50.01%.

A prisoner should question and prepare to understand how the presumption of effectiveness came to be. And, more importantly how does a layperson at law overcome being saddled with such a burden. The Supreme Court, in the *Strickland* decision, cites no controlling data, no professional research, or other facts to warrant a presumption of competence. The courts fact driven analysis in the *Strickland* decision cited *Michel v. Louisiana*, 350 U.S. 91, 100 L. Ed. 83, 76 S. Ct. 158 (1955): "The mere fact that a timely motion to quash was not filed does not overcome the presumption of effectiveness," United States ex rel. *Feeley v. Ragen*, 166 F. 2d. 976 (7th Cir. 1948).

In the *Feeley* case, the district court granted habeas relief based on (1) the bar association's find that Feeley's defense counsel's age had negatively affected counsel's mental abilities, and declaration that he was unfit to serve as a judge; (2) a lawyer of the Chicago Bar's testimony that Feeley's defense counsel was incapable of conducting an important criminal trial; and (3) the trial transcript's showing of several omissions by the attorney during the trial.

The Seventh Circuit reversed the district court's judgment holding that, "Whenever the court in good faith appoints or accepts the appearance of a member of the bar in good standing to represent a defendant, the presumption is that such counsel is competent. Otherwise, he would not be in good standing at the bar and accepted by the court." This is circular reasoning that means that, if an attorney is in good standing, then he can never be found to be incompetent (ineffective). Thus, the good standing label will protect him from all claims of ineffective assistance of counsel in collateral proceedings.

Now that you know where the baseless presumption in *Strickland* comes from, know also that a lawyer will never be found to be incompetent or ineffective. If this seems unclear to you it's because you are looking at the situation incorrectly. Although counsel error is likely the reason you are in prison, the problem is not your counsel. The problem, most likely, is that counsel error separated you from your Constitutional right. Thus, the root of the problem is a Constitutional violation, and counsel is only the "cause." Having your counsel declared incompetent or ineffective does little to help your situation. As satisfying as such a thing may sound, counsel's error is only part of the problem.

Having a lawyer declared incompetent or ineffective is as difficult as having a statute declared unconstitutional, and highly unlikely. Just as with invalidating a statute as unconstitutional, proving your lawyer is incompetent would require you to prove that he or she is incompetent, or ineffective, in every case he or she has ever represented, again highly unlikely. It's time to shift your point of view.

Regardless of how semantic this may sound; you must abandon the theory that all your problems are because your lawyer was ineffective. The true problem is that your counsel "provided ineffective assistance of counsel." Notice that in the first situation, much like in *Feeley*, the claim was against the lawyer personally. In the second the claim is against the assistance that counsel provided.

A claim of ineffective assistance of counsel should consist of three elements: 1) You have been deprived of a Constitutional right during a criminal proceeding; 2) It was due to counsel errors that the claim, or Constitutional violation, was not perfected for direct appeal, or counsel failed to raise the claim in direct appeal; and 3) The defendant was prejudiced by the deprivation of the Constitutional right. The defendant must be prepared to identify the Constitutional right he lost, what counsel did to cause it to be unreviewable, and the harm the defendant suffered by being deprived of the specified right.

CHAPTER THREE

IDENTIFYING INEFFECTIVE ASSISTANCE OF COUNSEL

A defendant who wishes to raise a claim of ineffective assistance of counsel must identify with particular counsel's error, along with prejudice, as in *Strickland*. First and foremost, however, there exists one class of defendants who have no right to raise an ineffectiveness claim.

PRO SE REPRESENTATION

Pro se is a Latin term that is loosely translated "in favor for self." This term, in a court, means that the defendant is representing himself. As confident such a gesture would seem it also means that the defendant has no right to make a Constitutional claim of ineffective assistance of counsel. In all courts a defendant has an absolute right to conduct his own business. In federal law this right is codified as 28 U.S.C. 1654. Unfortunately, when a criminal defendant decides to conduct his or her own business, he or she has waived their sixth amendment right to have the assistance of counsel for their defense. The Supreme Court has noted that a defendant who exercises his right to conduct his own defense cannot thereafter complain that the quality of the defense amounted to a denial of effective assistance of counsel, see *McKaskle v. Wiggins*, 465 U. S. 168, 79 L. Ed. 2d 122, 104 S. Ct. 944 (1984), for assessing the effect of standby defense counsel's unsolicited participation in a criminal trial on the defendant's right to conduct his own defense.

RETAINED COUNSEL

The right to the effective assistance of counsel, provided by The Sixth Amendment, applies to the service provided by all lawyers who represent a client in any criminal proceedings. This right is enjoyed by all criminal defendants without regard to whether counsel was selected and paid for by the defendant himself or appointed by a federal or state government.

The argument, that a defendant who hires his or her own counsel is entitled to a lower level of protection by the sixth amendments right to counsel, is often raised by the government in state proceedings. This argument, that the conduct of retained counsel does not involve state action, was rejected by the Supreme Court in *Cuyler v. Sullivan*, 466 U.S. 335, 64 L.Ed. 2d 333, 100 S.Ct. 1708. It's a common misconception that most counsel, whether retained or appointed, will protect the rights of the defendants. Experience has shown however, that often-retained counsel, just like appointed counsel, will not provide effective assistance of counsel simply because such assistance proves to be labor intensive on the part of the lawyer. It's because of this common professional norm that, the Supreme Court has ruled that, the vital guarantee of the sixth amendment would stand for nothing if the defendant's uniformed decision to hire a private lawyer could forfeit his or her right to the full Constitutional protection of the sixth amendment, see also *Evitts v. Lucey*, 469 U.S. 387,83 L. Ed. 2d 821. 105 S.Ct. 830 (1985) and *Mickens v. Taylor*, 535 U. S. 162, 152 L. Ed. 2d 291. 122 S. Ct. 1237 (2002).

EXAMINE COUNSEL PERFORMANCE

When it comes to claims for post-conviction relief, ineffective assistance of counsel ranks as the number one most often asserted claim. In federal proceedings it is the only claim that cannot be attacked, as waived, after the, time for direct appeal has expired. Thus, in federal criminal proceedings the claim of ineffective assistance of counsel automatically satisfies the procedural default rule, see *Massaro v. United States*, 538 U.S. 500 (1983).

Prisoners whose defense counsel was unsuccessful should examine their lawyer's performance carefully. The common perception in today's legal community is that a lawyer must do as little as possible to justify the highest obtainable fee. The lower the cost of litigation, the higher the profit margin will be. When evaluating counsel's performance for possible failures to meet professional standards, the prisoner must compare counsel's conduct to the written procedural standard. Remember that every court has a set of procedural rules for every stage of all proceedings. The procedural rules are the court's way of following due process. A defendant must always get the rules and read them one by one. Make notes of the differences between counsel's conduct and that required by the rules. Broken rules are signs of ineffective assistance of counsel, and denial of the due process right to be heard.

Evaluating counsel's performance is the beginning of a claim development process. Because this is a part of claim development it is important to apply the two-prong *Strickland* test, while you examine counsel's conduct, in every stage. But also, a prisoner should take each possible claim one step further; he or she should review the possible claim through the lens of their due process right to be heard. Thus, he or she must be sure to be prepared to explain how the error prevented them from presenting a viable defense. This is a necessary consideration because a defendant who wishes to raise a claim of ineffective assistance of counsel bears a heavy burden. The defendant is required to provide proof to establish that counsel's performance was constitutionally deficient.

Even though a defendant faces a high standard when raising an ineffective assistance of counsel claim, there are nevertheless strong advantages to doing so. When a defendant raises an ineffectiveness claim instead of one in conjunction with a constitutional claim, where counsel obstructed a defendant's due process right to present his or her defense, they may overcome other procedural barriers, for example. Although, it has been previously held that a prisoners fourth amendment claim may not be reviewed in a federal proceeding wherein a prisoner seeks post-conviction relief, where the state court has provided an opportunity for full and fair review of that claim; it has also been held that this procedural bar does not apply to a sixth amendment claim of ineffective assistance of counsel based on counsel failure to have previously raised the fourth amendment issue.

During this initial evaluation stage, a prisoner should examine the conduct of others involved in the proceeding as well. In the past there have been cases where the trial judge and/or the prosecutor have been determined to have interfered with the defense as to violate a defendant's Constitutional rights. Consider whether appointed counsel had adequate time to prepare for trial; it has been held that the late appointment of counsel in a state prosecution, under certain circumstances, had made it impossible for appointed counsel to provide the effective assistance of counsel. In the preparation or trial and/or sentencing in a capital case the untimely appointment of counsel constitutes a denial of due process of law.

The appointment of counsel by a trial court, where counsel was ordered to represent multiple defendants, may also violate a defendant's right to the assistance of counsel. In any event where counsel objects to multiple representations on the ground that such representation presents the possibility of a conflict of interest, and the court fails to take steps to determine the seriousness of the risk; the court may well have obstructed the defendants' right to due process of law itself.

Although this chapter is set out to specifically instruct the layman, as well as the professional, how to identify ineffective assistance of counsel; you may also, herein, discover the initial basis for your own claim for post-conviction relief. Therefore, before moving on to claim development, in specific stages of the criminal process; this chapter will also set out in finer detail how the Supreme Court views an attorney's representation. In an attempt to successfully make a claim that an attorney's performance violated a prisoner's constitutional right to the effective assistance of counsel, the prisoner must show that counsel's representation was substandard in some particular way.

The Supreme Court has laid down some general rules, to be followed by all who seek post-conviction relief, for determining if an attorney's representation in a criminal case is so deficient that it constitutes a violation of the constitutional requirements. The remainder of this chapter will set out some factors which may be considered while making that determination.

A CLOSER LOOK AT STRICKLAND

When qualifying a claim, for post-conviction relief, that counsel's assistance was constitutionally ineffective and that reversal of the subsequent conviction was required; the claim must be evaluated as required by *Strickland v. Washington*, 466 U.S. 668 (1984). The benchmark must be whether the lawyers' conduct undermined the proper functioning of the adversarial process to the point that the trial could not be relied upon as producing a just result. Additionally, the proper standard for evaluating attorney performance is whether counsel's assistance could be considered reasonably effective under prevailing professional norms. The Supreme Court directs all district courts that evaluate claims of ineffective assistance of counsel, to judge the reasonableness of counsel's challenged conduct against the facts of the particular case, viewed as it could have been at the time of the misconduct.

In *Darden v. Wainwright*, 91 L.Ed. 2d 144, 106 S.Ct. 2464 (1986), the Supreme Court quoting *Strickland*, similarly held that judicial scrutiny of counsel's performance must be highly deferential, and that a fair assessment of attorney performance required that every effort be made to eliminate the distorting effect of hindsight and to reconstruct the circumstances of counsel's perspective at the time. See also *Kimmelman v. Morrison*, 91 L.Ed. 2d 305, 106 S.Ct. 2574 (1986).

In *Murray v. Carrier*, 91 L.Ed. 2d 397, 106 S.Ct. 2639 (1986), the court noted that a defendant's right to the effective assistance of counsel may be violated by an isolated error by counsel if that error is sufficiently egregious and prejudicial.

To show that ineffective assistance of counsel violated the sixth amendment a criminal defendant must show a reasonable probability that, but not for counsel's unprofessional errors, the result of the proceeding would have been different, as in *Boyde v. California*, 494 U.S. 370, 108 L.Ed. 2d 316, 110 S.Ct. 1190 (1990). But in *Lee v. United States*, 198 L.Ed. 2d 476, 137 S. Ct. 1958 (2017, U. S.), holds that the sixth amendment guarantees defendant effective assistance of counsel at critical stage of criminal process, including when entering a guilty plea, even though the result would still end in guilt.

The sixth amendment guarantees reasonable competence, not perfect advocacy judged with the benefit of hindsight. Thus, even if omission of some issues by counsel is inadvertent rather than for tactical reasons, relief is not automatic, see *Yarbourough v. Gentry*, 540 U.S. 1, 157 L.Ed. 2d 1, 124 S. Ct. 1 (2003).

With respect to claims of ineffective assistance of counsel [in collateral relief proceedings], attorney negligence (1) is chargeable to the client; and (2) precludes relief unless conditions of 28 U.S.C. §2254(e)(2) – concerning federal *habeas corpus* relief for state prisoners – are satisfied, as in *Holland v. Jackson*, 159 L.Ed. 2d 683, 124 S.Ct. 2736 (2004, U.S.).

In preparing for the sentencing phase of a capital trial it is defense counsel's responsibility to counter the state's evidence of aggravated culpability with mitigating evidence. When faced with a claim that counsel failed to discharge the aforementioned duty, by providing constitutionally ineffective assistance of counsel; the courts apply the *Strickland* standard to determine the norms of adequate investigation. In judging the defense's investigation, as in applying *Strickland* generally, hindsight is discounted by (1) pegging adequacy to counsel's perspective at the time investigative decisions were made; and (2) giving a heavy measure of deference to counsel's judgments, see *Rompilla v. Beard*, 125 S.Ct. 2456, 162 L.Ed. 2d 360 (2005, U.S.).

The law does not require counsel to raise every available non-frivolous defense. Counsel also is not required to have tactical reason, beyond reasonable appraisal of a claim's dismal prospects for success, for recommending that weak claims be dropped altogether, see *Knowles v. Mirzagance*, 556 U.S. 111, 129 S.Ct. 1411, 173 L.Ed. 2d 251 (2009).

To successfully present a meaningful ineffective assistance of counsel claim in a collateral proceeding, a criminal defendant must meet both the deficient performance and the prejudice prong of *Strickland v. Washington*, 466 U.S. 668 (1984). To show deficient performance, a defendant must establish that counsel's representation fell below objective standard of reasonableness. In light of a variety of circumstances faced by the defense counsel and the range of legitimate decisions regarding how best to represent a criminal defendant, the performance inquiry must necessarily turn on whether counsel's assistance was reasonable considering all the circumstances. At all points, judicial scrutiny of counsel's performance must be highly deferential, as in *Wong v. Belmontes*, 175 L.Ed. 2d 328, 130 S.Ct. 383 (2009, U.S.); *Porter v. McCollum*, 175 L.Ed. 2d 398, 130 S.Ct. 447 (2009, U.S.); and *Premo v. Moore*, 131 S.Ct. 733, 178 L.Ed. 2d 649 (2011, U.S.).

Strickland v. Washington, 466 U.S. 668, does not guarantee perfect representation, only a reasonably competent attorney. Representation is constitutionally ineffective only if it so undermines the proper functioning of the adversarial process so that the defendant was denied a fair trial. Just as there is no expectation that competent counsel will be flawless strategist or tactician, an attorney may not be at fault for a reasonable miscalculation or lack of foresight or for failing to prepare for what appear to be remote possibilities, see *Harrington v. Richter*, 131 S.Ct 770, 178 L.Ed. 2d 624 (2011, U.S.).

In assessing the effectiveness of assistance of counsel, court must consider constitutionally protected independence of counsel and wide latitude counsel must have in making tactical decision. Beyond general requirement of reasonableness, specific guidelines are not appropriate. No particular set of detailed rules for counsel's conduct can satisfactorily take account of variety of circumstances faced by defense counselors range of legitimate decisions, as in *Cullen v. Pinhoister*, (2011, U.S.) 131 S.Ct. 1388, 179 L. Ed. 2d 557.

See *Lafler v. Cooper* (2012, U.S.) 182 L. Ed. 2d 398, 132 S.Ct. 1376, in which Supreme Court held that 28 U.S.C.S. §2254(d)(1) presented no bar to federal *habeas corpus* relief for accused who, after being convicted at trial of assault with intent to murder, claimed that his rejection of plea offer was based on ineffective assistance of counsel. He claimed that, among other matters, parties conceded fact of deficient performance, where accused rejected offer allegedly after attorney had convinced him that prosecution would be unable to establish intent to murder because victim had been shot below the waist.

Federal Constitution's Sixth Amendment did not guarantee right to perfect counsel; it promised only right to effective assistance. Judicial precedent held that lawyer's violation of ethical norms did not make lawyer per se ineffective, see *Burt v. Titlow*, (2013, U.S.) 134 S.Ct. 10, 187 L. Ed. 2d 348.

Accused's right under Federal Constitution's Sixth Amendment to counsel is violated if (1) trial attorney's performance falls below objective standard of reasonableness; and (2) there is reasonable probability that trial result would have been different absent deficient act or omission. Proper measure of attorney performance is reasonableness under circumstances and prevailing professional norms. Cases will arise where only reasonable and available defense strategy requires consultation with experts or introduction of expert evidence. Attorney's ignorance of point of law that is fundamental to case combined with failure to perform basic research on that point is quintessential example of unreasonable performance, as in *Hinton v. Alabama* (2014, U.S.) 134 S.Ct. 1081, 188 L. Ed. 2d 1.

In normal course, defendants claiming ineffective assistance of counsel must show that (1) counsel's performance was deficient; and (2) deficient performance prejudiced defense, see *Woods v. Donald*, (2015, U.S.) 191 L. Ed. 2d 464, 135 S.Ct. 1372.

INEFFECTIVE ASSISTANCE OF COUNSEL: OVERCOMING THE INEVITABLE

Defendant who asserts denial of effective assistance of counsel must show that, among other matters, counsel performed deficiently. This is high bar, such that lawyer had discharged constitutional responsibility so long as decisions fall within wide range of professionally competent assistance, as in *Buck v. Davis*, (2017, U.S.) 197 L. Ed. 2d 1, 137 S.Ct. 759.

To obtain relief on basis of ineffective assistance of counsel, defendant generally must show (1) deficient performance, i.e., that the attorney's error was so serious that counsel was not functioning as counsel guaranteed defendant by Federal Constitution's Sixth Amendment; and (2) that attorney's error prejudiced defense, see *Weaver v. Massachusetts* (2017, U.S.) 198 L. Ed. 2d 420, 137 S.Ct. 1899.

KELLY PATRICK RIGGS

CHAPTER FOUR

CONFLICT OF INTERESTS

This is a subject known to all courts but admitted by none of them. Even the most basic claim of conflict of interest is and/or should be a claim of ineffective assistance of counsel. This subject is also very personal to me because of the many conflicts in my own criminal case. The single most damaging conflict, however, is the conflict that a *pro se* litigant faces in a post-conviction relief proceeding, where even a federal judge will knowingly lie, obstructing justice, to protect the failed integrity of her court. I say her because my own judge in Birmingham Alabama, Karon Owen Bowdre, lied in her opinion where she denied my §22SS based on addressing only three of my four claims. I claimed, and proved, that a conflict of interest occurred in my criminal case. Federal public defender Glennon F. Threatt, Jr. had been tasked with representing a murder along with me, the author of this book, who was a witness to the murder. Mr. Threatt had gone so far as to enlist the services of a colleague named Sabra Barnett to attempt to kill me in Clay County Jail by providing information to her clients, see Case No.: 2:15-cv-8043-KOB, in the Northern District of Alabama. When this claim was particularized in my §2255, the judge herself manipulated the record by claiming that I only made three claims rather than four. She has loaned the integrity of her court to serve the ends of the interest of the lawyers involved, in an attempt to salvage their reputations and protect them from criminal prosecution.

In most criminal cases, especially those involving appointed counsel, a conflict of interest occurs. In many federal cases, I have noticed that an appointed panel lawyer will only go as far as to negotiate a plea agreement. One particular lawyer I know had told a mother of a criminal defendant that he wasn't paid enough to go to trial or to interview the eleven alibi witnesses, Mr. Jeffrey Bramer said that "Justice costs money, how much can you afford?"

These kinds of conflicts of interest occur much too often in the criminal courts of America. Unfortunately, most post-conviction courts will do all they can to conceal the trend of legal malpractice among defense lawyers. This is my encouragement to everyone to identify and present your claims of conflict of interest as a claim of ineffective assistance of counsel. Remember also that in doing so you must follow some basic rules.

The Supreme Court has set some general rules concerning the effect of an actual conflict of interest. The court has addressed and set out guidelines for you to follow while constructing a claim involving an actual, potential, or alleged conflict of interest, as it related to a defendant's right to the effective assistance of counsel. The court has determined that showing only the possibility of a conflict is not enough to prove that defense counsel provided ineffective assistance of counsel. But also, that prejudice is presumed if the defendant shows that defense counsel suffered a conflict of interest that had an adverse effect on his or her performance while representing said defendant.

While considering how a conflict of interest deprives a defendant of his right to the effective assistance of counsel; remember also that the Supreme Court has held that the right applies equally to both court appointed and privately retained lawyers, see *Cuyler v. Sullivan*, 446 U.S. 335 (1970).

> *Author's Note: One very powerful yet very unpopular claim that arises in a conflict of interest proceeding is the question of honest service violations, by the court itself, and violations of the public's trust by the lawyer. These two claims are despised by all district courts but are also very useful to a movant whose post-conviction proceeding is being purposely delayed by the court itself. A full copy of a petition for a writ of mandamus is available in the back of* Post-Conviction Relief: Winning Claims *published by Freebird Publishers.*

The Supreme Court has previously held that, when a trial court is aware or reasonably should be aware, that a conflict of interest exists between a defendant and his lawyer, the trial court has a duty to investigate that possibility. The court is to determine if the alleged conflict in fact exists, and if so, if it deprives the defendant of his right to the effective assistance of counsel. When a motion is filed in a district court concerning a conflict of interest one of two things should happen: 1) The court holds a hearing to determine if a conflict exists, and the effects of the conflict on the defendant's right; or 2) The defendant will be asked to sign a waiver to his right to conflict-free counsel. If the court was notified of the conflict and the court took no action, the court has committed an Honest Service violation, a criminal act.

The Supreme Court has held that as a general rule, where a conflict of interest serves to deprive a defendant of his right to the effective assistance of counsel, the defendant has the power to enter into an informed waiver of the right to conflict-free counsel. That power however, is not absolute, a trial court has the inherent authority to decline to accept such a waiver when the court believes that such a waiver will result in detriment to the defendant, see *Glasser v. United States*, 315 U.S. 60, 86 L.Ed. 680, 62 S.Ct. 457 (1942), and *Holloway v. Arkansas*, 435 U.S. 475, 55 L.Ed. 2d 426, 98 S.Ct. 1173 (1978).

What's interesting is that the Supreme Court has noted that a conflict of interest is a likely element any time a defendant is represented by a lawyer who has been hired and paid by a third party. But, to the contrary it allows a branch of the government; that is prosecuting a defendant in federal criminal cases; to appoint, pay for, and control a defendant's lawyer on a regular basis, see *Wood v. Georgia*, 450 U.S. 261, 67 L.Ed. 2d 220, 101 S.Ct. 1097 (1981).

A great deal of the Supreme Court cases involving conflicts of interests and a defendant's right to the effective assistance of counsel have involved counsel's representation of multiple defendants charged with the same offense. It has been held by the Supreme Court that: a lawyer's representation of a defendant who has been charged with the same crime as a defendant represented by the lawyer's law partner is the same as a single lawyer's representation of more than one defendant charged with the same crime. This is a common practice which the court has routinely held, is not a conflict of interest in itself. Thus, is not considered an automatic denial of a defendant's right to the effective assistance of counsel.

Occasionally a lawyer's strategy can constitute a conflict of interest that deprives a defendant of his right to the effective assistance of counsel. One very specific situation is where one lawyer represents two defendants, in the same case, at separate trials. In the event the lawyer advises one defendant not to testify, on his own behalf, because such testimony would have an adverse effect on another client in a different trial; the lawyer may have suffered a debilitating conflict of interest. If a lawyer's decision is influenced by considerations of an upcoming trial of the defendant's co-defendant, the first defendant has been deprived of his right to the effective assistance of counsel. This rule applies in most situations where defense counsel is required to divide his loyalties, forcing the lawyer to choose which defendant receives his effective assistance.

Equally, a defendant is deprived of his right to the effective assistance of counsel if; his lawyer decided to call no witnesses, who are available to testify on his behalf, where the lawyer's decision is influenced by the considerations of upcoming trials of the defendant's co-defendants, who are also represented by the same lawyer. Correspondingly, the Supreme Court has previously determined that the failure of a lawyer, who represented two clients in the same prosecution to make an objection to testimony that was unfavorable to one client because the objection could be harmful to the lawyers other client did in fact show that a conflict of interest existed.

PRESUMING PREJUDICE

The Supreme Court has previously held that prejudice to the defendant should be presumed if the defendant proves that his or her lawyer suffered a conflict of interest that adversely affected the lawyer's ability in representing the defendant. Thus, in the event the defendant shows that his lawyer's conflict prevented the defendant from exercising his due process right to defend himself, then his sixth amendment right to the effective assistance of counsel has been violated as well. The Constitutional right to counsel is so basic to a fair trial that its infraction can never be treated as harmless error.

Finding that a district court's appointment of a defendant's lawyer to perform as counsel for his co-defendant, where both defendants were on trial for conspiracy to defraud the government, had created a conflict of interest. The Supreme Court decided that the conflict of interest was enough to require that the defendant's conviction be vacated without a necessity to establish the level of prejudice suffered by the defendant. This indicated that a showing of a conflict of interest involving the defendant's lawyer had created a presumption of prejudice. The right to the assistance of counsel guaranteed by the sixth amendment contemplated that such assistance be untrammeled and unimpaired by a court requiring that one lawyer simultaneously represents conflicting interests. According to the Supreme Court, if the right to the assistance of counsel meant less than this, then a valuable Constitutional safeguard would have been substantially impaired, see *Glasser v. United States*, 315 U.S. 60, 86 L.Ed. 680 S.Ct. 457 (1942).

The Supreme Court indicated that, when a conflict of interest involving an accused's counsel is shown, prejudice arising from this conflict is presumed for purposes of determining whether the accused has been deprived of the effective assistance of counsel. The sixth amendment's guarantee to the assistance of counsel was among those Constitutional rights so basic to a fair trial that their infraction could never be treated as harmless error, see *Holloway v. Arkansas*, 435 U.S. 475, 55 L.Ed. 2d 426, 98 S.Ct. 1173 (1978).

In many cases, showing an actual conflict of interest has been held has been necessary to establish a violation of a defendant's sixth amendment right to the effective assistance of counsel. Once a defendant has shown that a conflict of interest actually affected the adequacy of his or her representation, he or she did not have to prove prejudice in order to obtain relief, see *Cuyler v. Sullivan*, 446 U.S. 335, 64 L.Ed. 2d 333, 100 S.Ct. 1708 (1970).

In *Flanagan v. United States*, 465 U.S. 259, 79 L.Ed. 2d 288, 104 S.Ct. 1051 (1984), the Supreme Court said, that no showing of prejudice was necessary to obtain reversal, when a trial court had denied counsel's request to be replaced because of a conflict of interest. Under such circumstances prejudice to the defense was presumed.

In *Strickland v. Washington*, 466 U.S. 668, the Supreme Court said, that prejudice as to the defendant is presumed only if the defendant demonstrates that (1) Counsel had actively represented conflicting interest, and (2) an actual conflict of interest had adversely affected counsel's performance. A defendant's counsel owes the defendant a duty to avoid conflicts of interests.

In *Satterwhite v. Texas*, 486 U.S. 249, 100 L.Ed. 2d 284, 108 S.Ct. 1792 (1988), the Supreme Court noted with respect to a defendant's right to the effective assistance of counsel, that prejudice to the accused resulting from such a conflict is presumed if the accused demonstrates that (1) Counsel actively represented conflicting interests, and (2) an actual conflict of interest adversely affected counsel's performance, see also *Burden v. Zant*, 510 U.S. 132, 126 L.Ed. 2d 611, 114 S.Ct. 654 (1994); *Smith v. Robbins*, 528 U.S. 259, 145 L.Ed. 2d 756, 120 S.Ct. 746 (2000); and *Mickens v. Taylor*, 535 U.S. 162, 152 L.Ed. 2d 291, 122 S.Ct. 1237 (2002).

In *Mickens v. Taylor*, 535 U.S. 162, the court went on to say that an actual conflict for sixth amendment purposes is a conflict of interest that has an adverse effect on counsel's performance. A serious conflict of interest arises when an attorney's interest in avoiding damage to his or her own reputation is at odds with a client's strongest argument, for example that the attorney had abandoned his client. In the case referenced above, the petitioner was entitled to substitute his lawyer with un-conflicted counsel under 18 U.S.C. §3599(e) because the petitioner's appointed attorney missed a filing deadline. Thus, the petitioner (1) had a right to an opportunity to show entitlement to equitable tolling on the basis of appointed counsel's failure; and (2) having his attorney make an argument concerning the attorney's own failure would have created a conflict of interest, see *Christeson v. Roper*, 190 L.Ed. 2d 763, 135 S.Ct. 891 (2015, U.S.).

COURTS INVESTIGATIVE DUTY

Every criminal case in America has the potential to create a conflict of interests. Thus, the effective assistance of counsel guarantee does not require a trial court to initiate inquiries into the possibility of a conflict of interests between the defendant and his or her lawyer, in every case. The court does, however, have a duty to investigate when the court is aware or reasonably should be aware, of a possible conflict of interest between a defendant and his lawyer. This means that when a motion concerning a conflict of interests is filed the court has a duty to conduct a hearing. In the event a motion was not filed a defendant, in some sets of circumstances, may rely solely on the events of the proceeding to establish that a court was aware or reasonably should have been aware. Be prepared, in most cases a judge will play stupid to avoid the claim. For example, on December 20, 2013, Chief district Judge Karon Owen Bowdre denied receiving a letter. In the letter she, and the U.S. Marshal's service, were warned that a plan existed to kill Sambo Hazelrig. The judge held a hearing at which she claimed that the letter must have been lost in the mail. But the hearing being scheduled was proof that the court got the letter in which the hearing was requested. Sambo Hazelrig was ultimately murdered in 2015 during a robbery of his home, identical to the robbery that had been planned.

In *Holloway v. Arkansas*, 435 U.S. 475, the Supreme Court reversed the convictions of three co-defendants. They had been convicted in a state court trial in which the three co-defendants had been represented by one single lawyer. The lawyer had moved the court to appoint separate counsel for each defendant because of the possibility of a conflict of interest. The court, however, rejected the lawyer's request without first investigating the possibility of a conflict of interest. The failure of the court created a reversible error.

According to the Supreme Court the lawyer's joint representation of the defendants confronted him with a risk of representing conflicting interest, which triggered the court's obligation to either appoint separate counselor to take adequate steps to ascertain whether the risk of a conflict of interest was too remote to warrant separate counsel. Thus, the court's failure to exercise its duty to investigate did deprive the co-defendants of their right to the assistance of counsel. The Supreme Court went on to reject the argument that its decision would be the equivalent of transferring, to defense counsel, the authority of the trial judge to rule on the existence or risk of a conflict and the need to appoint separate counsel. The court also observed that its decision did not preclude the trial court from exploring the validity of the basis of defense counsel's claims regarding a conflict of interest.

In *Wheat v. United States*, 486 U.S. 153, 100 L.Ed. 2d 140, 108 S.Ct. 1692 (1988), the Supreme Court said that a court that is confronted with, and alerted to, a possible conflict of interest involving an accused's counsel, had to take adequate steps to ascertain whether such a conflict warranted separate counsel, see also *Wood v. Georgia*, 450 U.S. 261 (1981) and *Mickens v. Taylor*, 535 U.S. 162 (2002).

PART TWO
CHAPTER FIVE

IDENTIFYING CLAIMS STAGE-BY-STAGE

Without a clear definition as to what ineffective assistance of counsel is or is not. Your assessment must be made as a product of comparison. You must compare your counsel's conduct to what is expected under due process, to get a clear picture. Again, a right to the effective assistance of counsel attaches only to defendants in a criminal case, according to the fifth and sixth amendment to the Constitution of the United States. Thus, you will only be concerned with the criminal rules of procedure and the associated statutes. As an example, this section will particularize what your reasonable expectation of counsel conduct is under the law in a federal criminal case. This book goes on to list the federal rules of criminal procedure in section three for your own personal study.

Be aware also that this book serves as a guide to both pre-trial defendants and post-conviction litigants. Therefore, you will find steps that may not pertain to your particular situation. Please employ good judgment as this attempt is made to help as many people as possible. The next big issue before you begin is to get on the same· page with the court. When you appear in a hearing for the first time, you will hear, or you did hear, words that were familiar to you. You might even know the definition. But in many cases, you will be wrong. That's because the courts have designated different meanings to words we already know. They do this to get you to agree to things you don't understand. Take for example the word "Court." How many of us have said we "were present in court." That simply is not possible except in a few limited circumstances. The "Court" under the federal rules of criminal procedure is not a place, a room, or a building. The Court is in fact a person under Fed. R. Crim. P., Rule l(b)(2) "'Court' means a federal judge performing functions authorized by law."

Take your time to remember back to the impeachment of former President William Jefferson Clinton, "that depends on what your definition of 'is' 'is.'" Remember also that he made a big deal out of "I did not have sexual relations with that woman." These statements by our own former president should be a lesson to all of us, know what the words really mean in legalese before we use them. Please let me suggest that you read all of rule one of the Federal Rules of Criminal Procedure before going on.

Next, keep in mind that there are a few basic principles that govern in any criminal proceeding. The first is that under the Constitution's sixth amendment, a person accused of a crime has a right to have the assistance of counsel for his or her defense. Although this subject has been sufficiently covered in previous chapters, it's important to know that the right, to the effective assistance of counsel, applies to the partial appeal of the accused defendant. Thus, with respect to a direct appeal, as of right, from his or her criminal conviction/the right to the effective assistance of counsel is a constitutional guarantee under the due process clause.

> *Author's Note: What I believe to be the most important issue concerning the right to the effective assistance of counsel, is that a defendant has no right to counsel to make an ineffectiveness claim in a federal criminal case. In my opinion, it is very important for a pro se litigant, who is filing under 28 U.S.C. §2255, to consider his claims thoroughly. I suggest that all federal defendants consider whether their case may be appropriate for a claim that: the failure to appoint counsel side- stepped Congress's intent in 18 U.S.C. §3006A, which demands that an indigent defendant be appointed counsel in all appeals, see 18 U.S.C. §3006A(c).*

For those of you who are making a claim of ineffective assistance of counsel in a 28 U.S.C. §2255 proceeding, you most likely will be forced to do so without the assistance of counsel. If you have no counsel in the development of your ineffectiveness claim, you have a constitutional issue. §2255 is the equivalent of a direct appeal for an ineffectiveness claim. Thus, the lower court's misguided view of *Massaro v. United States*, 538 U.S. 500 (2003), has circumvented the constitutional due process right to the effective assistance of counsel in federal criminal cases, concerning claims of ineffective assistance of counsel.

The following cases support that a defendant has the right to the assistance of counsel on the defendant's direct appeal, as of right from his or her conviction:

- *Ellis v. United States* (1958) 356 US 674, 2 L.Ed. 2d 1060, 78 S. Ct. 974 (Sixth Amendment)

- *Douglas v. California* (1963) 372 US 353, 9 L. Ed. 2d 811, 83 S. Ct. 814, reh, den. 373 US 905, 10 L. Ed. 2d. 200, 83 S. Ct. 1288 (due process and equal protection clause of Fourteenth Amendment)

- *Swenson v. Bosler* (1967) 386 US 258, 18 L. Ed. 2d 33, 87 S. Ct. 996 (due process and equal protection clause of Fourteenth Amendment)

- *Anders v. California* (1967) 386 US 738, 18 L. Ed. 2d 493, 87 S. Ct. 1396, reh. den. 388 us 924, 18 L. Ed. 2d 1377,87 S. Ct. 2094 (Sixth Amendment and due process and equal protection clause of Fourteenth Amendment)

- *Entsminger v. Iowa* (1967) 386 US 748, 18 L. Ed. 2d 501, 87 S. Ct. 1402 (due process and equal protection clause of Fourteenth Amendment)

- *McConnell v. Rhay* (1968) 393 US 2, 21 L. Ed. 2d 2, 89 S. Ct. 32 (due process and equal protection clause of Fourteenth Amendment)

- *Arsenault v. Massachusetts* (1968) 393 US 5, 21 L. Ed. 2d 5, 89 S. Ct. 35 (due process and equal protection clause of Fourteenth Amendment)

- *Ross v. Moffitt* (1974) 417 US 600, 41 L. Ed. 2d 341, 94 S. Ct. 2437 (due process and equal protection clause of Fourteenth Amendment)

- *Bounds v. Smith* (1977) 430 US 817, 52 L. Ed. 2d 72, 97 S. Ct. 1491 (due process and equal protection clause of Fourteenth Amendment)

- *Evitts v. Lucey* (1985) 469 US 387, 83 L. Ed. 2d 821, 105 S. Ct. 830, reh den. 470 US 1065, 84 L. Ed. 2d 841, 105 S. Ct. 1783 (due process and equal protection clause of Fourteenth Amendment)

- *Smith v. Murray* (1986) 477 US 527, 91 L. Ed. 2d 434, 106 S. Ct. 2661 (Sixth Amendment)

- *McCoy v. Court of Appeals*, Dist. 1 (1988) 486 US 429, 100 L. Ed. 2d 440, 108 S. Ct. 1895 (Sixth Amendment)

- *Penson v. Ohio* (1988) 488 US 75, 102 L. Ed. 2d 300, 109 S. Ct. 346 (due process and equal protection clause of Fourteenth Amendment)

- *Murray v. Giarratano* (1989, US) 106 L. Ed. 2d 1, 109 S. Ct. 2765 (Sixth Amendment and due process and equal protection clause of Fourteenth Amendment).

CHAPTER SIX

DUTY TO INVESTIGATE

It doesn't matter if you are preparing to move the court for post-conviction relief or you are preparing yourself for trial. In either instance you are or already have discovered that a number of events had already transpired before obtaining the services of counsel in your criminal case. Thus, your lawyer's first duty in a criminal case is the duty to investigate. Although thorough investigation is counsel's most critical duty; it is also the most egregious error committed by counsel in most cases. For those of you who are currently awaiting trial, know that this is the most important part of your case. Also know that in cases of prepaid or court appointed counsel, this is the most commonly neglected duty that counsel faces. Keep in mind that under these circumstances counsel has either already received all he is going to get, or the court limits the amount of money counsel is allowed to bill. Thus counsel, in most cases, will choose the path of least resistance to get the case to a quick resolution.

A thorough and creative investigation is required in every case to launch a meaningful defense. It is also counsel's legal and ethical responsibility to perform such an investigation. The investigation must include a number of regularly scheduled and meaningful consultations with the defendant. Counsel must conduct interviews with all people who may become potential witnesses for either the defense or the prosecution, and conduct complete and continuing discovery, see *Powell v. Alabama*, 287 U.S. 45 (1932).

The American Bar Association specifically identified a duty to provide a thorough investigation as an essential and ethical obligation, see ABA standards for Criminal Justice 4-4.1 (1980). It is counsel's duty to strive for the best result for every client, "the duty to investigate exists regardless of the accused's admission or statements to the lawyer, of fact constituting guilt or the accused's stated desire to plead guilty," *id.* The Criminal Justice System, in theory, is designed to release the people whom the government cannot prove to be guilty beyond a reasonable doubt.

The responsibility to provide investigation or to make a reasonable decision that make certain particular investigations unnecessary, is clarified in the following cases:

- *Strickland v. Washington*, 466 U.S. 668, 691 (1984) (The Sixth Amendment requires investigation and preparation, not only to exonerate, but also to secure and protect the rights of the accused. Such constitutional rights are granted to the innocent and guilty alike, and failure to investigate and file appropriate motions is ineffective.)
- *Kimmelman v. Morrison*, 477 U.S. 365 (1986) (failure to investigate and present fourth amendment claim was constitutionally ineffective).

It is a lawyer's responsibility to learn as much as he can about every case. Counsel must do so as soon as possible, because time is of the essence. The speed or lack thereof, to provide a meaningful investigation has an irreversible effect on the outcome of a criminal case. Physical evidence gets misplaced, memories fade, and witnesses have been known to move away or die. Counsel can never obtain too many details concerning the facts and circumstances in a criminal case.

ELEMENTS OF INVESTIGATION

Contrary to popular belief, the reading of a case file is not the end of counsel's duty to investigate. For those of you who are preparing for trial, you must remember that it is your freedom at stake and 99% of all lawyers don't care if you go home or go to prison. Therefore, I recommend that every criminal defendant remain diligent and demand continued investigation from your lawyer.

Client Interview – An effective lawyer's first step in any case is an initial interview with his client. Every lawyer has his own unique way of talking to a new client, but there are some basic issues that must be covered:

- The client should be advised concerning attorney-client privilege. That means that a client's conversations with his lawyer are confidential. And that all phone calls and mail are monitored going in and out of jail.

- The first counsel interview is not a good time to attempt an in-depth review of the case. Ordinarily, the first time that counsel meets a client is in a jail or in a courtroom, thus emotions are high, and things must be allowed time to calm down.

- The first private interview should be extensive. The exchange of information from a client to his lawyer should be free flowing. Nothing should be taken for granted, all doubts should be satisfied. Counsel who is professional will consider involving the client in his investigation as counsel's agent, especially in seeking out witnesses and other issues of relations to the case. A defendant should also be aware that failure to assist counsel will, in almost every case, cause more harm than good to the defense.

- Both counsel and the client should make every effort to stay in regular contact. When the defendant is in pre-trial custody, counsel should visit the defendant no less than once a month, and more often in a case where the right to a public speedy trial is invoked.

Discovery – Obtaining the government's discovery material is a very important preliminary step in any criminal case. But what has proven to be critical, in many criminal cases, is counsel's duty to discuss discovery issues with his client. In almost all federal criminal cases the government has been proven to be far less than forthcoming. Thus, the time spent discussing discovery issues with a defendant is indispensable. A defendant's memory can often lead counsel to seek other available discovery items.

Crime Scene Investigation – Law enforcement agencies employ people who are well trained and, in most cases, quite professional. But defense counsel should visit the crime scene to clarify any gaps that may be produced by assumptions. A personal inspection of the scene of an incident is always informative. It's best to see the scene under conditions that are similar to those at the time of the incident. It's important for the counsel to inspect the scene as soon as possible. Counsel should ensure that details can be memorialized by photographs. It's important for a defendant to ask counsel if he employs an investigator, and if not, the defendant should suggest that one be employed.

Defense Witnesses – Counsel should interview every possible defense witness quickly. Although, alibi witnesses and other obviously important witnesses are interviewed; those who seem to be less important should be interviewed as well. Those witnesses who can corroborate even a small part of the defense's case are equally important. Witnesses who appear to be of lesser importance can often provide leads for other witnesses. All meaningful witness interviews should be memorialized in a witness statement. Failure to interview exculpatory witnesses and to present their testimony is ineffectiveness.

Criminal Record – Counsel should review the criminal records of all witnesses involved in a criminal case. Even the full criminal history of the defendant is of great value in making decisions concerning counsel's advice to his client.

Prosecution Witnesses – The defense, as opposed to defense counsel, should attempt to interview all government witnesses as early as possible. The interviews should be conducted by counsel in the presence of an investigator who is employed by the defense. In the alternative, a defense investigator may interview hostile witnesses by themselves. Counsel should not, however, interview hostile witnesses by himself. An investigator should be present because in the event the witness changes his or her testimony, from the interview statement, only an investigator can serve as an impeaching witness. Counsel may never serve as an impeaching witness.

Physical Evidence – Physical evidence takes on many forms, the most important is tangible evidence. Tangible evidence is evidence that can be any physical thing. Likewise, it can be moved, lost, or preserved. Counsel's duty during investigation is to immediately find and preserve all tangible evidence whenever possible. The wide variety of tangible evidence often depends on what type of crime the defendant is accused of. Crimes of violence and other offenses that involve a weapon usually involve a tangible object such as a gun, a knife, or other dangerous item. Burglaries usually involve signs of forced entry where the tangible evidence is damage property. In burglaries, the evidence of the offense should be photographed. Thus, depending on the charged offense, the list of different types of tangible or physical evidence is limitless.

Other types of investigation, beyond the initial investigation, are covered in a later chapter.

CHAPTER SEVEN

PLEA AGREEMENTS IN GENERAL

This chapter is placed before the chapter that covers the discovery process on purpose. The reason it does is to aid those of you who are using this book as a pre-trial guide. The bottom line is that if your defense counsel advises you to plead guilty before he receives the discovery material in your case; he is already providing ineffective assistance of counsel.

The next significant problem with the practice of guilty determinations by plea agreement is that most are induced by coercion. The general practice of plea bargaining became widely acceptable during the 1970s. Crime was alleged to be on the rise although it was simply the result of over criminalization. Prior to 1970, the Supreme Court had rejected a large number of guilty pleas that were induced by threats of greater punishment or offers of false promises of leniency.

In 1970 however, the Supreme Court changed its view to a 180 degree turn about. The High Court had ruled that it did not violate the Constitution when prosecutors offered inducements to encourage a defendant to plead guilty. Less than ten years later, the Supreme Court was bending over backward to defend the practice of inducing defendants to plead guilty. Not even a threat of life in prison was enough to find that a defendant had been coerced. Thus, coercion became the practice to encourage defendants to give up their right to trial. The unfortunate part, and what's relevant to this book, is that ordinarily your own defense lawyer is in on the ruse.

Another issue due great consideration is that plea agreements contain a wide variety of complex waivers. Plea agreements for the most part require that a defendant give up a number of fundamental rights, such as the right to trial by a jury, the right to the presumption of innocence, and a right to appeal the conviction. The courts consistently uphold convictions where defendants knowingly and willingly enter waivers that forfeit such rights.

There is absolutely no Constitutional right to plead guilty. Nor does any federal law exist that provides authority for any court to accept a plea agreement. In the federal system it is the Federal Rules of Criminal Procedure that govern an attorney's conduct during the guilty plea process, see Fed. R. Crim. P., Rule 11. Without guidance from the Constitution or any federal law, it is Rule 11 alone that dictates what is, and what is not, appropriate under due process when it comes to this obscure practice. Consequently, there is no bright line requirement concerning counsel's conduct during this phase of the criminal procedure. Therefore, to lodge any meaningful claim of ineffective assistance of counsel, after entering a guilty plea, the defendant must fully understand what can be expected from the process.

After reading the Federal Rules of Criminal Procedures, Rule number eleven, and I strongly suggest that you do, remember that most of its requirements are placed on that of the presiding judge. Yes, the very same judge you will be asking to vacate your sentence. Needless to say, there remains no element of rule eleven that a federal court somewhere has not violated, and not one of those violations will be actionable. The problem with guilty plea errors rests with a phenomenon called pre-plea conduct. That's to say that you cannot make a claim against anything your attorney may have done wrong prior to the court accepting the plea agreement. That is the reason for the dogmatic performance that the defendant is a party to when pleading guilty before the court. It's the judges themselves who are trying to make a record to prove a defendant is happy with his counsel. At the end of every change of plea hearing the judge asks the defendant if he or she is happy with the services provided by defense counsel. That one answer will haunt all defendants in every §2255 proceeding, which follows a guilty plea.

With that in mind, let's take a look at what you can do about it. First, understand that a defendant has a Sixth Amendment right to the effective assistance of counsel during the plea-bargaining process. In *Jae Lee v. United States*, 582 U.S. _____ (2017), the Supreme Court held that: "When a defendant claims that his counsel's deficient performance deprived him of a trial by causing him to accept a plea, the defendant can show prejudice by demonstrating a 'reasonable probability that, but for counsel's errors, he would not have pleaded guilty and would have insisted on going to trial.' [See] *Hill v. Lockhart*, 474 U.S. 52, 59, 106 S. Ct. 366, 88 L. Ed. 2d 203."

A challenge claiming ineffective assistance of counsel after a guilty plea is subject to the *Strickland* two-part test. Some claims that have prevailed include elements such as the following:

- failure to inform the defendant about a favorable plea offer;

- inappropriately advising acceptance or refusal of a plea agreement;

- misinforming a defendant as to the possible consequences of pleading guilty; or

- failure to object and/or advise his client that the court has followed the procedure set out in Fed. R. Crim. P., Rule 11.

In situations such as these, a defendant must meet the *Strickland* test, he must establish that there is a reasonable probability that, but for counsel's unprofessional errors, the outcome of the plea agreement process would have been different had he have had competent advice from qualified counsel. The Constitutional basis for a claim of ineffective assistance, after a guilty plea, must be that: the defendant was deprived of his due process right to "a speedy and public trial …" because of his counsel's deficient performance.

A claim of conflict of interest during plea negotiation is another real and actionable claim. The competition for jobs in the legal field as an attorney is fierce. Most of the larger firms scout law schools searching out the next big hot-shot lawyers, offering jobs and internships to students with high grade point averages. Many corporate firms in the larger cities offer huge salaries to all attorneys who can turn billable hours. Usually leaving the lesser equipped attorneys, who barely passed the bar exam, to scratch out a living on court appointments under the criminal justice act.

Ill-equipped attorneys thrive on plea agreement waivers that protect them from pre-plea-conduct, which usually includes bad plea advice. The exception however is a claim that directly challenges the lawyer's advice to plead guilty as a conflict of interest. Criminal defendants have a constitutional right to the effective, conflict-free, assistance of counsel at every stage of a criminal proceeding, see the Sixth Amendment to the U.S. Constitution; *Alabama v. Shelton*, 535 U.S. 654 (2002); and *Strickland v. Washington*, 466 U.S. 668, 687 (1984). When faced with a claim that counsel's advice to enter a plea agreement waiver protected the lawyer from pre-plea conduct, the defense lawyer is put in a position that he cannot defend. Had this question have been raised before entering into a plea agreement the lawyer would be forced to explain the quality of representation he had provided up to that point. This claim raised in post-conviction relief proceedings draws into question every step of the pre-plea representation that counsel had provided. The conflict of interest that is usually intertwined with all plea discussions between counsel and defendant is comparable to a doctor handing a sedated patient a liability waiver as the patient is being rolled into surgery. Perhaps even more disturbing is an attorney requiring his client to enter into an agreement that would restrict the lawyer's malpractice liability.

The next conflict of interest, second only to the pre-plea-conduct waiver, is that requirement that a defendant state his or her satisfaction with counsel on the record. Most plea agreements and/or change of plea hearings contains a general agreement that the "defendant also acknowledges his complete satisfaction with the representation and advice received from his undersigned attorney." All criminal defense attorneys who do not object, amend, or otherwise declare that he had no part in such a requirement is ineffective because of a conflict of interest.

Finally, in the event that these previous steps have not been considered, or the record is silent as to the issues, the defendant has grounds to make a meaningful ineffective assistance of counsel claim in a post-conviction proceeding. The defendant seeking to advance an ineffectiveness claim should point out that the defendant was deprived of counsel, in violation of the constitutions Sixth Amendment, as to that part of the plea agreement, which made that portion of the agreement and/or its waivers unenforceable. For more examples concerning plea agreements review the following cases:

RODNEY CLASS, PETITIONER V. UNITED STATES
583 US, 138 S. CT. , 200 L. ED. 20 37
ARGUED OCTOBER 4, 2017; DECIDED FEBRUARY 21, 2018

DECISION

Guilty plea, by itself, did not bar federal criminal defendant from challenging constitutionality of statute of conviction on direct appeal.

SUMMARY

Holdings: [1] – A guilty plea by itself did not bar a federal criminal defendant from challenging the constitutionality of the statute of conviction on direct appeal; [2] – Petitioner did not relinquish his right to appeal the district court's constitutional determinations simply by pleading guilty because petitioner's constitutional claims did not contradict the terms of the indictment or the written plea agreement, and the claims did not focus upon case-related constitutional defects that occurred prior to the entry of the guilty plea. The claims called into question the government's power to constitutionally prosecute him because the claims challenged the government's power to criminalize petitioner's (admitted) conduct; [3] – Petitioner could have pursued his constitutional claims on direct appeal.

Judgment reversed; Case remanded; 6-3 Decision; 1 Dissent

JAE LEE, PETITIONER V. UNITED STATES
582 U.S., 137 S.CT., 198 L. ED. 2D 476
ARGUED MARCH 28, 2017; DECIDED JUNE 23, 2017

DECISION

Alien who pleaded guilty to federal drug-possession charge after assurance by counsel that plea, which subjected alien to mandatory deportation, would not result in deportation was entitled to vacation of conviction and sentence under 28 U.S.C.S. §2255 because alien demonstrated prejudice from deficient erroneous advice.

SUMMARY

Holdings: [l] – Defendant had adequately demonstrated a reasonable probability that, but for counsel's erroneous advice, he would have rejected a guilty plea where his plea colloquy and surrounding circumstances showed deportation was the determinative issue in his decision to accept the plea, and it was not irrational to reject the plea deal when there was some chance of avoiding deportation, however remote.

Judgment reversed; case remanded; 6-2 Decision; 1 dissent

Held: Lee has demonstrated that he was prejudiced by his counsel's erroneous advice. Pp. ___-___ , 198 L. Ed. 2d, at 484-489.

(a) When a defendant claims that his counsel's deficient performance deprived him of a trial by causing him to accept a plea, the defendant can show prejudice by demonstrating a "reasonable probability that, but for counsel's errors, he would not have pleaded guilty and would have insisted on going to trial." [See] *Hill v. Lockhart*, 474 U.S. 52, 59, 106 S. Ct. 366, 88 L. Ed. 2d 203.

Lee contends that he can make this showing because he never would have accepted a guilty plea had he known the result would be deportation. The Government contends that Lee cannot show prejudice from accepting a plea where his only hope at trial was that something unexpected and unpredictable might occur that would lead to acquittal. Pp. at 484-486. I 198 L. Ed. 2d,

(b) The Government makes two errors in urging the adoption of a per se rule that a defendant with no viable defense cannot show prejudice from the denial of his right to trial. First, it forgets that categorical rules are ill suited to an inquiry that demands a "case-by-case examination" of the "totality of the evidence." *Williams v. Taylor*, 529 U.S. 362, 391, 120 S. Ct. 1495, 146 L. Ed. 2d 389 (internal quotation marks omitted); *Strickland*, 466 U.S., at 695, 104 S. Ct. 2052, 80 L. Ed. 2d 674. More fundamentally, it overlooks that the *Hill v. Lockhart* inquiry focuses on a defendant's decision making, which may not turn solely on the likelihood of conviction after trial.

The decision whether to plead guilty also involves assessing the respective consequences of a conviction after trial and by plea, see INS v. St. Cyr, 533 U.S. 289, 322-323, 121 S. Ct. 2271, 150 L. Ed. 2d 347. When those consequences are, from the defendant's perspective, similarly dire, even the smallest chance of success at trial may look attractive. For Lee, deportation after some time in prison was not meaningfully different from deportation after somewhat less time; he says he accordingly would have rejected any plea leading to deportation in favor of throwing a "Hail Mary" at trial. Pointing to *Strickland*, the Government urges that "[a] defendant has no entitlement to the luck of a lawless decision maker" 466 U.S., at 695, 104 S. Ct. 2052, 80 L. Ed. 2d 674. That statement, however, was made in the context of discussing the presumption of reliability applied to judicial proceedings, which has no place where, as here, a defendant was deprived of a proceeding altogether. When the inquiry is focused on what an individual defendant would have done, the possibility of even a highly improbable result may be pertinent to the extent it would have affected the defendant's decision making. Pp.___-___ , 198 L. Ed. 2d, at 486-487.

(c) Courts should not upset a plea solely because of post hoc assertions from a defendant about how he would have pleaded but for his attorney's deficiencies. Rather, they should look to contemporaneous evidence to substantiate a defendant's expressed preferences. In the unusual circumstances of this case, Lee has adequately demonstrated a reasonable probability that he would have rejected the plea had he known that it would lead to mandatory deportation: Both Lee and his attorney testified that "deportation was the determinative issue" to Lee; his responses during his plea colloquy confirmed the importance he placed on deportation; and he had strong connections to the United States, while he had no ties to South Korea.

The Government argues that Lee cannot "convince the court that a decision to reject the plea bargain would have been rational under the circumstances," *Padilla v. Kentucky*, 559 U.S. 356, 372, 130 S. Ct. 1473, 176 L. Ed. 2d 284, since deportation would almost certainly result from a trial. Unlike the government, this Court cannot say that it would be irrational for someone in Lee's position to risk additional prison time in exchange for holding on to some chance of avoiding deportation. Pp. ___-___ , 198 L. Ed. 2d, at 487-489. 825 F.3d 311, reversed and remanded.

TIMOTHY LEE HURST, PETITIONER V. FLORIDA
577 U.S., 136 S. CT. , 193 L. ED. 2D 504
ARGUED OCTOBER 13, 2015; DECIDED JANUARY 12, 2016

DECISION

Florida's sentencing scheme, requiring judge to determine at separate hearing whether sufficient aggravating circumstances existed to justify imposing death penalty, violated Federal Constitution's Sixth Amendment, which required jury to find each fact necessary to impose death penalty.

SUMMARY

Holdings: [1] – Defendant's death sentence violated the Sixth Amendment where the maximum punishment he could have received without any judge-made findings was life in prison without parole, a judge had increased his authorized punishment based on her own fact-finding, and the existence of an advisory jury verdict did not impact whether Fla. Stat. §921.141(3) required a judge to make the critical findings necessary to impose the death penalty; [2] – *Spaziano v. Florida*, 468 U.S. 447 (1984), and *Holdwin v. Florida*, 490 U.S. 638 (1989), were overruled to the extent they allowed a sentencing judge to find an aggravating circumstance, independent of a jury's fact-finding, that was necessary for imposition of the death penalty; [3] – The State's harmless error assertion was not considered as there was no reason to depart from the usual practice of leaving it for the state court's consideration.

Judgment reversed; case remanded. 8-1 decision, 1 concurrence, 1 dissent

SYLLABUS

Under Florida law, the maximum sentence a capital felon may receive on the basis of a conviction alone is life imprisonment. He may be sentenced to death, but only if an additional sentencing proceeding "results in findings by the court that such person shall be punished by death," Fla. Stat. §775.082(1). In that proceeding, the sentencing judge first conducts an evidentiary hearing before a jury. §921.141(1). Next, the jury, by majority vote, renders an "advisory sentence." §921.141(2). Notwithstanding that recommendation, the court must independently find and weigh the aggravating and mitigating circumstances before entering a sentence of life or death. §921.141 (3).

A Florida jury convicted petitioner Timothy Hurst of first-degree murder for killing a co-worker and recommended the death penalty. The court sentenced Hurst to death, but he was granted a new sentencing hearing on appeal. At resentencing, the jury again recommended death, and the judge again found the facts necessary to sentence Hurst to death. The Florida Supreme Court affirmed, rejecting Hurst's argument that his sentence violated the Sixth Amendment in light of *Ring v. Arizona*, 536 U.S. 584, 122 S. Ct. 2482, 153 L. Ed. 2d 556, in which this court found unconstitutional an Arizona capital sentencing scheme that permitted a judge rather than the jury to find the facts necessary to sentence a defendant to death.

Held: Florida's capital sentencing scheme violates the Sixth Amendment in light of Ring. Pp.___-___ , 193 L. Ed. 2d, at 510-514.

(a) Any fact that "expose[s] the defendant to a greater punishment than that authorized by the jury's guilty verdict" is an "element" that must be submitted to a jury, *Apprendi v. New Jersey*, 530 U.S. 466, 494, 120 S. Ct. 2348, 147 L. Ed. 2d 435. Applying *Apprendi* to the capital punishment context, the Ring Court had little difficulty concluding that an Arizona judge's independent fact-finding exposed ring to a punishment greater than the jury's guilty verdict authorized, 536 U.S., at 604, 120 S. Ct. 2348, 147 L. Ed. 2d 435. Ring's analysis applies equally here. Florida requires not the jury but a judge to make the critical findings necessary to impose the death penalty. That Florida provides an advisory jury is immaterial, see *Walton v. Arizona*, 497 U.S. 639, 648, 110 S. Ct. 3047, 111 L. Ed. 2d 511. As with Ring,

Hurst had the maximum authorized punishment he could receive increased by a judge's own fact-finding. Pp.___-___ , 193 L. Ed. 2d, at 510-511.

(b) Florida's counterarguments are rejected. Pp.___-___ , 193 L. Ed. 2d, at 511-514.

(1) In arguing that the jury's recommendation necessarily included an aggravating circumstance finding, Florida fails to appreciate the judge's central and singular role under Florida law, which makes the court's findings necessary to impose death and makes the jury's function advisory only. The State cannot now treat the jury's advisory recommendation as the necessary factual finding required by Ring. Pp. ___-___ , 193 L. Ed. 2d, at 511-512.

(2) Florida's reliance on *Blakely v. Washington*, 542 U.S. 296, 124 S. Ct. 2531, 159 L. Ed. 2d 403, is misplaced. There, this Court stated that under *Apprendi*, a judge may impose any sentence authorized "on the basis of the facts … admitted by the defendant," 542 U.S., at 303, 124 S. Ct. 2531, 159 L. Ed. 2d 403. Florida alleges that Hurst's counsel admitted the existence of a robbery, but Blakely applied *Apprendi* to facts admitted in a guilty plea, in which the defendant necessarily waived his right to a jury trial, while Florida has not explained how Hurst's alleged admissions accomplished a similar waiver. In any event, Hurst never admitted to either aggravating circumstance alleged by the State, Pp.___-___ , 193 L. Ed. 2d, at 512.

(3) That this Court upheld Florida's capital sentencing scheme in *Hildwin v. Florida*, 490 U.S. 638, 109 S. Ct. 2055, 104 L. Ed. 2d 728, and *Spaziano v. Florida*, 468 U.S. 477, 104 S. Ct. 3154, 82 L. Ed. 2d 340, does not mean that stare decisis compels the Court to do so here, see *Alleyne v. United States*, 570 U.S., 133 S. Ct. 2151, 186 L. Ed. 2d 314 (Sotomayor, J., concurring). Time and subsequent cases have washed away the logic of *Spaziano* and *Hildwin*. Those decisions are thus overruled to the extent they allow a sentencing judge to find an aggravating circumstance, independent of a jury's fact-finding, that is necessary for imposition of the death penalty. Pp.___-___ , 193 L. Ed. 2d, at 512-513.

(4) The State's assertion that any error was harmless is not addressed here, where there is no reason to depart from the Court's normal pattern of leaving such considerations to state courts. P.___ , 193 L. Ed. 2d, at 513.

147 So. 3d 435; reversed and remanded

SAMUEL JAMES JOHNSON, PETITIONER V. UNITED STATES
ARGUED NOVEMBER 5, 2014, REARGUED APRIL 20, 2015, DECIDED JUNE 26, 2015

DECISION

Imposing increased sentence under residual clause of 18 U.S.C.S. §924(e) (2) (B), Armed Career Criminal Act of 1984, held to violate Fifth Amendment's guarantee of due process because residual clause denied fair notice to defendants and invited arbitrary enforcement by judges.

SUMMARY

Holdings:[1] – Where defendant pleaded guilty to being a felon in possession of a firearm in violation of 18 U.S.C.S. §922(g) and received a 15-year prison term under the Armed Career Criminal Act, remand was warranted because imposing an increased sentence under 18 U.S.C.S. §924(e)(2)(B)'s residual clause violated the Fifth Amendment's guarantee of due process since the indeterminacy of the wide-ranging inquiry required by the residual clause both denied fair notice to defendants and invited arbitrary enforcement by judges; [2] – The residual clause did not survive the prohibition of vague criminal laws, because the residual clause left grave uncertainty about how to estimate the risk posed by a crime and left uncertainty about how much risk it took for a crime to qualify as a violent felony; [3] – Standing by prior decisions would undermine the goals that stare decisis was meant to serve.

Judgment reversed and case remanded; 6-3 decision; 2 concurrences; 1 dissent

Held: Imposing an increased sentence under ACCA's residual clause violates due process. Pp.___-___ , 192 L. Ed. 2d, at 577-584.

(a) The Government violates the Due Process Clause when it takes away someone's life, liberty, or property under a criminal law so vague that it fails to give ordinary people fair notice of the conduct it punishes, or so standardless that it invites arbitrary enforcement. *Kolender v. Lawson*, 461 U.S. 352, 357-358, 103 S. ct. 1855, 75 L. Ed. 2d 903. Courts must use the "categorical approach" when deciding whether an offense is a violent felony, looking "only to the fact that the defendant has been convicted of crimes falling within certain categories, and not to the facts underlying the prior convictions." *Taylor v. United States*, 495 U.S. 575, 600, 110 S. Ct. 2143, 109 L. Ed. 2d 607. Deciding whether the residual clause covers a crime thus requires a court to picture the kind of conduct that the crime involves in "the ordinary case ..." and to judge whether that abstraction presents a serious potential risk of physical injury. James, supra, at 208, 127 S. ct. 1586, 167 L. Ed. 2d 532. Pp.___-___ , 192 L. Ed. 2d, at 577-578.

(b) Two features of the residual clause conspire to make it unconstitutionally vague. By tying the judicial assessment of risk to a judicially imagined "ordinary case" of a crime rather than to real-world facts or statutory elements, the clause leaves grave uncertainty about how to estimate the risk posed by a crime, see *James*, supra, at 211, 127 S. Ct. 1586, 167 L. Ed. 2d 532. At the same time, the residual clause leaves uncertainty about how much risk it takes for a crime to qualify as a violent felony. Taken together, these uncertainties produce more unpredictability and arbitrariness than the Due Process Clause tolerates. This Court's repeated failure to craft a principled standard out of the residual clause and the lower courts' persistent inability to apply the clause in a consistent way confirm its hopeless indeterminacy. Pp.___-___ , 192 L. Ed. 2d, at 578-581.

(c) This Court's cases squarely contradict the theory that the residual clause is constitutional merely because some underlying crimes may clearly pose a serious potential risk of physical injury to another, see, e.g., *United States v. L. Cohen Grocery Co.*, 255 U.S. 81, 89, 41 S. Ct. 298, 65 L. Ed. 516. Holding the residual clause void for vagueness does not put other criminal laws that use terms such as "substantial risk" in doubt, because those laws generally require gauging the riskiness of an individual's conduct on 'a particular occasion, not the riskiness of an idealized ordinary case of the crime. Pp.___-___ , 192 L. Ed. 2d, at 581-583.

(d) The doctrine of stare decisis does not require continued adherence to James and Sykes. Experience leaves no doubt about the unavoidable uncertainty and arbitrariness of adjudication under the residual clause. James and Sykes opined about vagueness without full briefing or argument. And continued adherence to those decisions would undermine, rather than promote, the goals of evenhandedness, predictability, and consistency served by stare decisis, Pp.___-___ , 192 L. Ed. 2d, at 583-584. 526 Fed. Appx. 708, reversed and remanded.

CAROL ANNE BOND, PETITIONER v. UNITED STATES
572 U.S. 844, 134 S. CT. 2077, 189 L. ED. 2D 1
ARGUED NOVEMBER 5, 2013, DECIDED JUNE 2, 2014

DECISION

Chemical Weapons Convention Implementation Act provision (18 U.S.C.S. §229(a)) held not to cover wholly in-state use of arsenic-based compound and commonly used photography chemical.

SUMMARY

Petitioner was convicted of possessing and using a chemical weapon, in violation of 18 U.S.C.S. §229(a). The United States Court of Appeals for the third Circuit rejected petitioner's constitutional challenge, holding that 18 U.S.C.S. §229 was necessary and proper to carry into effect the Convention on the Prohibition of the Development, Production, Stockpiling, and Use of Chemical Weapons and on their Destruction. *Certiorari* was granted.

Because the federal constitutional structure left local criminal activity primarily to the states, judicial precedent generally declined to read federal law as intruding on that responsibility, unless Congress clearly indicated that the law should have had such reach. The Chemical Weapons Convention Implementation Act contained no such clear indication where the general definition of chemical weapon, although defined broadly, was not a clear statement that Congress meant the statute to reach local criminal conduct. The chemicals used by the petitioner were not of the sort that an ordinary person would have associated with instruments of chemical warfare. Moreover, state laws were sufficient to prosecute petitioners. Thus, §229 was read consistent with the principles of federalism inherent in the federal constitutional structure.

The judgment was reversed; the case was remanded for further proceedings; 6-3 Decision; 3 concurrences

Held: Section 229 does not reach Bond's simple assault. Pp.___-___, 189 L. Ed. 2d, at 10-18.

(a) The parties debate whether section 229 is a necessary and proper means of executing the Federal Government's power to make treaties, but "normally [this] Court will not decide a constitutional question if there is some other ground upon which to dispose of the case," *Escambia County v. McMillan*, 466 U.S. 48, 51, 104 S. Ct. 1577, 80 L. Ed. 2d 36 (*per curiam*). Thus, this Court starts with Bond's argument that section 229 does not cover her conduct. Pp.___-___, 189 L. Ed. 2d, at 10-11.

(b) This Court has no need to interpret the scope of the international Chemical Weapons convention in this case. The treaty specifies that a signatory nation should implement its obligations "in accordance with its constitutional processes." Art. VII (1), 1974, U.N.T.S. 331. Bond was prosecuted under a federal statute, which, unlike the treaty, must be read consistent with the principles of federalism inherent in our constitutional structure. Pp.___-___, 189 L. Ed. 2d, at 11-18.

   (1) A fair reading of section 229 must recognize the duty of "federal courts to be certain of Congress's intent before finding that federal law overrides" the "usual constitutional balance of federal and state powers," *Gregory v. Ashcroft*, 501 U.S. 452, 460, 111 S. Ct. 2395, 115 L. Ed. 2d 410. This principle applies to federal laws that punish local criminal activity, which has traditionally been the responsibility of the States. This Court's precedents have referred to basic principles of federalism in the Constitution to resolve ambiguity in federal statutes, see, e.g., *United States v. Bass*, 404 U.S. 336, 92 S. Ct. 515, 30 L. Ed. 2d 488; *Jones v. United States*, 529 U.S. 848, 120 S. Ct. 1904, 146 L. Ed. 2d 902. Here, the ambiguity in the statute derives from the improbably broad reach of the key statutory definition, given the term – "chemical weapon" –that is being defined, the deeply serious consequences of adopting such a boundless reading, and the lack of any apparent need to do so in light of the context from which the statute arose-a treaty about chemical warfare and terrorism, not about local assaults; Thus, the Court can reasonably insist on a clear indication that congress intended to reach purely local crimes before interpreting section 229's expansive language in a way that intrudes on the States' police power. Pp.___-___, 189 L. Ed. 2d, at 11-14.

   (2) No such clear indication is found in section 229. An ordinary speaker would not describe Bond's feud-driven act of spreading irritating chemicals as involving a "chemical weapon." And the chemicals at issue here bear little resemblance to those whose prohibition was the object of an international Convention. Where the breadth of a statutory definition creates ambiguity, it is

appropriate to look to the ordinary meaning of the term being defined (here, "chemical weapon") in settling on a fair reading of the statute, see *Johnson v. United States*, 559 U.S. 133, 130 S. Ct. 1265, 176 L. Ed. 2d 1.

The Government's reading of section 229 would transform a statute concerned with acts of war, assassination, and terrorism into a massive federal anti-poisoning regime that reaches the simplest of assaults. In light of the principle that congress does not normally intrude upon the States' police power, this court is reluctant to conclude that Congress meant to punish Bond's crime with a federal prosecution for a chemical weapons attack. In fact, only a handful of prosecutions have been brought under section 229, and most of those involved crimes not traditionally within: The States' purview, e.g., terrorist plots.

Pennsylvania's laws are sufficient to prosecute assaults like bonds, and there is no indication in section 229 that Congress intended to abandon its traditional "reluctance to define as a federal crime conduct readily denounced as criminal by the States," Bass, supra, at 349, 92 S. Ct. 515, 30 L. Ed. 2d 488. That principle goes to the very structure of the Constitution, and "protects the liberty of the individual from arbitrary power." See *Bond v. United States*, 564 U.S. ___-___ , 131 S. Ct. 2355, 180 L. Ed. 2d 269. The global need to prevent chemical warfare does not require the Federal Government to reach into the kitchen cupboard. Pp.___-___ , 189 L. Ed. 2d, at 14-18.

681 F.3d 149; reversed and remanded

CHAPTER EIGHT

REVIEW OF PRETRIAL STAGES

There are a number of ways for a criminal case to begin. It can start from the issuance of a warrant, the determination or indictment from a grand jury, or from an instant offense. This chapter, however, focuses on a criminal case that stems from an instant offense. In such a case where an individual is arrested before the issuance of a warrant and there is no indictment, a determination of probable cause must be made. In an ordinary case such a determination is made by a magistrate judge in a Preliminary Hearing.

PRELIMINARY HEARING

The right to a preliminary hearing is established by law and therefore is not a constitutional right. Nonetheless it is now held to be a critical stage in a criminal proceeding. Thus, a criminal defendant has a due process right to the effective assistance of counsel. This stage of the case is also where most criminal lawyers start making life changing mistakes by choosing the predetermined path of least resistance.

The first indication that a lawyer did or is going to provide ineffective assistance, at the preliminary hearing stage, is marked by his advice to waive the right to a preliminary examination all together. What most lawyers don't tell criminal defendants is how important the preliminary hearing really is. A defendant is allowed, and often encouraged, to waive his or her right to a preliminary hearing. These waivers are always accepted by the court because the waiver almost always guarantees the court a conviction by plea agreement. Although, the formalities of such waivers are required; the court in most cases accepts a written waiver presented by defense counsel.

What most defendants in preliminary hearings don't know, and few lawyers advise their client, is that the prosecutor has the burden of proof at the preliminary hearing. The government, or state, need not prove a defendant's guilt beyond a reasonable doubt during a preliminary hearing. It must, however, establish that probable cause exists. The probable cause must show not only that a crime was committed but also that the particular defendant committed it. This one issue, in almost all internet crimes, gives rise to an ineffectiveness claim. Defense lawyers don't demand that the government show proof of the defendant's identity at the time of offense as opposed to his or her identity at arrest. In most internet sting operations, an agent entices someone to engage in a foolish conversation. The agent then sets up a meeting at a local business, and then arrests the first man they see that fits the description. Thus, the government shows proof of who they arrest rather than who was on the other end of the computer communication. What's most disturbing is that many men in prison today took a guilty plea to protect their minor children from the predators who work in law enforcement.

The American Criminal Justice System has set out a number of safeguards that stops the prosecution of innocent people. When looking at the trial process as a whole, one may discover that the preliminary hearing is the first opportunity to stop the process. The specific purpose of the preliminary hearing is to give the person arrested the opportunity to challenge the probable cause given to arrest them. In short, the preliminary hearing is a test the prosecutor must pass to justify putting any person through the judicial machinery.

An effective attorney knows that his preparation of a criminal case at the preliminary hearing can set course, good or bad, for the entire trial process. Counsel's best efforts in preparation for the preliminary hearing stage are absolutely essential to both the entire defense strategy in the case, as well as the overall defense as a whole. Contrary to the belief of most appointed lawyers, the days of waiting to see what the prosecution could produce are over. Today, the preliminary hearing is often the most critical stage of the trial process.

EFFECTIVE PREPARATION FOR PRELIMINARY HEARING

Trial counsel should treat the preparation for the preliminary hearing with the same level of care as he would the trial. Let there be no question the defense case should be determined by the facts of the case. It is therefore critical that defense counsel should immediately begin to gather and categorize by importance, the facts. Documents, witnesses and other materials that will be presented at the preliminary hearing should be considered as well. The best way for defense counsel to prepare for a preliminary hearing is by consulting with his client. In all situations, the client will likely know a great deal more about the facts of the case than the attorney will.

To be clear, a claim of ineffective assistance of counsel, claiming deficient performance at a preliminary hearing, can only be raised by defendants who did go to trial. Also know that an independent claim of ineffective assistance of counsel at a preliminary hearing is not grounds for relief. What this claim will do is add to the pattern of deficient performance of defense counsel. Note in the following cases the determination of relief is based on the claims presented:

- There is no basis for defendant filing motion to dismiss complaint containing felony charges for failing to contain probable cause for arrest before expiration of period provided in Fed. R. Crim. P. 5.1 for preliminary hearing or indictment; in instant case, defense counsel characterized motion to dismiss as request for magistrate to reconsider her finding that there was probable cause to arrest defendant; however, motions for reconsideration were governed by N.D. Cal. Civ. R. 7-9, pursuant to N.D. Cal. Crim. R. 2-1, and motion to dismiss in instant case did not meet requirements of N.D. Ca. Civ. R. 7-9 in various ways; there does not appear to be any good reason to create such non-statutory motion when law already provides means of assuring that defendant is not long detained if there is no probable cause for his detention after his arrest; specifically, if defendant who has been arrested on less than probable cause is in custody, he is adequately protected by requirement that within ten days of his initial appearance, magistrate judge at preliminary hearing or grand jury must find probable cause to believe offense was committed, see *United States v. Kang*, 489 F. Supp. 2d 1095 (N.D. Cal. 2007).

- Preliminary hearing is not only occasion upon which Government must justify continued detention by showing of probable cause, but also opportunity for accused to rebut that showing and it is as much arrestee's prerogative to endeavor to minimize probable cause as it is Government's to undertake to maximize it, and both sides must be indulged reasonably in their efforts as in *Coleman v. Burnett*, 477 F. 2d 1187, 155 US App DC 302 (D.C. Cir. 1973).

- Failure to issue subpoenas for material witnesses which defendant had timely requested deprives him of proper preliminary hearing and if point is properly and timely pressed, denial of hearing cannot be excused by pointing to intervening grand jury indictment, see *Ross v. Sirica*, 380 F. 2d 557, 127 US App DC 10 (D.C. Cir. 1967).

- Denial of right to call witness at preliminary hearing whose testimony is material to issue of probable cause is not only contravention of Rule 5.1(a) but also deprivation which reaches constitutional magnitude by its infringement of Sixth Amendment guaranty of effective assistance of counsel at every critical stage of criminal proceeding, in *United States v. King*, 482 F. 2d 768, 157 US App DC 179 (D.C. Cir. 1973).

GRAND JURY

The Grand Jury is traditionally known to be a buffer between the government and the rights of the people. In today's criminal justice system, however, that is not true. The primary job of the grand jury is almost the same as the magistrate judge at the preliminary hearing. The difference being that the magistrate decides if a case goes to the grand jury; and the grand jury decides if a case goes to trial. The standard for a grand jury decision is to decide or confirm that probable cause exists as to every element of the charged offense.

In its beginning, the grand jury was designed to serve a supervisory function. It had the authority to investigate willful and corrupt misconduct of the government and its officials. Today, however, the government supervises the grand jury, an action that guarantees an indictment against anyone the government chooses. This occurs because of presumptions. Even though the court has a supervisory power over the grand jury, it is a power rarely exercised. Most commonly the court leaves the government to conduct all proceedings before the grand jury and the court presumes that the government conducts itself professionally. Unfortunately, it's the court's presumption, coupled with the theory of grand jury secrecy, that has reduced the function of the grand jury to nothing more than a bad joke.

The secrecy of the grand jury was established for good reason. It was designed to protect the grand jurors from intimidation by the government, prevent the accused from evading arrest, and prevent the accused from threatening the witnesses against him. But today, secrecy only serves the interests of the prosecution. The discovery process of the grand jury helps only the government in gaining evidence and testimony from additional witnesses. The secrecy surrounding the grand jury proceeding deprives the defendant of an equal advantage by denying him and his counsel access to the proceeding. Ultimately, grand jury secrecy denies the defendant a transcript of the proceeding. Thus, the defendant has no way of knowing if the government even bothered to convene a grand jury or if the indictment is simply manufactured at the prosecutor's office. If your lawyer failed, or refuses, to challenge the existence of the grand jury he or she is ineffective. This, however, will not serve as a stand-alone claim unless it is lodged in a pre-trial motion. If your lawyer refuses to make the motion, write to your court immediately and inform your judge that your lawyer is ineffective.

> *Author's Note: In 2013, a large group of pre-trial detainees lodged an effort to discover if a grand jury was in-fact, In service at the time that hundreds of indictments were handed down, in the Northern District of Alabama. To no surprise, not one appointed defense lawyer would move the court to order the government to produce the grand jury minutes. When the defendants made their motion in pro se, the district court declared that the government would never have conducted themselves corruptly. The defendants then offered a reward to anyone, in the Northern District of Alabama, that had been called to serve on any federal grand jury. They offered $5000.00 to anyone who could prove that they had been summoned. They received not one shred of evidence that a grand jury had been convened in 2013 or the two years previous.*

In the event you are now planning to go to trial, remind your lawyer that the policy of grand jury secrecy is not absolute. A defendant may move to obtain a full transcript of the government witnesses' grand jury testimony, to compare to what the witness will testify to at trial. Remember also that, Federal Rules of Criminal Procedure, Rule 6 (e) allows disclosure of the grand jury materials to the defendant (among other) upon the filing of a motion to dismiss an indictment for matters that occurred before the grand jury.

In *Carison v. United States*, the Seventh Circuit held that, because a grand jury is a part of the judicial process, a member of the public has standing to assert a claim to grand jury transcripts because they are public records to which the public may seek access.

INDICTMENT

An indictment is the formal accusation, handed down by a grand jury that describes the criminal charges it finds. It is required to be in a written form so that it may be presented to both the court and the defendant. The Fifth Amendment and the Federal Rules of Criminal Procedure, Rule 7(a), require that a federal prosecution must be started by an indictment. The Sixth Amendment requires that the defendant receive notice of the accusation, i.e. a copy of the indictment.

This stage of the pre-trial process provides little in the way of claims development to someone filing for post-conviction relief. It does, however, provide a great deal to those of you who are in the pre-trial stage of a criminal proceeding. For those of you who are innocent it is important to demand that your counsel move to dismiss the indictment immediately. If he refuses, he is ineffective as defense counsel. This claim must be raised at or before your arraignment.

> *Author's Note: This is a really good time to face reality. From this point of your life forward it will be important for you to decide if you are truly innocent, or you believe that they can't prove you guilty. The facts are that, if you are indeed guilty, your own attorney will help the government convict you. Thus, if you are guilty don't piss them off by causing them to perform work they ordinarily wouldn't have to. They can be quite creative. If you are guilty, face the music and plead guilty, thereby minimizing your sentence. If you fight your lawyer knowing that you are guilty, your sentence will be much higher than anyone would normally expect, see the chapter for binding plea agreements.*

VINDICTIVE INDICTMENTS

A subject of specific interest to defendants who challenge their indictments is vindictive prosecution or vindictive indictments. Where a defendant has successfully moved to dismiss an indictment, a subsequent indictment that contains additional or nearly identical charges is, in some cases, brought by the government. Such indictments are subject to a meaningful attack as vindictive. The idea is: that a defendant may not be penalized for exercising a legal right, see *North Carolina v. Pearce*, 395 U.S. 711 (1969) (harsher sentence on retrial after successful appeal only allowed if objective, non-vindictive reasons are stated).

In *Blackledge v. Perry*, 417 U.S. 21 (1974), the defendant was convicted of a misdemeanor, but appealed and was granted a jury trial de novo in a higher court. The prosecutor then indicted him for a felony. The Supreme Court ruled that the increase in charges violated due process because it penalized the defendant for the exercise of his right to appeal, even though there was "no evidence that the prosecutor acted in bad faith or maliciously in seeking a felony indictment." *id.* at 28. Due process forbids even the appearance of vindictiveness, which should be presumed from the filing of additional charges after the defendant asserts a right, see *United States v. Schiller*, 424 A.2d 51, 56-57 (D.C. 1980).

Upon a defense motion to dismiss for prosecutorial vindictiveness, if the court determines that the prosecutor's actions give rise to the realistic likelihood of vindictiveness, then the government must rebut the presumption of vindictiveness by explaining its decision, as in *United States v. Goodwin*, 457 U.S. 368, 373 (1982); *Schiller*, 424 A.2d 51, 56-57. In determining whether the government has met its burden, the court should consider (1) the nature of the case; (2) the status of the case; (3) the nature of the right asserted by the defendant; (4) the type of vindictiveness alleged; and (5) the nature of the harm involved, see *Schiller*, 424 A.2d at 56; and also *United States v. Mahdi*, 777 A.2d 814 (D.C. 2001) (clarifying standard and procedures for consideration of claims of prosecutorial vindictiveness). Any time a motion to dismiss a complaint or indictment has been granted, and a new indictment increases the charges, defense counsel should consider filing a motion to dismiss because of prosecutorial vindictiveness.

WAIVER OF INDICTMENT

In a federal prosecution, a defendant may be prosecuted by information if the defendant waives prosecution by indictment, see Federal Rules of Criminal Procedure, Rule 7(b). If you claim to be innocent and planning to prove your case at a speedy and public trial, do not waive your right to prosecution by indictment. If, however, you are guilty and plan to plead guilty it may be a good idea to waive your right to an indictment.

Anytime a defendant is guilty, a good attorney will seek ways to minimize his client's sentence exposure. This can be done in a number of ways. Your attorney may seek leniency based on your substantial assistance to the government, your agreement to plead guilty in exchange to drop charges, your plea to a lesser included offense, or a number of other options. In this process, your attorney may suggest that a defendant waive a few constitutional rights. In such a case, your attorney's advice may be very good advice. When you plan to plead guilty, the government will give you a little more benefit in exchange for your assistance in making their job easier.

SPEEDY TRIAL

The constitution of the United States provides that, "in all criminal prosecutions, the accused shall enjoy the right to a speedy and public trial …," see the Sixth Amendment. This right was later clarified by the United States Congress with the enactment of the Speedy Trial Act of 1974, later amended in 1979.

The right to a speedy trial is available to defendants for the sole purpose of bringing a timely resolution to criminal proceedings. Because of the Speedy Trial Act, a defendant can no longer be jailed until his expected sentence is served in pre-trial detention. But this right must be invoked by the defendant. As with all other constitutional and statutory rights, the court will not protect the right to a speedy trial unless you ask them to do so. Again, if you are guilty and looking for a deal, sit back and enjoy the ride. If however, you are going to trial, make sure your lawyer moves for a "speedy and public trial."

The Speedy Trial Act is in theory, to protect the rights of the accused. In today's system that is not particularly true. If it were, all lawyers would move to secure this right for their client. In most cases an appointed lawyer will ask you to sign a speedy trial waiver during your first meeting. He or she will spout off about many reasons to waive the right but be aware that the waiver only helps in securing a guilty verdict. If the government's case was sound, they would be pushing for a quick resolution. This stage as well as some of the previous, is not grounds by itself to base a claim of ineffective assistance of counsel. It will, however, help to set a pattern of ineffectiveness. For clarification of The Speedy Trial Act, read the following statute:

§3161. TIME LIMITS AND EXCLUSIONS

(a) In any case involving a defendant charged with an offense, the appropriate judicial officer, at the earliest practicable time, shall, after consultation with the counsel for the defendant and the attorney for the Government, set the case for trial on a day certain, or list it for trial on a weekly or other short-term calendar at a place within the judicial district, so as to assure a speedy trial.

(b) Any information or indictment charging an individual with the commission of an offense shall be filed within thirty days from the date on which such individual was arrested or served with a summons in connection with such charges. If an individual has been charged with a felony in a district in which no grand jury has been in session during such thirty-day period, the period of time for filing of the indictment shall be extended an additional thirty days.

(c) (1) In any case in which a plea of not guilty is entered, the trial of a defendant charged in an information or indictment with the commission of an offense shall commence within seventy days from the filing date (and making public) of the information or indictment, or from the date the defendant has appeared before a judicial officer of the court in which such charge is pending, whichever date last occurs. If a defendant consents in writing to be tried before a magistrate [United States magistrate judge] on a complaint, the trial shall commence within seventy days from the date of such consent.

(2) Unless the defendant consents in writing to the contrary, the trial shall not commence less than thirty

days from the date on which the defendant first appears through counselor expressly waives counsel and elects to precede *pro se*.

(d) (1) If any indictment or information is dismissed upon motion of the defendant, or any charge contained in a complaint filed against an individual is dismissed or otherwise dropped, and thereafter a complaint is filed against such defendant or individual charging him with the same offense or an offense based on the same conduct or arising from the same criminal episode, or an information or indictment is filed charging such defendant with the same offense or an offense based on the same conduct or arising from the same criminal episode, the provisions of subsections (b) and (c) of this section shall be applicable with respect to such subsequent complaint, indictment, or information, as the case may be.

(2) If the defendant is to be tried upon an indictment or information dismissed by a trial court and reinstated following an appeal, the trial shall commence within seventy days from the date the actions occasioning the trial becomes final, except that the court retrying the case may extend the period for trial not to exceed one hundred and eighty days from the date the, action occasioning the trial becomes final if the unavailability of witnesses or other factors resulting from the passage of time shall make trial within seventy days impractical. The periods of delay enumerated in section 3161(h) [18 USCS §3l61(h)] are excluded in computing the time limitations specified in this section. The sanctions of section 3162 [18 USCS §3162] apply to this subsection.

(e) If the defendant is to be tried again following a declaration by the trial judge of a mistrial or following an order of such judge for a new trial, the trial shall commence within seventy days from the date the actions occasioning the retrial becomes final. If the defendant is to be tried again following an appeal or a collateral attack, the trial shall commence within seventy days form the date the action occasioning the retrial becomes final, except that the court retrying the case may extend the period for retrial not to exceed one hundred and eighty days from the date the action occasioning the retrial becomes final if unavailability of witnesses or other factors resulting from passage of time shall make trial within seventy days impractical. The periods of delay enumerated in section 3161(h) [18 USCS §3161(h)] are excluded in computing the time limitations specified in this section. The sanctions of section 3162 [18 USCS §3162] apply to this subsection.

(f) Notwithstanding the provisions of subsection (b) of this section, for the first twelve-calendar-month period following the effective date of this section as set forth in section 3163(a) of this chapter [18 USCS §3163][,] the time limit imposed with respect to the period between arrest and indictment by subsection (b) of this section shall be sixty days, for the second such twelve-month period such time limit shall be forty-five days and for the third such period such time limit shall be thirty-five days.

(g) Notwithstanding the provisions of subsection (c) of this section, for the first twelve-calendar-month period following the effective date of this section as set forth in section 3163(b) of this chapter [18 USCS §3163(b)], the time limit with respect to the period between arraignment and trial imposed by subsection (c) of this section shall be one hundred and eighty days, for the second such twelve-month period such time limit shall be one hundred and twenty days, and for the third such period such time limit with respect to the period between arraignment and trial shall be eighty days.

(h) The following periods of delay shall be excluded in computing the time within which an information or an indictment must be filed, or in computing the time within which the trial of any such offense must commence:

(1) Any period of delay resulting from other proceedings concerning the defendant, including but not limited to –

(A) delay resulting from any proceeding, including any examinations, to determine the mental competency or physical capacity of the defendant;

(B) delay resulting from trial with respect to other charges against the defendant;

(C) delay resulting from any interlocutory appeal

(D) delay resulting from any pretrial motion, from the filing of the motion through the conclusion of the hearing on, or other prompt disposition of, such motion;

(E) delay resulting from any proceeding relating to the transfer of a case or the removal of any defendant from another district under the Federal Rules of Criminal Procedure;

(F) delay resulting from transportation of any defendant from another district, or to and from places of examination or hospitalization, except that any time consumed in excess of ten days from the date an order of removal or an order directing such transportation, and the defendant's arrival at the destination shall be presumed to be unreasonable;

(G) delay resulting from consideration by ·the court of a proposed plea agreement to be entered into by the defendant and the attorney for the Government; and

(H) delay reasonably attributable to any period, not to exceed thirty days, during which any proceeding concerning the defendant is actually under advisement by the court.

(2) Any period of delay during which prosecution is deferred by the attorney for the Government pursuant to written agreement with the defendant, with the approval of the court, for the purpose of allowing the defendant to demonstrate his good conduct.

(3) (A) Any period of delay resulting from the absence or unavailability of the defendant or an essential witness.

(B) For purposes of subparagraph (A) of this paragraph, a defendant or an essential witness shall be considered absent when his whereabouts are unknown and, in addition, he is attempting to avoid apprehension or prosecution or his whereabouts cannot be determined by due diligence. For purposes of such subparagraph, a defendant or an essential witness shall be considered unavailable whenever his whereabouts are known but his presence for trial cannot be obtained by due diligence, or he resists appearing at or being returned for trial.

(4) Any period of delay resulting from the fact that the defendant is mentally incompetent or physically unable to stand trial.

(5) If the information or indictment is dismissed upon motion of the attorney for the government and thereafter a charge is filed against the defendant for the same offense, or any offense required to be joined with that offense, any period of delay from the date the charge was dismissed to the date the time limitation would commence to run as to the subsequent charge had there been no previous charge.

(6) A reasonable period of delay when the defendant is joined for trial with a codefendant as to whom the time for trial has not run and no motion for severance has been granted.

(7) (A) Any period of delay resulting from a continuance granted by any judge on his own motion or at the request of the defendant or his counselor at the request of the attorney for the Government, if the judge granted such continuance on the basis of his findings that the ends of justice served by taking such action outweigh the best interest of the public and the defendant in a speedy trial. No such period of delay resulting from a continuance granted by the court in accordance with this paragraph shall be excludable under this subsection unless the court sets forth, in the record of the case, either

orally or in writing, its reasons for finding that the ends of justice served by the granting of such continuance outweigh the best interests of the public and the defendant in a speedy trial.

(B) The factors, among other, which a judge shall consider in determining whether to grant a continuance under subparagraph (A) of this paragraph in any case are as follows:

    (i) Whether the failure to grant such a continuance in the proceeding would be likely to make a continuation of such proceeding impossible or result in a miscarriage of justice.

    (ii) Whether the case is so unusual or so complex due to the number of defendants, the nature of the prosecution, or the existence of novel questions of fact or law, that it is unreasonable to expect adequate preparation for pretrial proceedings or for the trial itself within the time limits established by this section.

    (iii) Whether, in a case in which arrest precedes indictment, delay in the filing of the indictment is caused because the arrest occurs at a time such that it is unreasonable to expect return and filing of the indictment within the period specified in section 3161(b) [18 USCS §3161(b)] or because the fact upon which the grand jury must base its determination are unusual or complex.

    (iv) Whether the failure to grant such a continuance in a case which, taken as a whole, is not so unusual or so complex as to fall within clause (ii), would deny the defendant reasonable time to obtain counsel, would unreasonably deny the defendant or the Government continuity of counsel, or would deny counsel for the defendant or the attorney for the Government the reasonable time necessary for effective preparation, taking into account the exercise of due diligence.

    (C) No continuance under subparagraph (A) of this paragraph shall be granted because of general congestion of the court's calendar, or lack of diligent preparation or failure to obtain available witnesses on the part of the attorney for the Government.

(8) Any period of delay, not to exceed one year, ordered by a district court upon an application of a party and a finding by a preponderance of the evidence that an official request, as defined in section 3292 of the title [18 USCS §3292], has been made for evidence of any such offense and that it reasonably appears, or reasonably appeared at the time the request was made, that such evidence is, or was, in such foreign country.

(i) If trial did not commence within the time limitation specified in section 3161 [18 USCS §3161] because the defendant had entered a plea of guilty or *nolo contendere* subsequently withdrawn to any or all charges in an indictment or information, the defendant shall be deemed indicted with respect to all charges therein contained within the meaning of section 3161 [18 USCS §3161] on the day the order permitting withdrawal of the plea becomes final.

(j) (1) If the attorney for the Government knows that a person charged with an offense is serving a term of imprisonment in any penal institution, he shall promptly –

    (A) undertake to obtain the presence of the prisoner for trial; or

    (B) cause a detainer to be filed with the person having custody of the prisoner and request him to so advise the prisoner and to advise the prisoner of his right to demand trial.

(2) If the person having custody of such a prisoner receives a detainer, he shall promptly advise the prisoner of the charge and of the prisoner's right to demand trial. If at any time thereafter the prisoner informs the person having custody that he does demand trial, such person shall cause notice to that effect to be sent promptly to the attorney for the Government who caused the detainer to be filed.

(3) Upon receipt of such notice, the attorney for the Government shall promptly seek to obtain the presence of the prisoner for trial.

(4) When the person having custody of the prisoner receives from the attorney for the Government a properly supported request for temporary custody of such prisoner for trial, the prisoner shall be made available to that attorney for the government (subject, in cases of inter jurisdictional transfer, to any right of the prisoner to contest the legality of his delivery).

(k) (1) If the defendant is absent (as defined by subsection (h)(3)) on the day set for trial, and the defendant's subsequent appearance before the court on a bench warrant or other process or surrender to the court occurs more than 21 days after the day set for trial, the defendant shall be deemed to have first appeared before a judicial officer of the court in which the information or indictment is pending within the meaning of subsection (c) on the date of the defendant's subsequent appearance before the court.

(2) If the defendant is absent (as defined by subsection (h)(3)) on the day set for trial, and the defendant's subsequent appearance before the court on a bench warrant or other process or surrender to the court occurs not more than 21 days after the day set for trial, the time limit required by subsection (c), as extended by subsection (h), shall further extended by 21 days.

ARRAIGNMENT

The arraignment is the first stage of the criminal process, where a defendant can raise a meaningful, stand alone, claim of ineffective assistance of counsel. If you review the Supreme Court case of *Powell v. Alabama*, 287 U.S. 24 (1932), you will find that the Sixth Amendment guarantee does not apply only to trial. But the court noted that the phase of the criminal proceedings where the constitutional right to the effective assistance of counsel is the most critical is, "the time of … arraignment until the beginning of … trial, when consultation, thorough-going investigation and preparation [are] vitally important." The court added that defendants were "as much entitled to such aid during that period as at the trial itself."

In a federal criminal proceeding you will discover that the arraignment is governed by the Federal Rules of Criminal Procedure, Rule 10. Also, the arraignment is the specific stage of the criminal process where the defendant is officially made aware of the charges against him. A defendant should never waive his or her right to arraignment. He or she may discover that the government is misapplying a statute, simply by listening to the charges as recited by the court as opposed to some appointed lawyers.

A very good example of a statute that is often misapplied is in the application of 18 U.S.C. §2422(b) as an all-inclusive sexual abuse statue. In reading this troubling statute you find that its plain language criminalizes the act of enticing a minor to commit a sexual act for which the minor could be charged. Such conduct would include prostitution and/or the production of child pornography. In both instances, the minor would be chargeable. The government however applies the statute to criminalize all sexual acts by excising the words "for which any person can be charged with a criminal offense." You will find that, in most indictments charging a violation of 18 U.S.C. §2422(b), the government replaces the words "any person" with the word "defendant" effectively changing the conduct that the statute actually criminalizes. Unfortunately, if you waive your arraignment, you would not be able to raise the claim that 18 U.S.C. §2422(b) is unconstitutionally void for vagueness.

At arraignment, the defendant will enter a plea of not guilty after which the court will set the trial schedule. The defendant will then have twenty days after the status hearing to file all pretrial challenges.

Therefore, immediately after arraignment, counsel must read the indictment carefully, comparing it to the strict reading of the statue as well as the conduct that the government has accused. In many cases, the indictment charges a defendant with the wrong offense among other errors. Many of these errors are the result of the government submitting erroneous indictments to the grand jury. The question however, is why the grand jury would actually approve an erroneous document. The most obvious answer is rather simple, the grand jury, if one is actually convened, doesn't actually read the indictment. This raises an interesting claim that, the grand jury does not act independently of the prosecution. The other possibility is that the grand jury may have read the indictment but failed to notice the error. That suggests that the grand jury was not adequately informed of the law and the evidence. As you may imagine, counsel's failure to find such an error gives rise to a very good post-conviction claim of ineffective assistance of counsel.

Needless to say, a speedy trial demand and a challenge to the constitutionality of the statute should be made at arraignment and renewed at every stage that follows. A pretrial defendant should not remain silent about speedy trial demands when the government moves for continuances. Such silence could ultimately result in forfeiture of the speedy trial right altogether. When objecting to a continuance, counsel should move for an immediate trial. If a co-defendant requests a continuance, counsel should move for severance and immediate trial.

- A criminal defendant's right to counsel under the Federal Constitution's Sixth Amendment attaches by the time of his examination by a court-appointed psychiatrist, where the defendant's indictment and arraignment and the appointment of defense counsel have all occurred prior to that examination. *Satterwhite v. Texas* (1998) 486 U.S. 249, 100 L. Ed. 2d 284, 108 S. Ct. 1792.

- The right, under the Federal Constitution's Sixth Amendment, to the assistance of counsel in all criminal prosecutions is offense-specific; the right cannot be invoked once for all future prosecutions, since it does not attach until the initiation of adversary judicial criminal proceedings by formal charge, preliminary hearing, indictment, information, or arraignment; just as the right is offense-specific, so also its effect of invalidating, subsequent to the attachment and invocation of the right, any waivers of the right during police-initiated custodial interviews is offense-specific. *McNeil v. Wisconsin* (1991) 501 U.S. 171, 115 L. Ed. 2d 158, 111 S. Ct. 2204.

- In *Stovall v. Denno* (1967) 388 U.S. 293, 18 L. Ed. 2d 1199, 87 S. Ct. 1967, it was recognized that the Supreme Court's rulings establishing the right to counsel at some forms of arraignment were entitles to retroactive application. The Sixth Amendment does not require the appointment of counsel before indictment for indigent inmates confined in administrative detention while being investigated for criminal activities. *United States v. Gouveia* (1984) 467 U.S. 180, 81 L. Ed. 2d 146, 104 S. Ct. 2292.

- Defendant's sixth Amendment right to assistance of counsel is violated by admission at trial of incriminating statements made by him after indictment to his codefendant, secret government informant, at meeting to plan defense strategy for upcoming trial with his codefendant, who, unknown to defendant, was wearing body wire transmitting device which enabled police to record incriminating statements; fact that police had other, legitimate reasons for listening to defendant's conversation with this codefendant at meeting, namely, to investigate defendant's alleged plan to kill the state's witness and to insure codefendant's safety, does not justify admission of incriminating statements; to allow admission of evidence obtained from defendant in violation of his Sixth Amendment rights whenever police assert an alternative, legitimate reason for their surveillance invites abuse by law-enforcement personnel in form of fabricated investigations and risks evisceration of Sixth Amendment right. *Maine v. Moulton* (1985) 474 U.S. 159, 88 L. Ed. 2d 481, 106 S. Ct. 477.

PRETRIAL INEFFECTIVE ASSISTANCE

This is a very common occurrence in the federal criminal justice system. It most commonly occurs in cases of appointed counselor when counsel is prepaid. The cause is counsel's need to get the case to speedy resolution and avoid losing money by having to do more work than he will be paid for. Therefore, counsel will outright refuse to file any meaningful pretrial motions. This conduct by counsel is an act of ineffective assistance of counsel, in cases of actual innocence and unethical charging practices.

To overcome pretrial ineffective assistance of counsel a defendant must make the claim before trial and/or entering a plea agreement. If a defendant claims that counsel is providing ineffective assistance before the trial or plea agreement, the court must, before trial or acceptance of plea agreement, "conduct an inquiry sufficient to determine the truth and scope of the defendant's allegations," *Monroe v. United States*, 389 R. 2d 811 (D.C. 1978); see also *McFadden v. United States*, 614 A. 2d 11, 15 (D.C. 1992); *Nelson v. United States*, 601 A. 2d 582, 591 (D.C. 1991); *Gordon v. United States*, 582 A. 2d 944, 945-47 (D.C. 1990); *Farrell v. United States*, 391 A. 2d 755, 760-61 (D.C. 1978).

> *[W]hen a defendant requests new counsel, based on pre-trial ... ineffectiveness, several weeks before trial, and the trial court conducts no inquiry, this court will remand for findings on the issue. The court will also remand when the defendant has made a pretrial request for new counsel immediately before trial but no inquiry has been made, and thus there is no basis on which to determine whether the claim may have merit. On the other hand, if "there is sufficient evidence on the record to sustain the ruling of the trial court in spite of the court's failure to make a proper inquiry before ruling," this court will affirm. We will reverse outright, however, where there is obvious prejudice, or when the trial court's conclusions are unsupported by the pre-trial record.*
>
> – *McFadden*, 614 A. 2d at 17-18 (citations omitted).

On post-conviction review, if no pre-trial findings were made, the government must prove by clear and convincing evidence that the defendant was accorded representation at trial by an attorney who was prepared within the requisite range of competence, in *Matthews v. United States*, 459 A. 2d 1063 (D.C. 1983). Specifically, it must show that counsel (1) conferred with the defendant as often as necessary and advised the client of his or her rights, (2) elicited from the defendant matters of defense and ascertained whether any potential defenses were available, and (3) conducted both factual and legal investigation sufficiently in advance to permit reflection and to determine whether matters of defense could be developed, *Monroe*, 389 A. 2d at 821.

CHAPTER NINE

ENTERING A PLEA AGREEMENT

Regardless of a defendant's intentions, the thoughts on his lawyer's mind are usually guilty plea at all cost and then sentencing. A guilty plea leads to a quick and final end to most criminal cases. The thought of most defense lawyers is that all defendants are guilty, and a guilty plea protects the public. Other benefits are reduced caseloads for both the prosecution and the defense bar. But, most importantly it will save the expense of defending the case at trial.

There are no controlling laws or special courses designed to guide an attorney while he decides who deserves to go to trial or when. It has been suggested that it is a skill learned only through practice and experience. Until that experience is gained, it is American families who are victimized and their children who suffer at the hand of ignorance. Plea bargains are surprisingly common. An estimated 160,000 people behind bars today may have admitted to crimes that they did not commit, all because of the ineffectiveness of a lawyer who chose the predetermined path of least resistance. In a recent article federal judge Jed. S. Rakoff is quoted as saying that, "Criminologists estimate that between 2 and 8 percent of convicted felons, from 40,000 to 160,000 people, are innocent of the crime to which they pleaded guilty." In the Federal Criminal Justice System, it is the Federal Rules of Criminal Procedure, Rule 11, which provides the only guidance to all involved in seeking plea agreements.

Author's Note: One of the most compelling yet ignored issues concerning plea agreements is the incarceration of a person who is actually innocent. Such an act is a direct violation of the most overlooked due process amendment. The Thirteenth Amendment to the Constitution of the United States states that:

"Neither slavery nor involuntary servitude, except as a punishment for crime whereof the party shall have been duly convicted, shall exist within the United States or any place subject to their jurisdiction."

The language of the Thirteenth Amendment is clear in its meaning that the incarceration of the innocent is prohibited under the "Constitution, and the laws of the United States which shall be made in pursuance thereof." Thus, any court, prosecutor, or defense lawyer who knowingly aids in the incarceration of an innocent person is in fact subject to a criminal conviction under the laws of the United States, see 18 U.S.C. §242.

Therefore, it is counsel's duty, as an officer of the court, to determine whether his client is actually guilty. In today's practice of law however, there is the erroneous belief that there may exist situations where a practical approach would require a guilty plea from someone who is actually innocent. Under the Constitution and the ethical practice of law, this theory is absurd. There are circumstances where an innocent defendant may believe that he must plead guilty due to other concerns. Those concerns may include adverse publicity, injury to their families, sentence of incarceration upon conviction, and/or financial ruin. Ultimately, the choice to plead guilty belongs to the defendant; but defense counsel has an ethical obligation to advise his client against the plea, as well as alert the court to any potential miscarriage of justice.

Counsel's first obligation is to find out what his client's position is. In a great majority of cases counsel will find, through attorney client visits, that most defendants are indeed guilty of something. But the defendant may actually be mischarged. In cases such as these, the attorney must find a charge contained within the charging instrument that is agreeable to all the parties in his or her plea negotiation.

UNDERSTANDING THE CHARGING STATUTE

Once a defendant, who is actually guilty, decides to enter a guilty plea there are a few things to consider before be accepts any particular plea agreement. First the defendant must be made aware of the reach of the charging statute. He must have a good understanding of the essential elements of the charged offense as they relate to the facts as well as the law. It is important to not only be aware of the statute's limitations, but also the lesser included offenses, in order to determine if the defendant has been overcharged. The government is also notorious for padding an indictment with additional charges to make sure that they have bargaining room. A related issue is unexpected enhancement, which will likely increase a defendant's sentence. This factor is particularly common in drug and child pornography cases.

AN ACCURATE FACTUAL BASIS

Most defendants, whose cases have little to no evidence, are encouraged, and sometimes even coerced, to plead guilty. To make up for the lack of evidence, the government will pad the factual basis with conduct that didn't actually happen. They do this for the sole purpose of causing prejudice against the judge. A judge who is thoroughly outraged with a grossly over-exaggerated factual basis won't bother to see if there is in fact any evidence to support a guilty plea. The unfortunate side to this tactic is that the conduct, even if removed, will later become relevant conduct that will be considered at sentencing. Therefore, even if a defendant has the conduct removed, he will still be sentenced for it.

DROPPED CHARGES

One of the most common bargaining tools that the government USCS is the ruse of dropping charges. They do this by stating their intent, under Rule 11(c)(I)(A), in motion "to dismiss, other charges." The government then goes on to draft an agreement, under 11(c)(I)(B), that states that the government will recommend, or agree not to oppose the defendant's request, that a particular sentence or sentencing range is appropriate or "that a particular provision of the sentencing guidelines, or policy statement, or sentencing factor does or does not apply (such a recommendation or request does not bind the court)." What this last part, the part in parenthesis, does is nullify any and all benefit offered by the government. This type of plea agreement is known as a non-binding plea agreement. This type of agreement should be avoided because, even though the charge is dropped, the judge will sentence a defendant for the conduct in the dropped charge anyway.

BINDING PLEA AGREEMENTS

When a defendant faces the facts and determines that he cannot win at trial because he is indeed guilty, it can be beneficial to enter a plea agreement. Unfortunately, if a defendant signs the wrong kind, he or she is likely to be sentenced more harshly than if they were to have lost at trial.

In the beginning, the plea-bargaining procedure was designed to provide a defendant with a method to reduce his sentence exposure. The way it was intended to work was to offer the defendant a lower sentence in exchange for his acceptance of an expedited process. The plea agreement, which like all other contracts, ordinarily set out all the conditions of the agreement in print, was then signed by the defendant, the defense counsel, and the prosecution. Afterward the court was left to only sentence the defendant and file the appropriate judgment and commitment order.

Somewhere along the line however, the courts and the government transformed the prison system into a lucrative enterprise that sustains a large portion of the American economy. The courts now seek higher sentences and most often from the lowest-level offenders; the government lobbies for charges that include longer sentences, stricter laws, and the criminalization of more and more conduct. One of those changes included allowing non-binding plea agreements, leaving all the relating expenditures to be paid by the taxpayers, a cost of nearly $800 billion a year.

The answer to this troubling issue is by demanding a binding plea agreement. At the inception of the plea agreement process they were all binding. But today the prosecutors, in seeking higher sentences by deception, offer non-binding plea agreements first. Your lawyer will advise you that the government will want a higher sentence in a binding agreement, which is true. That's because they already know how long of a sentence the judge will hand down. The estimate given to a defendant by his counsel and the government is only a number to entice the defendant to plead guilty in the first place. Therefore, to know what sentence you actually face and to have it guaranteed regardless of budgets, quotas, and the judge's new boat payment, *demands a binding plea agreement.*

IN THE FEDERAL SYSTEM

As with most other courts, in any state jurisdiction, a defendant has the right to the effective assistance of counsel, in front of a federal court, while making a plea agreement. Again, there is no constitutional right to a plea agreement. Also remember that it is the Federal Rules of Criminal Procedure, not the law, which governs the plea agreement process. It is Rule 11 that governs the conduct of the attorneys, the defendants, and the judges during the process. For example, the court (A.K.A. the judge) may not participate in the negotiation of, or the encouraging of the defendant to take, a plea bargain. When a judge does get involved, and all do at some point or another, they are in violation of Rule 11(c)(1). Although, the violation is an obvious due process violation; it will not produce automatic relief from the plea agreement. In such a case the reviewing court, usually the court of appeals in the circuit, will read the district court docket. The panel of that court will then determine that the defendant entered the agreement willfully and affirm the conviction. The reviewing court is supposed to look at all the events that transpired in the district court in an effort to determine the impact of that particular error on the defendant's decision to plead guilty. The court should consider whether it was reasonably probable that, without the judge's interference, the defendant would have exercised his right to go to trial. This claim will always lose in a direct appeal. That's because the defendant's defense counsel is not providing the effective assistance of counsel that the defendant is guaranteed under the Constitution of the United States. What the lawyer should have done or would be doing at that particular point is object to the court's interference, thus denying the court the opportunity to become a problem in the first place. Moreover, the defendant's lawyer was duty bound to report the incident to the Public Integrity Section of the Department of Justice, because the judge is depriving the defendant of his civil rights, a criminal violation of 18 U.S.C. §242.

THE DEFENDANT'S RIGHTS UNDER F. R. CRIM. P., RULE 11

Most plea agreements in federal prosecutions are not binding on other courts in the state. In addition, the entry of a plea agreement in one federal district is not binding on any other federal district except for the one in which the plea agreement is accepted. This is a very serious part of plea agreements. In most agreements, this element will be vaguely listed and should be thoroughly explained to a defendant by his counsel.

The next most serious issue of plea agreements is that most plea agreements are not binding on the court they are in, either. If a defendant enters a non-conditional plea of guilty, he or she admits to all of the elements of the charged offense, without regard to what the truth may actually be. The defendant also waives many of his or her Constitutional rights, most of which they don't yet understand. Because of the built-in admissions and waivers, pleas must be made knowingly and willingly. The defendant must also have the advice of counsel and the defendant must be competent to enter a plea. By entering a plea of guilty, the defendant agrees to waive a number of constitutional rights, such as:

- The right to a jury trial;
- The right to confront the accuser;

- The right to not be a witness against himself;
- The right to call witnesses in his own defense;
- The right to make a claim that counsel provided ineffective assistance in his advice to enter a guilty plea that was to the benefit of defense counsel himself; etc.

A guilty plea does not waive jurisdictional challenges to convictions such as the failure of an indictment to charge an offense or lack of subject matter jurisdiction. This claim, however, will not be heard by the district court. Federal judges are well practiced in ignoring justice, so that they may fill their conviction and budgetary quotas. The claim must be filed at every opportunity, nonetheless. And in the end, it will be a claim of ineffective assistance of counsel for not detecting the courts (corruption) error. Again, make a claim of subject matter jurisdiction every step of the way. That way it is preserved to claim as an ineffective assistance of counsel, claim, for counsel's failure to act on the error.

If an attorney is providing you with effective assistance of counsel, he will preserve all constitutional claims for appeal. This preservation can be secured in one of two ways. First, a defendant, with the sound advice of counsel, may plead not guilty and proceed through trial. He or she is therefore denied any benefits of a plea agreement. Second, in order to avoid such a problem, the court may accept a conditional plea agreement. A defendant may enter a conditional plea that reserves the right to appeal specific pretrial motions that would ordinarily be waived. In the event the defendant wins his appeal, the defendant then has the undisputable right to withdraw his guilty plea.

BINDING PLEA AGREEMENT (FEDERAL)

As has been previously stated, a plea agreement is a contract. It will, without waiver, bind the defendant to the whims of the court and the government, who have absolutely no concern for justice. Unless the defendant demands a binding plea agreement, he or she will enjoy no guarantee of anything but a long prison sentence ln a federal institution. Binding plea agreements under Rule 11(c)(1)(C) are not favored by the court. That's because it informs the defendant, up front, how long the court intends to sentence him for. When the length of sentence becomes an issue during the plea negotiation process, the defense lawyer and the government are required to be honest about the expected outcome of the case.

In the ordinary federal case, a defense lawyer will always inform the defendant of his base offense level, as found in the United States sentencing Guidelines. For example, the base offense level for the unlawful possession of cocaine is level 6 (see U.S.S.G. Chapter Two).

The defendant's counsel will then show the defendant a copy of the sentencing table in chapter 5 of the guidelines. Finding that the defendant has one previous drug offense, for possession of cocaine, and one speeding ticket gives him four criminal history points. Counsel shows the defendant that four points places him in Category Three. Reading the Sentencing Table like an elementary school times table; the lawyer shows the defendant that 6 criminal history points, cross sectioned under Category Three, gives a guideline sentencing range of two-to-eight months.

Defense counsel then advises his client that a plea agreement will most likely have him out of the county jail in a matter of a few short months, this statement is technically true. The defendant, eager to get back home, agrees to plead guilty. The government drafts an open plea agreement that only include that the government will not pursue additional charges. Everyone signs and the court accepts the plea agreement. The court then turns the case over to the United States probation office who eagerly seeks the longest sentence possible under the law. What counsel failed to tell his client, the defendant, is that monitory budgets are determined based on the numbers of months handed down in criminal sentences. With an open plea a probation officer can turn an expected sentence of two-to-eight months into a sentence of twenty years to life.

Once all is completed, the defendant is brought into a courtroom to be sentenced. What the defendant discovered was that with just a few enhancements, which are normal under the U.S.S.G., his adjusted base offense level is now much higher. The defendant's lawyer failed to mention the drug quantity table which, with the drug about of 450 kilograms over the previous fifteen years, turned his base offense level of 6 to an adjusted offense level of 38. Thus, counsel's advice of two-to-eight months was grossly misleading. With an actual adjusted offense level of 38 the defendant was subjected to a range of 292 to 365 months in prison, an over twenty-year minimum guideline sentence.

It is not enough for your lawyer to be right about the expected sentencing exposure. A defendant must also get a binding agreement, *in writing*, before he can have any reasonable expectation of the outcome. With a binding plea agreement that specifies a particular number of months, a defendant can have an avenue for recourse when the government and the court fail to keep their word. Read the following Supreme Court decision.

SANTOBELLO v. NEW YORK
404 US 257, 30 L ED 2D 427, 92 8 CT 496
ARGUED NOVEMBER 15, 1971, DECIDED DECEMBER 20, 1971

SUMMARY

After being indicted on two felony counts under New York statutes, and after negotiation with the prosecuting attorney, the defendant withdrew his not guilty plea and entered a guilty plea to a lesser included offense, the prosecutor agreeing to make no recommendation as to the sentence to be imposed. The New York trial court accepted the guilty plea and set a date for a sentencing hearing, which was subsequently postponed, and at which a new prosecuting attorney appeared and apparently being ignorant of his colleague's commitment, recommended that the maximum one-year sentence be imposed. Although defendant objected and sought adjournment of the sentencing hearing, the judge stated that he was not influenced by the prosecutor's recommendation and imposed the maximum sentence on the basis of a presentence report. The Supreme Court of New York, Appellate Division, First Department, affirmed the conviction (35 App div 2d 1084, 316 NYS 2d 194), and the defendant was denied leave to appeal to the New York Court of Appeals.

On *certiorari*, the United States Supreme Court vacated the judgment and remanded the case. In an opinion by Burger, Ch. J., it was held (1) in expressing the unanimous view of the court, that the disposition of criminal charges by agreement between the prosecutor and the accused-which was an essential component of the administration of justice, to be encouraged when properly administered-must be attended by safeguards, that when a guilty plea rested in significant degree on a promise of the prosecutor, so that it could be said to be part of the inducement, such promise must be fulfilled, and that the state court's affirmance of the conviction was improper in the case at bar, it being immaterial that the breach of agreement by the prosecution was inadvertent, and (2) in expressing the view of four of the seven members of the court, that the case should be remanded to the state court to decide whether the circumstances of the case required only that there be specific performance of the agreement on the plea, with the defendant being resentence before a different judge, or whether the relief sought by the defendant as to withdrawing his guilty plea should be granted.

Douglas, J., concurring, joined the opinion of the court, and expressed the view that where a "plea bargain" was not kept by the prosecutor, the sentence must be vacated and the state court should decide in light of the circumstances of each case whether due process required (1) that there be specific performance of the plea bargain, or (2) that the defendant be given the option to go to trial on the original charges, the defendant's preference to be given considerable, if not controlling, weight in choosing the appropriate remedy.

SYLLABUS

After negotiations with the prosecutor, petitioner withdrew his previous not-guilty plea to two felony counts and pleaded guilty to a lesser-included offense, the prosecutor having agreed to make no recommendation as to sentence. At petitioner's appearance for sentencing many months later a new prosecutor recommended the maximum sentence, which the judge (who stated that he was uninfluenced by that recommendation) imposed. The petitioner attempted unsuccessfully to withdraw his guilty plea, and his conviction was affirmed on appeal.

Held: The interest of justice and proper recognition of the prosecution's duties in relation to promises made in connection with any agreement on a plea of guilty require that the judgment be vacated and that the case be remanded to the state courts for further consideration as to whether the circumstances require only that there be specific performance of the agreement on the plea (in which case petitioner should be resentenced by a different judge), or petitioner should be afforded the relief he seeks of withdrawing his guilty plea.

35 App Div. 2d 1084, 316 NYS2d 194, vacated and remanded

CHANGE OF PLEA HEARING

The change of plea hearing is where it all happens. This is where the defendant's constitutional rights are waived and the lawyers, for both the defense and the prosecution set a barrier between themselves and a meaningful claim of ineffective assistance of counsel. In *Blackledge v. Allison*, 431 U.S. 63 (1977), the Supreme Court said that the representations of an accused, the accused's lawyer, and the federal prosecutor at [a] hearing where a guilty plea is entered, as well as any findings by the judge who accepts the plea, constitute a formidable barrier in any subsequent collateral proceeding attacking the validity of the plea under 28 U.S. §2255. The Supreme Court went on to say that such a solemn declaration in open court carry a strong presumption of verity, and that the subsequent presentation of conclusory allegations unsupported by specifics is subject to summary dismissal, as are contentions that in the face of the record are wholly incredible.

The worst thing that a defense lawyer will do to a client, who is a first-time offender, is to ask for his or her trust, only then to advise the defendant to enter a non-binding plea. When a lawyer is asking for blind trust, as opposed to providing full disclosure to the defendant, the lawyer is hiding something. That something, in most cases, is a life altering consequence of words that the defendant doesn't understand. Watch particularly for lawyers who ask defendants to lie about something in the change of plea hearing. When a lawyer is asking a defendant to lie to a court, the lawyer is trying to obtain a higher sentence. Remember that court appointed lawyers are rewarded for obtaining easy guilty pleas. What the courts don't tell you is that the lawyers who have track records of getting defendants to plea out quickly are rewarded with more appointments than other lawyers. Under 18 U.S.C. §3006A, an appointed lawyer is paid $7,000 for each guilty plea. Imagine for a moment a lawyer's annual pay of only ten cases a month. "Most appointed lawyers under the Criminal Justice Act, perform ten to twenty-five guilty pleas per month," Jeffrey Brammer, CJA lawyer in the Northern District of Alabama.

The Federal Rules of Criminal Procedure, Rule 11 requires that the terms of a plea agreement be disclosed in open court. This is the change of plea hearing. The hearing is a dogmatic ritual that is held for the sole purpose of denying later claims. The hearing is the equivalent of a modern-day liars' club. Every lawyer in the room, defense; prosecution; and the judge is going to lie about something. The trick is in getting the defendant to lie along with them. The most damaging two lies that the defendant can be coerced into telling is that one, he understands what is happening (and I can guarantee you, that no first timer and layman at law could possibly understand what all is happening); and two, that he is satisfied with his lawyer.

The rule allows a court to accept a plea agreement, reject the agreement, or postpone its decision until it has examined the presentence report. Rule 11 also sets out a list of steps that a court must follow, to be sure that a guilty plea is made knowingly and willingly. Understand that this process is a sham designed to give the appearance of compliance with the Constitution, when in fact it is unconstitutional. A guilty plea can be found to be involuntary if there was prosecutorial misconduct or if the defendant can prove that he or she entered the agreement because of fear. This aspect sounds promising because almost all first timers suffer from the fear set on them by their own lawyers. But it's the court that wants the conviction final that decides if the defendant suffered from fear.

A defendant who argues that he or she entered the plea agreement unknowingly and/or unwillingly must overcome a strong, and often times one-sided, presumption that the plea was in fact valid. Just a hint, a claim that the plea is invalid points to the obvious corruption of the court that will be deciding the claim. Always consider that it was the advice of the lawyer that caused you to plea guilty. And had the defendant have known that his interest had to compete with the financial interest of his or her own lawyer, the defendant would have demanded a speedy public trial.

The court must also be convinced that there is a factual basis for the plea. That is not to say that the factual basis has to be true. This is often time, a grossly misunderstood issue. In most cases, a prosecutor is going to offer a factual basis. That makes it easy for a court to be convinced one exists, the government-provided one. The next step is that defense counsel will convince the defendant to agree that it is in fact accurate. Thus, a lie becomes the truth. Do not let a lawyer convince you to lie in open court. This will only harm you later. For a full list of the requirements to accept a plea agreement, see Federal Rules of Criminal Procedure, Rule 11 (b).

WITHDRAWING A GUILTY PLEA

Once a plea of guilty has been accepted by a district court it is not likely that it will let go of its prize. Rule 11 provides that a defendant may withdraw a plea of guilty under very limited circumstances, see Rule 11(d). This allowance is in theory only. In today's high-pressure legal system, a federal judge will not allow a defendant to withdraw a plea agreement even when a defendant is actually innocent, see *United States v. Kelly Riggs*, case no.: 2:12-cr-297-KOB-JEO, Northern District of Alabama. Again, in theory, and taught as today's defense tactics, if the defendant moves to withdraw a plea agreement before sentencing, the court will grant it upon a showing of a fair and just reason. This is untrue. Lawyers of today are taught that the denial of a motion to withdraw a plea is reviewed under an abuse of discretion standard. This is not true either. In reality and practice in the federal courts of today, the denial of a motion to withdraw a plea agreement will not be reviewed at all.

In most cases the defense lawyer who advised a defendant to plead guilty will not support a motion to withdraw the guilty plea because it causes a conflict of interests. The court will not appoint replacement counsel unless the defendant, a layman at law, can show cause for the withdrawal by litigating the motion on his own.

In a case where withdrawal of the guilty plea is pursued, the defendant must claim pretrial (sentence) ineffective assistance of counsel to prevail in his motion. The defendant will have his last chance of success by arguing the conflict of interests to obtain new counsel. Caution must also be exercised with new counsel especially if he advised the defendant to withdraw the motion. Many CJA lawyers will have the defendant sign a withdrawal motion then never file a new motion. Or the counsel will advise that it's easier to wait for the appeal to seek a withdrawal of the plea agreement.

Bottom line, if a defendant filed a motion to withdraw his or her guilty plea, the court most likely denied the motion. Although, the denial is no doubt an abuse of discretion; the appeals court isn't going to or did not hear the claim. The ultimate problem that the defendant has or is facing is that defense counsel is ineffective because of conflict of interest. Keep in mind that if counsel gets the defendant through to sentencing, he will make $7,000 for about ten hours of work. If, however, counsel is successful in withdrawing the plea agreement then counsel will be paid the same $7,000 for a nearly one hundred hours of work. Thus, counsel faces a choice: $70 an hour, or $700 an hour. In a criminal case where a withdrawal of a guilty plea is warranted, the defense lawyer is impermissibly required to labor under a conflict of interests.

Again, the courts of today do not allow the withdrawal of guilty pleas. Please note, in the following case, that failure to follow Federal Rules of Criminal Procedure are no longer held to impact the validity of plea agreements:

UNITED STATES V. ENOGWE
U.S. APP LEXIS 42747 (5TH CIR. 1994)
DISPOSITION: AFFIRMED IN PART AND VACATED AND REMANDED IN PART.
OPINION

Per curiam:

I   Loveday Enogwe pleaded guilty to conspiring to import more than 100 grams of heroin in violation of 21 U.S.C. §§ 963 and 960(b)(2). Jens Bakker, Enogwe's counsel, wanted to withdraw from the case because Enogwe felt that Bakker had forced him to plead despite his innocence. A magistrate granted Bakker's motion to withdraw and appointed Roswald Shrull to replace him. At sentencing, the district court asked Enogwe whether he wanted to withdraw his plea. Enogwe said that he d*id.* The court denied Enogwe's motion and sentenced him to 236 months imprisonment and 5 years supervised release and fined him $2,000. Enogwe appealed.

II   Enogwe argues that the district court violated Fed. R. Crim. P. 11 by not informing him that five years was the mandatory minimum sentence and that $2 million was the statutory fine.

Any judicial deviation from Rule 11 procedures could not have materially impacted Enogwe's plea. First of all, the plea agreement identified the minimum prison term. In addition, the court told Enogwe that he faced a sentence of five to 40 years, implying a minimum of five years. Moreover, the PSR stated that the minimum prison term should not be less than five years and the maximum fine should not exceed $2 million. At the sentencing hearing, Enogwe did not allege that he had been misled about the minimum sentence or maximum fine.

As well, Enogwe stated during the plea colloquy that he had discussed with his counsel how the Sentencing Guidelines applied to his case. Enogwe pleaded guilty to importing more than 100 grams of heroin, which, under the Guidelines, corresponds to an offense level of 26. U.S.S.G. § 2Dl.l(c)(9). An offense level of 26, combined with a criminal history category of I, the lowest possible, results in a minimum sentence of 63 months, more than the five-year minimum.

More than that, the court's statement about the maximum fine could not possibly have affected Enogwe's plea. The court suggested that the fine would exceed $2 million only if Enogwe gained more than $1 million or caused someone to lose more than $1 million. There is no evidence that Enogwe's offense involved this much money. Even if we assumed that the sentencing court strayed from Rule 11 procedures, it would not have materially affected Enogwe's decision to plead guilty.

III Enogwe alleges that the district court erred in preventing him from withdrawing his guilty plea under Fed. R. Crim. P. 11(d), which provides for the withdrawal of a plea for any fair and just reason. Enogwe, however, has no absolute right to withdraw his plea. *United States v. Badger*, 925 F.2d 101, 103 (5th Cir. 1991). We review the court's resolution of a Rule 11(d) motion for abuse of discretion. *United States v. Gaitan*, 954 F.2d 1005, 1011 (5th Cir. 1992).

The court should have weighed seven factors in determining whether to permit Enogwe to withdraw his plea: (1) whether the defendant has asserted his innocence; (2) whether withdrawal would prejudice the Government; (3) whether the defendant delayed in filing the motion and if so, the reason for the delay; (4) whether withdrawal would substantially inconvenience the court; (5) whether adequate assistance of counsel was available to the defendant; (6) whether the plea was knowing and voluntary; and (7) whether withdrawal would waste judicial resources, *Badger*, 925 F.2d at 104. As "(n)o single factor or combination of factors mandates a particular result," the court should have based its decision on the totality of the circumstances, *id.*

The court concluded that only Enogwe's claim of innocence weighed in his favor, though not enough to permit withdrawal of the plea, as Enogwe had delayed in asserting it. In addition, the court found that the pressure to plead guilty experienced by Enogwe was no different than that influencing any defendant who wants to avoid the vagaries of trial. Moreover, the court saw arrayed against Enogwe's claim of innocence the substantial time and money already spent by the government and the court. The court did not abuse its discretion in making this determination.

IV Enogwe claims that the district court erred in accepting his plea because there was insufficient evidence to support the plea as required by Fed. R. Crim. P. 11(f). We review the court's acceptance of Enogwe's plea for clear error, *United States v. Adams*, 961 F.2d 505, 508 (5th Cir. 1992).

The court had to ascertain specific facts supporting each element of the offense, *id.* To prove conspiracy to import heroin, the government had to demonstrate (1) an agreement to import; (2) the defendant's knowledge of the agreement; and (3) the defendant's voluntary participation in the agreement, *United States v. Ojebode*, 957 F.2d 1218, 1223 (5th Cir. 1992), *cert. denied*, 507 U.S. 923, 113 S. Ct. 1291, 122 L. Ed. 2d 683 (1993). As the record established the elements of the offense, the court did not violate Rule 11(f) or commit a clear error in accepting Enogwe's plea.

V Enogwe argues that he was denied effective assistance of counsel because Bakker ignored his request to file a motion to withdraw his plea, had no time to prepare for trial, and forced him to plead. Enogwe, however, made this argument to the district court when he challenged the voluntariness of his plea. Given the way Enogwe presented this issue, the court did not compile a record on the ineffective assistance of counsel claim. "As there is no record adequate to test the merits of Enogwe's assertion, we decline to consider it on direct appeal," *United States v. Navejar*, 963 F.2d 732, 735 (5th Cir 1992); *United States v. Higdon*, 832 F.2d 312, 313-14 (5th Cir 1987), *cert. denied*, 484 U.S. 1075, 108 S. Ct. 1051, 98 L. Ed. 2d 1013 (1988).

VI Enogwe alleges that the district court erred by adopting the PSR, which stated that his offense involved 7.28 kilograms of heroin, an amount corresponding to an offense level of 34. U.S.S.G. 2D1.1(c)(5). Enogwe thinks that he should have received an offense level of 26, based on the amount of heroin detailed in the superseding information. "We review the court's determination of the amount of drugs involved in the offense for clear error," *United States v. Byrd*, 898 F.2d 450, 452 (5th Cir. 1990).

The court had to calculate the base offense level using drugs not specified in a count of conviction if they related to the same conduct as the count of conviction. U.S.S.G. §lBl.3; Byrd, 898 F.2d at 452. The factual record established Enogwe's involvement in three smuggling efforts that appear to be part of the same conduct. Enogwe had to demonstrate that the information forming the basis for his sentence was materially untrue, inaccurate, or unreliable. *United States v. Angulo*, 927 F.2d 202, 205 (5th Cir. 1991). He has not cast doubt on the amount of drugs that the court factored into the sentence.

Although the PSR suggests that the smuggling effort involved 5.28 kilograms of heroin rather than 7.28 kilograms, this fact is harmless error. The offense level of 34, which the court assigned, corresponds to at least three kilograms but less than ten kilograms of heroin, U.S.S.G. §2D1.1 (c)(5), so even if the court had taken 5.28 kilograms as the amount involved, Enogwe would still have been within the same sentencing range. The court did not clearly err in determining the amount of drugs involved in the offense.

VII   Enogwe claims that the district court failed to specify that his federal sentence should run concurrently with his state sentence for the same offense. A defendant may be prosecuted and sentenced by both federal and state governments if he violated the law of each sovereign. *United States v. Brown*, 920 F.2d 1212, 1217 (5th Cir 1991). This holding harkens back to 18 U.S.C. §3584(a), which provides in pertinent part:

(a)   Imposition of concurrent or consecutive terms. If multiple terms of imprisonment are imposed on a Defendant at the same time, or if a term of imprisonment is imposed on a Defendant who is already subject to an undischarged term of imprisonment, the terms may run concurrently or consecutively. Multiple terms of imprisonment imposed at the same time run concurrently unless the court orders or the statute mandates that the terms are to run consecutively. Multiple terms of imprisonment imposed at different times run consecutively unless the court orders that the terms are to run concurrently, 18 U.S.C. §3584(a). Whether the sentence should be concurrent or consecutive rests with the sound discretion of the court, subject to 18 U.S.C. §3553(a), which provides in pertinent part:

The court, in determining the particular sentence to be imposed, shall consider

(1) the nature and circumstances of the offense and the history and characteristics of the defendant;

(2) the need for the sentence imposed – (A) to reflect the seriousness of the offense, to promote respect for the law, and to provide just punishment for the offense; (B) to afford adequate deterrence to criminal conduct; (C) to protect the public from further crimes of the defendant; and (D) to provide the defendant with needed educational or vocational training, medical care, or other correctional treatment in the most effective manner;

(3) the kinds of sentences available;

(4) the kinds of sentence and sentencing range established for the applicable category of offense committed by the applicable category of defendant as set forth in the guidelines that are issued by the Sentencing Commission pursuant to 28 U.S.C. 994(a)(1) that are in effect on the date the defendant is sentenced;

(5) any pertinent policy statement issued by the Sentencing Commission pursuant to 28 U.S.C. 994(a)(2) that is in effect on the date the defendant is sentenced;

(6) the need to avoid unwarranted sentence disparities among defendants with similar records who have been found guilty of similar conduct; and

(7) the need to provide restitution to any victims of the offense. 18 U.S.C. §3553(a). If the court considered these factors and found sufficient reason to impose a consecutive sentence, then it could have done so, *Brown*, 920 F.2d at 1217, though the Sentencing Guidelines might cabin its discretion somewhat. U.S.S.G. §§ 5Gl.3(b), 5Gl.3(c).

Enogwe thinks that he should not receive a consecutive sentence because the federal offense resulted from the same conduct that led to the state sentence. Unfortunately, neither the record nor the court clearly discussed the relationship between the federal and state penalties. In addition, the court did not explain whether Enogwe's federal sentence should run concurrently or consecutively to the state sentence. Finally, the court did not consider the effect of § 5G1.3 on the federal sanction. We vacate and remand the sentence so the court can provide the information needed to ascertain the propriety of a concurrent or consecutive sentence.

Affirmed in Part and Vacated and Remanded in Part

CHAPTER TEN

SOME IMPORTANT THOUGHTS

For those of you who did, or who will be going to trial, there are some things that you need to know. Of course, you have a right to the effective assistance of counsel in the trial preparation stage. A defendant also has an absolute right to assist his or her defense lawyer in that preparation. No matter who, the stress of the criminal justice process will cause a defendant to forget things that may be critical to his defense. That is why Federal Rules of Criminal Procedure, Rule 16 provides that, "Upon a defendant's request, the government must disclose to the defendant …" a great many things. This statement is plain in saying that the right to discovery belongs to the defendant and not defense counsel. If a defendant is going through trial, he needs his discovery material in his possession. The defendant must study every aspect of his discovery material so he might better guide his attorney.

DISCOVERY

An effective defense lawyer will make sure that his defendant has possession of the discovery material in the beginning of trial preparation. An ineffective defense lawyer will claim the defendant has no need for his discovery material. The lawyer may claim that it will create a dangerous situation. He may be correct – the material may be dangerous to the guilty plea he is going to advise the defendant to sign. Also don't be naive; there are situations where sensitive materials can cause problems for some pretrial detainees in county jails. This most commonly occurs in cases of sexual offenses and major drug conspiracies. Again, a criminal defendant should never discuss aspects of his case with anyone other than his defense team. And never discuss elements of a potential defense over the jailhouse phone or in a letter to your lawyer. If it is discussed on the phone or in a letter, the government will record it and it will not be covered under attorney client privilege.

RULE 16

Rule 16 provides a criminal defendant, in a federal case, access to four broad categories of materials. Upon the defendant's request, he or she may obtain: (1) The defendant's own statements to police; (2) The defendant's own prior criminal record; (3) All documents related to the case; and (4) The results of scientific tests.

A defendant should always demand, and counsel should always obtain, by request, copies of statements made by the defendant and the defendant's prior criminal record. This request by the defendant and his counsel does not give the prosecution any right to demand reciprocal discovery from the defense. Reciprocal discovery will be discussed thoroughly throughout this chapter.

To be clear, there is no shame in admitting that you don't know what a particular word means. Knowing what some words mean may very well save you from decades of future incarceration. But to be clear, the word reciprocal means mutually shared. In other words, if the government gives a defendant certain discovery material, then the defendant must give materials to the government, such as with a request for documents and/or reports of examinations. The government in most cases will gladly comply with the defense request. But that gives the government the right to obtain the same reports from examinations performed by the defense.

Before requesting documents and reports under Rule l6(a)(1)(E), (F) or (G), a defendant must discuss with counsel the cost or benefit of having to supply the same materials to the government. If the defendant is going to trial because he or she is innocent, then the defendant has nothing to lose by reciprocal discovery but be sure by consulting with counsel.

MOTION OF DISCOVERY

The words "Motion of Discovery" and other similar variations are things you will or have in the past heard from other detainees. To be clear, asking your attorney for a "Motion of Discovery" will get you nowhere fast. When a defendant is represented by a lawyer who is providing ineffective assistance of counsel, the lawyer will or has employed word games to deny you your right of obtain your own discovery; therefore, if you ask for a "Motion of Discovery," that is exactly what he will give you. If this is or has happened to you, your lawyer is or was providing ineffective assistance of counsel. Remember, what you want is your "Discovery Material."

In nearly all jurisdictions the court has a standing order that requires the prosecution to hand over all the discovery materials that go to probable cause, to the defendant. Such an order advances the purpose of Rule 16 in that it dictates a duty to the prosecution requiring disclosure even prior to a defendant's request. However, to avoid any misunderstandings, the defense should present a written request for disclosure of particular items. The defense should serve the prosecution with a copy of the request by filing it with the clerk.

Most standing discovery orders also include a continuing duty of disclosure. This provides an illusion that a criminal case would be decided on guilt and fact instead of on passion and prejudice. This continual duty means that if either the defense or the prosecution discovers additional evidence or material before trial, they are obligated to disclose its existence promptly. This obligation covers any evidence or material that is subject to discovery or inspection and that was previously requested, or the court ordered the production of. This means that the defense should have requested all materials and evidence that could have been related to the case, regardless of any standing discovery order issued by a court.

CONTENTS OF A DISCOVERY REQUEST

Again, the defense must request that the government provide all evidence and discovery material in a written request filed with the clerk. This filing puts the court on notice that the defense is playing by the rules, regardless of the conduct of the average prosecutor. The request should cover the categories of evidence and materials that follow:

- *Statements of the defendant* – The effect of a prior statement by the defendant can change the entire defense strategy. That is why Rule 16 requires the government to disclose, after request four different types of statements by the defendant: (1)The Defendant's oral statement made before or after arrest in response to interrogation by a person that the defendant knew was a government agent, if the government intends to use the statement at trial; (2) Defendant's written or recorded statement within the government's possession custody or control about which the attorney for the government knows or could know, which contains the substance of relevant oral statements made before or after arrest, if the defendant made the statement in response to interrogation by a person known to be a government agent; (3) Recorded testimony of the defendant before a grand jury related to the offense charged; and (4) If the defendant is an organization, any statement where the government contends that the person making the statement was legally able to bind the defendant because of that person's position as the defendant's director, officer, employee, or agent.

- *The Defendant's Prior Record* – The defendant's prior criminal record should be requested. This request, like the request for statements, does not require the defendant to provide any information to the government. The defendant will not receive much value from the defendant's record as he or she prepares for trial. But the prosecutor is required to provide the defendant's record of prior conviction and the F.B.I. "rap sheet." Inaccuracies should be detected and contested. The prosecutor will use the defendant's prior convictions at trial to establish a pattern of behavior. And the court will use the prior record to enhance the defendant's sentence, if convicted. Therefore, be thorough and challenge inaccuracies in the record now. If your lawyer won't listen, write to the judge.

- *Documents and Tangible Items* – The right to obtain documents and tangible items is a powerful discovery tool that should be used. However, a defendant should also be aware that Rule 16(a)(I)(E) is a part of the rule that provides the government a right to reciprocal discovery. With that said, a defendant should move to obtain all discovery material made available under this rule. The rule requires that, upon request, the government *must* permit the defendant to copy or inspect documents and things falling into the following categories: (1) Those material to the preparation of the defendant's defense; (2) Those intended for use by the government as evidence in chief at the trial; and (3) Those obtained or belonging to the defendant.

- *Documents Material to the Defense* – Federal Rules of Criminal Procedure, Rule 16(a)(1)(E) provides that a defendant has a right to obtain all documents that are material to the preparation of his defense. In requesting disclosure under this portion of Rule 16, the defendant is seeking to get all documents relevant to his or her case. Prosecutors in most cases will withhold a few relevant documents to surprise the defense at trial. Prosecutors like these will not use the document in their case-in-chief. Thus, the defense will see the document for the first time during the defense's case or in rebuttal. This part of Rule 16 gives rise to two different ineffective assistance of counsel claims.

  When a defendant is caught unaware of certain documents, for the first time at trial; the lawyer for the defense should object. The prosecution will or did claim ignorance of the nature of the defense. What defense counsel should have done is reduce the likelihood of such a surprise by specifying the nature of documents and other things that will be material to the defense. When requesting documents and tangible items that are material to the defense, the defendant should request evidence which supports the prosecution's case along with evidence that supports the defense. An attorney who fails to make the appropriate request or object to new documents is ineffective.

- *Documents or Tangible Things that Were Taken from the Defendant* – This category should seem self-explanatory in most cases. If it belongs to the defendant, he has a right to obtain it regardless of if the government plans to use it or not. There is one exception however, in a case of computers and child pornography, the defendants should reconsider. There are a small number of cases out there where counsel obtained the discovery items and were then charged with possessing them. The government alleges that the contraband was not associated.

- *Reports and Examinations* – Rule 16(a)(1)(F) is relatively clear as well. When the government conducts a test, the results are obtainable. The result of almost any scientific procedure is discoverable by the defendant if it is material to the preparation of the defense. It is also discoverable by the defendant if it is intended for use by the government as evidence in its case at trial. There is, however, an exception to this rule. Forensic examinations of computers will not be considered as scientific tests or experiments if the court views it as a report prepared for trial, which is exempt from discovery under Fed. R. Crim. P., Rule 16(a)(2).

- *Expert Witnesses* – Expert witnesses can be particularly troubling to a defense at trial. Ordinarily, when the government hires an expert, the expert is willing to support the government's position for a fee, regardless of its veracity. Therefore, Rule 16(a)(l)(G) makes the intended testimony discoverable. The government must, upon the defendant's request, give the defendant a written statement of any expert testimony that the government intends to present in its case at trial. The written statement is required to describe the expert's opinions. The foundations and reasons for those opinions, and the expert's qualifications. The purpose of this part of Rule 16 is to "minimize surprise that often results from unexpected expert testimony, reduce the need for continuances, and to provide the opponent with a fair opportunity to test the merit of the expert's testimony through focused cross-examination." Because of the government's sharp increase in the use of both scientific and non-scientific expert testimony, a lawyer who fails to prepare by basic discovery is ineffective. This chapter is not an all-inclusive list of available discovery claims. You will also find ideas for claims by reading the Federal Rules of evidence, which are available at the end of chapter eleven. It is also beneficial to review this Supreme Court case that follows.

KIMMELMAN V. MORRISON
477 US 365, 91 L Ed 2d 305, 106 S Ct 2574 (1986)

DECISION

Restrictions on *habeas corpus* review of Fourth Amendment claims held not applicable to Sixth Amendment claim that assistance of counsel was ineffective because of incompetent representation on Fourth Amendment issues.

SUMMARY

Counsel for an accused rapist failed to request any discovery from the prosecution, and therefore was not aware that police had seized a bedsheet from the accused's apartment, where the rape had allegedly occurred, until after the accused's bench trial before a New Jersey Superior Court had begun. After a police officer testified regarding the seizure, counsel moved to suppress the sheet and related testimony on the ground that the police had acted without a warrant in violation of the Fourth Amendment, but the trial judge refused to entertain that motion because it was untimely under state law. In so holding, the judge rejected counsel's assertion that the prosecution had been obligated to disclose its case to the defense even without a discovery request, and also rejected counsel's excuse that he had not expected to go to trial because he had been told that the alleged victim did not wish to proceed. The accused appealed his ensuing conviction, alleging ineffective assistance of counsel; but the state appellate courts affirmed, and the Superior Court denied his request for post-conviction relief. The United States District Court for the District of New Jersey, however, granted the accused's petition for a writ of *habeas corpus*, holding (l) that it was precluded from considering the merits of the accused's Fourth Amendment claim under the rule of *Stone v. Powell* (1976) 428 US 465, 49 L Ed 2d 1067, 96 S Ct 3037, since it had not been alleged that the accused had been denied an opportunity to fully and fairly litigate that claim; but (2) that trial counsel's conduct in regard to that claim had deprived the accused of the effective assistance of counsel to which he was entitled under the Sixth Amendment (579 F Supp 796) the United States Court of Appeals for the Third Circuit vacated the District Court's decision and remanded for further proceedings, holding (1) that *Stone v. Powell* did not preclude consideration of the accused's Sixth Amendment claim; and (2) that counsel's performance had been incompetent enough to support such a claim; but (3) that the District Court should reconsider, in the light of intervening decisions, whether the accused had been prejudiced by this incompetence (752 F.2d 918).

On *certiorari*, the United States Supreme Court affirmed the judgment of the Court of Appeals. In an opinion by Brennan, J., joined by White, Marshall, Blackmun, Stevens, and O'Connor, JJ., it was held (1) that the rule of *Stone v. Powell* does not apply to Sixth Amendment claims of ineffective assistance of counsel that are founded primarily on incompetent representation with respect to a Fourth Amendment issue; and (2) that trial counsel's conduct in failing to file a timely suppression motion, under the circumstances presented, fell below the level of reasonable professional assistance and was thus constitutionally deficient; but (3) that the record was not sufficient to permit a determination whether the accused had been prejudiced, in the sense that there was a reasonable probability that the result of the trial would have been different absent counsel's error.

Powell, J., joined by Burger, Ch. J., and Rehnquist, J., concurred in the judgment, expressing the view (1) that *Stone v. Powell* does not bar consideration of ineffective assistance of counsel claims on federal *habeas corpus*; (2) that counsel's representation in this case was constitutionally deficient; and (3) that although the admission of illegally seized by reliable evidence might never be prejudicial for purposes of an ineffective assistance claim, the Court of Appeals should not be reversed on that ground because the issue had not been raised in the courts below or in the petition for *certiorari*.

Syllabus

At respondent's bench trial in a New Jersey court resulting in his conviction of rape, a police officer testified that a few hours after the rape she accompanied the victim to respondent's apartment where the rape had occurred; that he was not there but another tenant let them into respondent's apartment; and that the officer seized a sheet from respondent's bed. At such point in the testimony, respondent's counsel sought to suppress introduction of the sheet and any testimony about it on the ground that the officer had seized it without a search warrant in violation of the Fourth Amendment, but the judge ruled that counsel's suppression motion was late under the applicable New Jersey Court Rule. The judge rejected counsel's attempt to justify his omission on the grounds that he had not heard of the seizure until the day before, when the trial began; that it was the State's obligation to inform him of its case, even though he made no pretrial request for discovery, which would have revealed the search and seizure; and that he had not expected to go to trial because he had been told that the victim did not wish to proceed. Respondent retained new counsel after the trial and, on appeal, alleged ineffective assistance of counsel at the trial and error in the trial court's refusal to entertain the suppression motion during the trial. The appellate court rejected the claims and affirmed respondent's conviction. Thereafter respondents unsuccessfully sought post-conviction relief from the trial judge on the same grounds. He then obtained *habeas corpus* relief in Federal District Court, which held, inter alia, that he had established his ineffective- assistance claim. The Court of Appeals concluded that *Stone v. Powell*, 428 US 465, 49 L Ed 2d 1067, 96 S Ct 3037-which held that federal courts should withhold habeas review where the State has provided an opportunity for full and fair litigation of a Fourth Amendment claim-should not be extended to bar federal habeas consideration of sixth Amendment claims based on counsel's alleged failure to competently litigate Fourth Amendment claims. Reviewing the District Court's determination of ineffective assistance under the test established by the intervening decision in *Strickland v. Washington*, 466 US 668, 80 L Ed 2d 674, 104 S Ct 2052 – which held that, to establish ineffective assistance, the defendant must prove both incompetence of counsel and prejudice – the court of Appeals determined that respondent's trial counsel had been "grossly ineffective," but vacated and remanded for the District court to consider whether, under the standards set forth in *Strickland*, respondent had been prejudiced by his attorney's incompetence.

Held: (1) The restriction on federal habeas review of Fourth Amendment claims announced in *Stone v. Powell*, supra, does not extend to Sixth Amendment ineffective-assistance-of-counsel claims which are founded primarily on incompetent representation with respect to a Fourth Amendment issue. Federal courts may grant habeas relief in appropriate cases, regardless of the nature of the underlying attorney error.

(a) Respondent's Sixth Amendment claim is not in fact a Fourth Amendment claim directly controlled by *Stone*, as petitioners assert. The two claims are distinct, both in nature and in the requisite elements of proof.

(b) Nor are the rationale and purposes fully applicable to a Sixth Amendment claim that is based principally on defense counsel's failure to litigate a Fourth Amendment claim competently. *Stone* held that the remedy for Fourth Amendment violations provided by the exclusionary rule is not a personal constitutional right, but instead is predominately a judicially created structural remedy designed to safeguard Fourth Amendment rights generally through its deterrent effect; the rule has minimal utility in the context of federal collateral proceedings. Here, respondent sought direct federal habeas protection of his fundamental personal right to effective assistance of counsel, and collateral review is frequently the only means through which an accused can effectuate that right. Moreover, there is no merit to the contention that a defendant should not be allowed to vindicate through federal habeas review his right to effective assistance of counsel where counsel's primary error is failure to make a timely request for the exclusion of illegally seized evidence that is often the most probative information bearing on the defendant's guilt or innocence.

(c) Petitioners' prediction that every Fourth Amendment claim that fails in state court will be fully litigated in federal habeas proceedings in Sixth Amendment guise, and that, as a result, many state-cour judgments will be disturbed, is incorrect because it ignores the rigorous standard which *Strickland v. Washington*, supra, erects for ineffective-assistance claims. Although a meritorious Fourth Amendment issue is necessary to the success of a Sixth Amendment claim like the respondent's, a good Fourth Amendment claim also will not earn a prisoner federal habeas relief. Only those habeas petitioners who can prove under *Strickland* that they have been denied a fair trial by the gross incompetence of their attorneys are entitled to the writ and be retrial without the challenged evidence.

(2) Respondent satisfied the incompetence prong of the test for ineffective assistance of counsel set forth in *Strickland*, and the Court of Appeals did not err in remanding the case to the District Court for a determination of prejudice under *Strickland*'s standard.

(a) While the failure to file a suppression motion does not constitute per se ineffective assistance of counsel, the record clearly reveals that respondent's attorney failed to file a timely suppression motion, not due to trial strategy considerations, but because he was unaware of the search, and of the State's intention to introduce the bedsheet into evidence, due to his failure to conduct any pretrial discovery. Such failure here was not, as required under *Strickland*, reasonable and in accord with prevailing professional norms.

(b) with respect to the prejudice prong of the *Strickland* test, there is no merit to petitioners' contention that a statement made by the trial judge at post-trial hearing on respondent's motion for bail pending appeal constituted a finding that even if the bedsheet had been excluded, he would have found respondent guilty, and that such finding was a subsidiary finding of historical fact that respondent was not prejudiced by his attorney's incompetence, entitled under 28 USC §2254(d) [28 USCS § 2254(d)] to a presumption of correctness in federal habeas proceedings. The record here is not sufficiently complete to enable this Court to apply *Strickland*'s prejudice prong directly to the facts of the case, and the remand to the District Court for redetermination of prejudice was proper.

752 F.2d 918, affirmed

JENCKS MATERIAL

Another important issue of discovery is the issue of Jencks material. The Jencks act, 18 U.S.C. §3500, requires that the prosecution turn over to the defense any statement made by a government witness that relates to the substance of the witness' testimony. The discovery of such Jencks material is an effective tool, defense counsel should always seek to obtain prior statements for cross-examination.

Jencks Requirements – To obtain the Jencks material, counsel for the defense must show that four conditions are met: (1) the material is in the possession of the government; (2) that the defense has made a request to obtain the Jencks material; (3) the material is a "statement" as defined in 18 U.S.C. §3500(e); and (4) the statement does relate to the subject matter of the witness' testimony on direct examination. The government's attorney needs not have had the material in its possession. Possession by any government or investigative agency satisfies the requirement.

18 U.S.C. § 3500

§ 3500: Demands for production of statements and reports of witnesses

(a) In any criminal prosecution brought by the United States, no statement or report in the possession of the United States which was made by a government witness or prospective Government witness (other than the defendant) shall be the subject of subpoena, discovery, or inspection until said witness has testified on direct examination in the trial of the case.

(b) After a witness called by the United States has testified on direct examination, the court shall, on motion of the defendant, order the United States to produce any statement (as hereinafter defined) of the witness in the possession of the United States that relates to the subject matter as to which the witness has testified. If the entire contents of any such statement relate to the subject matter of the testimony of the witness, the court shall order it to be delivered directly to the defendant for his examination and use.

(c) If the United States claims that any statement ordered to be produced under this section contains matter which does not relate to the subject matter of the testimony of the witness, the court shall order the United States to deliver such statement for the inspection of the court in camera. Upon such delivery the court shall excise the portions of such statement which do not relate to the subject matter of the testimony of the witness. With such material excised, the court shall then direct delivery of such statement to the defendant for his use. If, pursuant to such procedure, any portion of such statement is withheld from the defendant and the defendant objects to such withholding, and the trial is continued to an adjudication of the guilt of the defendant, the entire text of such statement shall be preserved by the United States and, in the event the defendant appeals, shall be made available to the appellate court for the purpose of determining the correctness of the ruling of the trial judge. Whenever any statement is delivered to a defendant pursuant to this section, the court in its discretion, upon application of said defendant, may recess proceedings in the trial for such time as it may determine to be reasonably required for the examination of such statement by said defendant and his preparation for its use in the trial.

(d) If the United States elects not to comply with an order of the court under subsection (b) or (c) hereof to deliver to the defendant any such statement, or such portion thereof as the court may direct, the court shall strike from the record the testimony of the witness, and the trial shall proceed unless the court in its discretion shall determine that the interests of justice require that a mistrial be declared.

(e) The term "statement," as used in subsections (b), (c), and (d) of this section In relation to any witness called by the United States, means –

(1) a written statement made by said witness and signed or otherwise adopted or approved by him;

(2) a stenographic, mechanical, electrical, or other recording, or a transcription thereof, which is substantially verbatim recital of an oral statement made by said witness and recorded contemporaneously with the making of such oral statement; or

(3) a statement, however taken or recorded, or a transcription thereof, if any, made by said witness to a grand jury.

CHAPTER ELEVEN

CLAIMS RELATED TO OBJECTIONS

An objection is a powerful tool in any criminal proceeding. Properly used, an objection can change the course of questioning at trial or preserve an important issue for direct appeal. Some objections must be made timely, or the error will be considered to have been waived during appellate review. This chapter is *not* written as an encouragement to defendants to wage their own objections during a criminal trial. This chapter is written to alert all defendants to counsel's responsibility to raise proper and timely objections. This chapter also serves to assist post-conviction movants in determining whether counsel was ineffective when he or she did, or did not, properly object. There are many aspects of a criminal trial. But one of the most difficult aspects to understand is the art of raising an objection. An objection is most commonly used to limit the content of highly irrelevant and prejudicial questions or the improper introduction of evidence. The government may be effectively limited in its efforts by raising a well-placed, properly formed, and clearly stated objections. This chapter provides the defendant and the post-conviction movant with an understanding of counsel's responsibility to object and how to base a claim on the failure to do so.

There are also consequences to poorly asserted objections. An improperly raised objection that is overruled could create the appearance to the jury that the defense is trying to conceal guilt. Repeated and unnecessary objections can serve only to waste time, thereby irritating the jury along with the presiding judge.

Generally, defense counsel should make an objection only when an improper question or answer was offered and the failure to object would harm the defense. Also, know that an objection may have been made simply to interrupt the flow of a line of questions made by the government. However, keep in mind that an objection without a strong stated foundation can be meaningless, thus a claim of ineffectiveness.

An objection should be made immediately after the conduct occurred. A delay of only minutes will cause the objection to be meaningless. And defense counsel should be prepared to give the foundation for his or her objection, and an answer to the government's explanation.

USE OF OBJECTIONS

Objections must be evaluated by looking at two points of view: the first is a technical point of view, meaning what action is objectionable; and the second a tactical point of view, meaning when to make or forgo technically proper objections.

Having technical knowledge is important because even the best objection can get overruled if the lawyer is unable to support it with recent or controlling case law. A well-informed lawyer is vital because his or her objections, or failure to do so, will inevitably affect how the jury views the defendant.

Basic rule of objecting – A lawyer must know how to support the objection that he or she has raised. Being able to state and explain the basis of an objection is the next most important thing to knowing when to object in the first place. The basis of an objection doesn't have to be long, but it has to be clear. A basic difference to consider is the difference between objections to the form of a question, and to the content expected in the answer to the question.

Objecting to questions – An objection to the form of a question can control the way the government examines a witness. If sustained – meaning that the court supports or agrees with the objection – the objection does not forbid the questioning into a given area. But it does require the government to rephrase the question. Some very common grounds for such objections are:

(1) "Leading" – Suggestions to what the answer should be;

(2) "Confusing," "ambiguous," or "misleading" – meaning that the witness or the jury may misunderstand the question or the answer:

(3) "Argumentative" – Meaning that it argues with the witness' earlier testimony or uses the examination to suggest or preview the government's closing argument;

(4) "Repetitious" or "asked and answered" – That means that the expected answer has already been given or it has been answered thoroughly by the response to a previous question by the government;

(5) "Compound question" – The government is asking two or more questions at the same time. Ordinarily, compound questions would require different answers.

(6) "The government assumes facts not in the evidence" – self-explanatory; and

(7) "The government is interrupting the witness."

Objecting to answers – When the government's questions are answered, they (the answers) can sometimes contain information that is misleading to the jury. Thus, defense counsel must raise an objection. Objections to the information contained in a witness's answer, is an attempt to exclude harmful or misleading information from the trial. If the objection is sustained it will stop any further questions concerning the objectionable subject. Some of the most common grounds for this type of objection (objection to the substance of the answer) are that the answer would be:

(1) "Irrelevant" – the answer will not provide any information that will aid in resolving the dispute before the court;

(2) "Hearsay" – The answer will contain or rely on and/or imply that an out-of-court statement is truthful.

(3) "Speculative" – The answer is not based on a witness's first-hand knowledge, meaning that the witness is being called to guess about what is correct;

(4) "Lacking foundation" – The answer will be inadmissible until other facts have been provided, such as the qualification by or of an expert, memory failure, or authenticity of a document; and

(5) "Opinion" – Much like a "speculative" answer, the expected answer will contain information that is not based on fact. Or based on opinion or hypothetical facts where the witness is not qualified as an expert on that particular subject.

Remember also that there is no reason to object if the answer is not likely to cause any harm to the defense. But, the failure to object to a certain line of questioning that does not seem to harm the defense at first but later becomes damaging may cause a court to overrule a later objection as waived. The remainder of this chapter contains a full copy of the Federal Rules of Evidence.

FEDERAL RULES OF EVIDENCE
Effective July 1, 1975, as amended to December 1, 2018

Rule 101. Scope; Definitions

(a) SCOPE. These rules apply to proceedings in United States courts. The specific courts and proceedings to which the rules apply, along with exceptions, are set out in Rule 1101.

(b) DEFINITIONS. In these rules:

    (1) "civil case" means a civil action or proceeding;

    (2) "criminal case" includes a criminal proceeding;

    (3) "public office" includes a public agency;

    (4) "record" includes a memorandum, report, or data compilation;

(5) a "rule prescribed by the Supreme Court" means a rule adopted by the Supreme Court under statutory authority; and

(6) a reference to any kind of written material or any other medium includes electronically stored information.

Rule 102. Purpose

These rules should be construed so as to administer every proceeding fairly, eliminate unjustifiable expense and delay, and promote the development of evidence law, to the end of ascertaining the truth and securing a just determination.

Rule 103. Rulings on Evidence

(a) PRESERVING A CLAIM OF ERROR. A party may claim error in a ruling to admit or exclude evidence only if the error affects a substantial right of the party and:

(1) if the ruling admits evidence, a party, on the record:

(A) timely objects or moves to strike; and

(B) states the specific ground, unless it was apparent from the context; or

(2) if the ruling excludes evidence, a party informs the court of its substance by an offer of proof, unless the substance was apparent from the context.

(b) NOT NEEDING TO RENEW AN OBJECTION OR OFFER OF PROOF. Once the court rules definitively on the record – either before or at trial – a party need not renew an objection or offer of proof to preserve a claim of error for appeal.

(c) COURT'S STATEMENT ABOUT THE RULING; DIRECTING AN OFFER OF PROOF. The court may make any statement about the character or form of the evidence, the objection made, and the ruling. The court may direct that an offer of proof be made in question-and-answer form.

(d) PREVENTING THE JURY FROM HEARING INADMISSIBLE EVIDENCE. To the extent practicable, the court must conduct a jury trial so that inadmissible evidence is not suggested to the jury by any means.

(e) TAKING NOTICE OF PLAIN ERROR. A court may take notice of a plain error affecting a substantial right, even if the claim of error was not properly preserved.

Rule 104. Preliminary Questions

(a) IN GENERAL. The court must decide any preliminary question about whether a witness is qualified, a privilege exists, or evidence is admissible. In so deciding, the court is not bound by evidence rules, except those on privilege.

(b) RELEVANCE THAT DEPENDS ON A FACT. When the relevance of evidence depends on whether a fact exists, proof must be introduced sufficient to support a finding that the fact does exist. The court may admit the proposed evidence on the condition that the proof be introduced later.

(c) CONDUCTING A HEARING SO THAT THE JURY CANNOT HEAR IT. The court must conduct any hearing on a preliminary question so that the jury cannot hear it if:

(1) the hearing involves the admissibility of a confession;

(2) a defendant in a criminal case is a witness and so requests; or

(3) justice so requires.

(d) CROSS-EXAMINING A DEFENDANT IN A CRIMINAL CASE. By testifying on a preliminary question, a defendant in a criminal case does not become subject to cross-examination on other issues in the case.

(e) EVIDENCE RELEVANT TO WEIGHT AND CREDIBILITY. This rule does not limit a party's right to introduce before the jury evidence that is relevant to the weight or credibility of other evidence.

Rule 105. Limiting Evidence That Is Not Admissible Against Other Parties or for Other Purposes

If the court admits evidence that is admissible against a party or for a purpose – but not against another party or for another purpose – the court, on timely request, must restrict the evidence to its proper scope and instruct the jury accordingly.

Rule 106. Remainder of or Related Writings or Recorded Statements

If a party introduces all or part of a writing or recorded statement, an adverse party may require the introduction, at that time, of any other part – or any other writing or recorded statement – that in fairness ought to be considered at the same time.

Rule 201. Judicial Notice of Adjudicative Facts

(a) SCOPE. This rule governs judicial notice of an adjudicative fact only, not a legislative fact.

(b) KINDS OF FACTS THAT MAY BE JUDICIALLY NOTICED. The court may judicially notice a fact that is not subject to reasonable dispute because it:

(1) is generally known within the trial court's territorial jurisdiction; or

(2) can be accurately and readily determined from sources whose accuracy cannot reasonably be questioned.

(c) TAKING NOTICE. The court:

(1) may take judicial notice on its own; or

(2) must take judicial notice if a party requests it and the court is supplied with the necessary information.

(d) TIMING. The court may take judicial notice at any stage of the proceeding.

(e) OPPORTUNITY TO BE HEARD. On timely request, a party is entitled to be heard on the propriety of taking judicial notice and the nature of the fact to be noticed. If the court takes judicial notice before notifying a party, the party, on request, is still entitled to be heard.

(f) INSTRUCTING THE JURY. In a civil case, the court must instruct the jury to accept the noticed fact as conclusive. In a criminal case, the court must instruct the jury that it may or may not accept the noticed fact as conclusive.

Rule 301. Presumptions in Civil Cases Generally

In a civil case, unless a federal statute or these rules provide otherwise, the party against whom a presumption is directed has the burden of producing evidence to rebut the presumption. But this rule does not shift the burden of persuasion, which remains on the party who had it originally.

Rule 302. Applying State Law to Presumptions in Civil Cases

In a civil case, state law governs the effect of a presumption regarding a claim or defense for which state law supplies the rule of decision.

Rule 401. Test for Relevant Evidence

Evidence is relevant if:

(a) it has any tendency to make a fact more or less probable than it would be without the evidence; and

(b) the fact is of consequence in determining the action.

Rule 402. General Admissibility of Relevant Evidence

Relevant evidence is admissible unless any of the following provides otherwise:

- the United States Constitution;
- a federal statute;
- these rules; or
- other rules prescribed by the Supreme Court.

Irrelevant evidence is not admissible.

Rule 403. Excluding Relevant Evidence for Prejudice, Confusion, Waste of Time, or Other Reasons

The court may exclude relevant evidence if its probative value is substantially outweighed by a danger of one or more of the following: unfair prejudice, confusing the issues, misleading the jury, undue delay, wasting time, or needlessly presenting cumulative evidence.

Rule 404. Character Evidence; Crimes or Other Acts

(a) CHARACTER EVIDENCE.

(1) *Prohibited Uses.* Evidence of a person's character or character trait is not admissible to prove that on a particular occasion the person acted in accordance with the character or trait.

(2) *Exceptions for a Defendant or Victim in a Criminal Case.* The following exceptions apply in a criminal case:

(A) a defendant may offer evidence of the defendant's pertinent trait, and if the evidence is admitted, the prosecutor may offer evidence to rebut it;

(B) subject to the limitations in Rule 412, a defendant may offer evidence of an alleged victim's pertinent trait, and if the evidence is admitted, the prosecutor may:

(i) offer evidence to rebut it; and

(ii) offer evidence of the defendant's same trait; and

(C) in a homicide case, the prosecutor may offer evidence of the alleged victim's trait of peacefulness to rebut evidence that the victim was the first aggressor.

(3) *Exceptions for a Witness.* Evidence of a witness's character may be admitted under Rules 607, 608, and 609.

(b) CRIMES, PRONGS, OR OTHER ACTS.

(1) *Prohibited Uses.* Evidence of a crime, prong, or other act is not admissible to prove a person's character in order to show that on a particular occasion the person acted in accordance with the character.

(2) *Permitted Uses; Notice in a Criminal Case.* This evidence may be admissible for another purpose, such as proving motive, opportunity, intent, preparation, plan, knowledge, identity, absence of mistake, or lack of accident. On request by a defendant in a criminal case, the prosecutor must:

(A) provide reasonable notice of the general nature of any such evidence that the prosecutor intends to offer at trial; and

(B) do so before trial – or during trial if the court, for good cause, excuses lack of pretrial notice.

Rule 405. Methods of Proving Character

(a) BY REPUTATION OR OPINION. When evidence of a person's character or character trait is admissible, it may be proved by testimony about the person's reputation or by testimony in the form of an opinion. On cross-examination of the character witness, the court may allow an inquiry into relevant specific instances of the person's conduct.

(b) BY SPECIFIC INSTANCES OF CONDUCT. When a person's character or character trait is an essential element of a charge, claim, or defense, the character or trait may also be proved by relevant specific instances of the person's conduct.

Rule 406. Habit; Routine Practice

Evidence of a person's habit or an organization's routine practice may be admitted proving that on a particular occasion the person or organization acted in accordance with the habit or routine practice. The court may admit this evidence regardless of whether it is corroborated or whether there was an eyewitness.

Rule 407. Subsequent Remedial Measures

When measures are taken that would have made an earlier injury or harm less likely to occur, evidence of the subsequent measures is not admissible to prove: • negligence; • culpable conduct; • a defect in a product or its design; or • a need for a warning or instruction. But the court may admit this evidence for another purpose, such as impeachment or – if disputed – proving ownership, control, or the feasibility of precautionary measures.

Rule 408. Compromise Offers and Negotiations

(a) PROHIBITED USES. Evidence of the following is not admissible – on behalf of any party – either to prove or disprove the validity or amount of a disputed claim or to impeach by a prior inconsistent statement or a contradiction:

(1) furnishing, promising, or offering – or accepting, promising to accept, or offering to accept – a valuable consideration in compromising or attempting to compromise the claim; and

(2) conduct or a statement made during compromise negotiations about the claim – except when offered in a criminal case and when the negotiations related to a claim by a public office in the exercise of its regulatory, investigative, or enforcement authority.

(b) EXCEPTIONS. The court may admit this evidence for another purpose, such as proving a witness's bias or prejudice, negating a contention of undue delay, or proving an effort to obstruct a criminal investigation or prosecution.

Rule 409. Offers to Pay Medical and Similar Expenses

Evidence of furnishing, promising to pay, or offering to pay medical, hospital, or similar expenses resulting from an injury is not admissible to prove liability for the injury.

Rule 410. Pleas, Plea Discussions, and Related Statements

(a) PROHIBITED USES. In a civil or criminal case, evidence of the following is not admissible against the defendant who made the plea or participated in the plea discussions:

(1) a guilty plea that was later withdrawn;

(2) a *nolo contendere* plea;

(3) a statement made during a proceeding on either of those pleas under Federal Rule of Criminal Procedure 11 or a comparable state procedure; or

(4) a statement made during plea discussions with an attorney for the prosecuting authority if the discussions did not result in a guilty plea or they resulted in a later-withdrawn guilty plea.

(b) EXCEPTIONS. The court may admit a statement described in Rule 410(a)(3) or (4):

(1) in any proceeding in which another statement made during the same plea or plea discussions has been introduced, if in fairness the statements ought to be considered together; or

(2) in a criminal proceeding for perjury or false statement, if the defendant made the statement under oath, on the record, and with counsel present.

Rule 411. Liability Insurance

Evidence that a person was or was not insured against liability is not admissible to prove whether the person acted negligently or otherwise wrongfully. But the court may admit this evidence for another purpose, such as proving a witness's bias or prejudice or proving agency, ownership, or control.

Rule 412. Sex-Offense Cases: The Victim's Sexual Behavior or Predisposition

(a) PROHIBITED USES. The following evidence is not admissible in a civil or criminal proceeding involving alleged sexual misconduct:

(1) evidence offered to prove that a victim engaged in other sexual behavior; or

(2) evidence offered to prove a victim's sexual predisposition.

(b) EXCEPTIONS.

(1) *Criminal Cases*. The court may admit the following evidence in a criminal case:

(A) evidence of specific instances of a victim's sexual behavior, if offered to prove that someone other than the defendant was the source of semen, injury, or other physical evidence;

(B) evidence of specific instances of a victim's sexual behavior with respect to the person accused of the sexual misconduct, if offered by the defendant to prove consent or if offered by the prosecutor; and

(C) evidence whose exclusion would violate the defendant's constitutional rights.

(2) *Civil Cases*. In a civil case, the court may admit evidence offered to prove a victim's sexual behavior or sexual predisposition if its probative value substantially outweighs the danger of harm to any victim and of unfair prejudice to any party. The court may admit evidence of a victim's reputation only if the victim has placed it in controversy.

(c) PROCEDURE TO DETERMINE ADMISSIBILITY.

(1) *Motion*. If a party intends to offer evidence under Rule 412(b), the party must:

(A) file a motion that specifically describes the evidence and states the purpose for which it is to be offered;

(B) do so at least 14 days before trial unless the court, for good cause, sets a different time;

(C) serve the motion on all parties; and

(D) notify the victim or, when appropriate, the victim's guardian or representative.

(2) *Hearing*. Before admitting evidence under this rule, the court must conduct an in-camera hearing and give the victim and parties a right to attend and be heard. Unless the court orders otherwise, the motion, related materials, and the record of the hearing must be and remain sealed.

(d) DEFINITION OF "VICTIM." In this rule, "victim" includes an alleged victim.

Rule 413. Similar Crimes in Sexual-Assault Cases

(a) PERMITTED USES. In a criminal case in which a defendant is accused of a sexual assault, the court may admit evidence that the defendant committed any other sexual assault. The evidence may be considered on any matter to which it is relevant.

(b) DISCLOSURE TO THE DEFENDANT. If the prosecutor intends to offer this evidence, the prosecutor must disclose it to the defendant, including witnesses' statements or a summary of the expected testimony. The prosecutor must do so at least 15 days before trial or at a later time that the court allows for good cause.

(c) EFFECT ON OTHER RULES. This rule does not limit the admission or consideration of evidence under any other rule.

(d) DEFINITION OF "SEXUAL ASSAULT." In this rule and Rule 415, "sexual assault" means a crime under federal law or under state law (as "state" is defined in 18 U.S.C. § 513) involving:

(1) any conduct prohibited by 18 U.S.C. chapter 109A;

(2) contact, without consent, between any part of the defendant's body – or an object – and another person's genitals or anus;

(3) contact, without consent, between the defendant's genitals or anus and any part of another person's body;

(4) deriving sexual pleasure or gratification from inflicting death, bodily injury, or physical pain on another person; or

(5) an attempt or conspiracy to engage in conduct described in subparagraphs (1)–(4).

Rule 414. Similar Crimes in Child-Molestation Cases

(a) PERMITTED USES. In a criminal case in which a defendant is accused of child molestation, the court may admit evidence that the defendant committed any other child molestation. The evidence may be considered on any matter to which it is relevant.

(b) DISCLOSURE TO THE DEFENDANT. If the prosecutor intends to offer this evidence, the prosecutor must disclose it to the defendant, including witnesses' statements or a summary of the expected testimony. The prosecutor must do so at least 15 days before trial or at a later time that the court allows for good cause.

(c) EFFECT ON OTHER RULES. This rule does not limit the admission or consideration of evidence under any other rule.

(d) DEFINITION OF "CHILD" AND "CHILD MOLESTATION." In this rule and Rule 415:

(1) "child" means a person below the age of 14; and

(2) "child molestation" means a crime under federal law or under state law (as "state" is defined in 18 U.S.C. § 513) involving:

(A) any conduct prohibited by 18 U.S.C. chapter 109A and committed with a child;

(B) any conduct prohibited by 18 U.S.C. chapter 110;

(C) contact between any part of the defendant's body – or an object – and a child's genitals or anus;

(D) contact between the defendant's genitals or anus and any part of a child's body;

(E) deriving sexual pleasure or gratification from inflicting death, bodily injury, or physical pain on a child; or

(F) an attempt or conspiracy to engage in conduct described in subparagraphs (A)–(E).

Rule 415. Similar Acts in Civil Cases Involving Sexual Assault or Child Molestation

(a) PERMITTED USES. In a civil case involving a claim for relief based on a party's alleged sexual assault or child molestation, the court may admit evidence that the party committed any other sexual assault or child molestation. The evidence may be considered as provided in Rules 413 and 414.

(b) DISCLOSURE TO THE OPPONENT. If a party intends to offer this evidence, the party must disclose it to the party against whom it will be offered, including witnesses' statements or a summary of the expected testimony. The party must do so at least 15 days before trial or at a later time that the court allows for good cause.

(c) EFFECT ON OTHER RULES. This rule does not limit the admission or consideration of evidence under any other rule.

Rule 501. Privilege in General

The common law – as interpreted by United States courts in the light of reason and experience – governs a claim of privilege unless any of the following provides otherwise:

- the United States Constitution;
- a federal statute; or
- rules prescribed by the Supreme Court.

But in a civil case, state law governs privilege regarding a claim or defense for which state law supplies the rule of decision.

Rule 502. Attorney-Client Privilege and Work Product; Limitations on Waiver

The following provisions apply, in the circumstances set out, to disclosure of a communication or information covered by the attorney-client privilege or work-product protection.

(a) DISCLOSURE MADE IN A FEDERAL PROCEEDING OR TO A FEDERAL OFFICE OR AGENCY, SCOPE OF A WAIVER. When the disclosure is made in a federal proceeding or to a federal office or agency and waives the attorney-client privilege or work-product protection, the waiver extends to an undisclosed communication or information in a federal or state proceeding only if:

(1) the waiver is intentional;

(2) the disclosed and undisclosed communications or information concern the same subject matter; and

(3) they ought in fairness to be considered together.

(b) INADVERTENT DISCLOSURE. When made in a federal proceeding or to a federal office or agency, the disclosure does not operate as a waiver in a federal or state proceeding if:

(1) the disclosure is inadvertent;

(2) the holder of the privilege or protection took reasonable steps to prevent disclosure; and

(3) the holder promptly took reasonable steps to rectify the error, including (if applicable) following Federal Rule of Civil Procedure 26(b)(5)(B).

(c) DISCLOSURE MADE IN A STATE PROCEEDING. When the disclosure is made in a state proceeding and is not the subject of a state-court order concerning waiver, the disclosure does not operate as a waiver in a federal proceeding if the disclosure:

(1) would not be a waiver under this rule if it had been made in a federal proceeding; or

(2) is not a waiver under the law of the state where the disclosure occurred.

(d) CONTROLLING EFFECT OF A COURT ORDER. A federal court may order that the privilege or protection is not waived by disclosure connected with the litigation pending before the court – in which event the disclosure is also not a waiver in any other federal or state proceeding.

(e) CONTROLLING EFFECT OF A PARTY AGREEMENT. An agreement on the effect of disclosure in a federal proceeding is binding only on the parties to the agreement, unless it is incorporated into a court order.

(f) CONTROLLING EFFECT OF THIS RULE. Notwithstanding Rules 101 and 1101, this rule applies to state proceedings and to federal court-annexed and federal court-mandated arbitration proceedings, in the circumstances set out in the rule. And notwithstanding Rule 501, this rule applies even if state law provides the rule of decision.

(g) DEFINITIONS. In this rule:

(1) "attorney-client privilege" means the protection that applicable law provides for confidential attorney-client communications; and

(2) "work-product protection" means the protection that applicable law provides for tangible material (or its intangible equivalent) prepared in anticipation of litigation or for trial.

Rule 601. Competency to Testify in General

Every person is competent to be a witness unless these rules provide otherwise. But in a civil case, state law governs the witness's competency regarding a claim or defense for which state law supplies the rule of decision.

Rule 602. Need for Personal Knowledge

A witness may testify to a matter only if evidence is introduced sufficient to support a finding that the witness has personal knowledge of the matter. Evidence to prove personal knowledge may consist of the witness's own testimony. This rule does not apply to a witness's expert testimony under Rule 703.

Rule 603. Oath or Affirmation to Testify Truthfully

Before testifying, a witness must give an oath or affirmation to testify truthfully. It must be in a form designed to impress that duty on the witness's conscience.

Rule 604. Interpreter

An interpreter must be qualified and must give an oath or affirmation to make a true translation.

Rule 605. Judge's Competency as a Witness

The presiding judge may not testify as a witness at the trial. A party need not object to preserve the issue.

Rule 606. Juror's Competency as a Witness

(a) AT THE TRIAL. A juror may not testify as a witness before the other jurors at the trial. If a juror is called to testify, the court must give a party an opportunity to object outside the jury's presence.

(b) DURING AN INQUIRY INTO THE VALIDITY OF A VERDICT OR INDICTMENT.

(1) *Prohibited Testimony or Other Evidence.* During an inquiry into the validity of a verdict or indictment, a juror may not testify about any statement made or incident that occurred during the jury's deliberations; the effect of anything on that juror's or another juror's vote; or any juror's mental processes concerning the verdict or indictment. The court may not receive a juror's affidavit or evidence of a juror's statement on these matters.

(2) *Exceptions.* A juror may testify about whether:

(A) extraneous prejudicial information was improperly brought to the jury's attention;

(B) an outside influence was improperly brought to bear on any juror; or

(C) a mistake was made in entering the verdict on the verdict form.

Rule 607. Who May Impeach a Witness

Any party, including the party that called the witness, may attack the witness's credibility.

Rule 608. A Witness's Character for Truthfulness or Untruthfulness

(a) REPUTATION OR OPINION EVIDENCE. A witness's credibility may be attacked or supported by testimony about the witness's reputation for having a character for truthfulness or untruthfulness, or by testimony in the form of an opinion about that character. But evidence of truthful character is admissible only after the witness's character for truthfulness has been attacked.

(b) SPECIFIC INSTANCES OF CONDUCT. Except for a criminal conviction under Rule 609, extrinsic evidence is not admissible to prove specific instances of a witness's conduct in order to attack or support the witness's character for truthfulness. But the court may, on cross-examination, allow them to be inquired into if they are probative of the character for truthfulness or untruthfulness of:

(1) the witness; or

(2) another witness whose character is the witness being cross-examined has testified about.

By testifying on another matter, a witness does not waive any privilege against self-incrimination for testimony that relates only to the witness's character for truthfulness.

Rule 609. Impeachment by Evidence of a Criminal Conviction

(a) IN GENERAL. The following rules apply to attacking a witness's character for truthfulness by evidence of a criminal conviction:

(1) for a crime that, in the convicting jurisdiction, was punishable by death or by imprisonment for more than one year, the evidence:

(A) must be admitted, subject to Rule 403, in a civil case or in a criminal case in which the witness is not a defendant; and

(B) must be admitted in a criminal case in which the witness is a defendant, if the probative value of the evidence outweighs its prejudicial effect to that defendant; and

(2) for any crime regardless of the punishment, the evidence must be admitted if the court can readily determine that establishing the elements of the crime required proving – or the witness's admitting – a dishonest act or false statement.

(b) LIMIT ON USING THE EVIDENCE AFTER 10 YEARS. This subdivision (b) applies if more than 10 years have passed since the witness's conviction or release from confinement for it, whichever is later. Evidence of the conviction is admissible only if:

(1) its probative value, supported by specific facts and circumstances, substantially outweighs its prejudicial effect; and

(2) the proponent gives an adverse party reasonable written notice of the intent to use it so that the party has a fair opportunity to contest its use.

(c) EFFECT OF A PARDON, ANNULMENT, OR CERTIFICATE OF REHABILITATION. Evidence of a conviction is not admissible if:

(1) the conviction has been the subject of a pardon, annulment, certificate of rehabilitation, or other equivalent procedure based on a finding that the person has been rehabilitated, and the person has

not been convicted of a later crime punishable by death or by imprisonment for more than one year; or

    (2) the conviction has been the subject of a pardon, annulment, or other equivalent procedure based on a finding of innocence.

(d) JUVENILE ADJUDICATIONS. Evidence of a juvenile adjudication is admissible under this rule only if:

    (1) it is offered in a criminal case;

    (2) the adjudication was of a witness other than the defendant;

    (3) an adult's conviction for that offense would be admissible to attack the adult's credibility; and

    (4) admitting the evidence is necessary to fairly determine guilt or innocence.

(e) PENDENCY OF AN APPEAL. A conviction that satisfies this rule is admissible even if an appeal is pending. Evidence of the pendency is also admissible.

Rule 610. Religious Beliefs or Opinions

Evidence of a witness's religious beliefs or opinions is not admissible to attack or support the witness's credibility.

Rule 611. Mode and Order of Examining Witnesses and Presenting Evidence

(a) CONTROL BY THE COURT; PURPOSES. The court should exercise reasonable control over the mode and order of examining witnesses and presenting evidence so as to:

    (1) make those procedures effective for determining the truth;

    (2) avoid wasting time; and

    (3) protect witnesses from harassment or undue embarrassment.

(b) SCOPE OF CROSS EXAMINATION. Cross-examination should not go beyond the subject matter of the direct examination and matters affecting the witness's credibility. The court may allow inquiry into additional matters as if on direct examination.

(c) LEADING QUESTIONS. Leading questions should not be used on direct examination except as necessary to develop the witness's testimony. Ordinarily, the court should allow leading questions:

    (1) on cross-examination; and

    (2) when a party calls a hostile witness, an adverse party, or a witness identified with an adverse party.

Rule 612. Writing Used to Refresh a Witness's Memory

(a) SCOPE. This rule gives an adverse party certain options when a witness USCS a writing to refresh memory:

    (1) while testifying; or

    (2) before testifying, if the court decides that justice requires the party to have those options.

(b) ADVERSE PARTY'S OPTIONS; DELETING UNRELATED MATTER. Unless 18 U.S.C. § 3500 provides otherwise in a criminal case, an adverse party is entitled to have the writing produced at the hearing, to inspect it, to cross-examine the witness about it, and to introduce in evidence any portion that relates to the witness's testimony. If the producing party claims that the writing includes unrelated matter, the court must examine the writing in camera, delete any unrelated portion, and order that the rest be delivered to the adverse party. Any portion deleted over objection must be preserved for the record.

(c) FAILURE TO PRODUCE OR DELIVER THE WRITING. If a writing is not produced or is not delivered as ordered, the court may issue any appropriate order. But if the prosecution does not comply in a criminal case, the court must strike the witness's testimony or – if justice so requires – declare a mistrial.

Rule 613. Witness's Prior Statement

(a) SHOWING OR DISCLOSING THE STATEMENT DURING EXAMINATION. When examining a witness about the witness's prior statement, a party need not show it or disclose its contents to the witness. But the party must, on request, show it or disclose its contents to an adverse party's attorney.

(b) EXTRINSIC EVIDENCE OF A PRIOR INCONSISTENT STATEMENT. Extrinsic evidence of a witness's prior inconsistent statement is admissible only if the witness is given an opportunity to explain or deny the statement and an adverse party is given an opportunity to examine the witness about it, or if justice so requires. This subdivision (b) does not apply to an opposing party's statement under Rule 801(d)(2).

Rule 614. Court's Calling or Examining a Witness

(a) CALLING. The court may call a witness on its own or at a party's request. Each party is entitled to cross-examine the witness.

(b) EXAMINING. The court may examine a witness regardless of who calls the witness.

(c) OBJECTIONS. A party may object to the court's calling or examining a witness either at that time or at the next opportunity when the jury is not present.

Rule 615. Excluding Witnesses

At a party's request, the court must order witnesses excluded so that they cannot hear other witnesses' testimony. Or the court may do so on its own. But this rule does not authorize excluding:

(a) a party who is a natural person;

(b) an officer or employee of a party that is not a natural person, after being designated as the party's representative by its attorney;

(c) a person whose presence a party shows to be essential to presenting the party's claim or defense; or

(d) a person authorized by statute to be present.

Rule 701. Opinion Testimony by Lay Witnesses

If a witness is not testifying as an expert, testimony in the form of an opinion is limited to one that is:

(a) rationally based on the witness's perception;

(b) helpful to clearly understanding the witness's testimony or to determining a fact in issue; and

(c) not based on scientific, technical, or other specialized knowledge within the scope of Rule 702.

Rule 702. Testimony by Expert Witnesses

A witness who is qualified as an expert by knowledge, skill, experience, training, or education may testify in the form of an opinion or otherwise if:

(a) the expert's scientific, technical, or other specialized knowledge will help the trier of fact to understand the evidence or to determine a fact in issue;

(b) the testimony is based on sufficient facts or data;

(c) the testimony is the product of reliable principles and methods; and

(d) the expert has reliably applied the principles and methods to the facts of the case.

Rule 703. Bases of an Expert's Opinion Testimony

An expert may base an opinion on facts or data in the case that the expert has been made aware of or personally observed. If experts in the particular field would reasonably rely on those kinds of facts or data in forming an opinion on the subject, they need not be admissible for the opinion to be admitted. But if the facts or data would otherwise be inadmissible, the proponent of the opinion may disclose them to the jury only if their probative value in helping the jury evaluate the opinion substantially outweighs their prejudicial effect.

Rule 704. Opinion on an Ultimate Issue

(a) IN GENERAL – NOT AUTOMATICALLY OBJECTIONABLE. An opinion is not objectionable just because it embraces an ultimate issue.

(b) EXCEPTION. In a criminal case, an expert witness must not state an opinion about whether the defendant did or did not have a mental state or condition that constitutes an element of the crime charged or of a defense. Those matters are for the trier of fact alone.

Rule 705. Disclosing the Facts or Data Underlying an Expert's Opinion

Unless the court orders otherwise, an expert may state an opinion – and give the reasons for it – without first testifying to the underlying facts or data. But the expert may be required to disclose those facts or data on cross-examination.

Rule 706. Court-Appointed Expert Witnesses

(a) APPOINTMENT PROCESS. On a party's motion or on its own, the court may order the parties to show cause why expert witnesses should not be appointed and may ask the parties to submit nominations. The court may appoint any expert that the parties agree on and any of its own choosing. But the court may only appoint someone who consents to act.

(b) EXPERT'S ROLE. The court must inform the expert of the expert's duties. The court may do so in writing and have a copy filed with the clerk or may do so orally at a conference in which the parties have an opportunity to participate. The expert:

(1) must advise the parties of any findings the expert makes;

(2) may be deposed by any party;

(3) may be called to testify by the court or any party; and

(4) may be cross-examined by any party, including the party that called the expert.

(c) COMPENSATION. The expert is entitled to a reasonable compensation, as set by the court. The compensation is payable as follows:

(1) in a criminal case or in a civil case involving just compensation under the Fifth Amendment, from any funds that are provided by law; and

(2) in any other civil case, by the parties in the proportion and at the time that the court directs – and the compensation is then charged like other costs.

(d) DISCLOSING THE APPOINTMENT TO THE JURY. The court may authorize disclosure to the jury that the court appointed the expert.

(e) PARTIES' CHOICE OF THEIR OWN EXPERTS. This rule does not limit a party in calling its own experts.

Rule 801. Definitions That Apply to This Article; Exclusions from Hearsay

(a) STATEMENT. "Statement" means a person's oral assertion, written assertion, or nonverbal conduct, if the person intended it as an assertion.

(b) DECLARANT. "Declarant" means the person who made the statement.

(c) HEARSAY. "Hearsay" means a statement that:

(1) the declarant does not make while testifying at the current trial or hearing; and

(2) a party offers evidence to prove the truth of the matter asserted in the statement.

(d) STATEMENTS THAT ARE NOT HEARSAY. A statement that meets the following conditions is not hearsay:

(1) *A Declarant-Witness's Prior Statement*. The declarant testifies and is subject to cross-examination about a prior statement, and the statement:

(A) is inconsistent with the declarant's testimony and was given under penalty of perjury at a trial, hearing, or other proceeding or in a deposition;

(B) is consistent with the declarant's testimony and is offered:

(i) to rebut an express or implied charge that the declarant recently fabricated it or acted from a recent improper influence or motive in so testifying; or

(ii) to rehabilitate the declarant's credibility as a witness when attacked on another ground; or

(C) identifies a person as someone the declarant perceived earlier.

(2) *An Opposing Party's Statement*. The statement is offered against an opposing party and:

(A) was made by the party in an individual or representative capacity;

(B) is one the party manifested that it adopted or believed to be true;

(C) was made by a person whom the party authorized to make a statement on the subject;

(D) was made by the party's agent or employee on a matter within the scope of that relationship and while it existed; or

(E) was made by the party's coconspirator during and in furtherance of the conspiracy. The statement must be considered but does not by itself establish the declarant's authority under (C); the existence or scope of the relationship under (D); or the existence of the conspiracy or participation in it under (E).

Rule 802. The Rule Against Hearsay

Hearsay is not admissible unless any of the following provides otherwise:

- a federal statute;
- these rules; or
- other rules prescribed by the Supreme Court.

Rule 803. Exceptions to the Rule Against Hearsay – Regardless of Whether the Declarant Is Available as a Witness

The following are not excluded by the rule against hearsay, regardless of whether the declarant is available as a witness:

(1) *Present Sense Impression*. A statement describing or explaining an event or condition, made while or immediately after the declarant perceived it.

(2) *Excited Utterance*. A statement relating to a startling event or condition, made while the declarant was under the stress of excitement that it caused.

(3) *Then-Existing Mental, Emotional, or Physical Condition*. A statement of the declarant's then-existing state of mind (such as motive, intent, or plan) or emotional, sensory, or physical condition (such as

mental feeling, pain, or bodily health), but not including a statement of memory or belief to prove the fact remembered or believed unless it relates to the validity or terms of the declarant's will.

(4) Statement Made for Medical Diagnosis or Treatment. A statement that:

   (A) is made for – and is reasonably pertinent to – medical diagnosis or treatment; and

   (B) describes medical history; past or present symptoms or sensations; their inception; or their general cause.

(5) Recorded Recollection. A record that:

   (A) is on a matter the witness once knew about but now cannot recall well enough to testify fully and accurately;

   (B) was made or adopted by the witness when the matter was fresh in the witness's memory; and

   (C) accurately reflects the witness's knowledge. If admitted, the record may be read into evidence but may be received as an exhibit only if offered by an adverse party.

(6) Records of a Regularly Conducted Activity. A record of an act, event, condition, opinion, or diagnosis if:

   (A) the record was made at or near the time by – or from information transmitted by – someone with knowledge;

   (B) the record was kept in the course of a regularly conducted activity of a business, organization, occupation, or calling, whether or not for profit;

   (C) making the record was a regular practice of that activity;

   (D) all these conditions are shown by the testimony of the custodian or another qualified witness, or by a certification that complies with Rule 902(11) or (12) or with a statute permitting certification; and

   (E) the opponent does not show that the source of information or the method or circumstances of preparation indicate a lack of trustworthiness.

(7) *Absence of a Record of a Regularly Conducted Activity*. Evidence that a matter is not included in a record described in paragraph (6) if:

   (A) the evidence is admitted to prove that the matter did not occur or exist;

   (B) a record was regularly kept for a matter of that kind; and

   (C) the opponent does not show that the possible source of the information or other circumstances indicate a lack of trustworthiness.

(8) *Public Records*. A record or statement of a public office if:

   (A) it sets out:

      (i) the office's activities;

      (ii) a matter observed while under a legal duty to report, but not including, in a criminal case, a matter observed by law-enforcement personnel; or

      (iii) in a civil case or against the government in a criminal case, factual findings from a legally authorized investigation; and

   (B) the opponent does not show that the source of information or other circumstances indicate a lack of trustworthiness.

(9) *Public Records of Vital Statistics*. A record of a birth, death, or marriage, if reported to a public office in accordance with a legal duty.

(10)*Absence of a Public Record.* Testimony – or a certification under Rule 902 – that a diligent search failed to disclose a public record or statement if:

    (A) the testimony or certification is admitted to prove that

        (i) the record or statement does not exist; or

        (ii) a matter did not occur or exist, if a public office regularly kept a record or statement for a matter of that kind; and

    (B) in a criminal case, a prosecutor who intends to offer a certification provides written notice of that intent at least 14 days before trial, and the defendant does not object in writing within 7 days of receiving the notice – unless the court sets a different time for the notice or the objection.

(11)*Records of Religious Organizations Concerning Personal or Family History.* A statement of birth, legitimacy, ancestry, marriage, divorce, death, relationship by blood or marriage, or similar facts of personal or family history, contained in a regularly kept record of a religious organization.

(12)*Certificates of Marriage, Baptism, and Similar Ceremonies.* A statement of fact contained in a certificate:

    (A) made by a person who is authorized by a religious organization or by law to perform the act certified;

    (B) attesting that the person performed a marriage or similar ceremony or administered a sacrament; and

    (C) purporting to have been issued at the time of the act or within a reasonable time after it.

(13)*Family Records.* A statement of fact about personal or family history contained in a family record, such as a Bible, genealogy, chart, engraving on a ring, inscription on a portrait, or engraving on an urn or burial marker.

(14)*Records of Documents That Affect an Interest in Property.* The record of a document that purports to establish or affect an interest in property if:

    (A) the record is admitted to prove the content of the original recorded document, along with its signing and its delivery by each person who purports to have signed it;

    (B) the record is kept in a public office; and

    (C) a statute authorizes recording documents of that kind in that office.

(15)*Statements in Documents That Affect an Interest in Property.* A statement contained in a document that purports to establish or affect an interest in property if the matter stated was relevant to the document's purpose – unless later dealings with the property are inconsistent with the truth of the statement or the purport of the document.

(16)*Statements in Ancient Documents.* A statement in a document that was prepared before January 1, 1998, and whose authenticity is established.

(17)*Market Reports and Similar Commercial Publications.* Market quotations, lists, directories, or other compilations that are generally relied on by the public or by persons in particular occupations.

(18)*Statements in Learned Treatises, Periodicals, or Pamphlets.* A statement contained in a treatise, periodical, or pamphlet if:

    (A) the statement is called to the attention of an expert witness on cross-examination or relied on by the expert on direct examination; and

(B) the publication is established as a reliable authority by the expert's admission or testimony, by another expert's testimony, or by judicial notice. If admitted, the statement may be read into evidence but not received as an exhibit.

(19) *Reputation Concerning Personal or Family History.* A reputation among a person's family by blood, adoption, or marriage – or among a person's associates or in the community – concerning the person's birth, adoption, legitimacy, ancestry, marriage, divorce, death, relationship by blood, adoption, or marriage, or similar facts of personal or family history.

(20) *Reputation Concerning Boundaries or General History.* A reputation in a community – arising before the controversy – concerning boundaries of land in the community or customs that affect the land, or concerning general historical events important to that community, state, or nation.

(21) *Reputation Concerning Character.* A reputation among a person's associates or in the community concerning the person's character.

(22) *Judgment of a Previous Conviction.* Evidence of a final judgment of conviction if:

(A) the judgment was entered after a trial or guilty plea, but not a *nolo contendere* plea;

(B) the conviction was for a crime punishable by death or by imprisonment for more than a year;

(C) the evidence is admitted to prove any fact essential to the judgment; and

(D) when offered by the prosecutor in a criminal case for a purpose other than impeachment, the judgment was against the defendant.

The pendency of an appeal may be shown but does not affect admissibility.

(23) *Judgments Involving Personal, Family, or General History, or a Boundary.* A judgment that is admitted to prove a matter of personal, family, or general history, or boundaries, if the matter:

(A) was essential to the judgment; and

(B) could be proved by evidence of reputation.

(24) [Other Exceptions.] [Transferred to Rule 807.]

Rule 804. Exceptions to the Rule Against Hearsay – When the Declarant Is Unavailable as a Witness

(a) CRITERIA FOR BEING UNAVAILABLE. A declarant is considered to be unavailable as a witness if the declarant:

(1) is exempted from testifying about the subject matter of the declarant's statement because the court rules that a privilege applies;

(2) refuses to testify about the subject matter despite a court order to do so;

(3) testifies to not remembering the subject matter;

(4) cannot be present or testify at the trial or hearing because of death or a then-existing infirmity, physical illness, or mental illness; or

(5) is absent from the trial or hearing and the statement's proponent has not been able, by process or other reasonable means, to procure:

(A) the declarant's attendance, in the case of a hearsay exception under Rule 804(b)(1) or (6); or

(B) the declarant's attendance or testimony, in the case of a hearsay exception under Rule 804(b)(2), (3), or (4).

But this subdivision (a) does not apply if the statement's proponent procured or wrongfully caused the declarant's unavailability as a witness in order to prevent the declarant from attending or testifying.

(b) THE EXCEPTIONS. The following are not excluded by the rule against hearsay if the declarant is unavailable as a witness:

(1) *Former Testimony*. Testimony that:

(A) was given as a witness at a trial, hearing, or lawful deposition, whether given during the current proceeding or a different one; and

(B) is now offered against a party who had – or, in a civil case, whose predecessor in interest had – an opportunity and similar motive to develop it by direct, cross-, or redirect examination.

(2) *Statement Under the Belief of Imminent Death*. In a prosecution for homicide or in a civil case, a statement that the declarant, while believing the declarant's death to be imminent, made about its cause or circumstances.

(3) *Statement Against Interest*. A statement that:

(A) a reasonable person in the declarant's position would have made only if the person believed it to be true because, when made, it was so contrary to the declarant's proprietary or pecuniary interest or had so great a tendency to invalidate the declarant's claim against someone else or to expose the declarant to civil or criminal liability; and

(B) is supported by corroborating circumstances that clearly indicate its trustworthiness, if it is offered in a criminal case as one that tends to expose the declarant to criminal liability.

(4) *Statement of Personal or Family History*. A statement about:

(A) the declarant's own birth, adoption, legitimacy, ancestry, marriage, divorce, relationship by blood, adoption, or marriage, or similar facts of personal or family history, even though the declarant had no way of acquiring personal knowledge about that fact; or

(B) another person concerning any of these facts, as well as death, if the declarant was related to the person by blood, adoption, or marriage or was so intimately associated with the person's family that the declarant's information is likely to be accurate.

(5) [Other Exceptions.] [Transferred to Rule 807.]

(6) *Statement Offered Against a Party That Wrongfully Caused the Declarant's Unavailability*. A statement offered against a party that wrongfully caused – or acquiesced in wrongfully causing – the declarant's unavailability as a witness and did so intending that result.

Rule 805. Hearsay Within Hearsay

Hearsay within hearsay is not excluded by the rule against hearsay if each part of the combined statements conforms with an exception to the rule.

Rule 806. Attacking and Supporting the Declarant's Credibility

When a hearsay statement – or a statement described in Rule 801(d)(2)(C), (D), or (E) – has been admitted in evidence, the declarant's credibility may be attacked, and then supported, by any evidence that would be admissible for those purposes if the declarant had testified as a witness. The court may admit evidence of the declarant's inconsistent statement or conduct, regardless of when it occurred or whether the declarant had an opportunity to explain or deny it. If the party against whom the statement was admitted calls the declarant as a witness, the party may examine the declarant on the statement as if on cross-examination.

Rule 807. Residual Exception

(a) IN GENERAL. Under the following circumstances, a hearsay statement is not excluded by the rule against hearsay even if the statement is not specifically covered by a hearsay exception in Rule 803 or 804:

    (1) the statement has equivalent circumstantial guarantees of trustworthiness;

    (2) it is offered as evidence of a material fact;

    (3) it is more probative on the point for which it is offered than any other evidence that the proponent can obtain through reasonable efforts; and

    (4) admitting it will best serve the purposes of these rules and the interests of justice.

(b) NOTICE. The statement is admissible only if, before the trial or hearing, the proponent gives an adverse party reasonable notice of the intent to offer the statement and its particulars, including the declarant's name and address, so that the party has a fair opportunity to meet it.

Rule 901. Authenticating or Identifying Evidence

(a) IN GENERAL. To satisfy the requirement of authenticating or identifying an item of evidence, the proponent must produce evidence sufficient to support a finding that the item is what the proponent claims it is.

(b) EXAMPLES. The following are examples only – not a complete list – of evidence that satisfies the requirement:

    (1) *Testimony of a Witness with Knowledge.* Testimony that an item is what it is claimed to be.

    (2) *Nonexpert Opinion About Handwriting.* A nonexpert's opinion that handwriting is genuine, based on a familiarity with it that was not acquired for the current litigation.

    (3) *Comparison by an Expert Witness or the Trier of Fact.* A comparison with an authenticated specimen by an expert witness or the trier of fact.

    (4) *Distinctive Characteristics and the Like.* The appearance, contents, substance, internal patterns, or other distinctive characteristics of the item, taken together with all the circumstances.

    (5) *Opinion About a Voice.* An opinion identifying a person's voice – whether heard firsthand or through mechanical or electronic transmission or recording – based on hearing the voice at any time under circumstances that connect it with the alleged speaker.

    (6) *Evidence About a Telephone Conversation.* For a telephone conversation, evidence that a call was made to the number assigned at the time to:

        (A) a particular person, if circumstances, including self-identification, show that the person answering was the one called; or

        (B) a particular business, if the call was made to a business and the call related to business reasonably transacted over the telephone.

    (7) *Evidence About Public Records.* Evidence that:

        (A) a document was recorded or filed in a public office as authorized by law; or

        (B) a purported public record or statement is from the office where items of this kind are kept.

    (8) *Evidence About Ancient Documents or Data Compilations.* For a document or data compilation, evidence that it:

        (A) is in a condition that creates no suspicion about its authenticity;

        (B) was in a place where, if authentic, it would likely be; and

(C) is at least 20 years old when offered.

(9) *Evidence About a Process or System.* Evidence describing a process or system and showing that it produces an accurate result.

(10) *Methods Provided by a Statute or Rule.* Any method of authentication or identification allowed by a federal statute, or a rule prescribed by the Supreme Court.

Rule 902. Evidence That Is Self-Authenticating

The following items of evidence are self-authenticating; they require no extrinsic evidence of authenticity in order to be admitted:

(a) *Domestic Public Documents That Are Sealed and Signed.* A document that bears:

(1) a seal purporting to be that of the United States; any state, district, commonwealth, territory, or insular possession of the United States; the former Panama Canal Zone; the Trust Territory of the Pacific Islands; a political subdivision of any of these entities; or a department, agency, or officer of any entity named above; and

(2) a signature purporting to be an execution or attestation.

(b) *Domestic Public Documents That Are Not Sealed but Are Signed and Certified.* A document that bears no seal if:

(1) it bears the signature of an officer or employee of an entity named in Rule 902(1)(A); and

(2) another public officer who has a seal and official duties within that same entity certifies under seal – or its equivalent – that the signer has the official capacity and that the signature is genuine.

(c) *Foreign Public Documents.* A document that purports to be signed or attested by a person who is authorized by a foreign country's law to do so. The document must be accompanied by a final certification that certifies the genuineness of the signature and official position of the signer or attester – or of any foreign official whose certificate of genuineness relates to the signature or attestation or is in a chain of certificates of genuineness relating to the signature or attestation. The certification may be made by a secretary of a United States embassy or legation; by a consul general, vice consul, or consular agent of the United States; or by a diplomatic or consular official of the foreign country assigned or accredited to the United States. If all parties have been given a reasonable opportunity to investigate the document's authenticity and accuracy, the court may, for good cause, either:

(1) order that it be treated as presumptively authentic without final certification; or

(2) allow it to be evidenced by an attested summary with or without final certification.

(d) *Certified Copies of Public Records.* A copy of an official record – or a copy of a document that was recorded or filed in a public office as authorized by law – if the copy is certified as correct by:

(1) the custodian or another person authorized to make the certification; or

(2) a certificate that complies with Rule 902(1), (2), or (3), a federal statute, or a rule prescribed by the Supreme Court.

(e) *Official Publications.* A book, pamphlet, or other publication purporting to be issued by a public authority.

(f) *Newspapers and Periodicals.* Printed material purporting to be a newspaper or periodical.

(g) *Trade Inscriptions and the Like.* An inscription, sign, tag, or label purporting to have been affixed in the course of business and indicating origin, ownership, or control.

(h) *Acknowledged Documents*. A document accompanied by a certificate of acknowledgment that is lawfully executed by a notary public or another officer who is authorized to take acknowledgments.

(i) *Commercial Paper and Related Documents*. Commercial paper, a signature on it, and related documents, to the extent allowed by general commercial law.

(j) *Presumptions Under a Federal Statute*. A signature, document, or anything else that a federal statute declares to be presumptively or prima facie genuine or authentic.

(k) *Certified Domestic Records of a Regularly Conducted Activity*. The original or a copy of a domestic record that meets the requirements of Rule 803(6)(A)–(C), as shown by a certification of the custodian or another qualified person that complies with a federal statute or a rule prescribed by the Supreme Court. Before the trial or hearing, the proponent must give an adverse party reasonable written notice of the intent to offer the record – and must make the record and certification available for inspection – so that the party has a fair opportunity to challenge them.

(l) *Certified Foreign Records of a Regularly Conducted Activity*. In a civil case, the original or a copy of a foreign record that meets the requirements of Rule 902(11), modified as follows: the certification, rather than complying with a federal statute or Supreme Court rule, must be signed in a manner that, if falsely made, would subject the maker to a criminal penalty in the country where the certification is signed. The proponent must also meet the notice requirements of Rule 902(11).

(m) *Certified Records Generated by an Electronic Process or System*. A record generated by an electronic process or system that produces an accurate result, as shown by a certification of a qualified person that complies with the certification requirements of Rule 902(11) or (12). The proponent must also meet the notice requirements of Rule 902(11).

(n) *Certified Data Copied from an Electronic Device, Storage Medium, or File*. Data copied from an electronic device, storage medium, or file, if authenticated by a process of digital identification, as shown by a certification of a qualified person that complies with the certification requirements of Rule 902(11) or (12). The proponent also must meet the notice requirements of Rule 902(11).

Rule 903. Subscribing Witness's Testimony

A subscribing witness's testimony is necessary to authenticate a writing only if required by the law of the jurisdiction that governs its validity.

Rule 1001. Definitions That Apply to This Article

In this article:

(a) A "writing" consists of letters, words, numbers, or their equivalent set down in any form.

(b) A "recording" consists of letters, words, numbers, or their equivalent recorded in any manner.

(c) A "photograph" means a photographic image or its equivalent stored in any form.

(d) An "original" of a writing or recording means the writing or recording itself or any counterpart intended to have the same effect by the person who executed or issued it. For electronically stored information, "original" means any printout – or other output readable by sight – if it accurately reflects the information. An "original" of a photograph includes the negative or a print from it.

(e) A "duplicate" means a counterpart produced by a mechanical, photographic, chemical, electronic, or other equivalent process or technique that accurately reproduces the original.

Rule 1002. Requirement of the Original

An original writing, recording, or photograph is required in order to prove its content unless these rules or a federal statute provides otherwise.

Rule 1003. Admissibility of Duplicates

A duplicate is admissible to the same extent as the original unless a genuine question is raised about the original's authenticity, or the circumstances make it unfair to admit the duplicate.

Rule 1004. Admissibility of Other Evidence of Content

An original is not required, and other evidence of the content of a writing, recording, or photograph is admissible if:

(a) all the originals are lost or destroyed, and not by the proponent acting in bad faith;

(b) an original cannot be obtained by any available judicial process;

(c) the party against whom the original would be offered had control of the original; was at that time put on notice, by pleadings or otherwise, that the original would be a subject of proof at the trial or hearing; and fails to produce it at the trial or hearing; or

(d) the writing, recording, or photograph is not closely related to a controlling issue.

Rule 1005. Copies of Public Records to Prove Content

The proponent may use a copy to prove the content of an official record – or of a document that was recorded or filed in a public office as authorized by law – if these conditions are met: the record or document is otherwise admissible; and the copy is certified as correct in accordance with Rule 902(4) or is testified to be correct by a witness who has compared it with the original. If no such copy can be obtained by reasonable diligence, then the proponent may use other evidence to prove the content.

Rule 1006. Summaries to Prove Content

The proponent may use a summary, chart, or calculation to prove the content of voluminous writings, recordings, or photographs that cannot be conveniently examined in court. The proponent must make the originals or duplicates available for examination or copying, or both, by other parties at a reasonable time and place. And the court may order the proponent to produce them in court.

Rule 1007. Testimony or Statement of a Party to Prove Content

The proponent may prove the content of a writing, recording, or photograph by the testimony, deposition, or written statement of the party against whom the evidence is offered. The proponent need not account for the original.

Rule 1008. Functions of the Court and Jury

Ordinarily, the court determines whether the proponent has fulfilled the factual conditions for admitting other evidence of the content of a writing, recording, or photograph under Rule 1004 or 1005. But in a jury trial, the jury determines – in accordance with Rule 104(b) – any issue about whether:

(a) an asserted writing, recording, or photograph ever existed;

(b) another one produced at the trial or hearing is the original; or

(c) other evidence of content accurately reflects the content.

Rule 1101. Applicability of the Rules

(a) To Courts and Judges. These rules apply to proceedings before:

- United States district courts;

- United States bankruptcy and magistrate judges;
- United States courts of appeals;
- the United States Court of Federal Claims; and
- the district courts of Guam, the Virgin Islands, and the Northern Mariana Islands.

(b) TO CASES AND PROCEEDINGS. These rules apply in:

- civil cases and proceedings, including bankruptcy, admiralty, and maritime cases;
- criminal cases and proceedings; and
- contempt proceedings, except those in which the court may act summarily.

(c) RULES ON PRIVILEGE. The rules on privilege apply to all stages of a case or proceeding.

(d) EXCEPTIONS. These rules – except for those on privilege – do not apply to the following:

(1) the court's determination, under Rule 104(a), on a preliminary question of fact governing admissibility;

(2) grand-jury proceedings; and

(3) miscellaneous proceedings such as:

- extradition or rendition;
- issuing an arrest warrant, criminal summons, or search warrant;
- a preliminary examination in a criminal case;
- sentencing;
- granting or revoking probation or supervised release; and
- considering whether to release on bail or otherwise.

(e) OTHER STATUTES AND RULES. A federal statute or a rule prescribed by the Supreme Court may provide for admitting or excluding evidence independently from these rules.

Rule 1102. Amendments

These rules may be amended as provided in 28 U.S.C. § 2072.

Rule 1103. Title

These rules may be cited as the Federal Rules of Evidence.

CHAPTER TWELVE

Pretrial Motions

The purpose of this chapter is to provide a prisoner, or a pretrial defendant, with the basic knowledge of how a defense lawyer should use the pretrial motion process. Therefore, this chapter will focus on the types of pretrial motions that could or should be filed before trial.

Motions are formal written or oral requests that ask the court to provide specific forms of relief. Most motions are filed before the particular proceeding that they are expected to affect. For example, pretrial motions are filed before the trial begins. Most pretrial motions are filed with the expectation to either avoid a trial, reduce the number of issues that are in controversy, or to better situate the defense in preparation of the trial. This chapter is designed to alert a criminal defendant to the various motions that may be, or should have been, made in a criminal case.

Also be aware that no defendant, in any one criminal case, can expect that all of these forms of relief could possibly apply, nor is this a complete list of all possible motions. But also know that an attorney who files no pretrial motions is, or has, provided ineffective assistance of counsel. A basic principle of motion practice is that it is without limits. Anytime an attorney or a defendant faces a new set of facts in the case, the attorney should consider whether there is any relief to request. It does not matter that no law or Supreme Court case supports a particular position. Thus, this chapter is not included to provide a limited number of pretrial motions, it is provided to give the defendant and *pro se* petitioner an idea about how the practice should be approached by defense counsel.

Time Limits – All courts and jurisdictions, whether state or federal, have a set schedule for filing almost all motions. Normally, the time limits are related to a given period from the date of arraignment, or a number of days prior to trial. Time limits may also be set from the time of reasonable discovery of the facts upon which the request is made. Rule 12 of the Federal Rules of Criminal Procedure sets the time limits in the Federal Criminal Justice System.

A pretrial motion, by nature, must be filed before the trial begins. Often, the court will set a schedule for the filing of pretrial motions. The schedule should be followed by defense counsel; the failure to do so is ineffectiveness. The Federal Rules of Criminal Procedure, Rule 12(c), provides a federal court with the discretion to establish a date for the filing of all Rule 12 pretrial motions. Specifically, "the court may, at the arraignment or as soon afterward as practicable, set a deadline for the parties to make pretrial motions and may also schedule a motion hearing." Generally, a schedule for motions is set at the initial appearance or at a pretrial calendar conference in front of the district court judge whom the case is assigned to.

Finally, defense counsel should also make an effort to raise every claim that he can in one motion. Many courts require counsel to file an omnibus pretrial motion, which means that all possible claims are to be contained in a single set of moving papers. Once an omnibus motion is filed, additional motions on the defendant's behalf will be rejected. Failure to include a claim in the omnibus motion often will result in the waiver of that particular claim.

Types of motions that must be raised pretrial – Although creative legal minds spawn new types of motions every day you will find that Rule 12 allows for three basic categories of motions. The first category is made of the five types of motions that *must* be brought pretrial, under the rule. This first category is most likely the most important category, because Rule 12 is unforgiving in their regard. The second category of pretrial motions is made up of the motions that *may* be brought pretrial. Pay special attention to the difference between *must* and *may*. The third category of motions is made up of the motions that are strictly regulated under Rule 12, but that can be brought pretrial.

- *Defects in the prosecution* – This first type deals with claims of "defects in the institution of the prosecution …" Such claims include errors that occurred at the time that the government presented the case to the grand jury that is serious enough to make any produced indictment invalid. Because of the secrecy under which the government holds the grand jury, the only likely claim is that the grand jury indicted based on false information. This can be identified when the listed conduct of the offense does not rise to a violation of the criminal statute, based on the essential elements of the charged offense.

- *Defect in the pleadings* – The second type deals with claims of "defects in the indictment or information …" These are claims that raise issues with the form and sufficiency of the documents upon which the prosecution is based. Pretrial motions that raise these types of claims usually contain accusations that a pleading is invalid because it was not prepared properly and, thus should be dismissed. Defects can most commonly include the following: (a) misjoinder; (b) duplicity, or multiplicity; (c) an improper amendment to the pleadings; or (d) vague or insufficient language in the documents.

- *Suppression of Evidence* – The third type of pretrial motions are similar to some of the objections discussed in an earlier chapter. Motion for the suppression of evidence *must* be raised before trial. These motions are often focused on fourth amendment issues where the defendant claims that the evidence was illegally secured, and as such, is due to be suppressed under the Exclusionary Rule. Motions of this type can also be based on Fifth Amendment claims concerning the right against self-incrimination, or the Sixth Amendment rights to counsel and confrontation. Such motions can seek suppression of: (a) statements that the defendant made to law enforcement officers; (b) physical evidence seized from the defendant's person or his property; and/or (c) identifications of the defendant that were made by persons who will be called to testify at trial.

- *Motions for Severance* – The fourth type of motion that *must* be made in pretrial motions are motions for severance, under Rule 14 of the Federal Rules of Criminal Procedure. A motion for severance must be made before trial because it has the potential to change the defendants who are subject to the trial itself. Such a motion raises the issue that the defendant will be prejudiced at trial because he or she is placed in a situation with people known or suspected of more serious criminal conduct. Severance may become an issue where a co-defendant is accused of multiple offenses that are unrelated to a specific defendant.

- *Motions for Discovery* – The fifth and final type of pretrial motion that *must* be filed pretrial, is the Rule 16 motion for discovery. Although, the Rule 16 discovery motions were covered in an earlier chapter, it's raised again here because of the importance of counsel's duty of continual discovery. Again, the court most likely has a standing discovery order. Defense counsel has likely filed a request for additional discovery categories with the clerk. But counsel's duty to discover and investigate did not end there, and I have not yet encountered one federal prosecutor who has turned over the entire discovery. Therefore, a defense lawyer must remain vigilant to discover other types of evidence. On May 29, 2019, *U.S.A. Today* released a front-page story about an innocent man who spent 33 years in prison for a murder he did not commit. In that case, the defendant was prejudiced by mishandled evidence that his lawyer failed to discover.

  In the last days allowed for pretrial motions, defense counsel should file an additional discovery motion seeking the materials that he suspects that the government will use but has failed to disclose. This motion should be filed because the failure to disclose will provide grounds for the defendant's appeal.

Motions that may be brought pretrial – The five types of motions that were just covered *must* be brought in pretrial motions. But Rule 12 also allows a number of other issues in pretrial motions as well. Rule 12 states in part that, "Any defense, objection, or request that the court can determine without a trial on the merits" may be raised in a pretrial motion. Thus, a court has the authority to address issues that can be resolved, that do not require the resolution of the ultimate issue at trial. In other words, the court can resolve any issue that does not determine the defendant's guilt or innocence, and therefore, *may* be raised in a pretrial motion.

Other types of pretrial motions – In this third category of pretrial motion, are motions other than those that either *may* be made or *must* be made under Rule 12. Rule 12 of the Federal Rules of Criminal Procedure allows for other issues to be raised in pretrial motions. This subpart will describe a few of the most common motions filed.

- *Motions to change venue* – Under Fed. R. Crim. P. Rule 21, a defendant is allowed to have a pending criminal action transferred to another district. The court has the authority to grant the motion "if the court is satisfied that so great a prejudice against the defendant exists in the transferring district that the defendant cannot obtain a fair or impartial trial" in the district where the offense was committed. A transfer is also allowed "for the convenience of the parties, any victim, and the witnesses and in the interest of justice." Rule 21 then allows that "a motion to transfer … may be made at or before arraignment or at any other time as the court or these rules prescribe."

Author's Note: A motion to change venue should be filed no later than the date the court sets for the filing of pretrial motions. Be aware that the federal courts seek convictions not justice. That is why the court allows the prosecution to demonize a defendant in the press while, at the same time, places a "hush order" on the defendant. The motion should be filed none the less to preserve the issue for appeal. If counsel failed to raise the issue, counsel is providing ineffective assistance of counsel.

The most common reason for filing a motion requesting a change of venue is because the defendant cannot receive a fair trial in the district of offense because of the prosecutor's pretrial publicity of the case. This type of situation is most common in major drug conspiracy cases and that of child sexual exploitation, i.e. child pornography and related offenses. Most courts will deny this motion pretrial, directing that the motion be renewed at trial. Again, the courts allow the government to create prejudice in the press and usually will not allow a transfer of a defendant who is not wealthy or influential in the community.

- *Notice of insanity defense* – Although not a motion, notices must also be served in accordance with the time limits set by Rule 12 and the court. Rule 12.2 requires that when a defendant intends to claim a defense of insanity, he or she "must so notify an attorney for the government in writing within the time provided for filing a pretrial motion, or at any later time the court sets, and file a copy of the notice with the clerk." If the defense fails to comply with the required time limits, then he or she cannot raise a defense that claims insanity.

  Also, the rules require that a defendant file, in accordance with the established time limits, any notice of their intention to offer expert testimony related to their mutual condition at trial. Under Rule 12.2(d), the failure to provide notice as required can result in having the expert's testimony excluded.

- *Motion in Limine* – There are always issues to be resolved before trial. A fair number of these issues are not addressed in the Federal Rules of Criminal Procedure. These issues can be raised in pretrial motion, nonetheless. This category of issues is most often raised by *in limine* motions which are made right before the trial. More specifically, a lawyer can move to preclude specific matters in evidence that the prosecution may want to present at trial. The idea of raising an issue by making a motion *in limine* is that counsel can receive an advance decision from the court making certain evidence inadmissible at trial. One good example of this kind of motion is one that asks to stop the government from using the defendant's criminal history at trial or limits the introduction of crime scene photographs. These issues are often raised best *in limine* because the evidence they are challenging is used only to cause prejudice with the jury. In other words, makes the jury want to punish somebody, no matter whom. When these issues are raised by motions *in limine* the government has little time to make up some ridiculous reason to allow the introduction of such evidence.

MOTION FOR BENCH TRIAL

The Federal Rules of Criminal Procedure, Rule 23, allows a criminal defendant to waive a "jury trial." This should not be confused with a "waiver of trial" altogether. To waive a jury trial under the rule is the method by which the defense requests a Bench Trial. This request ordinarily is required to be made in a motion that is accompanied by a written waiver under Rule 23. The waiver was or will be strictly construed because the right to a jury trial is a fundamental right which should not be carelessly surrendered.

The government will prefer a jury trial in every event where its case is weak. Juries are not made up of twelve people trained in law, they are twelve common people that the government's attorneys are expert at enraging. A bench trial should be considered when: against a defendant.

(1) The facts of the defendant's case would invoke anger, horror, fear, or repulsion on the part of the jury. Judges are used to hearing inflammatory details of terrible crimes.

(2) The defense to an accusation requires the presentation of complicated issues of law or sophisticated expert testimony. Jurors have little contact with the legal process prior to being seated on a panel. Thus, a defense that requires a difficult understanding of law is better suited for presentation to a judge.

(3) The strength of the defendant's case would lead the factfinder to an obvious legal conclusion. This is particularly true in cases where guilt hinges on the essential elements of the charged offense as opposed to the conduct of the defendant.

A jury lacks the experience that a judge is expected to possess. A judge has practice with the legal system, and therefore, provides an expectation that the law rather than passion will be controlling.

CHAPTER THIRTEEN

TRIAL

News Reporting – There is going to be a trial, and the defendant has a Sixth Amendment right to "a speedy and *public* ..." one. His right, however, is most often trampled on by a defendant's own lawyer. The last thing he or she wants is their lack of diligence or effective assistance broadcast on the nightly news. The right to a public trial is a Constitutional one, it is established to keep everyone involved honest, even the lawyers. Knowing this, most defense lawyers, especially those hired by the court under the Criminal Justice Act, will claim that "I fight cases in the court, not in the news." When you hear this or a closely related statement, know that your lawyer is hiding something.

The failure to demand a public trial creates some serious political, practical, and constitutional problems. The most important problem, second only to the defendant's right, is the public's interest in the administration of justice. The United States attorneys, defense lawyers, and judges live above the law for the most part, see the qualified immunity standards. Therefore, the only authority that these people answer to is the interest of the American people.

Not only is the public's interest in criminal trials the source of popular forms of entertainment, books and movies; it is also important news. it doesn't matter if it is a local or national case, the public's interest in the criminal process is spellbinding. The most thrilling element of the political arena is that of official corruption, and the public's interest in knowing that an estimated 40 percent of all prisoners are convicted of conduct that they did not commit.

Because of this great public interest in the criminal process, and the need of officials to keep it concealed, restrictions on reporting criminal trials are carefully scrutinized by the courts. In the words of our own Supreme Court justice *Douglas*, "A trial is a public event. What transpires in a courtroom is public property." The courts have held that news relating to criminal trials is an interest of the media, which should be preserved. But the courts often restrict any news from the defendant's perspective to reduce any injury to the reputation of the court or it's bar members. What most commonly occurs is that the court allows news releases by the government that serve only to demonize the defendant and taint the jury pool. Therefore, if defense counsel fails to demand and exercise the right to a public trial; he or she has provided constitutionally ineffective assistance of counsel.

Trial Preparation – The defense of a criminal prosecution is a big deal. In the federal system a defendant has a better chance of overcoming stage-four lung cancer than he does of overcoming a felony indictment. That is why the defense of a criminal case is an ongoing effort. From the very beginning of the case, defense counsel's focus should not be on one stage of the case, without reasonable consideration to trial preparation. Including any advice to plead guilty, all stages of the criminal process should be viewed through the lens of trial preparation. Even though pretrial preparation is not as exciting as the trial itself; the fact is that more cases are won by diligent preparation than by slick courtroom theatrics. The trial must be viewed from the perspective of the evidence in the case. It does not proceed in a vacuum; it should be affected by the available evidence and shaped in advance by pretrial preparation.

Unless the trial has been bargained away in a plea negotiation, or the charges were dismissed, the case will move forward on to trial. This is where diligent counsel will be effective by focusing his energies on trial preparation. When a case reaches this point, it is time to maximize both factual investigation and legal analysis. For example, if additional evidence is necessary to prove a point, the defense counsel should enlist investigators to seek it out. If you have ever watched a trial on television, you have seen the investigator enter the courtroom at the last minute to save the day. If a defendant is not getting this kind of service, he is suffering the effects of ineffective assistance of counsel.

Pretrial Conference – Federal rules of Criminal Procedure, Rule 17.1, provides that a party or the court "May hold one or more pretrial conferences." As can be seen here the rules permit a pretrial conference meaning it is not required. Rest assured that prior to any trial, a truly conscientious judge will hold a pretrial conference.

The variety of issues that can be resolved pretrial is almost unlimited. But consider also that the pretrial conference is not a replacement for motions that should have been brought under rule 12. The Rule 17.1 pretrial conference addresses issues that are more procedural, meaning the mechanics of fighting a complicated case. Also, the pretrial conference is meant to be a more relaxed atmosphere, another forum to discuss adverse pretrial evidentiary rulings. The pretrial conference is an opportunity to further assert the defendant's position concerning evidentiary matters and in the effort of continuing discovery.

The most harmful aspect of the pretrial conference is the defendant's failure to understand the stipulations. A *stipulation* is an agreement; a bargain, or condition – an agreement between opposing parties that certain facts are true. In a case of an affirmative defense, the defendant may "stipulate" that he did in fact commit the act; leaving only the reason for his actions in question.

The defendant must consent to a pretrial conference, usually as part of a final stipulation. A memorandum will be filed that specifies what matters have been agreed upon, usually in writing. Defense lawyers will often ask a defendant to sign an explicit waiver of the defendant's presence; this is a defensive step that helps the lawyer forestall any ineffective assistance of counsel claims. *Don't sign waivers*! If you already have, your failure to understand them is ineffective assistance of counsel.

Additional facts concerning the pretrial conference –

- The admissions made by the defendant and/or by his attorney at a pretrial conference may not be used at trial. The exception to this rule is that, if the admission is in writing and is signed by the defendant and his attorney, the admission then may be used against the defendant. *Do not sign admissions or stipulations before any trial*!

- In federal courts, the judge will demand that a pretrial conference be held. The most important issue for the court at the pretrial conference is to establish a clear schedule for the trial.

- The most important benefit for the parties of a pretrial conference is the timing and completion of discovery. This gives the defense an opportunity to raise disclosure issues in the presence of the judge, usually receiving an instant determination on the issue. Defense counsel should make and/or renew his demand for evidence that is exculpatory or is simply favorable to the case of the defense. Anything less is ineffective assistance of counsel.

- The pretrial conference is also the proper time and place to confirm the accuracy of transcripts of audio and video, or other recorded conversations for submission to the jury. The parties may also seek approval of the style and content of documentary "exhibit books" to be given to the jurors. Different from decisions made on bare pleadings, the pretrial conference provides some personalization to the process. Often a judge's exposure to the basic humanity of a defendant and his lawyer, in an informal pretrial setting, may cause him to be more inclined to reject the government's "convict at all costs" attitude on the grounds of plain fairness. When a well-prepared defense lawyer articulates a need for relief from unfair prejudice, or raises a fair and actual discovery requirement, the court is more likely to question the government's tactics and sense of fair play.

Jury Selection – Once all pretrial positioning is complete, the next step to actually conducting a trial is what is known to a layman as jury selection. The process in which a jury is selected is called "voir dire" in the legal community. *Voir dire* is defined as; a preliminary examination of a prospective juror, in order to determine his or her qualifications to serve as a juror.

Generally, the purpose of the *voir dire* process is to select a jury from a large group of people. The principle is to select a jury that will serve in a fair and impartial manner, judging the case solely on the basis of the facts presented at trial and the law as instructed by the judge. In its simplest terms, the jury selection process provides an opportunity for the lawyers on both sides and the court to remove jurors who display an inability to judge the case against the accused in a fair and impartial manner.

The court may conduct the examination itself; it may allow counsel to conduct it or allow counsel from both sides to share in the questioning. An appellate review of the manner of conducting *voir dire* is conducted under an "abuse of discretion" standard of review.

When evaluating counsel's effectiveness during jury selection, keep in mind that there is no such thing as a perfect juror. Additionally, it's a good idea to search court decisions that have ruled in a defendant's favor for guidance.

Opening statements – Although not considered to be evidence, the opening statements can be harmful to a defendant's case. The opening statement is most commonly nothing more than a simple discussion about the law and facts of a case. It is also, most often, counsel's first opportunity to address the jury directly; an opportunity to advise the jury about how the parties believe the jury should view the evidence.

The opening statements are brief discussions that serve to educate the jury in law and duty. They are also, usually, the longest remembered part of the criminal trial. The opening statements serve as the jury's first impression of the case that the parties intend to present. This is the first and most meaningful opportunity for a lawyer to present the most critical aspect of any trial; it is the time to tell the jury what the case is really all about.

Opening statements are important because they are the first meaningful opportunity for counsel to speak freely with the jury, the first time they will be directly addressed for an extended amount of time by counsel. Even though counsel addressed most of the jurors individually during the *voir dire* process, the opening statements is counsel's first opportunity to converse with the jury naturally. The ability to speak to the jury, as opposed to testing them, is as important as the right to cross-examine adverse witnesses.

It is well known, in most cases, that despite the jury's oath to the contrary, a great many jurors decide the case long before hearing any evidence. The opening statements are the time for the lawyers from both sides to give the jurors assurances about the lawyers, the accused, the criminal justice system, and the duty of the jury itself. The most important issue to relay to the jury, in the opening statement, is that they are there to try the government's evidence, not the defendant. The jury should be convinced by counsel's opening statement that their purpose is not to convict the defendant, but rather to hold the government, or the State, to its burden of proof beyond a reasonable doubt.

The government's opening statement – In most jurisdictions, the prosecuting attorney is required to make an opening statement. The prosecutor's most practiced skill is convincing the jury that the defendant is guilty. Their next effort is to convince the jury that the prosecution is protecting the people in that particular jurisdiction; in this the prosecuting attorney will seem very personal and sincere. In the Federal System especially the people go unrepresented because it is the government who is represented, they who have a financial interest in incarceration. The government is most often required to make an opening statement in a jury trial to "ensure the jurors' comprehension of what is about to transpire at trial," *Jackson v. United States*, 515 A. 2d 1133, 1134 (D.C. 1986). The government, however, is not required to give an opening statement in a bench trial. Contrary to the government's belief and practice, the purpose of an opening statement is to give the basic outlines of the case so the jury can comprehend the issues. It is not given to poison the minds of the jurors against the defendant.

Although, not rising to stand-alone ground for relief; defense counsel's failure to object to an improper opening statement by the government is ineffectiveness. Defense counsel must be vigilant to determine when to object to remarks in the government's opening statement. Defense counsel must consider the procedures of the presiding judge but should not allow improper remarks to go without objection.

Opening statement by the defense – The defense has a right to give an opening statement as well, regardless of whether or not evidence is provided in its case. The purpose of such an opening statement is to provide a convincing alternative view of the evidence and to persuade the jury of the defendant's innocence. The opening statement is an extremely critical moment in the trial process. It provides an opportunity for defense counsel to contradict the prosecutor's theory of the case and inject some truth into the criminal case. Defense counsel should give an opening statement that puts the prosecution on the defensive. Counsel should make every effort to take an early lead in the case by casting the evidence in a light more favorable to the defense. The opening statement is most effective when given immediately after the prosecutor's opening statement. Studies show a majority of jurors decide the issue of guilt and innocence based solely on the opening statements. If the jury hears only the government's side of the story, they are likely to convict. Thus, a defense opening statement must be given to show that the prosecutor is trying to pull one over on the jury. Anything less is ineffectiveness.

Although, in most cases the opening statements will not be a source of stand-alone ineffective assistance of counsel claim; there are some exceptions. For example, a defense lawyer should never promise the jury something that is not delivered. The opening statement is often used to humanize the defendant and to present him in a sympathetic light. But counsel should never offer a preview to such things, as a traumatic childhood, and then fail to deliver the full story. This is especially true in capital sentencing proceedings where life and death hang in the balance; see the Supreme Court decision that follows:

WIGGINS V. SMITH
539 US 510, 156 L ED 2D 471, 123 S CT 2527
DECIDED JUNE 26, 2003
DECISION

Federal *habeas corpus* court was held to have erred in upholding Maryland court's rejection of accused's claim of violation of sixth Amendment right to effective assistance of counsel with respect to capital-sentencing proceedings.

SUMMARY

An accused, who had been convicted of capital murder by a judge in the Baltimore County Circuit court of Maryland, elected to be sentenced by a jury. The two attorneys who were acting as the accused's defense counsel at the trial moved to bifurcate the sentencing, on the basis of counsel's purported desire (1) to prove that the accused had not killed the victim by the accused's own hand, and (2) then, if necessary to present a mitigation case. The state court denied the bifurcation motion. During the sentencing proceedings, one defense attorney, in her opening statement, told the jurors that they would hear about the accused's difficult life. However, defense counsel never introduced evidence about the accused's life history during the sentencing proceedings. Before closing arguments and outside the presence of the jury, the second attorney, in proffering to the court to preserve the bifurcation issue for appeal, (1) detailed the mitigation case that counsel would have presented, but (2) never mentioned the accused's life history or family background.

The jury sentenced the accused to death, and the Maryland Court of Appeals affirmed (324 Md 551, 597 A2d 1359).

The accused, represented by new counsel, petitioned the trial court for post-conviction relief, as the accused (1) alleged that his trial counsel had rendered ineffective assistance by failing to investigate, and to present mitigating evidence of, his dysfunctional background; and (2) presented a social worker's expert testimony about the accused's severe physical and sexual abuse by the accused's mother and by foster parents. One of the accused's trial attorneys testified that (1) he did not remember retaining a forensic social worker to prepare a social history before sentencing, despite the availability of state funds for that purpose; and (2) defense counsel had decided to focus on retrying the factual case and disputing the accused's direct responsibility for the murder. After the trial court had denied the petition for relief, the state Court of Appeals (1) determined that trial counsel had made a reasoned choice to use what they considered to be the accused's best defense; and (2) affirmed the trial court's denial of relief (352 Md 580, 724 A2d 1).

Subsequently, the accused filed, under 28 USCS § 2254, a petition for a writ of *habeas corpus* in the United States District Court for the District of Maryland. The District Court granted the accused relief (164 F Supp 2d 538). However, the United States Court of Appeals for the Fourth Circuit (1) concluded that trial counsel had reasonably made a strategic decision to focus on the accused's direct responsibility, and (2) reversed the District Court's judgment (288 F.3d 629).

On *certiorari*, the United States Supreme Court reversed and remanded. In an opinion by O'Conner, J., joined by Rehnquist, Ch. J., and Stevens, Kennedy, Souter, Ginsburg, and Breyer, JJ., it was held that:

(a) Trial counsel's failure to investigate the accused's background and to present mitigating evidence of the accused's unfortunate life history at the accused's capital-sentencing proceedings had violated the accused's right, under the Federal Constitution's Sixth Amendment, to the effective assistance of counsel, as such failure by trial counsel had (a) fallen below the standard of reasonableness under prevailing professional norms; and (b) prejudiced the accused's defense.

(b) The Federal Court of Appeals had erred in upholding the Maryland Court of Appeals' rejection of the accused's claim of ineffective assistance of counsel, as the Maryland Court of Appeals had (a) unreasonably applied the clearly established federal law created by the Supreme Court's holding, in *Strickland v. Washington* (1984) 446 US 668, 80 L Ed 2d 674, 104 S Ct 2052, concerning ineffective assistance; and (b) partially relied on an erroneous factual assumption

Held: The performance of Wiggins's attorneys at sentencing violated his Sixth Amendment right to effective assistance of counsel.

(a) A federal writ can be granted only if a state court decision "was contrary to, or involved an unreasonable application of, clearly established" precedents of this Court. 28 USC § 2254(d)(1) [28 USCS § 2254(d)(1)]. This "unreasonable application" prong permits the writ to be granted when a state court identifies the correct governing legal principle but unreasonably applies it to the facts of a petitioner's case, *Williams v. Taylor*, 529 US 362, 413, 146 L Ed 2d 389, 120 S Ct 1495. For this standard to be satisfied, the state court decision must have been "objectively unreasonable," *id.*, at 409, 146 L Ed 2d 389, 120 S Ct 1495, not just incorrect or erroneous. An ineffective assistance claim has two components: A petitioner must show that counsel's performance was deficient, and that the deficiency prejudiced the defense, *Strickland v. Washington*, 466 US 668, 687, 80 L Ed 2d 674, 104 S Ct 2052. Performance is deficient if it falls below an objective standard of reasonableness, which is defined in terms of prevailing professional norms. *Id.*, at 688, 80 L Ed 2d 674, 104 S Ct 2052. Here, as in *Strickland*, counsel claims that their limited investigation into petitioner's background reflected a tactical judgment not to present mitigating evidence and to pursue an alternative strategy instead. In evaluating petitioner's claim, this

Court's principal concern is not whether counsel should have presented a mitigation case, but whether the investigation supporting their decision not to introduce mitigating evidence of Wiggins's background was itself reasonable. The Court thus conducts an objective review of their performance, measured for reasonableness under prevailing professional norms, including a context-dependent consideration of the challenged conduct as seen from counsel's perspective at the time of that conduct. *Id.*, at 688, 80 L Ed 2d 674, 104 S Ct 2052. (b)

(b) Counsel did not conduct a reasonable investigation. Their decision not to expand their investigation beyond a presentence investigation (PSI) report and Baltimore City Department of Social Services (DSS) records fell short of the professional standards prevailing in Maryland in 1989. Standard practice In Maryland capital cases at that time included the preparation of a social history report. Although there were funds to retain a forensic social worker, counsel chose not to commission a report. Their conduct similarly fell short of the American Bar Association's capital defense work standards. Moreover, in light of the facts counsel discovered in the DSS records concerning Wiggins's alcoholic mother and his problems in foster care, counsel's decision to cease investigating when they did was unreasonable. Any reasonably competent attorney would have realized that pursuing such leads was necessary to making an informed choice among possible defenses, particularly given the apparent absence of aggravating factors from Wiggins's background. Indeed, counsel discovered no evidence to suggest that a mitigation case would have been counterproductive or that further investigation would have been fruitless, thus distinguishing this case from precedents in which this Court has found limited investigations into mitigating evidence to be reasonable. The record of the sentencing proceedings underscores the unreasonableness of counsel's conduct by suggesting that their failure to investigate thoroughly stemmed from inattention, not strategic judgment. Until the trial court denied their bifurcation motion, they had every reason to develop the most powerful mitigation case possible during the sentencing process itself, counsel did not focus exclusively on Wiggins's direct responsibility for the murder; rather they put on a halfhearted mitigation case instead the Maryland Court of Appeals' assumption that counsel's investigation was adequate reflected an unreasonable application of *Strickland*. In deferring to council's decision not to present every conceivable mitigation defense despite the fact that counsel based their alleged choice on an inadequate investigation, the Maryland Court of Appeals further unreasonably applied *Strickland*. And the court's conclusion that the social services records revealed incidences of sexual abuse, when they in fact did not, reflects "an unreasonable determination of the facts in light of evidence presented in the State court proceeding," 28 USC §2254(d)(2) [28 USCS § 2254(d)(2)]. Contrary to the State's and the United States' contention, the record as a whole does not support the conclusion that counsel conducted a more thorough investigation than the one this Court describes. Ultimately, this Court's conclusion that counsel's investigation was inadequate does not mean that *Strickland* requires counsel to investigate every conceivable line of mitigating evidence no matter how unlikely the effort would be to assist the defendant at sentencing. Nor does *Strickland* require counsel to present such evidence at sentencing in every case. Rather, the conclusion is based on the much more limited principle that "strategic choices made after less than complete investigation are reasonable: only to the extent that "reasonable professional judgments support the limitations on investigation." *Strickland*, supra, at 690-691, 80 L Ed 2d 674, 104 S Ct 2052.

(c) Counsel's failures prejudiced Wiggins's defense. To establish prejudice, a defendant must show that there is a reasonable probability that, but for counsel's unprofessional errors, the proceeding's result would have been different. *Strickland*, supra, at 694, 80 L Ed 2d 674, 104 S Ct 2052. This Court assesses prejudice by reweighing the aggravating evidence against the totality of the mitigating evidence adduced both at trial and in the habeas proceedings. *Williams v. Taylor*, supra, 397-398, 146 L Ed 2d 389, 120 S

Ct 1495. The mitigating evidence counsel failed to discover and present here is powerful. Wiggins experienced severe privation and abuse while in the custody of his alcoholic, absentee mother and physical torment, sexual molestation, and repeated rape while in foster care. His time spent homeless, and his diminished mental capacities further augment his mitigation case. He thus has the kind of troubled history relevant to assessing a defendant's moral culpability. *Penry v. Lynaugh*, 492 US 302, 319, 106 L Ed 2d 256, 109 S Ct 2934. Given the nature and extent of the abuse, there is a reasonable probability that a competent attorney, aware of this history, would have introduced it at sentencing, and that a jury confronted with such mitigating evidence would have returned with a different sentence. The only significant mitigating factor the jury heard was that Wiggins had no prior convictions. Had it been able to place his excruciating life history on the mitigating side of the scale, there is a reasonable probability that at least one juror would have struck a different balance. Wiggins had no record of violent conduct that the State could have introduced to offset this powerful mitigating narrative. Thus, the available mitigating evidence, taken as a whole, might well have influenced the jury's appraisal of his moral culpability. 288 F.3d 629, reversed and remanded.

Government's case in chief – After the opening statements are given, the government will proceed into its case-in-chief. The government's attorney will seek to introduce the defendant's confession, physical evidence, and eyewitness identifications at trial. As the applicable rules require, the prosecutor is bound to present the case against the defendant for the purpose of proving the defendant's guilt "beyond a reasonable doubt." During this process the prosecutor conducts direct examination of the government's witnesses in an effort to guide them through their testimony. This process is also instrumental as a tool to refocus the witness' attention on important details if she happens to stray too far from the central issue.

During the government's case-in-chief, defense counsel has the important duty to remain vigilant. He must determine if and when the government's questions become improper and object accordingly. The defendant also has an obligation to take notes to 1) remind his counsel of questionable issues when in private; and 2) keep notes as he prepares for his later claims of ineffective assistance of counsel.

Cross examination – The defendant has a right to cross-examine the government's witnesses. The rule of cross-examination is more than a trial rule used to maintain equality. It is an expressed right in the Confrontation Clause of the U.S. Constitutions Sixth Amendment. Cross examination helps to maintain the accuracy of the truth-determining process. Thus, an essential and basic requirement to ensure a fair trial, which is our country's constitutional goal, see *Chambers v. Mississippi*, 410 U.S. 284, 295 (1973); and *Davis v. Alaska*, 415 U.S. 308, 316 (1974), which emphasized the importance of cross-examination, calling it "the principle means by which the believability of a witness and the truth of his testimony are tested." Indeed, cross-examination is so essential that it's denial without waiver is "Constitutional error of the first magnitude and no amount of showing of want of prejudice [can] cure it," *Brookhart v. Janis*, 384 U.S. I, 3 (1966), see also *Davis*, 415 U.S., at 318; and *Smith v. Illinois*, 390 U.S. 129, 131 (1968).

The Decision to Cross-examine – Cross-examining and objecting in a trial are two skills that are learned on a personal level for all attorneys. Just like you will not find two lawyers who practice law exactly alike, likewise you will discover that no two trials are alike either. As lay people, most defendants have little-to-no chance of learning enough about the practice of law to make any meaningful changes while a trial is being conducted. But the defendant should be aware of things that seem out of place, and thus making notes in preparation of a future ineffectiveness claim.

With that in mind, know that the basic purpose of cross-examination is to: (1) support the defense theory by establishing additional facts that corroborate the evidence counsel plans to introduce through defense witnesses; (2) contradict the testimony provided by another government witness; or (3) discredit the testimony previously provided, on direct examination, by the witness being examined. There is an endless list of additional reasons that would prompt defense counsels to cross-examine a witness. Counsel may also wish to argue that only part of a witness' story should be discredited while other parts should be believed. As there may be hundreds of different examples that would justify these three reasons to cross-examine a witness, there has never been one that justifies a lay person interrupting a defense lawyer in the middle of a trial. Don't be the first.

First motion for Judgment of Acquittal – An age-old tactic exercised by many appointed lawyers who have been bullied into a trial by their client is to move for a motion for acquittal at the end of the government's case, only then to rest the case of the defense. This conduct is ineffective assistance of counsel. There is no sound reason to fail to defend one's client.

There is cause, however, to make the motion for acquittal after the government's case-in-chief. Nonetheless, if it is not granted then the defense counsel should launch into the case he or she has prepared for the defense.

Right to Present a Defense – Due process of law is the basic constitutional right to be heard in one's own defense at a fair trial. This means that a defendant has an unquestionable "right to present a defense, the right to present the defendant's version of the fact," *Washington v. Texas*, 388 U.S. 14, 19 (1967).

Right to Present Evidence – Very similar to the right to present a defense, is the right to present evidence in that defense. The most important due process right that the defendant possesses is the right to testify on his or her own behalf. The defendant has an absolute right to testify, guaranteed by the United States Constitution. Under the due process clause of both the Fifth and Fourteenth Amendments, the right to testify at one's own trial is essential in providing due process of law in today's criminal justice system. This basic right is personal and can be waived only by the defendant, see *Johnson v. United States*, 613 A.2d 888, 894 (D.C. 1992).

The sixth Amendment also guarantees the accused a "compulsory process for obtaining witnesses in his favor." This right is also, "fundamental and essential to a fair trial," which applies in both state as well as federal courts, see *Washington v. Texas*, 388 U.S. 14, 17-18 (1967). The right to present a defense combines together with the right to confront adversarial witnesses, and thus has constitutionalized "the right to a defense as we know it," *California v. Green*, 399 U.S. 149, 176 (1970).

> *The right to offer the testimony of witnesses, and to compel their attendance, if necessary, is in plain terms the right to present a defense, the right to present the defendant's version of the facts as well as the prosecutions to the jury so it may decide where the truth lies. Just as an accused has the right to confront the prosecution's witnesses for the purpose of challenging their testimony, he has the right to present his own witnesses to establish a defense. The right is a fundamental element of due process of law. – Washington v. Texas, 388 U.S., at 19.*

Second Motion for Judgment of Acquittal – A diligent or effective criminal defense lawyer will seek a judgment of acquittal three times. First, at the close of the government's evidence; second, after the close of all the evidence; and three, within 14 days after a guilty verdict or after the court discharges the jury, see the Federal Rules of Criminal Procedure, Rule 29. If these motions for a judgment of acquittal are not made, the defense lawyer provided constitutionally ineffective assistance of counsel.

In any trial, especially in federal court, the government will put on a spectacle worthy of a theatrical award yet providing little evidence warranting conviction. Thus, a defendant must learn to understand the difference between evidence that invokes fear or passion in the jury as opposed to evidence that proves guilt beyond a reasonable doubt. This difference is the root cause that allows the conviction of the innocent, in today's criminal justice system. This difference also places a unique responsibility on the presiding judge to decide if the evidence only permits the jury to speculate as to the defendant's guilt or proves guilt beyond a reasonable doubt. Although, the court has the authority to act on its own accord; in today's criminal justice system, it won't unless defense counsel files the appropriate Rule 29 motions. Therefore, counsel who fails to file timely Rule 29 motions has provided ineffective assistance of counsel.

Federal Rules of Criminal Procedure allows the filing of a motion for judgment of acquittal "after the evidence on either side is closed." In today's practice, the motion should be made at the end of the government's case and renewed after the closing of all evidence. Defense counsel should also move for judgment of acquittal when he or she files a motion for a new trial, which must be filed within 14 days after the jury's verdict. Rule 29(c). In today's American Criminal Justice System – especially the federal system where budgets are increased based on the length of sentences rather than justice – the Rule 29 motions are filed only as a formality and to preserve the lack of evidence issue for appeal. When defense counsel fails to move for a judgement of acquittal, he or she closes the issue of appealability concerning the sufficiency of the evidence claim.

In today's practice of criminal justice, almost all cases are resolved in guilty pleas based on agreement drafted by the prosecutions, leaving trials very rare. But, when a trial does happen, the process is slanted to favor conviction. This is best identified in the practice and procedure of Rule 29 motions. In theory, defense counsel should be familiar with the instructions and case law relating to each charge. Unfortunately, in most cases, counsel doesn't even read the statute of conviction. Counsel should also be familiar with the comments to the standard jury instructions to determine how well they relate to fact as well as law.

Because Rule 29 motions are not usually granted, counsel should submit a detailed and written memorandum at the time of the motion for judgment of acquittal. This will preserve the sufficiency of the evidence issue as an abuse of discretion rather than simply a jury error that won't be overturned.

Again, the Rule 29 procedure is simply a charade. It is a standard operating procedure for a judge to excuse the jury, at the close of the government's case, before allowing the defense to move for a judgment of acquittal. In a close case, this act will stop the jury from getting the truth concerning how the facts relate to the law and more likely to guarantee a conviction. Remember, the government prefers jury trials because lay persons don't understand the complexities of the law. The court then decided the motion of acquittal by denying it outright or by reserving judgment until after the case of the defense when it will be denied or reserved again until after conviction. This indecision by the judge is practiced to simply avoid any adversity with the prosecutor.

Ordinarily the judge reserves the motion at the close of the government's case, he then reserves at the end of the defense's case, then denies it after the jury's verdict. This whole process is practiced in a way to use the jury's verdict to divert responsibility to the jury. The theory is that the court should decide a Rule 29 motion on the basis of the evidence at the time the ruling was reserved. That is why a Rule 29 motion must be made at the end of the government's case. Defense counsel who decides to wait until after the verdict to file a Rule 29 motion loses this standard of review and thus is ineffective.

Closing Arguments – The defendant has a Constitutional right to an opportunity to give a closing argument, see *Herring v. New York*, 422 U.S. 853 (1975). Although, this right is waivable, it should never be waived. The closing argument is the defendant's opportunity to make a clear assertion of innocence, directly to the trier of fact, based on the presentation of the evidence and how it relates to the charging statute. It's only after all the evidence is given that defense counsel can paint a clear picture that proves innocence. More importantly, closing arguments is the last clear chance that counsel has to inform the trier of fact that their duty is to find guilt beyond a reasonable doubt based on the fact and evidence presented at trial.

There is no set structure or tactics required by rules concerning a closing argument; a defendant is therefore at the mercy of counsel's experience. But the closing argument should be logical and clear, above all compelling. It should be carefully rehearsed as opposed to a dry reading of notes. Defense counsel should consciously reach out to the jurors on a personal level to obtain their trust and respect. Counsel's personality should seem earnest and straightforward. He or she should use a conversational tone and avoid legal jargon and confusing phrases like "on the premise of …" Everything that counsel presents must convince the jury of his absolute and unwavering personal belief in his or her client's innocence. Anything less is ineffective assistance of counsel.

Jury Instructions – Jury instructions contain the basis of the law that the jurors swear to follow while they are deciding whether the defendant is guilty or not guilty. This is the very backbone of the due process right to a fair trial. The trial court, however, is most commonly fixed on conviction regardless of guilt or innocence and makes this clear in their jury instructions. Defense counsel has little say in the final jury instructions even when meaningful instructions are requested. Therefore, it is counsel's duty to object when the final jury instructions are improper, thus preserving the issue for direct appeal. Common errors in jury instructions are related to the essential elements of the charged offense. If counsel fails to object when the trial court shifts or misquotes the essential elements, then counsel is ineffective.

Deliberations of the Jury – Once the case is turned over to the jury for deliberation, a whole new set of circumstances comes into play. It is highly unlikely that a lay person would recognize any errors at that point of the proceeding, leaving the defendant's most important task being that of making good notes. Notes are important because errors can be found in instances of polling the jury, whether defense counsel moved to declare a mistrial, or impeaching the verdict in certain circumstances. As anyone can imagine, a jury's verdict of guilt is the end of the trial itself. The final motion for a judgment of acquittal should be filed within 14 days, but at that point the defendant is left with preparing for the next step of the trial process and in some circumstances can mean the difference between life and death.

CHAPTER FOURTEEN

SENTENCING

Sentencing is the apex of the trial process. This one single statement is the main purpose of the criminal justice system. Unknown to most Americans is that the Criminal Justice System, both State and Federal, is an 800 billion dollar a year business. This business if suddenly shut down, would likely cause an interruption in the American economy that would rival The Great Depression.

In the Federal Criminal Justice scheme alone, the U.S. Congress allocates 80 billion dollars a year to the Department of Justice. That money is then doled out to the 94 judicial districts around the country. Each district receives its annual budget, an about determined by the number of months of sentencing handed down by its judges rather than by size or population. The judicial district then pays out about ten percent (10) of what it collects to the prisons for holding each prisoner in a state of confinement. The amount paid to the prison alone is near to three thousand dollars a month per prisoner. Ninety percent of the 80-billion-dollar annual budget is deposited in private accounts of those government officials, and the friends and family thereof, which provide goods and services to the Federal Bureau of Prisons and the Department of Justice.

As you can see, the purpose of sentencing is to convert tax dollars into private funds. Another facet to this interesting dynamic is that prisoners complete their sentences and get released every day. To keep, at a minimum, the status quo, federal judges are required to replace prisoners as quickly as possible. If growth is desired in any judicial district, and they all wish to grow to add more and more jobs for family members, the judges must hand down longer sentences than the ones that were just completed or add to the prison population. This is why we: all hear about judges who desire to hand down "a million years," as opposed to dispensing justice or releasing one hundred innocent prisoners.

In the federal system, sentencing preparation begins right after conviction with a visit between the defendant and his lawyer. Pleasant enough, the lawyer gives the usual banter about his disbelief concerning the verdict, when in fact, 98% of all federal indictments end in conviction. Additionally, counsel advises that the defendant must also consider preparing for the sentencing phase. True enough on its face. However, most of the time counsel will advise his client to play up any possible addictions he may have. Counsel will advertise that doing so will gain sympathy from the judge and, in a case of drug addiction, gain a year off a sentence by qualifying for the Residential Drug Abuse Program (RDAP for short). This in most cases is not true at all. Only a select few are chosen by the Federal Bureau of Prisons to participate in RDAP, and even fewer yet qualify for the year off their sentences.

In these types of cases, the lawyer is preparing his client for the presentence Report Investigation. Please note that the Presentence Investigation (P.S.I) and the Presentence Report (P.S.R.) are two uniquely different things. The P.S.I. is an interview with a probation officer; the P.S.R. is the written summary of that interview. The P.S.R. is very important because this is the document that the U.S. Probation office will use when making its sentencing recommendations to the sentencing judge.

Additionally, it's the U.S. Probation Office who monitors the districts budgetary needs while handling sentencing recommendations. Just like a child making lemonade for nickels on a street corner; the U.S. Probation Office prepares a P.S.R., squeezing every available dollar out of an unsuspecting American's life and family. Also know that the defendant's defense lawyer has known the probation officer a lot longer than he has known his client, the defendant. Thus, he is much more likely to assist the probation officer in exacerbating the expected sentence exposure, than reducing it. A defendant should *never* exaggerate offense conduct, no matter who advises to do so. If the probation officer is asking about drug usage (or picture quantity in child pornography cases) he or she is trying to gain additional sentencing factors. A defendant should not lie, nor should he or she answer.

After a guilty plea, the defendant suffering ineffective assistance of counsel is almost guaranteed. This happens because counsel knows that the defendant is very limited in the claims that he can raise in either direct appeal or in post-conviction relief proceedings.

Defense counsel knows that the Sixth Amendment right, to the effective assistance of counsel, extends to counsel's advice, to the defendant, to accept a plea agreement. That right also encompasses consideration of plea offers that lapse or are rejected. That right applies to all critical stages of the criminal proceedings, see *Montejo v. Louisiana*, 556 U.S. 778 (2009); and *Hill v. Lockhart*, 474 U.S. 52 (1985), established that the *Strickland* two-part test governs all ineffective assistance of counsel claims in cases concerning plea bargains. In the context of plea bargains, the defendant must show that counsel had given him inadequate advice about his plea; and that he would have proceeded to trial had he received the proper advice. In short, counsel knows that he can provide ineffective assistance at the Presentence Report Investigation after a plea agreement because the defendant *cannot* raise a claim concerning sentencing after a plea agreement.

FEDERAL LAWS THAT GOVERN SENTENCING

§355l. Authorized Sentences

(a) *In general*. Except as otherwise specifically provided, a defendant who has been found guilty of an offense described in any Federal statute, including sections 13 and 1153 of this title [18 USCS §§ 13 and 1153], other than an Act of Congress applicable exclusively in the District of Columbia or the Uniform Code of Military Justice [10 USCS §§ 801 *et seq.*], shall be sentenced in accordance with the provisions of this chapter so as to achieve the purposes set forth in subparagraphs (A) through (D) of section 3553(a)(2) [18 USCS § 3553(a)(2)] to the extent that they are applicable in light of all the circumstances of the case.

(b) *Individuals*. An individual found guilty of an offense shall be sentenced, in accordance with the provisions of section 3553 [18 USGS § 3553] to –

(1) a term of probation as authorized by subchapter B 118 USCS §§ 3561 *et seq.*];

(2) a fine as authorized by subchapter e [18 USCS §§ 3571 *et seq.*]; or

(3) a term of imprisonment as authorized by subchapter D [18 USCS §§ 3581 *et seq.*].

> A sentence to pay a fine may be imposed in addition to any other sentence.

> A sanction authorized by section 3554, 3555" or 3556 [18 USCS § 3554, 3555, or 3556] may be imposed in addition to the sentence required by this subsection.

(c) *Organizations*. An organization found guilty of an offense shall be sentenced, in accordance with the provisions of section 3553 [18 USCS § 3553], to –

(1) a term of probation as authorized by subchapter B [18 USCS §§ 3561 *et seq.*]; or

(2) a fine as authorized by subchapter e [18 USCS §§ 3571 *et seq.*]. a sentence to pay a fine may be imposed in addition to a sentence to probation. A sanction authorized by section 3554, 3555, or 3556 [18 USCS § 3554, 3555, or 3556) may be imposed in addition to the sentence required by this subsection.

§ 3552. Presentence reports

(a) *Presentence investigation and report by probation officer*. A United States probation officer shall make a presentence investigation of a defendant that is required pursuant to the provision of Rule 32(c) of the

Federal Rules of Criminal Procedure, and shall, before the imposition of sentence, report the results of the investigation to the court.

(b) *Presentence study and report by Bureau of Prisons*. If the court, before or after its receipt of a report specified in subsection (a) or (c), desires more information that is otherwise available to it as a basis for determining the sentence to be imposed on a defendant found guilty of a misdemeanor or felony, it may order a study of the defendant. The study shall be conducted in the local community by qualified consultants unless the sentencing judge finds that there is a compelling reason for the study to be done by the Bureau of Prisons or there are no adequate professional resources available in the local community to perform the study. The period of the study shall be no more than sixty days. The order shall specify the additional information that the court needs before determining the sentence to be imposed. Such an order shall be treated for administrative purposes as a provisional sentence of imprisonment for the maximum term authorized by section 3581 (b)[18 USCS § 3581(b)] for the offense committed. The study shall inquire into such matters as are specified by the court and any other matters that the Bureau of Prisons or the professional consultants believe are pertinent to the factors set forth in section 3553(a) [18 USCS § 3553(a)]. The period of the study may, at the discretion of the court, be extended for an additional period by not more than sixty days. By the expiration of the period of the study, or by the expiration of any extension granted by the court, the United States marshal shall, if the defendant is in custody, return the defendant to the court for final sentencing. The Bureau of Prisons or the professional consultants shall provide the court with a written report of the pertinent results of the study and make to the court whatever recommendations the Bureau or the consultants believe will be helpful to a proper resolution of the case. The report shall include recommendations of the Bureau or the consultants concerning the guidelines and policy statements, promulgated by the Sentencing Commission pursuant to 28 U.S.C. 994(a), that they believe are applicable to the defendant's case. After receiving the report and the recommendations, the court shall proceed finally to sentence the defendant in accordance with the sentencing alternatives and procedures available under this chapter [18 USCS §§ 3551 *et seq.*].

(c) *Presentence examination and report by psychiatric or Psychological examiners*. If the court, before or after its receipt of a report specified in subsection 9 (a) or (b) desires more information than is otherwise available to it as a basis for determining the mental condition of the defendant, the court may order the same psychiatric or psychological examination and report thereon as may be ordered under section 4244(b) of this title [18 USCS § 4244(b)].

(d) *Disclosure of presentence reports*. The court shall assure that a report filed pursuant to this section is disclosed to the defendant, the counsel for the defendant, and the attorney for the Government at least ten days prior to the date set for sentencing, unless this minimum period is for the Government to use in collecting an assessment, criminal fine, forfeiture or restitution imposed.

§ 3553. Imposition of a sentence

(a) *Factors to be considered in imposing a sentence*. The court shall impose a sentence sufficient, but not greater than necessary, to comply with the purposes set forth in paragraph (2) of this subsection. The court, in determining the particular sentence to be imposed, shall consider –

   (1) the nature and circumstances of the offense and the history and characteristics of the defendant;

   (2) the need for the sentence imposed –

      (A) to reflect the seriousness of the offense, to promote respect for the law, and to provide just punishment for the offense;

(B) to afford adequate deterrence to criminal conduct;

(C) to protect the public from further crimes of the defendant; and

(D) to provide the defendant with needed educational or vocational training, medical care, or other correctional treatment in the most effective manner;

(3) the kinds of sentences available;

(4) the kinds of sentence and the sentencing range established for –

(A) the applicable category of offense committed by the applicable category of defendant as set forth in the guidelines –

(i) issued by the Sentencing Commission pursuant to section 994(a)(1) of title 28, United States Code, subject to any amendments made to such guidelines by act of Congress (regardless of whether such amendments have yet to be incorporated by the Sentencing Commission into amendments issued under section 994(p) of title 28); and

(ii) that, except as provided in section 3742(g) [18 USCS § 3742(g)], are in effect on the date the defendant is sentenced; or

(B) in the case of a violation of probation or supervised release, the applicable guidelines or policy statements issued by the Sentencing Commission pursuant to section 994(a)(3) of title 28, United States Code, taking into account any amendments made to such guidelines or policy statements by act of Congress (regardless of whether such amendments have yet to be incorporated by the Sentencing Commission into amendments issued under section 994(p) of title 28:

(5) any pertinent policy statement –

(A) issued by the Sentencing Commission pursuant to section 994(a)(2) of title 28, United States Code, subject to any amendments made to such policy statement by act of Congress (regardless of whether, such amendments have yet to be incorporated by the Sentencing Commission into amendments issued under section 994(p) of title 28); and

(B) that, except as provided in section 3742(g) [18 USCS § 3742(g)], is in effect on the date the defendant is sentenced. [;]

(6) the need to avoid unwarranted sentence disparities among defendants with similar records who have been found guilty of similar conduct; and

(7) the need to provide restitution to any victims of the offense.

(b) *Application of guidelines in imposing a sentence.*

(1) In general [*Caution: In United States v. Booker (2005) 543 US 220, 160 L Ed 2d 621, 125 S Ct 738, the Supreme Court held that 18 USCS §3553(b)(1), which makes the Federal Sentencing Guidelines mandatory, is incompatible with the requirements of the Sixth Amendment and therefore must be severed and excised from the Sentencing Reform Act of 1984.*] Except as provided in paragraph (2), the court shall impose a sentence of the kind, and within the range, referred to in subsection (a)(4) – unless the court finds that there exists an aggravating or mitigating circumstance of a kind, or to a degree, not: adequately taken into consideration by the Sentencing Commission in formulating the guidelines that should result in a sentence different from that described. In determining whether a circumstance was adequately taken into consideration, the court shall consider only the sentencing guidelines, policy statements, and official commentary of the Sentencing Commission. In the absence of an applicable sentencing guideline, the court shall impose an appropriate sentence,

having due regard for the purposes set forth in subsection (a)(2). In the absence of an applicable sentencing guideline in the case of an offense other than a petty offense, the court shall also have due regard for the relationship of the sentence imposed to sentences prescribed by guidelines applicable to similar offenses and offenders, and to the applicable policy statements of the Sentencing Commission.

(2) Child crimes and sexual offenses.

(A) Sentencing. In sentencing a defendant convicted of an offense under section 1201 [18 USCS § 1201] involving a minor victim, an offense under section 1591 [18 USCS § 1591], or an offense under chapter 71, 109A, 110, or 117 [18 USCS §§ 1460 *et seq.*, 2241 *et seq.*, 2251 *et seq.*, or 2421 *et seq.*], the court shall impose a sentence of the kind, and within the range, referred to in subsection (a)(4) unless –

(i) the court finds that there exists an aggravating circumstance of a kind, or to a degree, not adequately taken into consideration by the Sentencing Commission in formulating the guidelines that should result in a sentence greater than that described;

(ii) the court finds that there exists a mitigating circumstance of a kind or to a degree, that:

(I) has been affirmatively and specifically identified as a permissible ground of downward departure in the sentencing guidelines or policy statements issued under section 994(a) of title 28, taking account of any amendments to such sentencing guidelines or policy statements by Congress;

(II) has not been taken into consideration by the Sentencing Commission in formulating the guidelines; and

(III) should result in a sentence different from that described; or

(iii) the court finds, on motion of the Government, that the defendant has provided substantial assistance in the investigation or prosecution of another person who has committed an offense, and that this assistance established a mitigating circumstance of a kind, or to a degree, not adequately taken into consideration by the Sentencing Commission in formulating the guidelines that should result in a sentence lower than that described.

In determining whether a circumstance was adequately taken into consideration, the court shall consider only the sentencing guidelines, policy statements, and official commentary of the Sentencing Commission, together with any amendments thereto by act of Congress. In the absence of an applicable sentencing guideline, the court shall impose an appropriate sentence, having due regard for the purposes set forth in subsection (a)(2). In the absence of an applicable sentencing guideline in the case of an offense other than a petty offense, the court shall also have due regard for the relationship of the sentence imposed to sentences prescribed by guidelines applicable to similar offenses and offenders, and to the applicable policy statements of the Sentencing Commission, together with any amendments to such guidelines or policy statements by act of Congress.

(c) *Statement of reasons for imposing a sentence*. The court, at the time of sentencing, shall state in open court the reasons for its imposition of the particular sentence, and, if the sentence –

(1) is of the kind and within the range, described in subsection (a)(4), and that range exceeds 24 months, the reason for imposing a sentence at a particular point within the range; or

(2) is not of the kind, or is outside the range, described in subsection (a)(4), the specific reason for the imposition of a sentence different from that described, which reasons must also be stated with

specificity in a statement of reasons form issued under section 994(w)(1)(B) of title 28 [28 USCS § 994(w)(1)(B)], except to the extent that the court relies upon statements received in camera in accordance with Federal Rule of Criminal Procedure 32. In the event that the court relies upon statements received in camera in accordance with Federal Rule of Criminal Procedure 32 the court shall state that such statements were so received and that it relied upon the content of such statements.

If the court does not order restitution, or orders only partial restitution, the court shall include in the statement the reason therefor. The court shall provide a transcription or other appropriate public record of the court's statement of reasons, together with the order of judgment and commitment, to the Probation System and to the Sentencing Commission, [,] and, if the sentence includes a term of imprisonment, to the Bureau of Prisons.

(d) *Presentence procedure for an order of notice.* Prior to imposing an order of notice pursuant to section 3555 [18 USCS § 3555], the court shall give notice to the defendant and the Government that it is considering imposing such an order. Upon motion of the defendant or the Government, or on its own motion, the court shall –

(1) permit the defendant and the Government to submit affidavits and written memoranda addressing matters relevant to the imposition of such an order;

(2) afford counsel an opportunity in open court to address orally the appropriateness of the imposition of such an order; and

(3) include in its statement of reasons pursuant to subsection (c) specific reasons underlying its determinations regarding the nature of such an order.

Upon motion of the defendant or the Government, or on its own motion, the court may in its discretion employ any additional procedures that it concludes will not unduly complicate or prolong the sentencing process.

(e) *Limited authority to impose a sentence below a statutory minimum.* Upon motion of the Government, the court shall have the authority to impose a sentence below a level established by statute as a minimum sentence so as to reflect a defendant's substantial assistance in the investigation or prosecution of another person who has committed an offense. Such sentence shall be imposed in accordance with the guidelines and policy statements issued by the Sentencing Commission pursuant to section 994 of title 28, United States Code.

(f) *Limitation on applicability of statutory minimums in certain cases.* Notwithstanding any other provision of law, in the case of an offense under section 401, 404, or 406 of the Controlled Substances Act (21 U.S.C. 841, 844 846), section 1010 or 1013 of the Controlled Substance Import and: Export Act (21 U.S.C. 960, 963), or section 70503 or 705056 of title 46, the court shall impose a sentence pursuant; to guidelines promulgated by the United States Sentencing Commission under section 994 of title 28 without regard to any statutory minimum sentence, if the court finds at sentencing, after the Government has been afforded the opportunity to make a recommendation, that –

(1) the defendant does not have –

(A) more than 4 criminal history points, excluding any criminal history points resulting from a I-point offense, as determined under the sentencing guidelines;

(B) a prior 3-point offense, as determined under the sentencing guidelines; and

(C) a prior 2-point violent offense, as determined under the sentencing guidelines;

Information disclosed by a defendant under this subsection may not be used to enhance the sentence of the defendant unless the information relates to a violent offense.

(2) the defendant did not use violence or credible threats of violence or possess a firearm or other dangerous weapon (or induce another participant to do so) in connection with the offense;

(3) the offense did not result in death or serious bodily injury to any person;

(4) the defendant was not an organizer, leader, manager, or supervisor of others in the offense, as determined under the sentencing guidelines and was not engaged in a continuing criminal enterprise, as defined in section 408 of the Controlled Substances Act [21 USCS § 848]; and

(5) not later than the time of the sentencing hearing, the defendant has truthfully provided to the Government all the information and evidence the defendant has concerning the offense or offenses that were part of the same course of conduct or of a common scheme or plan, but the fact that the defendant has no relevant or useful other information to provide or that: the Government is already aware of the information shall not preclude a determination by the court that the defendant has complied with this requirement.

(g) *Definition of violent offense.* As used in this section, the term "violent offense" means a crime of violence, as defined in section 16 [18 USCS § 16], that is punishable by imprisonment.

§ 3554. Order of criminal forfeiture

The court, in imposing a sentence on a defendant who has been found guilty of an offense described in section 1962 of this title [18 USCS § 1962] or in title II or III of the Comprehensive Drug Abuse Prevention and Control Act of 1970 [21 USCS §§ 801 *et seq.* or 951 *et seq.*] shall order, in addition to the sentence that is imposed pursuant to the provisions of section 3551 [18 USCS § 3551], that the defendant forfeit property to the United States in accordance with the provisions of section 1963 of this title [18 USCS § 1963] or section 413 of the Comprehensive Drug Abuse and Control Act of 1970 [21 USCS § 853].

§ 3555. Order of notice to victims

The court, in imposing a sentence on a defendant who has been found guilty of an offense involving fraud or other intentionally deceptive practices, may order, in addition to the sentence that is imposed pursuant to the provision of section 3551 [18 USCS § 3551], that the defendant give reasonable notice and explanation of the conviction, in such form as the court may approve, to the victims of the offense. The notice may be ordered to be given by mail, by advertising in designated areas or through designated media, or by other appropriate means. In determining whether to require the defendant to give such notice, the court shall consider the factors set forth in sections 3553(a) [18 USCS § 3553(a)] to the extent that they are applicable and shall consider the cost involved in giving the notice as it relates to the loss caused by the offense, and shall not require the defendant to bear the costs of notice in excess of $20,000

§ 3556. Order of restitution

The court, in imposing a sentence on a defendant who has been found guilty of an offense shall order restitution in accordance with section 3663A [18 USCS § 3663A] and may order restitution in accordance with section 3663 [18 USCS § 3663]. The procedures under section 3664 [18 USCS § 3664] shall apply to all orders of restitution under this section.

§ 3557. Review of a sentence

The review of a sentence imposed pursuant to section 3551 [18 USCS § 3551] is governed by the provisions of section 3742 [18 USCS § 3742]

§ 3558. Implementation of a sentence

The implementation of a sentence imposed pursuant to section 3551 [18 USCS § 3551] is governed by the provisions of chapter 229 [18 USCS §§ 3601 *et seq.*].

§ 3559. Sentencing classification of offenses

(a) *Classification.* An offense that is not specifically classified by a letter grade in the section defining it, is classified if the maximum term of imprisonment authorized is –

    (1) life imprisonment, or if the maximum penalty is death, as a Class A felony;

    (2) twenty-five years or more, as a Class B felony;

    (3) less than twenty-five years but ten or more years, as a Class C felony;

    (4) less than ten years but five or more years, as a Class D felony;

    (5) less than five years but more than one year, as a Class E felony;

    (6) one year or less but more than six months, as a Class A misdemeanor;

    (7) six months or less but more than thirty days, as a Class B misdemeanor;

    (8) thirty days or less but more than five days, as a Class C misdemeanor; or

    (9) five days or less, or if no imprisonment is authorized, as an infraction.

(b) *Effect of classification.* Except as provided in subsection (c) an offense classified under subsection (a) carries all the incidents assigned to the applicable letter designation, except that, the maximum term of imprisonment is the term authorized by the law describing the offense.

(c) *Imprisonment of certain violent felons*

    (1) Mandatory life imprisonment- Notwithstanding any other provision of law, a person who is convicted in a court of the United States of a serious violent felony shall be sentenced to life imprisonment if –

        (A) the person has been convicted (and those convictions have become final) on separate prior occasions in a court of the United States or of a State of –

            (i) 2 or more serious violent felonies; or

            (ii) one or more serious violent felonies and one or more serious drug offenses; and

        (B) each serious violent felony or serious drug offense used as a basis for sentencing under this subsection, other than the first, was committed after the defendant's conviction of the preceding serious violent felony or serious drug offense.

    (2) Definitions. For purposes of this subsection –

        (A) the term "assault with intent to commit rape" means an offense that has as its elements engaging in physical contact with another person or using or brandishing a weapon against another person with intent to commit aggravated sexual abuse or sexual abuse (as described in sections 2241 and 2242 [18 USCS §§ 2241 and 2242]);

        (B) the term "arson" means an offense that has as its elements maliciously damaging or destroying any building, inhabited structure, vehicle, vessel, or real property by means of fire or an explosive;

        (C) the term "extortion" means an offense that has as its elements the extraction of anything of value from another person by threatening or placing that person in fear of injury to any person or kidnapping of any person;

(D) the term "firearms use" means an offense that has as its elements those described in section 924(c) or Stet(a) [18 USCS §924(c) or 929(a)], if the firearm was brandished, discharged, or otherwise used as a weapon and the crime of violence or drug trafficking crime during and relation to which the firearm was used was subject to prosecution in a court of the United States or a court of a State, or both;

(E) the term "kidnapping" means an offense that has as its elements the abduction, restraining, confining, or carrying away of another person by force or threat of force;

(F) the term "serious violent felony" means –

    (i) a Federal or State offense, by whatever designation and wherever committed, consisting of murder (as described in section 1111 [18 USCS § 1111]); manslaughter other than involuntary manslaughter (as described in section 1112 [18 USCS § 1112]); assault with intent to commit murder (as described in section Stet(a) [18 USCS § 113(a)]); assault with intent to commit rape; aggravated sexual abuse and sexual abuse (as described in sections 2241 and 2242 [18 USCS §§2241 and 2242]); abuse sexual contact (as described in section s 2244(a)(1) and (a)(2) [18 USCS § 2244(a)(1) and (a) (2)]); kidnapping; aircraft piracy (as described in section 46502 of Title 49); robbery (as described in section 2111, 2113, or 2118 [18 USCS § 2111, 2113· or 2118]); carjacking (as described in section 2119 [18 USCS § 2119]); extortion; arson; firearms use; firearms possession (as described in section 924(c)' [18 USCS § 924(c)]); or attempt, conspiracy, or solicitation to commit any of the above offenses; and

    (ii) any other offense punishable by a maximum term of imprisonment of 10 years or more that has an element the use, attempted use, or threatened use of physical force against the person of another or that, by its nature, involves a substantial risk that physical force against the person of another may be used in the course of committing the offense;

(G) the term "State" means a State of the United States, the District of Columbia, and a commonwealth, territory, or possession of the United States; and

(H) the term "serious drug offense" means –

    (i) an offense that is punishable under section 401(b)(1)(A) or 408 of the Controlled Substances Act (21 U.S.C. 841(b)(1)(A), 848) or section 1010(b)(1)(A) of the Controlled Substances Import and Export Act (21 U.S.C. 960(b)(1)(A)); or

    (ii) an offense under State law that, had the offense been prosecuted in a court of the United States, would have been punishable under section 401(b)(1)(A) or 408 of the Controlled Substances Act (21 U.S.C. 841(b)(1)(A), 848) or section 1010(b)(1)(A) of the Controlled Substances Import and Export Act (21 U.S.C. 960(b)(1)(A)).

(3) Non-qualifying felonies.

(A) Robbery in certain cases. Robbery, an attempt, conspiracy. or solicitation to commit robbery; or an offense described in paragraph (2)(F)(ii) shall not serve as a basis for sentencing under this subsection if the defendant establishes by clear and convincing evidence that –

    (i) no firearm or other dangerous weapon was used in the offense and no threat of use of a firearm or other dangerous weapon was involved ln the offense; and

    (ii) the offense did not result in death or serious bodily injury (as defined in section 1365 [18 USCS §1365]) to any person.

(B) Arson in certain cases. Arson shall not serve as a basis for sentencing under this subsection if the defendant establishes by clear and convincing evidence that –

(i) the offense posed no threat to human life; and

(ii) the defendant reasonably believed the offense posed no threat to human life.

(4) Information filed by United States Attorney. The provisions of section 411(a) of the Controlled Substances Act (21 D.S.C. 85l(a)) shall apply to the imposition of sentence under this subsection.

(5) Rule of construction. This subsection shall not be construed to preclude imposition of the death penalty.

(6) Special provision for Indian country. No person subject to the criminal jurisdiction of an Indian tribal government shall be subject to this subsection for any offense for which Federal jurisdiction is solely predicated on Indian country (as defined in section 1151 [18 USCS § 1151)) and which occurs within the boundaries of such Indian country unless the governing body of the tribe has elected that this subsection have effect over land and persons subject to the criminal jurisdiction of the tribe.

(7) Resentencing upon overturning of prior conviction. If the conviction for a serious violent felony or serious drug offense that was a basis for sentencing under this subsection is found, pursuant to any appropriate State or Federal procedure, to be unconstitutional or is vitiated on the explicit basis of innocence, or if the convicted person is pardoned on the explicit basis of innocence, the person serving a sentence imposed under this subsection shall be resentenced to any sentence that was available at the time of the original sentencing.

(d) *Death or imprisonment for crimes against children.*

(1) In general. Subject to paragraph (2) and notwithstanding any other provision of law, a person who is convicted of a Federal offense that is a serious violent felony (as defined in subsection (c)) or a violation of section 2422, 2423, or 2251 [18 USCS § 2422, 2423, or 2251) shall unless the sentence of death is imposed, be sentenced to imprisonment for life, if –

(A) the victim of the offense has not attained the age of 14 years;

(B) the victim dies as a result of the offense; and

(C) the defendant, in the court of the offense, engages in conduct described in section 3591(a)(2) (18 USCS § 3591(a)(2)).

(2) Exception. With respect to a person convicted of a Federal offense described in paragraph (1), the court may impose any lesser sentence that is authorized by law to take into account any substantial assistance provided by the defendant in the investigation or prosecution of another person who has committed an offense, in accordance with the Federal Sentencing Guidelines and the policy statements of the Federal Sentencing commission pursuant to section 994(p) of title 28, or for other good cause.

(e) *Mandatory life imprisonment for repeated sex offenses against children.*

(1) In general. A person who is convicted of a Federal sex offense in which a minor is the victim shall be sentenced to life imprisonment if the person has a prior sex conviction in which a minor was the victim, unless the sentence of death is imposed.

(2) Definitions. For the purposes of this subsection –

(A) the term "Federal sex offense" weans an offense under section 1591 [18 USCS § 1591] (relating to sex trafficking of children), 2241 [18 USCS § 2241] (relating to aggravated sexual abuse),

2242 [18 USCS § 2242] (relating to sexual abuse), 2244(a)(1) [18 USCS § 2244 (a) (1)] (relating to abusive sexual contact), 2245 [18 USCS § 2245] (relating to sexual abuse resulting in death), 2251 [18 USCS § 2251] (relating to sexual exploitation of children) 2251A [18 USCS §2251A] (relating to selling or buying of children), 2242(b) [18 USCS 2242(b)] (relating to coercion and enticement of a minor into prostitution), or 2423(a) [18 USCS § 2423(a)] (relating to transportation of minors);

(B) the term "State sex offense" means an offense under State law that is punishable by more than one year in prison and consists of conduct that would be a Federal sex offense if, to the extent or in the manner specified in the applicable provision of this title –

(i) the offense involved interstate or foreign commerce, or the use of the mails; or

(ii) the conduct occurred in any commonwealth, territory, or possession of the United States, within the special maritime and territorial jurisdiction of the United States, in a Federal: prison, or any land or building owned by, leased to, or otherwise used by or under the control of the government of the United States, or in the Indian country (as defined in section 1151 [18 USCS § 1151]);

(C) the term "prior sex conviction" means a conviction for which the sentence was imposed before the conduct occurred constituting the subsequent Federal sex offense, and which was for a Federal sex offense or a State sex offense;

(D) the term "minor" means an individual who has not attained the age of 17 years; and

(E) the term "State" has the meaning given that term in subsection (c)(2).

(3) Non-qualifying felonies. An offense described in section 2422(b) or 2423(a) [18 USCS § 2422(b) or 2423(a)] shall not serve as a basis for sentencing under this subsection if the defendant establishes by clear and convincing evidence that –

(A) the sexual act or activity was consensual and not for the purpose of commercial or pecuniary gain;

(B) the sexual act or: - activity would not be punishable by more than one year in prison under the law of the State in which it occurred; or

(C) no sexual act or activity occurred.

(f) *Mandatory minimum terms of imprisonment for violent crimes against children.* A person who is convicted of a Federal offense that is a crime of violence against the person of an individual who has not attained the age of 18 years shall, unless a greater mandatory minimum sentence of imprisonment is otherwise provided by law and regardless of any maximum term of imprisonment otherwise provided for the offense –

(1) if the crime of violence is murder, be imprisoned for life or for any term of years not less than 30, except that such person shall be punished by death or life imprisonment if the circumstances satisfy any of subparagraphs (A) through (D) of section 3591(a)(2) of this title [18 USCS § 3591(a)(2)];

(2) if the crime of violence is kidnapping (as defined in section 1201 [18 USCS § 1201]) or maiming (as defined in section Stet [18 USCS § 114]), be imprisoned for life or any term of years not less than 25; and

(3) if the crime of violence results in serious bodily injury (as defined in section 1365 [18 USCS § 1365]), or if a dangerous weapon was used during and in relation to the crime of violence, be imprisoned for life or for any term of years not less than 10.

(g) (1) If a defendant who is convicted of a felony offense (other than [an] offense of which an element is the false registration of a domain name) knowingly falsely registered a domain name and knowingly used that domain name in the course of that offense, the maximum imprisonment otherwise provided by law for that offense shall be doubled or increased by 7 years, whichever is less.

(2) As used in this section –

(A) the term "falsely registers" means registers in a manner that prevents the effective identification of or contact with the person who registers; and

(B) the term "domain name" has the meaning given that term is [in] section 45 of the Act entitled "An Act to provide for the registration and protection of trademarks used in commerce, to carry out the provisions of certain international conventions, and for other purposes" approved July 5, 1946 (commonly referred to as the "Trademark Act of 1946") (15 U.S.C- 1127).

SOME IMPORTANT THOUGHTS

Sentencing is governed by Law, Rules, and the United States Sentencing Guidelines, all passed with the expressed intent to bring uniformity to the sentencing process. As mentioned earlier, sentencing begins with the development of the pre-sentence report. This report should be, but not always is, a reflection of the defendant's conduct and the appropriate sentence for the conduct as illustrated in the sentencing guidelines. The single most fundamental aspect of sentencing is that it should be implemented based on accurate information. Thus, the court should begin by *correctly* calculating the applicable guidelines range, see *Gall v. United States* and the sentencing table that follows:

GALL V. UNITED STATES
5S2 US 38, 128 S CT 586, 169 L ED 2D 445 (2007)

DECISION

Federal Courts of Appeals held required to review all federal criminal sentences – whether inside, just outside, or significantly outside Federal sentencing Guidelines (18 U.S.C.S. Appx.) range-under deferential abuse – of discretion standard.

SUMMARY

Procedural Posture: Petitioner, an individual who pled guilty to conspiracy to distribute a mixture and substance containing methylenedioxy methamphetamine (ecstasy), sought *certiorari* review of a judgment from the United States Court of Appeals for the Eighth Circuit, which reversed and remanded the district court's decision to sentence petitioner to probation for a term of 36 months rather than imprisonment.

Overview: Petitioner joined an ongoing enterprise distributing ecstasy while in college, but he withdrew from the conspiracy after seven months and ceased all drug activity. Three and one-half years after withdrawing from the conspiracy, petitioner pled guilty to his participation. The court of appeals characterized the difference between the sentence of probation "and the bottom of petitioner's advisory Guidelines range of 30 months as extraordinary," and it held that the variance was not supported by extraordinary circumstances. Although the Court agreed that the court of appeals could take the degree of variance into account and consider the extent of a deviation from the Guidelines, the Court held that the court of appeals erred in requiring "extraordinary" circumstances. The court of appeals' rule requiring "proportional" justifications for departures was not consistent with *Booker*. Under the deferential abuse-of-discretion standard that applied to review of sentencing decisions, the Court found that the court of appeals failed to give due deference to the district court's reasoned and reasonable decision that the 18 U.S.C.S. § 3553(a) factors justified the sentence of probation.

The Court reversed the judgment of the court of appeals; 7-2 decision; 2 concurrences; 2 dissents

SYLLABUS

Petitioner Gall joined an ongoing enterprise distributing the controlled substance "ecstasy" while in college, but withdrew from the conspiracy after seven months, has sold no illegal drugs since, and has used no illegal drugs and worked steadily since graduation. Three and a half years after withdrawing from the conspiracy, Gall pleaded guilty to his participation. A presentence report recommended a sentence of 30 to 37 months in prison, but the District Court sentenced Gall to 36 months of probation, finding that probation reflected the seriousness of his offense, and that imprisonment was unnecessary because his voluntary withdrawal from the conspiracy and post offense conduct showed that he would not return to criminal behavior and was not a danger to society. The Eighth Circuit reversed the decision on the ground that a sentence outside the Federal Sentencing Guidelines range must be – and was not in this case – supported by extraordinary circumstances.

Held: (1) While the extent of the difference between a particular sentence and the recommended Guidelines range is relevant, courts of appeals must review all sentences-whether inside, just outside, or significantly outside the Guidelines range-under a deferential abuse-of-discretion standard.

(a) Because the Guidelines are now advisory, appellate review of sentencing decisions is limited to determining whether they are "reasonable," *United States v. Booker* I 543 U.S. 220, 125 S. Ct. 738, 160 L. Ed. 2d 621, and an abuse-of-discretion standard applies to appellate review of sentencing decisions. A district judge must consider the extent of any departure from the Guidelines and must explain the appropriateness of an unusually lenient or harsh sentence with sufficient justifications. An appellate court may take the degree of variance into account and consider the extent of a deviation from the Guidelines, but it may not require "extraordinary" circumstances or employ a rigid mathematical formula using a departure's percentage as the standard for determining the strength of the justification required for a specific sentence. Such approaches come too close to create an impermissible unreasonableness presumption for sentences outside the Guidelines range. The mathematical approach also suffers from infirmities of application. And both approaches reflect a practice of applying a heightened standard of review to sentences outside the Guidelines range, which is inconsistent with the rule that the abuse-of-discretion standard applies to appellate review of all sentencing decisions-whether inside or outside that range.

(b) A district court should begin by correctly calculating the applicable Guidelines range. The Guidelines are the starting point and initial benchmark but are not the only consideration. After permitting both parties to argue for a particular sentence, the judge should consider all of 18 U.S.C. 3553(a)'s factors to determine whether they support either party's proposal. He may not presume that the Guidelines range is reasonable but must make an individualized assessment based on the facts presented. If he decides on an outside-the-Guidelines sentence, he must consider the extent of the deviation and ensure that the justification is sufficiently compelling to support the degree of variation. He must adequately explain the chosen sentence to allow for meaningful appellate review and to promote the perception of fair sentencing. In reviewing the sentence, the appellate court must first ensure that the district court made no significant procedural errors and then consider the sentence's substantive reasonableness under an abuse- of-discretion standard, taking into account the totality of the circumstances, including the extent of a variance from the Guidelines range, but must give due deference to the district court's decision that the 3553(a) factors justify the variance. That the appellate court might have reasonably reached a different conclusion does not justify reversal.

2. On abuse-of-discretion review, the Eighth Circuit failed to give due deference to the District Court's reasoned and reasonable sentencing decision. Since the District Court committed no procedural error, the only question for the Circuit was whether the sentence was reasonable, i.e., whether the District Judge

abuse his discretion in determining that the 3553(a) factors supported the sentence and justified a substantial deviation from the Guidelines range. The Circuit gave virtually no deference to the District Court's decision that the variance was justified. The Circuit clearly disagreed with the District Court's decision, but it was not for the Circuit to decide de novo whether the justification for a variance is sufficient or the sentence reasonable.

446 F.3d 884, reversed

OTHER SENTENCING FACTORS

There are a multitude of factors that can reduce or extend a defendant's sentence. The application of those factors is regulated as well. However, courts around the country have routinely tested those limitations throughout history. One fine example is the court that sentenced Allen Ryan Alleyne. The Supreme Court decision that followed set some pivotal limitations concerning judge-found facts that affect increases in mandatory minimum sentences:

ALLEYNE V. UNITED STATES
570 US 99, 133 S CT 2151, 186 L ED 2D 314 (2013)

DECISION

Judge's finding of brandishing firearm during drug trafficking crime, resulting in increased sentence under 18 U.S.C.S. § 924(c)(1)(A), held to violate Federal Constitution's Sixth Amendment, as brandishing was "element" requiring submission to jury.

SUMMARY

Procedural Posture: Defendant was convicted of using or carrying a firearm in relation to a crime of violence under 18 U.S.C. § 924(c)(1)(A). However, the sentence was based on a finding that he brandished the firearm even though the jury did not find brandishing beyond a reasonable doubt. A district court overruled defendant's sentencing objection on the basis of *Harris v. United States* (2002) 536 U.S. 545, 122 S. Ct. 2406, 153 L. Ed. 2d 524, 2002 U.S. LEXIS 4652; the U.S. Court of Appeals for the Fourth Circuit affirmed. *Certiorari* was granted.

Overview: A § 924(c)(1)(A) conviction carried a mandatory minimum five-year sentence, which was increased to a seven-year minimum if the firearm was brandished. The jury form indicated that defendant used a firearm during and in relation to a crime of violence, but not that the firearm was brandished. The district and circuit courts relied on Harris, which held that judicial fact-finding that increased the mandatory minimum sentence for a crime was permissible under the Sixth Amendment. Because the finding of brandishing increased the penalty to which defendant was subjected, the Supreme Court held that it was an element of the offense, which had to be found by the jury beyond a reasonable doubt. As the judge, rather than the jury, found brandishing, the Court held that the sentence violated defendant's Sixth Amendment rights. The Supreme Court determined that the essential Sixth Amendment inquiry was whether a fact was an element of the crime. Because there was no logical basis to distinguish facts that raised the maximum sentence from those that increased the minimum sentence, the Court concluded that Harris was inconsistent with *Apprendi v. New Jersey* (2000) 530 U.S. 466, 120 S. Ct. 2358, 147 L. Ed. 2d 435, 2000 U.S. LEXIS 4304. Accordingly, the Supreme Court overruled Harris.

Outcome: The court vacated the circuit court's judgment with respect to defendant's sentence on the § 924(c)(1)(A) conviction and remanded the case for resentencing consistent with the jury's verdict.

5-4 Decision; 2 concurrences; 2 dissents

Petitioner Alleyne was charged, as relevant here, with using or carrying a firearm in relation to a crime of violence, 18 U.S.C. § 924(c)(1)(A), which carries a 5-year mandatory minimum sentence, § 924(c)(1)(A)(i), that increases to a 7-year minimum "if the firearm is brandished," § 924(c)(1)(A)(ii), and to a 10-year minimum "if the firearm is discharged," § 924(c)(1)(A)(iii). In convicting Alleyne, the jury form indicated that he had "[u]sed or carried a firearm during and in relation to a crime of violence," but not that the firearm was" [b]randished." When the presentence report recommended a 7-year sentence on the § 924(c) count, Alleyne objected, arguing that the verdict form clearly indicated that the jury did not find brandishing beyond a reasonable doubt and that raising his mandatory minimum sentence based on a sentencing judge's finding of brandishing would violate his Sixth Amendment right to a jury trial. The District Court overruled his objection, relying on this Court's holding in *Harris v. United States*, 536 U.S. 545, 122 S. Ct. 2406, 153 L. Ed. 2d 524, that judicial fact-finding that increases the mandatory minimum sentence for a crime is permissible under the Sixth Amendment. The Fourth Circuit affirmed, agreeing that Alleyne's objection was foreclosed by Harris.

Held: The judgment is vacated, and the case is remanded. Pp.___-___,186 L. Ed. 2d, at 326-331.

457 Fed. Appx. 348, vacated and remanded.

Justice Thomas delivered the opinion of the Court with respect to Parts I, III-B, III-C, and IV, concluding:

(1) Because mandatory minimum sentences increase the penalty for a crime, any fact that increases the mandatory minimum is an "element" that must be submitted to the jury. Accordingly, *Harris* is overruled. Pp.___-___, 186 L. Ed. 2d, at 326-330.

   (A) *Apprendi v. New Jersey*, 530 U.S. 466, 120 S. Ct. 2348, 147 L. Ed. 2d 435, concluded that any "facts that increase the prescribed range of penalties to which a criminal defendant is exposed" are elements of the crime, *id.*, at 490, 120 S. Ct. 2348, 147 L. Ed. 2d 435, and thus the Sixth Amendment provides defendants with the right to have a jury find those facts beyond a reasonable doubt, *id.*, at 484, 120 S. Ct. 2348, 147 L. Ed. 2d 435. *Apprendi*'s principle applies with equal force to facts increasing the mandatory minimum, for a fact triggering a mandatory minimum alters the prescribed range of sentences to which a criminal defendant is exposed. *id.*, at 490, 120 S. Ct. 2348, 147 L. Ed. 2d 435. Because the legally prescribed range is the penalty affixed to the crime, it follows that a fact increasing either end of the range produces a new penalty and constitutes an ingredient of the offense. It is impossible to dissociate the floor of a sentence range from the penalty affixed to the crime. The fact that criminal statutes have long specified both the floor and ceiling of sentence ranges is evidence that both define the legally prescribed penalty. It is also impossible to dispute that the facts increasing the legally prescribed floor aggravate the punishment, heightening the loss of liberty associated with the crime. Defining facts that increase a mandatory minimum to be part of the substantive offense enables the defendant to predict the legally applicable penalty from the face of the indictment, see *id.*, at 478-479, 120 S. Ct. 2348, 147 L Ed. 2d 435 and preserves the jury's historic role as an intermediary between the State and criminal defendants, see *United States v. Gaudin*, 515 U.S. 506, 510- 511, 115 S. Ct. 2310, 132 L. Ed 2d 444. In reaching a contrary conclusion, Harris relied on the fact that the 7-year minimum sentence could have been imposed with or without a judicial finding of brandishing, because the jury finding authorized a sentence of five years to life, 536 U.S., at 561, 122 S. Ct. 2406, 153 L. Ed. 2d 524, but that fact is beside the point. The essential Sixth Amendment inquiry is whether a fact is an element of the crime. Because the fact of brandishing aggravates the legally prescribed range of allowable sentences, it constitutes an element of a separate, aggravated offense that must be found by the jury, regardless of what sentence the defendant might have received had a different range been applicable. There is no basis in principle or logic to distinguish facts that raise the maximum from those that increase the minimum. Pp.___-___ , 186 L. Ed. 2d, at 326-330.

(B) This ruling does not mean that any fact that influences judicial discretion must be found by a jury. This Court has long recognized that broad sentencing discretion, informed by judicial fact-finding, does not violate the Sixth Amendment, see, e.g., *Dillon v. United States*, 560 U.S. , 130 S. Ct. 2683, 177 L. Ed. 2d 271. Pp. ___-___ ,186 L. Ed. 2d, at 330.

(2) Here, the sentencing range supported by the jury's verdict was five years' imprisonment to life, but the judge, rather than the jury, found brandishing. This increased the penalty to which Alleyne was subjected and violated his Sixth Amendment rights. Pp. ___-___ , 186 L. Ed. 2d, at 330-331.

Justice Thomas, joined by Justice Ginsburg, Justice Sotomayor, and Justice Kagan, concluded in Parts II and III-A:

(1) The Sixth Amendment right to trial "by an impartial jury," in conjunction with the Due Process Clause, requires that each element of a crime be proved to the jury beyond a reasonable doubt, *Gaudin*, 515 U.S., at 510, 115 S. Ct. 2310, 132 L. Ed. 2d 444. Several divided opinions of this Court have addressed the constitutional status of a "sentencing factor." In *McMillan v. Pennsylvania*, 477 U.S. 79, 86, 106 S. Ct. 2411, 91 L. Ed. 2d 67, the Court held that facts found to increase a mandatory minimum sentence are sentencing factors that a judge could find by a preponderance of the evidence. In *Apprendi*, however, the Court declined to extend McMillan to a New Jersey statute that increased the maximum term of imprisonment if the trial judge found that the crime was committed with racial bias, 530 U.S., at 4,0, 120 S. Ct. 2348, 147 L. Ed. 2d 435, finding that any fact that increased the prescribed statutory maximum sentence must be an "element' of the offense to be found by the jury. *id.*, at 483, n. 10, 490, 120 S. Ct. 2348, 147 L. Ed. 2d 435. Two years later in Harris, the Court declined to apply *Apprendi* to facts that increased the mandatory minimum sentence but not the maximum sentence. 536 U.S., at 557, 122 S. Ct. 2406, 153 L. Ed. 2d 524. Pp.__ , 186 L. Ed. 2d, at 322-324.

(2) The touchstone for determining whether a fact must be found by a jury beyond a reasonable doubt is whether the fact constitutes an element; of the charged offense. United States v. O'Brien, ~60 U.S. 218, 130 S. Ct. 2169, 116 L. Ed. 2d 979. *Apprendi*'s definition necessarily includes not only facts that increase the ceiling, but also those that increase the floor. At common law, the relationship between crime and punishment was clear. A sentence was prescribed for each offense, leaving judges with little sentencing discretion. If a fact was by law essential to the penalty, it was an element of the offense. There was a well-established practice of including in the indictment, and submitting to the jury, every fact that was a basis for imposing or increasing punishment. And this understanding was reflected in contemporaneous court decisions and treatises- Pp- 186 L. Ed. 2d, at 324-329. Justice Breyer, agreeing that *Harris v. United States*, 536 U-S_ 545, 122 S. Ct. 2406, 153 L. Ed. 2d 524, should be overruled, concluded that he continues to disagree with *Apprendi v. New Jersey*, 530 U.S. 466, 120 S. Ct. 2348, 147 L. Ed. 2d 435, because it fails to recognize the law's traditional distinction between elements of a crime and sentencing facts, but finds it highly anomalous to read *Apprendi* as insisting that juries find sentencing facts that permit a judge to impose a higher sentence while not insisting that juries find sentencing facts that require a judge to impose a higher sentence. Overruling Harris and applying *Apprendi*'s basic Jury- determination rule to mandatory minimum sentences would erase that anomaly- Where a maximum sentence is at issue, *Apprendi* means that a judge who wishes to impose a higher sentence cannot do so unless a jury finds the requisite statutory factual predicate. Where a mandatory minimum sentence is an issue, *Apprendi* would mean that the government cannot force a judge who

does not wish to impose a higher sentence to do so unless a jury finds the requisite statutory factual predicate. Pp.___-___ , 186 L. Ed. 2d, at 334-335.

SENTENCING TABLE
(in months of imprisonment)

Criminal History Category (Criminal History Points

Offense Level	I (0 or 1)	II (2 or 3)	III (4, 5, 6)	IV (7, 8, 9)	V (10, 11, 12)	VI (13 +)
1	0-6	0-6	0-6	0-6	0-6	0-6
2	0-6	0-6	0-6	0-6	0-6	1-7
3	0-6	0-6	0-6	0-6	2-8	3-9
4	0-6	0-6	0-6	2-8	4-10	6-12
5	0-6	0-6	1-7	4-10	6-12	9-15
6	0-6	1-7	2-8	6-12	9-15	12-18
7	0-6	2-8	4-10	8-14	12-18	15-21
8	0-6	4-10	6-12	10-16	15-21	18-24
9	4-10	6-12	8-14	12-18	18-24	21-27
10	6-12	8-14	10-16	15-21	21-27	24-30
11	8-14	10-16	12-18	18-24	24-30	27-33
12	10-16	12-18	15-21	21-27	27-33	30-37
13	12-18	15-21	18-24	24-30	30-37	33-41
14	15-21	18-24	21-27	27-33	33-41	37-46
15	18-24	21-27	24-30	30-37	37-46	41-51
16	21-27	24-30	27-33	33-41	41-51	46-57
17	24-30	27-33	30-37	37-46	46-57	51-63
18	27-33	30-37	33-41	41-51	51-63	57-71
19	30-37	33-41	37-46	46-57	57-71	63-78
20	33-41	37-46	41-51	51-63	63-78	70-87
21	37-46	41-51	46-57	57-71	70-87	77-96
22	41-51	46-57	51-63	63-78	77-96	84-105
23	46-57	51-63	57-71	70-87	84-105	92-115
24	51-63	57-71	63-78	77-96	92-115	100-125
25	57-71	63-78	70-87	84-105	100-125	110-137
26	63-78	70-87	78-97	92-115	110-137	120-150
27	70-87	78-97	87-108	100-125	120-150	130-162
28	78-97	87-108	97-121	110-137	130-162	140-175
29	87-108	97-121	108-135	121-151	140-175	151-188
30	97-121	108-135	121-151	135-168	151-188	168-210
31	108-135	121-151	135-168	151-188	168-210	188-235
32	121-151	135-168	151-188	168-210	188-235	210-262
33	135-168	151-188	168-210	188-235	210-262	235-293
34	151-188	168-210	188-235	210-262	235-293	262-327
35	168-210	188-235	210-262	235-293	262-327	292-365
36	188-235	210-262	235-293	262-327	292-365	324-405
37	210-262	235-293	262-327	292-365	324-405	360-life
38	235-293	262-327	292-365	324-405	360-life	360-life
39	262-327	292-365	324-405	360-life	360-life	360-life
40	292-365	324-405	360-life	360-life	360-life	360-life
41	324-405	360-life	360-life	360-life	360-life	360-life
42	360-life	360-life	360-life	360-life	360-life	360-life
43	life	life	life	life	life	life

Zone A (Offense Levels 1–8)
Zone B (Offense Levels 9–11)
Zone C (Offense Levels 12–13)
Zone D (Offense Levels 14–43)

CHAPTER FIFTEEN

DIRECT APPEAL

The direct appeal is the final stage in the trial process. Although, the defendant may seek a writ of *certiorari* from the Supreme Court of the United States; *Certiorari* is not a review that is a matter of right. The direct appeal in the United States Court of Appeals, however, is a matter of statutory right. A defendant will often suffer from ineffective assistance of counsel in this stage of the trial process as well; only because most lawyers don't understand this complex statutory right or simply don't care.

A criminal defendant has a very particular right to appeal his or her conviction. This right is set out clearly in a number of rules and laws in every jurisdiction, both state and federal. A defendant has the right of review in the courts of appeal to prevent the arbitrary enforcement of criminal law. But this right is not a Constitutional one. The Constitution of the United States imposes no obligation to provide appellate review of criminal convictions, see *McKane v. Durston*, 153 U.S. 684, 687, 38 L. Ed. 867, 14 S. Ct. 913 (1894). Once a statutory provision to appeal has been provided, however, a state may not "bolt the door to equal justice" to indigent defendants. *Griffin v. Illinois*, 351 U.S. 12, 24, 100 L. Ed. 891, 76 S. Ct. 585 (1956); See *id.*, at 23, 100 L. Ed. 891, 76 S. Ct. 585 (same) ("when a state deems it wise and just that convictions be susceptible to review by an appellate court, it cannot by force of its exaction draw a line which precludes convicted indigent persons … from securing such … review"). *Douglas v. California*, 372 U.S. 353, 9 L. Ed. 2d 811, 83 S. Ct. 814 (1963) relied on *Griffin*'s reasoning to hold that, in first appeals as of right, states must appoint counsel to represent indigent defendants. 372 U.S., at 357, 9 L. Ed. 2d 811, 83 S. Ct. 814, see also the holdings in *Halbert v. Michigan*, 545 US 605, 162 L Ed 2d 552, 125 S Ct 2582 (2005) that follow:

DECISION

Due process and equal protection clauses of Federal Constitution's Fourteenth Amendment held to require appointed counsel for indigent defendants, convicted on pleas, seeking access to Michigan Court of Appeals' first- tier review.

SUMMARY

In *Douglas v. California* (1963) 372 U.S. 353, 9 L. Ed. 2d 811, 83 S. Ct. 814, reh den 373 U.S. 905, 10 L. Ed. 2d 200, 83 S. Ct. 1288, the United States Supreme Court held that a state was required to appoint counsel for an indigent criminal defendant in a first appeal as of right, as the court noted that (1) an appeal of· right yielded an adjudication on the merits; and (2) prior to first-tier review, the defendant's claims had not been presented by a lawyer and passed upon by an appellate court. However, in *Ross v. Moffitt* (1974) 417 U.S. 600, 41 L. Ed. 2d 341, 94 S. Ct. 2347, it was held that a state was not required to appoint counsel for an indigent defendant seeking to pursue a second-tier discretionary appeal to a state's highest court-or, thereafter, *certiorari* review in the United States Supreme Court – as (1) at that stage, the reviewing court's function, rather than being primarily error correction, involved matters including whether (a) the issues presented were of significant public interest, (b) the cause involved legal principles of major significance to the state's jurisprudence, and (c) the decision below was in probable conflict with precedent of the state's highest court; and (2) a defendant aided by counsel in a first-tier appeal as of right would possess (a) a transcript or other record of trial proceedings, (b) a brief in an appellate court setting forth the defendant's claims, and (c) often, the appellate court's opinion disposing of the case.

Under Michigan's two-tier appellate system, the Michigan Supreme Court heard appeals by leave only, while the intermediate Michigan Court of Appeals adjudicated appeals as of right from criminal convictions, except that a defendant convicted on a plea of guilty or *nolo contendere* who sought review in the Michigan Court of Appeals was required to apply for leave to appeal.

131

During the plea colloquy of an accused who, in a Michigan trial court, pleaded *nolo contendere* to two counts of criminal sexual conduct, the trial court (1) advised the accused of instances in which, although an appeal would not be of right, the trial court "must" or "may" appoint appellate counsel; but (2) did not tell the accused that the trial court could not appoint counsel in any other circumstances, including the accused's case. After the accused's sentence was imposed, he moved to withdraw his plea. However, the trial court denied the motion.

Subsequently, the accused – asserting that (1) his sentence had been mis-scored, (2) he needed counsel to preserve the issue before undertaking an appeal, and (3) he had learned disabilities and was mentally impaired – twice asked the trial court to appoint counsel to help him prepare an application for leave to appeal to the Michigan Court of Appeals. The court denied both requests.

The accused then filed a *pro se* application for leave to appeal. The Michigan Court of Appeals denied the motion, and the Michigan Supreme Court declined review (469 Mich. 901, 669 N.@.2d 814).

On *certiorari* the United States Supreme Court vacated and remanded. In an opinion by Ginsburg, J., joined by Stevens, O'Connor, Kennedy, Souter, and Breyer, JJ., it was held that the due process and equal protection clauses of the Federal Constitution's Fourteenth Amendment required appointment of counsel to assist indigent defendants, convicted on pleas of guilty or *nolo contendere*, in applying for leave to appeal to the Michigan Court of Appeals. The case at hand was controlled by *Douglas* rather than *Ross*, as:

(1) In determining how to dispose of an application for leave to appeal, the Court of Appeals (a) necessarily performed some evaluation of the merits of the applicant's claims; and (b) provided the first, and likely the only direct review that the defendant's conviction and sentence would receive.

(2) Indigent defendants pursuing first-tier review in the Court of Appeals generally were ill equipped to represent themselves, for (a) a first-tier review applicant, forced to act *pro se*, would face a record un-reviewed by appellate counsel; and (b) without guides keyed to a court of review, a *pro se* applicant's entitlement to seek leave to appeal to might be more formal than real.

SYLLABUS

In *Douglas v. California*, 372 U.S. 353, 9 L. Ed. 2d 811, 83 S. Ct. 814, this Court held that, in criminal proceedings, a State must provide counsel for an indigent defendant in a first appeal as of right. Two considerations were key: (1) *An appeal "of right" yields an adjudication on the "merits," id.*, at 357, 9 L. Ed. 2d 811, 83 S. Ct. 814, and (2) first-tier review differs from subsequent appellate stages "at which the claims have once been presented by a lawyer and passed upon by an appellate court," *id.*, at 356, 9 L. Ed. 2d 811, 83 S. Ct. 814. Later, in *Ross v. Moffitt*, 417 U.S. 600, 41 L. Ed. 2d 341, 94 S. Ct. 2437, the Court held that a State need not appoint counsel to aid a poor person seeking to pursue a second-tier discretionary appeal to the State's highest court, or, thereafter, *certiorari* review in this Court. *id.*, at 610-612, 615-618, 41 L. Ed. 2d 341, 94 S. Ct. 2437. *The Douglas rationale does not extend to second-tier discretionary review*, the Court explained, *because, at that stage, error correction is not the reviewing court's prime function.* 417 U.S., at 615, 41 L. Ed. 2d 341, 94 S. Ct. 2437. Principal criteria for state high court review, *Ross* noted, include whether the issues presented are of significant public interest, whether the cause involves legal principles of major significance to the State's jurisprudence, and whether the decision below is in probable conflict with the high court's precedent, *ibid.* Further, a defendant who has received counsel's aid in a first-tier appeal as of right would be armed with a transcript or other record of trial proceedings, a brief in the appeals court setting forth his claims, and, often, that court's opinion disposing of the case, *ibid.*

Michigan has a two-tier appellate system. The State Supreme Court hears appeals by leave only. The intermediate Court of Appeals adjudicates appeals as of right form criminal convictions, except that a defendant convicted on a guilty or *nolo contendere* plea who seeks intermediate appellate court review must apply for leave to appeal. Under Michigan law, most indigent defendants convicted on a plea must proceed in prose in seeking leave to appeal to the intermediate court. In *People v. Bulger*, the Michigan Supreme Court held that the Fourteenth Amendment's Equal Protection and Due Process Clause do not secure a right to appointed counsel for plea-convicted defendants seeking review in the intermediate appellate court for these reasons: Such review is discretionary; plea proceedings are shorter, simpler, and more routine than trials; and a defendant entering a plea accedes to the State's fundamental interest in finality.

Petitioner Halbert pleaded *nolo contendere* to two counts of criminal sexual conduct. During Halbert's plea colloquy, the trial court advised him of instances in which it "must" or "may" appoint appellate counsel but failed to tell him that it could not appoint counsel in any other circumstances, including Halbert's own case. The day after his sentence was imposed, Halbert moved to withdraw his plea. Denying the motion, the trial court stated that Halbert's proper remedy was to appeal to the State Court of Appeals. Twice thereafter, Halbert asked the trial court to appoint counsel to help him prepare an application for leave to appeal to the intermediate court, stating that his sentence had been mis-scored, that he needed counsel to preserve the issue before undertaking an appeal, that he had learning disabilities and was mentally impaired, and that he had been obliged to rely on fellow inmates in preparing his *pro se* filings. The court denied Halbert's motion, citing Bulger. Halbert then filed a *pro se* application for leave to appeal, asserting sentencing error and ineffective assistance of counsel and seeking, inter alia, remand for appointment of appellate counsel The Court of Appeals denied leave "for lack of merit in the grounds presented." The Michigan Supreme Court declined review.

Held: The Due Process and Equal Protection clauses require the appointment of counsel for defendants convicted on their pleas, who seek access to first-tier review in the Michigan Court of Appeals.

Two aspects of the Michigan Court of Appeals' process following plea-based conviction compel the conclusion that *Douglas*, not *Ross*, controls here. First, in ruling on an application for leave to appeal, that court looks to the merits of the appellant's claims. Second, indigent defendants pursuing first-tier review in the Court of Appeals are generally ill equipped to represent themselves. A defendant who pleads guilty or *nolo contendere* in a Michigan court, although he relinquishes access to an appeal as of right, is entitled to apply for leave to appeal, and that entitlement is officially conveyed to him. Of critical importance, the intermediate appellate court, unlike the Michigan Supreme Court, sits as an error-correction instance. A court Rule provides that the intermediate court may respond to a leave application in a number of ways: It may grant or deny the application, enter a final decision, grant other relief, request additional material from the record, or require a certified concise statement of proceedings and facts from the lower court. The court's response to the leave application by any of these alternatives – including denial of leave – necessarily entails some evaluation of the merits of the applicant's claims.

This Court rejects Michigan's argument that *Ross* is dispositive here because review in the intermediate appellate court following a plea-based conviction is discretionary, given the necessity of filing an application for leave to appeal. The *Ross* Court recognized that leave-granting determinations by a State's highest court turn on considerations other than a lower court's commission of error, e.g., the involvement of a matter of "significant public interest," 417 U.S., at 615, 41 L. Ed. 2d 341, 94 S. Ct. 2437. Michigan's Supreme Court, like the highest courts of other States, sits not to correct errors in individual cases, but to decide matters of larger public import. By contrast, the intermediate court, as an error-correction instance, is guided in responding to leave to appeal applications by the merits of the particular defendant's claims, not by the general importance of the questions presented.

Whether formally categorized as the decision of an appeal or the disposal of a leave application, the intermediate appellate court's ruling on a plea-convicted defendant's claims provides the first, and likely the only, direct review the defendant's conviction and sentence will receive. Parties like Halbert, however, are disarmed in their endeavor to gain first-tier review. *Ross* emphasized that a defendant seeking State Supreme Court review following a first-tier appeal as of right earlier had the assistance of appellate counsel, who will have reviewed the trial court record, researched the legal issues, and prepared a brief reflecting that review and research, 417 U.S., at 615, 41 L. Ed. 2d 341, 94 S. Ct. 2437. Such a defendant may also be armed with an opinion of the intermediate appellate court addressing the issues counsel raised, Without such guides keyed to a court of review, a *pro se* applicant's entitlement to seek leave to appeal to Michigan's intermediate court may be more formal than real, Cf. *Swenswon v. Bosler*, 386 U.S. 258, 18 L. Ed. 2d 33, 87 S. Ct 996 (*per curiam*). Persons in Halbert's situation, many of whom have little education, learning disabilities, and mental impairments, are particularly handicapped as self-representatives, see *Kowalski v. Tesmer*, 543 U.S. 125, 140, 160 L. Ed. 2d 519, 125 S. Ct 564 (Ginsburg, J., dissenting). Further, appeals by defendants convicted on their pleas may be "no less complex than other appeals," *id.* at 141, 160 L. Ed. 2d 519, 125 S. Ct. 564. Michigan's complex procedures for seeking leave to appeal after sentencing on a plea, moreover, may intimidate the uncounseled, see *id.*, at 141, 142, 160 L. Ed. 2d 519, 125 S. Ct. 564. The State does have a legitimate interest in reducing its judiciary's workload but providing indigents with appellate counsel will yield applications easier to comprehend. Michigan's Court of Appeals would still have recourse to summary denials of leave applications in cases not warranting further review. And when a defendant's case presents no genuinely arguable issue, appointed counsel may so inform the court.

The Court disagrees with Michigan's contention that, even if Halbert had a constitutionally guaranteed right to appointed counsel for first-level appellate review, he waived that right by entering a *nolo contendere* plea. At the time he entered his plea, Halbert had not recognized right to appointed appellate counsel he could elect to forgo. Moreover, the trial court did not tell Halbert, simply and directly, that in his case, there would be no access to appointed counsel, *Cf. Iowa v. Tovar*, 541 U.S. 77, 81, 158 L. Ed. 2d 209, 124 S. Ct. 1379. Vacated and remanded this should make it clear that, under the Constitution of the United States, a person accused of a crime has a right to an appellate review and that he or she has a right to the assistance of counsel for that first-tier direct appeal. Because of the Fourteenth Amendment's due process clause, the federal right to counsel at direct appeal, has been declared to apply to state defendants as well. The Supreme Court has held that such a right is applicable to a defendant's direct appeal from his or her criminal conviction, and that this right to counsel means the right to the effective assistance of counsel.

Although, there are probably hundreds of different ways that appellate counsel could provide ineffective assistance of counsel; this chapter concentrates on the four main and re-occurring, methods that lawyers choose to provide ineffective assistance of counsel.

Failure to File a Notice of Appeal – Trial counsel will often fail to file a notice of appeal either by mistake, neglect, or on purpose. As harsh as this may sound, hundreds of lawyers will make a big production of his or her disbelief in the trial process. They will then placate the defendant by announcing their decision to appeal the conviction, only to fail to file the notice of appeal. Although this is a constitutional error, the court of appeals will hold the defendant to the obligation of filing a notice of appeal. Thus, no appeal will follow because of counsel's ineffectiveness.

> *Author's Note: I suggest that in all criminal cases, the defendant file his own notice of appeal. After a plea agreement a lawyer will tell the defendant that he has waived his right to appeal. This is just plain not true. True enough, a defendant who pleads guilty waives a number of rights. But he cannot possibly waive all his or her appeal rights. Read the case that follows:*

GARZA, JR. V. IDAHO
586 US ___ , 139 S CT ___ , 203 L ED 2D 77 (2019)
DECISION

Presumption of prejudice applied-where accused instructed his trial counsel to file notice of appeal, but trial counsel decided not to do so because accused's plea agreement included appeal waiver-regardless of whether accused signed waiver.

SUMMARY

Overview: *Holdings*: [1]-The presumption of prejudice recognized in *Roe v. Flores-Ortega*, 528 U.S. 470 (2000), applied regardless of whether a defendant had signed an appeal waiver. This ruling followed squarely from *Flores-Ortega* and from the fact that even the broadest appeal waiver did not deprive a defendant of all appellate claims. Accordingly, where an attorney performed deficiently in failing to file a notice of appeal despite the defendant's express instructions, prejudice was presumed with no further showing from the defendant of the merits of his underlying claims. Judgment reversed. 6-3 decision; 1 dissent.

SYLLABUS

Petitioner Gilberto Garza, Jr., signed two plea agreements, each arising from state criminal charges and each containing a clause stating that Garza waived his right to appeal. Shortly after sentencing, Garza told his trial counsel that he wished to appeal. Instead of filing a notice of appeal, counsel informed Garza that an appeal would be "problematic" given Garza's appeal waiver. After the time period for Garza to preserve an appeal lapsed, he sought state post-conviction relief, alleging that his trial counsel had rendered ineffective assistance by failing to file a notice of appeal despite his repeated requests. The Idaho trial court denied relief, and the Idaho Court of Appeals affirmed. Also affirming, the Idaho Supreme Court held that Garza could not show the requisite deficient performance by counsel and resulting prejudice. In doing so, the court concluded that the presumption of prejudice recognized in *Roe v. Flores-Ortega*, 528 U.S. 470, 120 s. Ct. 1029, 145 L. Ed. 2d 985, when trial counsel fails to file an appeal as instructed does not apply when the defendant has agreed to an appeal waiver.

Held: *Flores-Ortega*'s presumption of prejudice applies regardless of whether a defendant has signed an appeal waiver. Pp.___-___ , 203 L. Ed. 2d, at 85-92.

(a) Under *Strickland v. Washington*, 466 U.S. 668, 104 S. Ct. 2052, 80 L. Ed. 2d 674, a defendant who claims ineffective assistance of counsel must prove (1) "that counsel's representation fell below an objective standard of reasonableness," *id.*, at 687-688, 104 S. Ct. 2052, 80 L. Ed. 2d 674, and (2) that any such deficiency was "prejudicial to the defense," *id.*, at 692, 104 S. Ct. 2052, 80 L. Ed. 2d 674. However, "prejudice is presumed" in "certain Sixth Amendment contexts" *ibid.*, such as "when counsel's constitutionally deficient performance deprives a defendant of an appeal that he otherwise would have taken," *Flores-Ortega*, 528 U.S., at 484, 120 S. Ct. 1029, 145 L. Ed. 2d 985. Pp. ___-___ , 203 L. Ed. 2d, at 85.

(b) This case hinges on two procedural devices: appeal waivers and notices of appeal. No appeal waiver serves as an absolute bar to all appellate claims. Because a plea agreement is essentially a contract, it does not bar claims outside its scope and, like any contract, the language of appeal waivers can vary widely, leaving many types of claims un-waived. A waived appellate claim may also proceed if the prosecution forfeits or waives the waiver or if the Government breaches the agreement. Separately, some claims are treated as un-waivable. Most fundamentally, courts agree that defendants retain the right to challenge whether the waiver itself was knowing and voluntary.

The filing of a notice of appeal is "a purely ministerial task that imposes no great burden on counscl." *Flores-Ortega*, 528 U.S., at 474, 120 S. Ct. 1029, 145 L. Ed. 2d 985. Filing requirements reflect that appellate claims are likely to be ill defined or unknown at the filing stage. And within the division of labor between defendants and their attorneys, the "ultimate authority" to decide whether to "take an appeal" belongs to the· accused, *Jones v. Barnes*, 463 U.S. 745, 751, 103 S. Ct. 3308, 77 L. Ed. 2d 987. Pp. ___-___ , 203 L. Ed. 2d, at 85-87.

(c) Garza's attorney rendered deficient performance by not filing a notice of appeal in light of Garza's clear requests. Given the possibility that a defendant will end up raising claims beyond an appeal waiver's scope, simply filing a notice of appeal does not necessarily breach a plea agreement. Thus, counsel's choice to override Garza's instructions was not a strategic one. In any event, the bare decision whether to appeal is ultimately the defendants to make. Pp.___-___, 203 L. Ed. 2d, at 87-88.

(d) Because there is not dispute that Garza wished to appeal, a direct application of *Flores-Ortega*'s language resolves this case. *Flores-Ortega* reasoned that because a presumption of prejudice applies whenever "the accused is denied counsel at a critical stage," it makes greater sense to presume prejudice when counsel's deficiency forfeits an "appellate proceeding altogether," 528 U.S., at 483, 120 S. Ct 1029, 145 L. Ed. 2d 985. Because Garza retained a right to appeal at least some issues despite his waivers, he had a right to a proceeding and was denied that proceeding altogether as a result of counsel's deficient performance. That he surrendered many claims by signing appeal waivers does not change things. First, the presumption of prejudice does not bend because a particular defendant seems to have had poor prospects. See e.g., *Jae Lee v. United States*, 582 U.S. ___-___ , 137 S. Ct. 1958, 198 L. Ed. 2d 476. Second, while the defendant in *Flores-Ortega* did not sign an appeal waiver, he did plead guilty, which "reduces the scope of potentially appealable issues" on its own. 528 U.S., at 480, 120 S. Ct. 1029, 145 L. Ed. 2d 985. Pp. ___-___ , 203 L. Ed. 2d, at 88-89.

(e) Contrary to the argument by Idaho and the U.S. Government, as *amicus*, that Garza never "had a right" to his appeal and thus that any deficient performance by counsel could not have caused the loss of any such appeal, Garza did retain a right to his appeal; he simply had fewer possible claims than some other appellants. The Government also proposes a rule that would require a defendant to show-on a case-by-case basis-that he would have presented claims that would have been considered by the appellate court on the merits. his Court, however, has already rejected attempts to condition the restoration of a defendant's appellate rights forfeited by ineffective counsel on proof that the defendant's appeal had merit, see, e.g., *Rodriquez v. United States*, 395 U.S. 327, 330, 89 S. Ct. 1715, 23 L. Ed. 2d 340. Moreover, it is not the defendant's role to decide what arguments to press, making it especially improper to impose that role upon the defendant simply because his opportunity to appeal was relinquished by deficient counsel. And because there is not right to counsel in post-conviction proceedings and, thus, most applicants proceed *pro se*, the Government's proposal would be unfair, ill advised, and unworkable. Pp. ___-___ , 203 L. Ed. 2d, at 89-92.

162 Idaho 791, 405 p.3d 576, reversed and remanded

Failure to Give Appeal Advice – In almost all criminal cases it is trial counsel who has the obligation to advise his client that he, the defendant, has a right to appeal. No matter the circumstances a defendant who has been convicted and sentenced has the absolute right to appeal from a final sentence, see 18 U.S.C. § 3742. Counsel must provide sound advice as to whether a defendant should appeal as well.

> *Author's Note I've said it many times that if a defendant is guilty, he or she should enter a binding plea agreement that provides a reasonable sentence. If however, you did not enter a binding plea agreement, and the resulting sentence seems unreasonable, a defendant has the right to appeal. But*

that is not always the smartest thing to do. I have witnessed a number of cases where a defendant pleaded guilty and in exchange the government dropped a number of charges. Following a successful appeal, the government opted, as is their right, to charge the defendant with the dropped charges. Only after trial on the remaining charges did the defendant discover that he could receive a longer sentence on the charges that were dropped. I personally do not recommend that anyone who has outstanding charges, file a notice of appeal; unless the statutory maximum for the outstanding charges is lower than the sentence to be appealed from. Be careful, you might get the appeal you're wishing for.

Defense counsel should always advise his client concerning his right to appeal. That advice should include: the law that provides for appeal, the court rule that governs how an appeal should be taken, the court rule that governs when an appeal should be taken, and the statutory maximum sentence of any dropped charges. For federal defendants, counsel's advice should include the statute and Federal Rules of Appellate Procedure that follows:

§ 3742. Review of a sentence

(a) *Appeal by a defendant.* A defendant may file a notice of appeal in the district court for review of an otherwise final sentence if the sentence –

    (1) was imposed in violation of law;

    (2) was imposed as a result of an incorrect application of the sentencing guidelines; or

    (3) is greater than the sentence specified in the applicable guideline range to the extent that the sentences includes a greater fine or term of imprisonment, probation, or supervised release than the maximum established in the guideline range, or includes a more limiting condition of probation or supervised release under section 3565(b)(6) or (b)(11)[18 USCS § 3563(b)(6) or (b)(11)] than the maximum established in the guideline range; or

    (4) was imposed for an offense for which there is no sentencing guideline and is plainly unreasonable.

(b) *Appeal by the Government.* The Government may file a notice of appeal in the district court for review of an otherwise final sentence if the sentence –

    (1) was imposed in violation of law;

    (2) was imposed as a result of an incorrect application of the sentencing guidelines issued by the Sentencing Commission pursuant to 28 U.S.C. 994 (a);

    (3) is less than the sentence specified in the applicable guideline range to the extent that the sentence includes a lesser fine or term of imprisonment, probation, or supervised release than the minimum established in the guideline range, or includes a less limiting condition of probation or supervised release under section 3563(b)(6) or (b) (11) [18 USCS § 3563(b)(6) or (b) (11)] than the minimum established in the guideline range; or

    (4) was imposed for an offense for which there is no sentencing guideline and is plainly unreasonable. The Government may not further prosecute such an appeal without the personal approval of the Attorney General, the solicitor General, or a deputy solicitor general designated by the Solicitor General.

(c) *Plea agreements.* In the case of a plea agreement that includes a specific sentence under rule 11(e)(1)(C) of the Federal rules of Criminal Procedure –

    (1) a defendant may not file a notice of appeal under paragraph (3) or (4) of subsection (a) unless the sentence imposed is greater than the sentence set forth in such agreement; and

(2) the Government may not file a notice of appeal under paragraph (3) or (4) of subsection (b) unless the sentence imposes is less than the sentence set forth in such agreement.

(d) *Record on review.* If a notice of appeal is filed in the district court pursuant to subsection (a) or (b), the clerk shall certify to the court of appeals –

(1) that portion of the record in the case that is designated as pertinent by either of the parties;

(2) the presentence report; and

(3) the information submitted during the sentencing proceeding.

(e) *Consideration.* [*Caution: In* United States v. Booker *(2005) 543 US 220, 160 L Ed 2d 621, 125 S Ct 738, the Supreme Court held (1) that 18 USCS § 3553(b)(1), which makes the Federal Sentencing Guidelines mandatory, is incompatible with the requirements of the Sixth Amendment and therefore must be severed and excised from the Sentencing Reform Act of 1984, and (2) that 18 USCS § 3742(e), which depends upon the Guidelines' mandatory nature, also must be severed and excised.*] Upon review of the record, the court of appeals shall determine whether the sentence –

(1) was imposed in violation of law;

(2) was imposed as a result of an incorrect application of the sentencing guidelines;

(3) is outside the applicable guideline range, and

(A) the district court failed to provide the written statement of reasons required by section 3553(c) [18 USCS § 3553(c)];

(B) the sentence departs from the applicable guideline range based on a factor that –

(i) does not advance the objectives set forth in section 3553(a)(2) [18 USCS § 3553(a)(2)]; or

(ii) is not authorized under section 3553(b) [18 USCS § 3552(b)]; or

(iii) is not justified by the facts of the case; or

(C) the sentence departs to an unreasonable degree from the applicable guideline range, having regard for the factors to be considered in imposing a sentence, as set forth in section 3553(a) of, this title,:[18 ,USCS §3553(a)] and the reasons for the imposition of the particular sentence, as stated by the district court pursuant to the provision of section 3553 (c) [18 USCS § 3553(c)]; or

(4) was imposed for an offense for which there is no applicable sentencing guideline and is plainly unreasonable.

The court of appeals shall give due regard to the opportunity of the district court to judge the credibility of the witnesses and shall accept the findings of fact of the district court unless they are clearly erroneous and, except with respect to determinations under subsection (3)(A) or (3)(B), shall give due deference to the district court's application of the guidelines to the facts. With respect to determinations under subsection (3)(A) or (3)(B), the court of appeals shall review de novo the district court's application of the guidelines to the facts.

(f) *Decision and disposition.* If the court of appeals determine that –

(1) the sentence was imposed in violation of law or imposed as a result of an incorrect application of the sentencing guidelines, the court shall remand the case for further sentencing proceedings with such instructions as the court considers appropriate;

(2) the sentence is outside the applicable guideline range and the district court failed to provide the required statement of reasons in the order of judgment and commitment, or the departure is based on an impermissible factor, or is to an unreasonable degree, or the sentence was imposed for an offense

for which there is no applicable sentencing guideline and is plainly unreasonable, it shall state specific reasons for its conclusions and –

    (A) if it determines that the sentence is too high and the appeal has been filed under subsection (a), it shall set aside the sentence and remand the case for further sentencing proceedings with such instructions as the court considers appropriate, subject to subsection (g);

    (B) if it determines that the sentence is too low and the appeal has been filed under subsection (b), it shall set aside the sentence and remand the case for further sentencing proceedings with such instructions as the court considers appropriate, subject to subsection (g);

  (3) the sentence is not described in paragraph (1) or (2), it shall affirm the sentence.

(g) *Sentencing upon remand.* A district court to which a case is remanded pursuant to subsection (f)(1) or (f)(2) shall resentence a defendant in accordance with section 3553 [18 USCS § 3553] and with such instructions as may have been given by the court of appeals, except that –

  (1) In determining the range referred to in subsection 3553(a)(4), the court shall apply the guidelines issued by the Sentencing Commission pursuant to section 994(a)(1) of title 28, United States Code, and that were in effect on the date of the previous sentencing of the defendant prior to the appeal, together with any amendments thereto by any act of Congress that was in effect on such date; and

  (2) The court shall not impose a sentence outside the applicable guidelines range except upon a ground that – (A) was specifically and affirmatively included in the written statement of reasons required by section 3553(c) [18 USCS § 3553(c)] in connection with the previous sentencing of the defendant prior to the appeal; and (B) was held by the court of appeals, in remanding the case, to be a permissible ground of departure.

(h) *Application to a sentence by a magistrate [magistrate judge].* An appeal of an otherwise final sentence imposed by a United States magistrate [United States magistrate judge] may be taken to a judge of the district court, and this section shall apply (except for the requirement of approval by the Attorney General to the Solicitor General in the case of a Government appeal) as though the appeal were to a court of appeals from a sentence imposed by a district court.

(i) *Guidelines not expressed as a range.* For the purpose of this section, the term "guideline range" includes a guideline range having the same upper and lower limits.

(j) *Definitions.* For purposes of this section –

  (1) a factor is a "permissible" ground of departure if it –

    (A) advances the objectives set forth in section 3553(a)(2) [18 USCS § 3553(a)(2)]; and

    (B) is authorized under section 3553(b) [18 USCS § 3553(b)]; and

    (C) is justified by the facts of the case; and (2) a factor is an "impermissible" ground of departure if it is not a permissible factor within the meaning of subsection (j)(1).

Rule 3. Appeal as of Right – How Taken

(a) *Filing the Notice of Appeal.*

  (1) An appeal permitted by law as of right from a district court to a court of appeals may be taken only by filing a notice of appeal with the district clerk within the time allowed by Rule 4. At the time of filing, the appellant must furnish the clerk with enough copies of the notice to enable the clerk to comply with Rule 3(d).

(2) An appellant's failure to take any step other than the timely filing of a notice of appeal does not affect the validity of the appeal but is ground for only court of appeals to act as it considers appropriate, including dismissing the appeal.

(3) An appeal from a judgment by a magistrate judge in a civil case is taken in the same way as an appeal from any other district court judgment.

(4) An appeal by permission under 28 U.S.C. §1292(b) or an appeal in a bankruptcy case may be taken only in the manner prescribed by Rules 5 and 6, respectively.

(b) *Joint or Consolidated Appeals.*

(1) When two or more parties are entitled to appeal from a district- court judgment or order, and their interest makes joinder practicable, they may file a joint notice of appeal. They may then proceed on appeal as a single appellant.

(2) When the parties have filed separate timely notices of appeal, the appeals may be joined or consolidated by the court of appeals.

(c) *Contents of the Notice of Appeal.*

(1) The notice of appeal must:

(A) specify the party or parties taking the appeal by naming each one in the caption or body of the notice, but an attorney representing more than one party may describe those parties with such terms as "all plaintiffs," "the defendants," "the plaintiffs A, B, *et al.*," or "all defendants except X";

(B) designate the judgment, order, or part thereof being appealed; and (e) name the court to which the appeal is taken.

(2) A *pro se* notice of appeal is considered filed on behalf of the signer and the signer's spouse and minor children (if they are parties), unless the notice clearly indicates otherwise.

(3) In a class action, whether or not the class has been certified, the notice of appeal is sufficient if it names one person qualified to bring the appeal as representative of the class.

(4) An appeal must not be dismissed for informality of form or title of the notice of appeal, or for failure to name a party whose intent to appeal is otherwise clear from the notice.

(5) Form 1 in the Appendix of Forms is a suggested form of notice of appeal.

(d) *Serving the Notice of Appeal.*

(1) The district clerk must serve notice of the filing of a notice of appeal by mailing a copy to each party's counsel of record – excluding the appellant's – or, if a party is proceeding *pro se*, to the party's last known address. When a defendant in a criminal case appeals, the clerk must also serve a copy of the notice of appeal on the defendant, either by personal service or by mail addressed to the defendant. The clerk must promptly send a copy of the notice of appeal and of the docket entries – and any later docket entries – to the clerk of the court of appeals named in the notice. The district clerk must note, on each copy, the date when the notice of appeal was filed.

(2) If an inmate confined in an institution files a notice of appeal in the manner provided by Rule 4(c), the district clerk must also note the date when the clerk docketed the notice.

(3) The district clerk's failure to serve notice does not affect the validity of the appeal. The clerk must note on the docket the names of the parties to whom the clerk mails copies, with the date of mailing. Service is sufficient despite the death of a party or the party's counsel.

(e) *Payment of Fees*. Upon filing a notice of appeal, the appellant must pay the district clerk all required fees. The district clerk receives the appellate docket fee on behalf of the court of appeals.

Rule 4. Appeal as of Right – When Taken

(a) *Appeal in a civil case*.

(1) *Time for filing a notice of appeal*.

(A) In a civil case, except as provided ln Rules 4(a)(I)(B), 4(a)(4), and 4(c), the notice of appeal required by Rule 3 must be filed with the district clerk within 30 days after entry of the judgment or order appealed from.

(B) The notice of appeal may be filed by any party within 60 days after entry of the judgment or order appealed from if one of the parties is:

(i) the United States:

(ii) a United States agency;

(iii) a United States officer or employee sued in an official capacity; or

(iv) a current or former United States officer or employee sued in an individual capacity for an act or omission occurring in connection with duties performed on the United States' behalf – including all instances in which the United States represents that person when the judgment or order is entered or files the appeal for that person.

(C) An appeal from an order granting or denying an application for a writ of error *coram nobis* is an appeal in a civil case for purposes of Rule 4(a).

(2) *Filing before entry of judgment*. A notice of appeal filed after the court announces a decision or order – but before the entry of the judgment or order – is treated as filed on the date of and after the entry.

(3) *Multiple appeals*. If one party timely files a notice of appeal, any other party may file a notice of appeal within 14 days after the date when the first notice was filed, or within the time otherwise prescribed by this Rule 4(a), whichever period ends later.

(4) *Effect of a motion on a notice of appeal*.

(A) If a party files in the district court any of the following motions under the Federal Rules of Civil Procedure – and does so within the time allowed by those rules – the time to file an appeal runs for all parties from the entry of the order disposing of the last such remaining motion:

(i) for judgment under Rule 50(b);

(ii) to amend or make additional factual findings under Rule 52(b), whether or not granting the motion would alter the judgment;

(iii) for attorney's fees under Rule 54 if the district court extends the time to appeal under Rule 58;

(iv) to alter or amend the judgment under Rule 59;

(v) for a new trial under Rule 59; or

(vi) for relief under Rule 60 if the motion is filed no later than 28 days after the judgment is entered.

(B)

(i) If a party files a notice of appeal after the court announces or enters a judgment – but before it disposes of any motion listed in Rule (a)(4) (A) – the notice becomes effective to appeal a judgment or order, in whole or in part, when the order disposing of the last such remaining motion is entered.

(ii) A party intending to challenge an order disposing of any motion listed in Rule 4(a)(4)(A), or a judgment's alteration or amendment upon such a motion, must file a notice of appeal, or an amended notice of appeal – in compliance with Rule 3(c) – within the time prescribed by this Rule measured from the entry of the order disposing of the last such remaining motion.

(iii) No additional fee is required to file an amended notice.

(5) *Motion for extension of time.*

(A) The district court may extend the time to file a notice of appeal if:

(i) a party so moves no later than 30 days after the time prescribed by this Rule 4(a) expires; and

(ii) regardless of whether its motion is filed before or during the 30 days after the time prescribed by this Rule 4(a) expires, that party shows excusable neglect or good cause.

(B) A motion filed before the expiration of the time prescribed in Rule 4(a)(1) or (3) may be ex parte unless the court requires otherwise. If the motion is filed after the expiration of the prescribed time, notice must be given to the other parties in accordance with local rules.

(C) No extension under this Rule 4(a)(5) may exceed 30 days after the prescribed time or 14 days after the date when the order granting the motion is entered, whichever is later.

(6) *Reopening the time to file an appeal.* The district court may reopen the time to file an appeal for a period of 14 days after the date when its order to reopen is entered, but only if all the following conditions are satisfied:

(A) the court finds that the moving party did not receive notice under Federal Rule of Civil Procedure 77(d) of the entry of the judgment or order sought to be appealed within 21 days after entry;

(B) the motion is filed within 180 days after the judgment or order is entered or within 14 days after the moving party receives notice under Federal Rule of Civil Procedure 77(d) of the entry, whichever is earlier; and

(C) the court finds that no party would be prejudiced.

(7) *Entry defined.*

(A) a judgment or order is entered for purposes of this Rule 4(a);

(i) if Federal Rule of Civil Procedure 58(a) does not require a separate document, when the judgment or order is entered in the civil docket under Federal Rule of civil Procedure 79(a); or

(ii) if Federal Rule of Civil Procedure 58(a) requires a separate document, when the judgment or order is entered in the civil docket under Federal Rule of civil Procedure 79(a) and when the earlier of these events occurs:· the judgment or order is set forth on a separate document, or 150 days have run from entry of the judgment or order in the civil docket under Federal Rule of civil Procedure 79(a).

(B) A failure to set forth a judgment or order on a separate document when required by Federal Rule of civil Procedure 58(a) does not affect the validity of an appeal from that judgment or order.

(b) *Appeal in a Criminal case.*

   (1) *Time for filing a notice of appeal.*

      (A) In a criminal case, a defendant's notice of appeal must be filed In the district court within 14 days after the later of:

         (i) the entry of either the judgment or the order being appealed; or

         (ii) the filing of the government's notice of appeal.

      (B) When the government is entitled to appeal, its notice of appeal must be filed in the district court within 30 days after the later of:

         (i) the entry of the judgment or order being appealed; or

         (ii) the filing of a notice of appeal by any defendant.

   (2) *Filing before entry of judgment.* A notice of appeal filed after the court announces a decision, sentence, or order but before the entry of the judgment or order – is treated as filed on the date of and after the entry.

   (3) *Effect of a motion on a notice of appeal.*

      (A) If a defendant timely makes any of the following motions under the Federal Rules of Criminal Procedure, the notice of appeal from a judgment of conviction must be filed within 14 days after the entry of the order disposing of the last such remaining motion, or within 14 days after the entry of the judgment of conviction, whichever period ends later. This provision applies to a timely motion:

         (i) for judgment of acquittal under Rule 29;

         (ii) for a new trial under Rule 33, but if based on newly discovered evidence, only if the motion is made no later than 14 days after the entry of the judgment: or

         (iii) for arrest of judgment under Rule 34.

      (B) A notice of appeal filed after the court announces a decision, sentence, or order – but before it disposes of any of the motions referred to in Rule 4(b)(3)(A) – becomes effective upon the later of the following:

         (i) the entry of the order disposing of the last such remaining motion; or

         (ii) the entry of the judgment of conviction.

      (C) A valid notice of appeal is effective – without amendment to appeal from an order disposing of any of the motions referred to in Rule 4(b) (3) (A).

   (4) *Motion for extension of time.* Upon a finding of excusable neglect or good cause, the district court may before or after the time has expired, with or without motion and notice extend the time to file a notice of appeal for a period not to exceed 30 days from the expiration of the time otherwise prescribed by this Rule 4(b).

   (5) *Jurisdiction.* The filing of a notice of appeal under this rule 4(b) does not divest a district court of jurisdiction to correct a sentence under Federal Rule of Criminal Procedure 35(a), nor does the filing of a motion under 35(a) affect the validity of a notice of appeal filed before entry of the order disposing of the motion. The filing of a motion under Federal Rule of Criminal Procedure 35(a) does not suspend the time for filing a notice of appeal from a judgment of conviction.

   (6) *Entry defined.* A judgment or order is entered for purposes of this Rule 4(b) when it is entered on the criminal docket.

(c) *Appeal by an Inmate Confined in an Institution.*

    (1) If an institution has a system designed for legal mail, an inmate files a notice of appeal in either a civil or a criminal case, the notice is timely if it is deposited in the institution's internal mail system on or before the last day for filing and:

        (A) it is accompanied by:

            (i) a declaration in compliance with 28 U.S.C. § 1746 – or a notarized statement – setting out the date of deposit and stating that first-class postage is being prepaid; or

            (ii) evidence (such as a postmark or date stamp) showing that the notice was so deposited, and that postage was prepaid; or

        (B) the court of appeals exercises its discretion to permit the later filing of a declaration or notarized statement that satisfies Rule 4(c)(1)(A)(i).

    (2) If an inmate files the first notice of appeal in a civil case under this Rule 4(c), the 14-day period provided in Rule 4(a)(3) for another party to file a notice of appeal runs from the date when the district court dockets the first notice.

    (3) When a defendant in a criminal case files a notice of appeal under this rule 4(c), the 30-day period for the government to file its notice of appeal runs from the entry of the judgment or order appealed from or from the district court's docketing of the defendant's notice of appeal, whichever is later.

(d) *Mistaken Filing in the Court of Appeals.* If a notice of appeal in either a civil or a criminal case is mistakenly filed in the court of appeals, the clerk of that court must note on the notice the date when it was received and send it to the district clerk. The notice is then considered filed in the district court on the date so noted.

Failure to File a Timely Notice of Appeal – One of the most hostile acts of ineffectiveness is when a defense lawyer files a notice of appeal late. This happens more times than any defendant would imagine. In the event that a defendant figures out that his counsel had failed him, and then demands that counsel file the notice of appeal or the defendant files his own in *pro se*, the court of appeals will deny the defendant access to the court. This little game happens quite often leaving the defendant with no relief in the appeals court. Again, this is ineffectiveness, thus defendants should not assume that a defense attorney will do anything to assist his client after trial. A defendant should always file a notice of appeal if he or she believes it to be appropriate, it can always be voluntarily dismissed under Federal Rules of Appellant Procedure, Rule 42(a) or (b).

In the event an attorney files late the court record will reflect that counsel's conduct is unprofessional, leaving the defendant to file his or her claim in a post-conviction proceeding. The court will apply the *Strickland* two-part-test of "cause and prejudice." The record will reflect counsel's unprofessional conduct showing "cause," but the court will then turn to deny the claim on the prejudice prong. To overcome the second prong, the defendant must show that the claim at appeal had an effect on the fairness of the trial, and or, that he or she was deprived of trial. Next, the defendant must illustrate the prejudice that failing to file a timely notice of appeal resulted in.

The defendant must show that he had reason to appeal because he was deprived of a trial or a fair trial. He must then show that counsel was the "cause" that deprived the defendant of an appeal. And, that the defendant is "prejudiced" because he is forced to raise his issue in a post-conviction proceeding where he faces a more stringent standard of review, Le. "cause and prejudice." Finally, the defendant should remind the court that under today's standards he has no right to the appointment of counsel in collateral, post-conviction proceedings. Unlike the direct appeal that counsel deprived him of where he or she has a constitutional right to the appointment of counsel.

Counsel Abandonment on Direct Appeal – The Eleventh Circuit, of the United States Court of Appeals, has declared that direct appeal is a critical stage in the trial process; and therefore creates a Constitutional right to the effective assistance of counsel for that appeal, see *United States v. Roy*, 855 F. 3d 1133, 1147, (11th Cir. 2017), quoting *Harrington v. Gillis*, 456 F. 3d 118, 132 (3rd Cir. 2006) (noting that "an appeal is a critical stage of a criminal proceedings.") Accordingly, the Supreme Court in *Anders v. California*, (1967) 386 U.S. 738, not only barred counsel from abandoning a non-frivolous appeal, but also barred counsel from abandoning a non-frivolous issue on appeal.

Unfortunately, in today's criminal justice system thousands of attorneys abandon meaningful appellate claims routinely. Counsel who does this has provided constitutionally ineffective assistance of counsel. A defendant must also understand that not all attorneys conduct themselves unprofessionally. Thus, the defendant must understand the claims he or she believes can be raised in direct appeal. A direct appeal is neither the place to re-enact the trial, nor raise an ineffectiveness of counsel claim. Needless to say, some attorneys who withdraw from an appeal, and file the appropriate *Andes* brief, do so rightfully. What a defendant should concentrate on learning is what a sound appeal claim truly is.

To determine if defense counsel is ineffective for withdrawing from an appeal, a defendant should start his study by understanding the Supreme Court decision that follows:

ANDERS V. CALIFORNIA
386 US 738, 18 L ED 2D 493, 87 S CT 1396, REH DEN (1967)

SUMMARY

After the California District Court of Appeal had appointed counsel to conduct a first appeal to that court from an indigent's conviction, counsel informed the court by letter that after a study of the record and consultation with the accused, he had concluded that there was no merit to the appeal. The court denied the indigent's request for appointment of another attorney, after which the indigent filed his own brief *pro se*. The state responded and the indigent filed a reply brief. The conviction was affirmed. About 6 years later, the court denied the indigent's application for *habeas corpus*, stating that the earlier appeal had been without merit. The Supreme Court of California later denied without opinion the indigent's petition for *habeas corpus*. On *certiorari*, the Supreme Court of the United States reversed. In an opinion by Clark, J., expressing the views of six members of the court, it was held that the constitutional right to counsel requires that on an indigent's first appeal from his conviction, court-appointed counsel support the appeal to the best of his ability, requesting permission to withdraw only if he finds the case to be wholly frivolous, in which event he must file a brief referring to anything in the record that might arguably support the appeal. Stewart, J., joined by Black and Harlan, JJ., dissented on the grounds that if the record presented any arguable issues, a court-appointed lawyer would not deem the appeal to be wholly frivolous.

OPINION
[386 US 739]

Mr. Justice Clark delivered the opinion of the Court.

We are here concerned with the extent of the duty of a court-appointed appellate counsel to prosecute a first appeal from a criminal conviction, after that attorney has conscientiously determined that there is no merit to the indigent's appeal.

After he was convicted of the felony of possession of marijuana, petitioner sought to appeal and moved that the California District Court of Appeal appoint counsel for him. Such motion was granted; however, after a study of the record and consultation with petitioner, the appointed counsel concluded that there was no merit to the appeal. He so advised the court by letter and, at the same time, informed the court that petitioner wished

[386 US 740]

to file a brief in his own behalf. At this juncture, petitioner requested the appointment of another attorney. This request was denied, and the petitioner proceeded to file his own brief *pro se*. The State responded and petitioner filed a reply brief. On January 9, 1959, the District Court of Appeal unanimously affirmed the conviction, People v. Anders, 167 Cal App 2d 65, 333 P2d 854.

[1] On January 21, 1965, petitioner filed an application for a writ of *habeas corpus* in the District Court of appeal in which he sought to have his case reopened. In that application he raised the issue of deprivation of the right to counsel in his original appeal because of the court's refusal to appoint counsel at the appellate stage of the proceedings. The court denied the application on the same day, in a brief unreported memorandum opinion. The court stated that it "ha[d] again reviewed the record and [had] determined the appeal' [to be] without merit." The court also stated that "the procedure prescribed by In re Nash, 61 AC 538, was followed in this case ..." On June 25, 1965, petitioner submitted a petition for a writ of *habeas*

[386 US 741]

corpus to the Supreme Court of California, and the petition was denied without opinion by that court on July 14, 1965. Among other trial errors, petitioner claimed that both the judge and the prosecutor had commented on his failure to testify contrary to the holding of this Court in *Griffin v. California*, 380 US 609, 14 L Ed. 2d 106, 85 S Ct 1229 (1965).

We have concluded that California's action does not comport with fair procedure and lacks that equality that is required by the Fourteenth Amendment.

I.

[2][3][4] For a decade or more, a continuing line of cases has reached this Court concerning discrimination against the indigent defendant on his first appeal. Beginning with *Griffin v. Illinois*, 351 US 12, 100 L Ed 891, 76 S Ct 585, 55 ALR2d 1055 (1956) where it was held that equal justice was not afforded an indigent appellant where the nature of the review "depends on the amount of money he has," at 19, and continuing throughout *Douglas v. California*, 372 US 353, 9 L Ed 2d 811, 83 S Ct 814 (1963), this Court has consistently held invalid those procedures "where the rich man, who appeals as of right, enjoys the benefit of counsel's examination into the record, research of the law, and marshalling of arguments on his behalf, while the indigent, already burdened by a preliminary determination that his case is without merit, is forced to shift for himself." At 358, 9 L Ed 2d at 815. Indeed, in the federal courts, the advice of counsel has long been required whenever a defendant challenges a certification that an appeal is not taken in good faith, *Johnson v. United States*, 352 US 565, 1 L Ed 2d 593, 77 S Ct 550 (1957), and such representation must be in the role of an advocate, *Ellis v. United States*, 356 US 674, 675, 2 L Ed 2d 1060, 1061, 78 S Ct 974 (1958), rather than as *amicus curiae*. In *Ellis*, supra, we concluded:

"If counsel is convinced, after conscientious investigation, that the appeal is frivolous, of course, he may ask to withdraw on that account. If the court

[386 US 742]

is satisfied that counsel has diligently investigated the possible grounds of appeal, and agrees with counsel's evaluation of the case, then leave to withdraw may be allowed and leave to appeal may be denied." At 675, 2 L Ed. 2d at 1061.

In *Gideon v. Wainwright*, 372 US 335, 9 L Ed. 2d 799, 83 S Ct 792, 93 ALR2d (1963), the Sixth Amendment's requirement that "the accused shall enjoy the right … to have the Assistance of Counsel for his defense" was made obligatory on the States by the Fourteenth Amendment, the Court holding that "in our adversary system of criminal justice, any person hauled into court, who is too poor to hire a lawyer, cannot be assured a fair trial unless counsel is provided for him," at 344, 9 L Ed. 2d at 805. We continue to adhere to these principles.

II.

[5] In petitioner's case, his appointed counsel wrote the District Court of Appeal, stating:

"I will not file a brief on appeal as I am of the opinion that there is no merit to the appeal. I have visited and communicated with Mr. Anders and have explained my views and opinions to him. … [H]e wishes to file a brief in this matter on his own behalf."

The District Court of Appeal, after having examined the record, affirmed the conviction. We believe that counsel's bare conclusion, as evidence by his letter, was not enough. It smacks of the treatment that Eskridge received, which this Court condemned, that permitted a trial judge to withhold a transcript if he found that a defendant "has been accorded a fair and impartial trial, and in the Court's opinion no grave or prejudicial errors occurred therein," *Eskridge v. Washington State Board*, 357 US 214, 215, 2 L Ed. 2d 1269, 1270, 78 S Ct 1061 (1958). Such a procedure, this Court said, "cannot be an adequate substitute for the right to full appellate review available to all defendants"

[386 US 743]

who may not be able to afford such an expense, at 216, 2 L Ed. 2d at 1271. And in still another case in which "a state officer outside the judicial system" was given the power to deprive an indigent of his appeal by refusing to order a transcript merely because he thought the "appeal would be unsuccessful" we reversed, finding that such a procedure did not meet constitutional standards, *Lane v. Brown*, 372 US 477, 9 L Ed. 2d 892, 83 S Ct 768 (1963). Here the court appointed counsel had the transcript but refused to proceed with the appeal because he found no merit in it. He filed a no-merit letter with the District Court of Appeal whereupon the court examined the record itself and affirmed the judgment. On a petition for a writ of *habeas corpus* some six years later it found the appeal had no merit. It failed, however, to say whether it was frivolous or not, but, after consideration, simply found the petition to be "without merit." The Supreme Court, in dismissing this *habeas corpus* application, gave no reason at all for its decision, and so we do not know the basis for its action. We cannot say that there was a finding of frivolity by either of the California courts or that counsel acted in any greater capacity than merely as *amicus curiae*, which was condemned in *Ellis*, supra. Hence California's procedure did not furnish petitioner with counsel acting in the role of an advocate nor did it provide that full consideration and resolution of the matter as is obtained when counsel is acting in that capacity. The necessity for counsel so acting is highlighted by the possible disadvantage the petitioner suffered here. In his *pro se* brief, which was filed in 1959, he urged several trial errors but failed to raise the point that both the judge and prosecutor had commented to the jury regarding petitioner's failure to testify. In 1965, this Court in *Griffin v. California*, supra, outlawed California's comment rule, as embodied in Art. I, § 13, of the California Constitution.

[386 US 744]

III.

[6][7] The constitutional requirement of substantial equality and fair process can only be attained where counsel acts in the role of an active advocate in behalf of his client, as opposed to that of *amicus curiae*. The no-merit letter and the procedure it triggers do not reach that dignity. Counsel should, and can with

honor and without conflict, be of more assistance to his client and to the court. His role as advocate requires that he support his client's appeal to the best of his ability. Of course, if counsel finds his case to be wholly frivolous, after a conscientious examination of it, he should advise the court and request permission to withdraw. That request must, however, be accompanied by a brief referring to anything in the record that might arguably support the appeal. A copy of counsel's brief should be furnished to the indigent and time allowed him to raise any points that he chooses; the court-not counsel-then proceeds, after a full examination of all the proceedings, to decide whether the case is wholly frivolous. If it so finds it may grant counsel's request to withdraw and dismiss the appeal insofar as federal requirements are concerned, or proceed to a decision on the merits, if state law so requires. On the other hand, if it finds any of the legal points arguable on their merits (and therefore not frivolous) it must, prior to decision, afford the indigent the assistance of counsel to argue the appeal.

[386 US 745]

This requirement would not force appointed counsel to brief his case against his client but would merely afford the latter that advocacy which a non-indigent defendant is able to obtain. It would also induce the court to pursue all the more vigorously its own review because of the ready references not only to the record, but also to the legal authorities as furnished it by counsel. The no-merit letter, on the other hand, affords neither the client nor the court any aid. The former must shift entirely for himself, while the court has only the cold record which it must review without the help of an advocate. Moreover, such handling would tend to protect counsel from the constantly increasing charge that he was ineffective and had not handled the case with that diligence to which an indigent defendant is entitled. This procedure will assure penniless defendants the same rights and opportunities on appeal-as nearly as is practicable- as are enjoyed by those persons who are in a similar situation but who are able to afford the retention of private counsel. The judgment is reversed, and the case is remanded for further proceedings not inconsistent with this opinion.

PART THREE
CHAPTER SIXTEEN

FEDERAL RULES OF CRIMINAL PROCEDURE

This chapter introduces the reader to the heart and soul of the due process that is referred to in the Fifth and Thirteenth Amendments. The Fourteenth Amendment is also a due process amendment but, only the Fifth and the Thirteenth Amendments are controlling in the Federal Criminal Justice System. The Rules that follow govern the criminal trial procedure in federal court. Thus, it is the following of these rules that is believed to provide the fair trial required by the Constitution's due process requirement.

Rule 1. Scope; Definitions

(a) **Scope.**

   (1) ***In General.*** These rules govern the procedure in all criminal proceedings in the United States district courts, the United States courts of appeals, and the Supreme Court of the United States.

   (2) ***State or Local Judicial Officer.*** When a rule so states, it applies to a proceeding before a state or local judicial officer.

   (3) ***Territorial Courts.*** These rules also govern the procedure in all criminal proceedings in the following courts: (A) the district court of Guam; (B) the district court for the Northern Mariana Islands, except as otherwise provided by law; and (C) the district court of the Virgin Islands, except that the prosecution of offenses in that court must be by indictment or information as otherwise provided by law.

   (4) ***Removed Proceedings.*** Although these rules govern all proceedings after removal from a state court, state law governs a dismissal by the prosecution.

   (5) ***Excluded Proceedings.*** Proceedings not governed by these rules include:

     (A) the extradition and rendition of a fugitive;

     (B) a civil property forfeiture for violating a federal statute;

     (C) the collection of a fine or penalty;

     (D) a proceeding under a statute governing juvenile delinquency to the extent the procedure is inconsistent with the statute, unless Rule 20(d) provides otherwise;

     (E) a dispute between seamen under 22 U.S.C. §§ 256–258; and

     (F) a proceeding against a witness in a foreign country under 28 U.S.C. § 1784.

(b) **Definitions.** The following definitions apply to these rules:

   (1) "Attorney for the government" means:

     (A) the Attorney General or an authorized assistant;

     (B) a United States attorney or an authorized assistant;

     (C) when applicable to cases arising under Guam law, the Guam Attorney General or other person whom Guam law authorizes to act in the matter; and

     (D) any other attorney authorized by law to conduct proceedings under these rules as a prosecutor.

   (2) "Court" means a federal judge performing functions authorized by law.

   (3) "Federal judge" means:

     (A) a justice or judge of the United States as these terms are defined in 28 U.S.C. § 451;

(B) a magistrate judge; and

(C) a judge confirmed by the United States Senate and empowered by statute in any commonwealth, territory, or possession to perform a function to which a particular rule relates.

(4) "Judge" means a federal judge or a state or local judicial officer.

(5) "Magistrate judge" means a United States magistrate judge as defined in 28 U.S.C. §§ 631–639.

(6) "Oath" includes an affirmation.

(7) "Organization" is defined in 18 U.S.C. § 18.

(8) "Petty offense" is defined in 18 U.S.C. § 19.

(9) "State" includes the District of Columbia, and any commonwealth, territory, or possession of the United States.

(10) "State or local judicial officer" means:

(A) a state or local officer authorized to act under 18 U.S.C. § 3041; and

(B) a judicial officer empowered by statute in the District of Columbia or in any commonwealth, territory, or possession to perform a function to which a particular rule relates.

(11) "Telephone" means any technology for transmitting live electronic voice communication.

(12) "Victim" means a "crime victim" as defined in 18 U.S.C. § 3771(e).

(c) **Authority of a Justice or Judge of the United States.** When these rules authorize a magistrate judge to act, any other federal judge may also act.

Rule 2. Interpretation

These rules are to be interpreted to provide for the just determination of every criminal proceeding, to secure simplicity in procedure and fairness in administration, and to eliminate unjustifiable expense and delay.

Rule 3. The Complaint

The complaint is a written statement of the essential facts constituting the offense charged. Except as provided in Rule 4.1, it must be made under oath before a magistrate judge or, if none is reasonably available, before a state or local judicial officer.

Rule 4. Arrest Warrant or Summons on a Complaint

(a) **Issuance.** If the complaint or one or more affidavits filed with the complaint establish probable cause to believe that an offense has been committed and that the defendant committed it, the judge must issue an arrest warrant to an officer authorized to execute it. At the request of an attorney for the government, the judge must issue a summons, instead of a warrant, to a person authorized to serve it. A judge may issue more than one warrant or summons on the same complaint. If an individual defendant fails to appear in response to a summons, a judge may, and upon request of an attorney for the government must, issue a warrant. If an organizational defendant fails to appear in response to a summons, a judge may take any action authorized by United States law.

(b) **Form.**

(1) *Warrant.* A warrant must:

(A) contain the defendant's name or, if it is unknown, a name or description by which the defendant can be identified with reasonable certainty;

(B) describe the offense charged in the complaint;

(C) command that the defendant be arrested and brought without unnecessary delay before a magistrate judge or, if none is reasonably available, before a state or local judicial officer; and

(D) be signed by a judge.

(2) **Summons.** A summons must be in the same form as a warrant except that it must require the defendant to appear before a magistrate judge at a stated time and place.

(c) **Execution or Service, and Return.**

(1) **By Whom.** Only a marshal or other authorized officer may execute a warrant. Any person authorized to serve a summons in a federal civil action may serve a summons.

(2) **Location.** A warrant may be executed, or a summons served, within the jurisdiction of the United States or anywhere else a federal statute authorizes an arrest. A summons to an organization under Rule 4(c)(3)(D) may also be served at a place not within a judicial district of the United States.

(3) **Manner.**

(A) A warrant is executed by arresting the defendant. Upon arrest, an officer possessing the original or a duplicate original warrant must show it to the defendant. If the officer does not possess the warrant, the officer must inform the defendant of the warrant's existence and of the offense charged and, at the defendant's request, must show the original or a duplicate original warrant to the defendant as soon as possible.

(B) A summons is served on an individual defendant:

(i) by delivering a copy to the defendant personally; or

(ii) by leaving a copy at the defendant's residence or usual place of abode with a person of suitable age and discretion residing at that location and by mailing a copy to the defendant's last known address.

(C) A summons is served on an organization in a judicial district of the United States by delivering a copy to an officer, to a managing or general agent, or to another agent appointed or legally authorized to receive service of process. If the agent is one authorized by statute and the statute requires, a copy must also be mailed to the organization.

(D) A summons is served on an organization not within a judicial district of the United States:

(i) by delivering a copy, in a manner authorized by the foreign jurisdiction's law, to an officer, to a managing or general agent, or to an agent appointed or legally authorized to receive service of process; or

(ii) by any other means that gives notice, including one that is:

(a) stipulated by the parties;

(b) undertaken by a foreign authority in response to a letter rogatory, a letter of request, or a request submitted under an applicable international agreement; or

(c) permitted by an applicable international agreement.

(4) **Return.**

(A) After executing a warrant, the officer must return it to the judge before whom the defendant is brought in accordance with Rule 5. The officer may do so by reliable electronic means. At the request of an attorney for the government, an unexecuted warrant must be brought back to and canceled by a magistrate judge or, if none is reasonably available, by a state or local judicial officer.

(B) The person to whom a summons was delivered for service must return it on or before the return day.

(C) At the request of an attorney for the government, a judge may deliver an unexecuted warrant, an unserved summons, or a copy of the warrant or summons to the marshal or other authorized person for execution or service.

(d) **Warrant by Telephone or Other Reliable Electronic Means.** In accordance with Rule 4.1, a magistrate judge may issue a warrant or summons based on information communicated by telephone or other reliable electronic means.

Rule 4.1. Complaint, Warrant, or Summons by Telephone or Other Reliable Electronic Means

(a) **In General.** A magistrate judge may consider information communicated by telephone or other reliable electronic means when reviewing a complaint or deciding whether to issue a warrant or summons.

(b) **Procedures.** If a magistrate judge decides to proceed under this rule, the following procedures apply:

(1) *Taking Testimony Under Oath.* The judge must place under oath – and may examine – the applicant and any person on whose testimony the application is based.

(2) *Creating a Record of the Testimony and Exhibits.*

(A) *Testimony Limited to Attestation.* If the applicant does no more than attest to the contents of a written affidavit submitted by reliable electronic means, the judge must acknowledge the attestation in writing on the affidavit.

(B) *Additional Testimony or Exhibits.* If the judge considers additional testimony or exhibits, the judge must:

(i) have the testimony recorded verbatim by an electronic recording device, by a court reporter, or in writing;

(ii) have any recording or reporter's notes transcribed, have the transcription certified as accurate, and file it;

(iii) sign any other written record, certify its accuracy, and file it; and

(iv) make sure that the exhibits are filed.

(3) *Preparing a Proposed Duplicate Original of a Complaint, Warrant, or Summons.* The applicant must prepare a proposed duplicate original of a complaint, warrant, or summons, and must read or otherwise transmit its contents verbatim to the judge.

(4) *Preparing an Original Complaint, Warrant, or Summons.* If the applicant reads the contents of the proposed duplicate original, the judge must enter those contents into an original complaint, warrant, or summons. If the applicant transmits the contents by reliable electronic means, the transmission received by the judge may serve as the original.

(5) *Modification.* The judge may modify the complaint, warrant, or summons. The judge must then: (A) transmit the modified version to the applicant by reliable electronic means; or (B) file the modified original and direct the applicant to modify the proposed duplicate original accordingly.

(6) *Issuance.* To issue the warrant or summons, the judge must:

(A) sign the original documents;

(B) enter the date and time of issuance on the warrant or summons; and

(C) transmit the warrant or summons by reliable electronic means to the applicant or direct the applicant to sign the judge's name and enter the date and time on the duplicate original.

(c) **Suppression Limited.** Absent a finding of bad faith, evidence obtained from a warrant issued under this rule is not subject to suppression on the grounds that issuing the warrant in this manner was unreasonable under the circumstances.

Rule 5. Initial Appearance

(a) **In General.**

(1) *Appearance Upon an Arrest.*

(A) A person making an arrest within the United States must take the defendant without unnecessary delay before a magistrate judge, or before a state or local judicial officer as Rule 5(c) provides, unless a statute provides otherwise.

(B) A person making an arrest outside the United States must take the defendant without unnecessary delay before a magistrate judge, unless a statute provides otherwise.

(2) *Exceptions.*

(A) An officer making an arrest under a warrant issued upon a complaint charging solely a violation of 18 U.S.C. § 1073 need not comply with this rule if:

(i) the person arrested is transferred without unnecessary delay to the custody of appropriate state or local authorities in the district of arrest; and

(ii) an attorney for the government moves promptly, in the district where the warrant was issued, to dismiss the complaint.

(B) If a defendant is arrested for violating probation or supervised release, Rule 32.1 applies.

(C) If a defendant is arrested for failing to appear in another district, Rule 40 applies.

(3) *Appearance Upon a Summons.* When a defendant appears in response to a summons under Rule 4, a magistrate judge must proceed under Rule 5(d) or (e), as applicable.

(b) **Arrest Without a Warrant.** If a defendant is arrested without a warrant, a complaint meeting Rule 4(a)'s requirement of probable cause must be promptly filed in the district where the offense was allegedly committed.

(c) **Place of Initial Appearance; Transfer to Another District.**

(1) *Arrest in the District Where the Offense Was Allegedly Committed.* If the defendant is arrested in the district where the offense was allegedly committed:

(A) the initial appearance must be in that district; and

(B) if a magistrate judge is not reasonably available, the initial appearance may be before a state or local judicial officer.

(2) *Arrest in a District Other Than Where the Offense Was Allegedly Committed.* If the defendant was arrested in a district other than where the offense was allegedly committed, the initial appearance must be:

(A) in the district of arrest; or

(B) in an adjacent district if:

(i) the appearance can occur more promptly there; or

(ii) the offense was allegedly committed there, and the initial appearance will occur on the day of arrest.

(3) ***Procedures in a District Other Than Where the Offense Was Allegedly Committed.*** If the initial appearance occurs in a district other than where the offense was allegedly committed, the following procedures apply:

(A) the magistrate judge must inform the defendant about the provisions of Rule 20;

(B) if the defendant was arrested without a warrant, the district court where the offense was allegedly committed must first issue a warrant before the magistrate judge transfers the defendant to that district;

(C) the magistrate judge must conduct a preliminary hearing if required by Rule 5.1;

(D) the magistrate judge must transfer the defendant to the district where the offense was allegedly committed if:

(i) the government produces the warrant, a certified copy of the warrant, or a reliable electronic form of either; and

(ii) the judge finds that the defendant is the same person named in the indictment, information, or warrant; and (E) when a defendant is transferred and discharged, the clerk must promptly transmit the papers and any bail to the clerk in the district where the offense was allegedly committed.

(4) ***Procedure for Persons Extradited to the United States.*** If the defendant is surrendered to the United States in accordance with a request for the defendant's extradition, the initial appearance must be in the district (or one of the districts) where the offense is charged.

(d) **Procedure in a Felony Case.**

(1) ***Advice.*** If the defendant is charged with a felony, the judge must inform the defendant of the following:

(A) the complaint against the defendant, and any affidavit filed with it;

(B) the defendant's right to retain counsel or to request that counsel be appointed if the defendant cannot obtain counsel;

(C) the circumstances, if any, under which the defendant may secure pretrial release;

(D) any right to a preliminary hearing;

(E) the defendant's right not to make a statement, and that any statement made may be used against the defendant; and

(F) that a defendant who is not a United States citizen may request that an attorney for the government or a federal law enforcement official notify a consular officer from the defendant's country of nationality that the defendant has been arrested – but that even without the defendant's request, a treaty or other international agreement may require consular notification.

(2) ***Consulting with Counsel.*** The judge must allow the defendant reasonable opportunity to consult with counsel.

(3) ***Detention or Release.*** The judge must detain or release the defendant as provided by statute or these rules.

(4) ***Plea.*** A defendant may be asked to plead only under Rule 10.

(e) **Procedure in a Misdemeanor Case.** If the defendant is charged with a misdemeanor only, the judge must inform the defendant in accordance with Rule 58(b)(2).

(f) **Video Teleconferencing.** Video teleconferencing may be used to conduct an appearance under this rule if the defendant consents.

Rule 5.1. Preliminary Hearing

(a) **In General.** If a defendant is charged with an offense other than a petty offense, a magistrate judge must conduct a preliminary hearing unless:

   (1) the defendant waives the hearing;

   (2) the defendant is indicted;

   (3) the government files an information under Rule 7 (b) charging the defendant with a felony;

   (4) the government files an information charging the defendant with a misdemeanor; or

   (5) the defendant is charged with a misdemeanor and consents to trial before a magistrate judge.

(b) **Selecting a District.** A defendant arrested in a district other than where the offense was allegedly committed may elect to have the preliminary hearing conducted in the district where the prosecution is pending.

(c) **Scheduling.** The magistrate judge must hold the preliminary hearing within a reasonable time, but no later than 14 days after the initial appearance if the defendant is in custody and no later than 21 days if not in custody.

(d) **Extending the Time.** With the defendant's consent and upon a showing of good cause – taking into account the public interest in the prompt disposition of criminal cases – a magistrate judge may extend the time limits in Rule 5.1(c) one or more times. If the defendant does not consent, the magistrate judge may extend the time limits only on a showing that extraordinary circumstances exist, and justice requires the delay.

(e) **Hearing and Finding.** At the preliminary hearing, the defendant may cross-examine adverse witnesses and may introduce evidence but may not object to evidence on the ground that it was unlawfully acquired. If the magistrate judge finds probable cause to believe an offense has been committed and the defendant committed it, the magistrate judge must promptly require the defendant to appear for further proceedings.

(f) **Discharging the Defendant.** If the magistrate judge finds no probable cause to believe an offense has been committed or the defendant committed it, the magistrate judge must dismiss the complaint and discharge the defendant. A discharge does not preclude the government from later prosecuting the defendant for the same offense.

(g) **Recording the Proceedings.** The preliminary hearing must be recorded by a court reporter or by a suitable recording device. A recording of the proceeding may be made available to any party upon request. A copy of the recording and a transcript may be provided to any party upon request and upon any payment required by applicable Judicial Conference regulations.

(h) **Producing a Statement.**

   (1) *In General.* Rule 26.2(a)–(d) and (f) applies at any hearing under this rule, unless the magistrate judge for good cause rules otherwise in a particular case.

   (2) *Sanctions for Not Producing a Statement.* If a party disobeys a Rule 26.2 order to deliver a statement to the moving party, the magistrate judge must not consider the testimony of a witness whose statement is withheld.

Rule 6. The Grand Jury

(a) Summoning a Grand Jury.

(1) *In General.* When the public interest is so required, the court must order that one or more grand juries be summoned. A grand jury must have 16 to 23 members, and the court must order that enough legally qualified persons be summoned to meet this requirement.

(2) *Alternate Jurors.* When a grand jury is selected, the court may also select alternate jurors. Alternate jurors must have the same qualifications and be selected in the same manner as any other juror. Alternate jurors replace jurors in the same sequence in which the alternates were selected. An alternate juror who replaces a juror is subject to the same challenges, takes the same oath, and has the same authority as the other jurors.

(b) Objection to the Grand Jury or to a Grand Juror.

(1) *Challenges.* Either the government or a defendant may challenge the grand jury on the grounds that it was not lawfully drawn, summoned, or selected, and may challenge an individual juror on the ground that the juror is not legally qualified.

(2) *Motion to Dismiss an Indictment.* A party may move to dismiss the indictment based on an objection to the grand jury or on an individual juror's lack of legal qualification, unless the court has previously ruled on the same objection under Rule 6(b)(1). The motion to dismiss is governed by 28 U.S.C. § 1867(e). The court must not dismiss the indictment on the ground that a grand juror was not legally qualified if the record shows that at least 12 qualified jurors concurred in the indictment.

(c) Foreperson and Deputy Foreperson.
The court will appoint one juror as the foreperson and another as the deputy foreperson. In the foreperson's absence, the deputy foreperson will act as the foreperson. The foreperson may administer oaths and affirmations and will sign all indictments. The foreperson – or another juror designated by the foreperson – will record the number of jurors concurring in every indictment and will file the record with the clerk, but the record may not be made public unless the court so orders.

(d) Who May Be Present.

(1) *While the Grand Jury Is in Session.* The following persons may be present while the grand jury is in session: attorneys for the government, the witness being questioned, interpreters when needed, and a court reporter or an operator of a recording device.

(2) *During Deliberations and Voting.* No person other than the jurors, and any interpreter needed to assist a hearing-impaired or speech-impaired juror, may be present while the grand jury is deliberating or voting.

(e) Recording and Disclosing the Proceedings.

(1) *Recording the Proceedings.* Except while the grand jury is deliberating or voting, all proceedings must be recorded by a court reporter or by a suitable recording device. But the validity of a prosecution is not affected by the unintentional failure to make a recording. Unless the court orders otherwise, an attorney for the government will retain control of the recording, the reporter's notes, and any transcript prepared from those notes.

(2) *Secrecy.*

(A) No obligation of secrecy may be imposed on any person except in accordance with Rule 6(e)(2)(B).

(B) Unless these rules provide otherwise, the following persons must not disclose a matter occurring before the grand jury:

(i) a grand juror;

(ii) an interpreter;

(iii) a court reporter;

(iv) an operator of a recording device;

(v) a person who transcribes recorded testimony;

(vi) an attorney for the government; or

(vii) a person to whom disclosure is made under Rule 6(e)(3)(A)(ii) or (iii).

(3) ***Exceptions.***

(A) Disclosure of a grand-jury matter – other than the grand jury's deliberations or any grand juror's vote – may be made to:

(i) an attorney for the government for use in performing that attorney's duty;

(ii) any government personnel – including those of a state, state subdivision, Indian tribe, or foreign government – that an attorney for the government considers necessary to assist in performing that attorney's duty to enforce federal criminal law; or

(iii) a person authorized by 18 U.S.C. § 3322.

(B) A person to whom information is disclosed under Rule 6(e)(3)(A)(ii) may use that information only to assist an attorney for the government in performing that attorney's duty to enforce federal criminal law. An attorney for the government must promptly provide the court that impaneled the grand jury with the names of all persons to whom a disclosure has been made, and must certify that the attorney has advised those persons of their obligation of secrecy under this rule.

(C) An attorney for the government may disclose any grand-jury matter to another federal grand jury.

(D) An attorney for the government may disclose any grand-jury matter involving foreign intelligence, counterintelligence (as defined in 50 U.S.C. § 3003), or foreign intelligence information (as defined in Rule 6(e)(3)(D)(iii)) to any federal law enforcement, intelligence, protective, immigration, national defense, or national security official to assist the official receiving the information in the performance of that official's duties. An attorney for the government may also disclose any grand-jury matter involving, within the United States or elsewhere, a threat of attack or other grave hostile acts of a foreign power or its agent, a threat of domestic or international sabotage or terrorism, or clandestine intelligence gathering activities by an intelligence service or network of a foreign power or by its agent, to any appropriate federal, state, state subdivision, Indian tribal, or foreign government official, for the purpose of preventing or responding to such threat or activities.

(i) Any official who receives information under Rule 6(e)(3)(D) may use the information only as necessary in the conduct of that person's official duties subject to any limitations on the unauthorized disclosure of such information. Any state, state subdivision, Indian tribal, or foreign government official who receives information under Rule 6(e)(3)(D) may use the information only in a manner consistent with any guidelines issued by the Attorney General and the Director of National Intelligence.

(ii) Within a reasonable time after disclosure is made under Rule 6(e)(3)(D), an attorney for the government must file, under seal, a notice with the court in the district where the grand jury convened stating that such information was disclosed and the departments, agencies, or entities to which the disclosure was made.

(iii) As used in Rule 6(e)(3)(D), the term "foreign intelligence information" means:

(a) information, whether or not it concerns a United States person, that relates to the ability of the United States to protect against –

- actual or potential attack or other grave hostile acts of a foreign power or its agent;

- sabotage or international terrorism by a foreign power or its agent; or

- clandestine intelligence activities by an intelligence service or network of a foreign power or by its agent; or

(b) information, whether or not it concerns a United States person, with respect to a foreign power or foreign territory that relates to –

- the national defense or the security of the United States; or

- the conduct of the foreign affairs of the United States.

(E) The court may authorize disclosure – at a time, in a manner, and subject to any other conditions that it directs – of a grand-jury matter:

(i) preliminarily to or in connection with a judicial proceeding;

(ii) at the request of a defendant who shows that a ground may exist to dismiss the indictment because of a matter that occurred before the grand jury;

(iii) at the request of the government, when sought by a foreign court or prosecutor for use in an official criminal investigation;

(iv) at the request of the government if it shows that the matter may disclose a violation of State, Indian tribal, or foreign criminal law, as long as the disclosure is to an appropriate state, state-subdivision, Indian tribal, or foreign government official for the purpose of enforcing that law; or

(v) at the request of the government if it shows that the matter may disclose a violation of military criminal law under the Uniform Code of Military Justice, as long as the disclosure is to an appropriate military official for the purpose of enforcing that law.

(F) A petition to disclose a grand-jury matter under Rule 6(e)(3)(E)(i) must be filed in the district where the grand jury convened. Unless the hearing is ex parte – as it may be when the government is the petitioner – the petitioner must serve the petition on, and the court must afford a reasonable opportunity to appear and be heard to:

(i) an attorney for the government;

(ii) the parties to the judicial proceeding; and

(iii) any other person whom the court may designate.

(G) If the petition to disclose arises out of a judicial proceeding in another district, the petitioned court must transfer the petition to the other court unless the petitioned court can reasonably determine whether disclosure is proper. If the petitioned court decides to transfer, it must send to the transferee court the material sought to be disclosed, if feasible, and a written evaluation of the need for continued grand-jury secrecy. The transferee court must afford those persons identified in Rule 6(e)(3)(F) a reasonable opportunity to appear and be heard.

(4) *Sealed Indictment.* The magistrate judge to whom an indictment is returned may direct that the indictment be kept secret until the defendant is in custody or has been released pending trial. The clerk must then seal the indictment, and no person may disclose the indictment's existence except as necessary to issue or execute a warrant or summons.

(5) *Closed Hearing.* Subject to any right to an open hearing in a contempt proceeding, the court must close any hearing to the extent necessary to prevent disclosure of a matter occurring before a grand jury.

(6) *Sealed Records.* Records, orders, and subpoenas relating to grand-jury proceedings must be kept under seal to the extent and as long as necessary to prevent the unauthorized disclosure of a matter occurring before a grand jury.

(7) *Contempt.* A knowing violation of Rule 6, or of any guidelines jointly issued by the Attorney General and the Director of National Intelligence under Rule 6, may be punished as a contempt of court.

(f) **Indictment and Return.** A grand jury may indict only if at least 12 jurors concur. The grand jury – or its foreperson or deputy foreperson – must return the indictment to a magistrate judge in open court. To avoid unnecessary cost or delay, the magistrate judge may take the return by video teleconference from the court where the grand jury sits. If a complaint or information is pending against the defendant and 12 jurors do not concur in the indictment, the foreperson must promptly and in writing report the lack of concurrence to the magistrate judge.

(g) **Discharging the Grand Jury.** A grand jury must serve until the court discharges it, but it may serve more than 18 months only if the court, having determined that an extension is in the public interest, extends the grand jury's service. An extension may be granted for no more than 6 months, except as otherwise provided by statute.

(h) **Excusing a Juror.** At any time, for good cause, the court may excuse a juror either temporarily or permanently, and if permanently, the court may impanel an alternate juror in place of the excused juror.

(i) **"Indian Tribe" Defined.** "Indian tribe" means an Indian tribe recognized by the Secretary of the Interior on a list published in the Federal Register under 25 U.S.C. § 479a–1.

Rule 7. The Indictment and the Information

(a) **When Used.**

(1) *Felony.* An offense (other than criminal contempt) must be prosecuted by an indictment if it is punishable:

(A) by death; or

(B) by imprisonment for more than one year.

(2) *Misdemeanor.* An offense punishable by imprisonment for one year or less may be prosecuted in accordance with Rule 58(b)(1).

(b) **Waiving Indictment.** An offense punishable by imprisonment for more than one year may be prosecuted by information if the defendant – in open court and after being advised of the nature of the charge and of the defendant's rights – waives prosecution by indictment.

(c) **Nature and Contents.**

(1) *In General.* The indictment or information must be a plain, concise, and definite written statement of the essential facts constituting the offense charged and must be signed by an attorney for the government. It need not contain a formal introduction or conclusion. A count may incorporate by reference an allegation made in another count. A count may allege that the means by which the defendant committed the offense are unknown or that the defendant committed it by one or more specified means. For each count, the indictment or information must give the official or customary citation of the statute, rule, regulation, or other provision of law that the defendant is alleged to have violated. For purposes of an indictment referred to in section 3282 of title 18, United States Code, for which the identity of the defendant is unknown, it shall be sufficient for the indictment to describe the defendant as an individual whose name is unknown, but who has a particular DNA profile, as that term is defined in section 3282.

(2) *Citation Error.* Unless the defendant was misled and thereby prejudiced, neither an error in a citation nor a citation's omission is a ground to dismiss the indictment or information or to reverse a conviction.

(d) **Surplusage.** Upon the defendant's motion, the court may strike surplusage from the indictment or information.

(e) **Amending an Information.** Unless an additional or different offense is charged or a substantial right of the defendant is prejudiced, the court may permit an information to be amended at any time before the verdict or finding.

(f) **Bill of Particulars.** The court may direct the government to file a bill of particulars. The defendant may move for a bill of particulars before or within 14 days after arraignment or at a later time if the court permits. The government may amend a bill of particulars subject to such conditions as justice requires.

Rule 8. Joinder of Offenses or Defendants

(a) **Joinder of Offenses.** The indictment or information may charge a defendant in separate counts with 2 or more offenses if the offenses charged – whether felonies or misdemeanors or both – are of the same or similar character, or are based on the same act or transaction, or are connected with or constitute parts of a common scheme or plan.

(b) **Joinder of Defendants.** The indictment or information may charge 2 or more defendants if they are alleged to have participated in the same act or transaction, or in the same series of acts or transactions, constituting an offense or offenses. The defendants may be charged in one or more counts together or separately. All defendants need not be charged in each count

Rule 9. Arrest Warrant or Summons on an Indictment or Information

(a) **Issuance.** The court must issue a warrant – or at the government's request, a summons – for each defendant named in an indictment or named in an information if one or more affidavits accompanying the information establish probable cause to believe that an offense has been committed and that the defendant committed it. The court may issue more than one warrant or summons for the same defendant. If a defendant fails to appear in response to a summons, the court may, and upon request of an attorney for the government must, issue a warrant. The court must issue the arrest warrant to an officer authorized to execute it or the summons to a person authorized to serve it.

(b) **Form.**

(1) *Warrant.* The warrant must conform to Rule 4(b)(1) except that it must be signed by the clerk and must describe the offense charged in the indictment or information.

(2) **Summons.** The summons must be in the same form as a warrant except that it must require the defendant to appear before the court at a stated time and place.

(c) **Execution or Service; Return; Initial Appearance.**

   (1) *Execution or Service.*

     (A) The warrant must be executed, or the summons served as provided in Rule 4(c)(1), (2), and (3).

     (B) The officer executing the warrant must proceed in accordance with Rule 5(a)(1).

   (2) *Return.* A warrant or summons must be returned in accordance with Rule 4(c)(4).

   (3) *Initial Appearance.* When an arrested or summoned defendant first appears before the court, the judge must proceed under Rule 5.

(d) **Warrant by Telephone or Other Means.** In accordance with Rule 4.1, a magistrate judge may issue an arrest warrant or summons based on information communicated by telephone or other reliable electronic means.

Rule 10. Arraignment

(a) **In General.** An arraignment must be conducted in open court and must consist of:

   (1) ensuring that the defendant has a copy of the indictment or information;

   (2) reading the indictment or information to the defendant or stating to the defendant the substance of the charge; and then

   (3) asking the defendant to plead to the indictment or information.

(b) **Waiving Appearance.** A defendant need not be present for the arraignment if:

   (1) the defendant has been charged by indictment or misdemeanor information;

   (2) the defendant, in a written waiver signed by both the defendant and defense counsel, has waived appearance and has affirmed that the defendant received a copy of the indictment or information and that the plea is not guilty; and

   (3) the court accepts the waiver.

(c) **Video Teleconferencing.** Video teleconferencing may be used to arraign a defendant if the defendant consents.

Rule 11. Pleas

(a) **Entering a Plea.**

   (1) *In General.* A defendant may plead not guilty, guilty, or (with the court's consent) nolo contendere.

   (2) *Conditional Plea.* With the consent of the court and the government, a defendant may enter a conditional plea of guilty or nolo contendere, reserving in writing the right to have an appellate court review an adverse determination of a specified pretrial motion. A defendant who prevails on appeal may then withdraw the plea.

   (3) *Nolo Contendere Plea.* Before accepting a plea of nolo contendere, the court must consider the parties' views and the public interest in the effective administration of justice.

   (4) *Failure to Enter a Plea.* If a defendant refuses to enter a plea or if a defendant organization fails to appear, the court must enter a plea of not guilty.

(b) **Considering and Accepting a Guilty or Nolo Contendere Plea.**

(1) *Advising and Questioning the Defendant.* Before the court accepts a plea of guilty or nolo contendere, the defendant may be placed under oath, and the court must address the defendant personally in open court. During this address, the court must inform the defendant of, and determine that the defendant understands, the following:

(A) the government's right, in a prosecution for perjury or false statement, to use against the defendant any statement that the defendant gives under oath;

(B) the right to plead not guilty, or having already so pleaded, to persist in that plea;

(C) the right to a jury trial;

(D) the right to be represented by counsel – and if necessary, have the court appoint counsel – at trial and at every other stage of the proceeding;

(E) the right at trial to confront and cross-examine adverse witnesses, to be protected from compelled self-incrimination, to testify and present evidence, and to compel the attendance of witnesses;

(F) the defendant's waiver of these trial rights if the court accepts a plea of guilty or nolo contendere;

(G) the nature of each charge to which the defendant is pleading;

(H) any maximum possible penalty, including imprisonment, fine, and term of supervised release;

(I) any mandatory minimum penalty;

(J) any applicable forfeiture;

(K) the court's authority to order restitution;

(L) the court's obligation to impose a special assessment;

(M) in determining a sentence, the court's obligation to calculate the applicable sentencing-guideline range and to consider that range, possible departures under the Sentencing Guidelines, and other sentencing factors under 18 U.S.C. § 3553(a);

(N) the terms of any plea-agreement provision waiving the right to appeal or to collaterally attack the sentence; and

(O) that, if convicted, a defendant who is not a United States citizen may be removed from the United States, denied citizenship, and denied admission to the United States in the future.

(2) *Ensuring That a Plea Is Voluntary.* Before accepting a plea of guilty or nolo contendere, the court must address the defendant personally in open court and determine that the plea is voluntary and did not result from force, threats, or promises (other than promises in a plea agreement).

(3) *Determining the Factual Basis for a Plea.* Before entering judgment on a guilty plea, the court must determine that there is a factual basis for the plea.

(c) **Plea Agreement Procedure.**

(1) *In General.* An attorney for the government and the defendant's attorney, or the defendant when proceeding pro se, may discuss and reach a plea agreement. The court must not participate in these discussions. If the defendant pleads guilty or nolo contendere to either a charged offense or a lesser or related offense, the plea agreement may specify that an attorney for the government will:

(A) not bring, or will move to dismiss, other charges;

(B) recommend, or agree not to oppose the defendant's request, that a particular sentence or sentencing range is appropriate or that a particular provision of the Sentencing Guidelines, or policy statement, or sentencing factor does or does not apply (such a recommendation or request does not bind the court); or

(C) agree that a specific sentence or sentencing range is the appropriate disposition of the case, or that a particular provision of the Sentencing Guidelines, or policy statement, or sentencing factor does or does not apply (such a recommendation or request binds the court once the court accepts the plea agreement).

(2) *Disclosing a Plea Agreement.* The parties must disclose the plea agreement in open court when the plea is offered, unless the court for good cause allows the parties to disclose the plea agreement in camera.

(3) *Judicial Consideration of a Plea Agreement.*

(A) To the extent the plea agreement is of the type specified in Rule 11(c)(1)(A) or (C), the court may accept the agreement, reject it, or defer a decision until the court has reviewed the presentence report.

(B) To the extent the plea agreement is of the type specified in Rule 11(c)(1)(B), the court must advise the defendant that the defendant has no right to withdraw the plea if the court does not follow the recommendation or request.

(4) *Accepting a Plea Agreement.* If the court accepts the plea agreement, it must inform the defendant that to the extent the plea agreement is of the type specified in Rule 11(c)(1)(A) or (C), the agreed disposition will be included in the judgment.

(5) *Rejecting a Plea Agreement.* If the court rejects a plea agreement containing provisions of the type specified in Rule 11(c)(1)(A) or (C), the court must do the following on the record and in open court (or, for good cause, in camera):

(A) inform the parties that the court rejects the plea agreement;

(B) advise the defendant personally that the court is not required to follow the plea agreement and give the defendant an opportunity to withdraw the plea; and

(C) advise the defendant personally that if the plea is not withdrawn, the court may dispose of the case less favorably toward the defendant than the plea agreement contemplated.

(d) **Withdrawing a Guilty or Nolo Contendere Plea.** A defendant may withdraw a plea of guilty or nolo contendere:

(1) before the court accepts the plea, for any reason or no reason; or

(2) after the court accepts the plea, but before it imposes sentence if:

(A) the court rejects a plea agreement under Rule 11(c)(5); or

(B) the defendant can show a fair and just reason for requesting the withdrawal.

(e) **Finality of a Guilty or Nolo Contendere Plea.** After the court imposes sentence, the defendant may not withdraw a plea of guilty or nolo contendere, and the plea may be set aside only on direct appeal or collateral attack.

(f) **Admissibility or Inadmissibility of a Plea, Plea Discussions, and Related Statements.** The admissibility or inadmissibility of a plea, a plea discussion, and any related statement is governed by Federal Rule of Evidence 410.

(g) **Recording the Proceedings.** The proceedings during which the defendant enters a plea must be recorded by a court reporter or by a suitable recording device. If there is a guilty plea or a nolo contendere plea, the record must include the inquiries and advice to the defendant required under Rule 11(b) and (c).

(h) **Harmless Error.** A variance from the requirements of this rule is harmless error if it does not affect substantial rights.

Rule 12. Pleadings and Pretrial Motions

(a) **Pleadings.** The pleadings in a criminal proceeding are the indictment, the information, and the pleas of not guilty, guilty, and nolo contendere.

(b) **Pretrial Motions.**

(1) *In General.* A party may raise by pretrial motion any defense, objection, or request that the court can determine without a trial on the merits. Rule 47 applies to a pretrial motion.

(2) *Motions That May Be Made at Any Time.* A motion that the court lacks jurisdiction may be made at any time while the case is pending.

(3) *Motions That Must Be Made Before Trial.* The following defenses, objections, and requests must be raised by pretrial motion if the basis for the motion is then reasonably available, and the motion can be determined without a trial on the merits:

(A) a defect in instituting the prosecution, including:

(i) improper venue;

(ii) preindictment delay;

(iii) a violation of the constitutional right to a speedy trial;

(iv) selective or vindictive prosecution; and

(v) an error in the grand jury proceeding or preliminary hearing;

(B) a defect in the indictment or information, including:

(i) joining two or more offenses in the same count (duplicity);

(ii) charging the same offense in more than one count (multiplicity);

(iii) lack of specificity;

(iv) improper joinder; and

(v) failure to state an offense;

(C) suppression of evidence;

(D) severance of charges or defendants under Rule 14; and

(E) discovery under Rule 16.

(4) *Notice of the Government's Intent to Use Evidence.*

(A) *At the Government's Discretion.* At the arraignment or as soon afterward as practicable, the government may notify the defendant of its intent to use specified evidence at trial in order to afford the defendant an opportunity to object before trial under Rule 12(b)(3)(C).

(B) *At the Defendant's Request.* At the arraignment or as soon afterward as practicable, the defendant may, in order to have an opportunity to move to suppress evidence under Rule

12(b)(3)(C), request notice of the government's intent to use (in its evidence-in-chief at trial) any evidence that the defendant may be entitled to discover under Rule 16.

(c) **Deadline for a Pretrial Motion; Consequences of Not Making a Timely Motion.**

   (1) *Setting the Deadline.* The court may, at the arraignment or as soon afterward as practicable, set a deadline for the parties to make pretrial motions and may also schedule a motion hearing. If the court does not set one, the deadline is the start of trial.

   (2) *Extending or Resetting the Deadline.* At any time before trial, the court may extend or reset the deadline for pretrial motions.

   (3) *Consequences of Not Making a Timely Motion Under Rule 12(b)(3).* If a party does not meet the deadline for making a Rule 12(b)(3) motion, the motion is untimely. But a court may consider the defense, objection, or request if the party shows good cause.

(d) **Ruling on a Motion.** The court must decide every pretrial motion before trial unless it finds good cause to defer a ruling. The court must not defer ruling on a pretrial motion if the deferral will adversely affect a party's right to appeal. When factual issues are involved in deciding a motion, the court must state its essential findings on the record.

(e) **[Reserved]**

(f) **Recording the Proceedings.** All proceedings at a motion hearing, including any findings of fact and conclusions of law made orally by the court, must be recorded by a court reporter or a suitable recording device.

(g) **Defendant's Continued Custody or Release Status.** If the court grants a motion to dismiss based on a defect in instituting the prosecution, in the indictment, or in the information, it may order the defendant to be released or detained under 18 U.S.C. § 3142 for a specified time until a new indictment or information is filed. This rule does not affect any federal statutory period of limitations.

(h) **Producing Statements at a Suppression Hearing.** Rule 26.2 applies at a suppression hearing under Rule 12(b)(3)(C). At a suppression hearing, a law enforcement officer is considered a government witness.

Rule 12.1. Notice of an Alibi Defense

(a) **Government's Request for Notice and Defendant's Response.**

   (1) *Government's Request.* An attorney for the government may request in writing that the defendant notify an attorney for the government of any intended alibi defense. The request must state the time, date, and place of the alleged offense.

   (2) *Defendant's Response.* Within 14 days after the request, or at some other time the court sets, the defendant must serve written notice on an attorney for the government of any intended alibi defense. The defendant's notice must state:

      (A) each specific place where the defendant claims to have been at the time of the alleged offense; and

      (B) the name, address, and telephone number of each alibi witness on whom the defendant intends to rely.

(b) **Disclosing Government Witnesses.**

   (1) *Disclosure.*

(A) *In General.* If the defendant serves a Rule 12.1(a)(2) notice, an attorney for the government must disclose in writing to the defendant or the defendant's attorney:

    (i) the name of each witness – and the address and telephone number of each witness other than a victim – that the government intends to rely on to establish that the defendant was present at the scene of the alleged offense; and

    (ii) each government rebuttal witness to the defendant's alibi defense.

(B) *Victim's Address and Telephone Number.* If the government intends to rely on a victim's testimony to establish that the defendant was present at the scene of the alleged offense and the defendant establishes a need for the victim's address and telephone number, the court may:

    (i) order the government to provide the information in writing to the defendant or the defendant's attorney; or

    (ii) fashion a reasonable procedure that allows preparation of the defense and also protects the victim's interests.

(2) **Time to Disclose.** Unless the court directs otherwise, an attorney for the government must give its Rule 12.1(b)(1) disclosure within 14 days after the defendant serves notice of an intended alibi defense under Rule 12.1(a)(2), but no later than 14 days before trial.

(c) **Continuing Duty to Disclose.**

(1) *In General.* Both an attorney for the government and the defendant must promptly disclose in writing to the other party the name of each additional witness – and the address and telephone number of each additional witness other than a victim – if:

(A) the disclosing party learns of the witness before or during trial; and

(B) the witness should have been disclosed under Rule 12.1(a) or (b) if the disclosing party had known of the witness earlier.

(2) *Address and Telephone Number of an Additional Victim Witness.* The address and telephone number of an additional victim witness must not be disclosed except as provided in Rule 12.1 (b)(1)(B).

(d) **Exceptions.** For good cause, the court may grant an exception to any requirement of Rule 12.1(a)–(c).

(e) **Failure to Comply.** If a party fails to comply with this rule, the court may exclude the testimony of any undisclosed witness regarding the defendant's alibi. This rule does not limit the defendant's right to testify.

(f) **Inadmissibility of Withdrawn Intention.** Evidence of an intention to rely on an alibi defense, later withdrawn, or of a statement made in connection with that intention, is not, in any civil or criminal proceeding, admissible against the person who gave notice of the intention.

Rule 12.2. Notice of an Insanity Defense; Mental Examination

(a) **Notice of an Insanity Defense.** A defendant who intends to assert a defense of insanity at the time of the alleged offense must so notify an attorney for the government in writing within the time provided for filing a pretrial motion, or at any later time the court sets, and file a copy of the notice with the clerk. A defendant who fails to do so cannot rely on an insanity defense. The court may, for good cause, allow the defendant to file the notice late, grant additional trial-preparation time, or make other appropriate orders.

(b) **Notice of Expert Evidence of a Mental Condition.** If a defendant intends to introduce expert evidence relating to a mental disease or defect or any other mental condition of the defendant bearing on either (1) the issue of guilt or (2) the issue of punishment in a capital case, the defendant must – within the time provided for filing a pretrial motion or at any later time the court sets – notify an attorney for the government in writing of this intention and file a copy of the notice with the clerk. The court may, for good cause, allow the defendant to file the notice late, grant the parties additional trial-preparation time, or make other appropriate orders.

(c) **Mental Examination.**

    (1) *Authority to Order an Examination; Procedures.*

        (A) The court may order the defendant to submit to a competency examination under 18 U.S.C. § 4241.

        (B) If the defendant provides notice under Rule 12.2(a), the court must, upon the government's motion, order the defendant to be examined under 18 U.S.C. § 4242. If the defendant provides notice under Rule 12.2(b) the court may, upon the government's motion, order the defendant to be examined under procedures ordered by the court.

    (2) *Disclosing Results and Reports of Capital Sentencing Examination.* The results and reports of any examination conducted solely under Rule 12.2(c)(1) after notice under Rule 12.2(b)(2) must be sealed and must not be disclosed to any attorney for the government or the defendant unless the defendant is found guilty of one or more capital crimes and the defendant confirms an intent to offer during sentencing proceedings expert evidence on mental condition.

    (3) *Disclosing Results and Reports of the Defendant's Expert Examination.* After disclosure under Rule 12.2(c)(2) of the results and reports of the government's examination, the defendant must disclose to the government the results and reports of any examination on mental condition conducted by the defendant's expert about which the defendant intends to introduce expert evidence.

    (4) *Inadmissibility of a Defendant's Statements.* No statement made by a defendant in the course of any examination conducted under this rule (whether conducted with or without the defendant's consent), no testimony by the expert based on the statement, and no other fruits of the statement may be admitted into evidence against the defendant in any criminal proceeding except on an issue regarding mental condition on which the defendant:

        (A) has introduced evidence of incompetency or evidence requiring notice under Rule 12.2(a) or (b)(1), or

        (B) has introduced expert evidence in a capital sentencing proceeding requiring notice under Rule 12.2(b)(2).

(d) **Failure to Comply.**

    (1) *Failure to Give Notice or to Submit to Examination.* The court may exclude any expert evidence from the defendant on the issue of the defendant's mental disease, mental defect, or any other mental condition bearing on the defendant's guilt or the issue of punishment in a capital case if the defendant fails to:

        (A) give notice under Rule 12.2(b); or

        (B) submit to an examination when ordered under Rule 12.2(c).

    (2) *Failure to Disclose.* The court may exclude any expert evidence for which the defendant has failed to comply with the disclosure requirement of Rule 12.2(c)(3).

(e) **Inadmissibility of Withdrawn Intention.** Evidence of an intention as to which notice was given under Rule 12.2(a) or (b), later withdrawn, is not, in any civil or criminal proceeding, admissible against the person who gave notice of the intention.

Rule 12.3. Notice of a Public-Authority Defense

(a) **Notice of the Defense and Disclosure of Witnesses.**

(1) *Notice in General.* If a defendant intends to assert a defense of actual or believed exercise of public authority on behalf of a law enforcement agency or federal intelligence agency at the time of the alleged offense, the defendant must so notify an attorney for the government in writing and must file a copy of the notice with the clerk within the time provided for filing a pretrial motion, or at any later time the court sets. The notice filed with the clerk must be under seal if the notice identifies a federal intelligence agency as the source of public authority.

(2) *Contents of Notice.* The notice must contain the following information:

(A) the law enforcement agency or federal intelligence agency involved;

(B) the agency member on whose behalf the defendant claims to have acted; and

(C) the time during which the defendant claims to have acted with public authority.

(3) *Response to the Notice.* An attorney for the government must serve a written response on the defendant or the defendant's attorney within 14 days after receiving the defendant's notice, but no later than 21 days before trial. The response must admit or deny that the defendant exercised the public authority identified in the defendant's notice.

(4) *Disclosing Witnesses.*

(A) *Government's Request.* An attorney for the government may request in writing that the defendant disclose the name, address, and telephone number of each witness the defendant intends to rely on to establish a public-authority defense. An attorney for the government may serve the request when the government serves its response to the defendant's notice under Rule 12.3(a)(3), or later, but must serve the request no later than 21 days before trial.

(B) *Defendant's Response.* Within 14 days after receiving the government's request, the defendant must serve on an attorney for the government a written statement of the name, address, and telephone number of each witness.

(C) *Government's Reply.* Within 14 days after receiving the defendant's statement, an attorney for the government must serve on the defendant or the defendant's attorney a written statement of the name of each witness – and the address and telephone number of each witness other than a victim – that the government intends to rely on to oppose the defendant's public-authority defense.

(D) *Victim's Address and Telephone Number.* If the government intends to rely on a victim's testimony to oppose the defendant's public-authority defense and the defendant establishes a need for the victim's address and telephone number, the court may: (i) order the government to provide the information in writing to the defendant or the defendant's attorney; or (ii) fashion a reasonable procedure that allows for preparing the defense and also protects the victim's interests.

(5) *Additional Time.* The court may, for good cause, allow a party additional time to comply with this rule.

(b) **Continuing Duty to Disclose.**

(1) **In General.** Both an attorney for the government and the defendant must promptly disclose in writing to the other party the name of any additional witness – and the address, and telephone number of any additional witness other than a victim – if:

(A) the disclosing party learns of the witness before or during trial; and (B) the witness should have been disclosed under Rule 12.3(a)(4) if the disclosing party had known of the witness earlier.

(2) **Address and Telephone Number of an Additional Victim- Witness.** The address and telephone number of an additional victim-witness must not be disclosed except as provided in Rule 12.3(a)(4)(D).

(c) **Failure to Comply.** If a party fails to comply with this rule, the court may exclude the testimony of any undisclosed witness regarding the public-authority defense. This rule does not limit the defendant's right to testify.

(d) **Protective Procedures Unaffected.** This rule does not limit the court's authority to issue appropriate protective orders or to order that any filings be under seal.

(e) **Inadmissibility of Withdrawn Intention.** Evidence of an intention as to which notice was given under Rule 12.3(a), later withdrawn, is not, in any civil or criminal proceeding, admissible against the person who gave notice of the intention.

Rule 12.4. Disclosure Statement

(a) **Who Must File.**

(1) **Nongovernmental Corporate Party.** Any nongovernmental corporate party to a proceeding in a district court must file a statement that identifies any parent corporation and any publicly held corporation that owns 10% or more of its stock or states that there is no such corporation.

(2) **Organizational Victim.** Unless the government shows good cause, it must file a statement identifying any organizational victim of the alleged criminal activity. If the organizational victim is a corporation, the statement must also disclose the information required by Rule 12.4(a)(1) to the extent it can be obtained through due diligence.

(b) **Time to File; Later Filing.** A party must:

(1) file the Rule 12.4(a) statement within 28 days after the defendant's initial appearance; and

(2) promptly file a later statement if any required information changes.

Rule 13. Joint Trial of Separate Cases

The court may order that separate cases be tried together as though brought in a single indictment or information if all offenses and all defendants could have been joined in a single indictment or information.

Rule 14. Relief from Prejudicial Joinder

(a) **Relief.** If the joinder of offenses or defendants in an indictment, an information, or a consolidation for trial appears to prejudice a defendant or the government, the court may order separate trials of counts, sever the defendants' trials, or provide any other relief that justice requires.

(b) **Defendant's Statements.** Before ruling on a defendant's motion to sever, the court may order an attorney for the government to deliver to the court for camera inspection any defendant's statement that the government intends to use as evidence.

Rule 15. Depositions

(a) When Taken.

   (1) ***In General.*** A party may move that a prospective witness be deposed in order to preserve testimony for trial. The court may grant the motion because of exceptional circumstances and in the interest of justice. If the court orders the deposition to be taken, it may also require the deponent to produce at the deposition any designated material that is not privileged, including any book, paper, document, record, recording, or data.

   (2) ***Detained Material Witness.*** A witness who is detained under 18 U.S.C. § 3144 may request to be deposed by filing a written motion and giving notice to the parties. The court may then order that the deposition be taken and may discharge the witness after the witness has signed under oath the deposition transcript.

(b) Notice.

   (1) ***In General.*** A party seeking to take a deposition must give every other party reasonable written notice of the deposition's date and location. The notice must state the name and address of each deponent. If requested by a party receiving the notice, the court may, for good cause, change the deposition's date or location.

   (2) ***To the Custodial Officer.*** A party seeking to take the deposition must also notify the officer who has custody of the defendant of the scheduled date and location.

(c) Defendant's Presence.

   (1) ***Defendant in Custody.*** Except as authorized by Rule 15(c)(3), the officer who has custody of the defendant must produce the defendant at the deposition and keep the defendant in the witness's presence during the examination, unless the defendant:

     (A) waives in writing the right to be present; or

     (B) persists in disruptive conduct justifying exclusion after being warned by the court that disruptive conduct will result in the defendant's exclusion.

   (2) ***Defendant Not in Custody.*** Except as authorized by Rule 15(c)(3), a defendant who is not in custody has the right upon request to be present at the deposition, subject to any conditions imposed by the court. If the government tenders the defendant's expenses as provided in Rule 15(d) but the defendant still fails to appear, the defendant – absent good cause – waives both the right to appear and any objection to the taking and use of the deposition based on that right.

   (3) ***Taking Depositions Outside the United States Without the Defendant's Presence.*** The deposition of a witness who is outside the United States may be taken without the defendant's presence if the court makes case-specific findings of all the following:

     (A) the witness's testimony could provide substantial proof of a material fact in a felony prosecution;

     (B) there is a substantial likelihood that the witness's attendance at trial cannot be obtained;

     (C) the witness's presence for a deposition in the United States cannot be obtained;

     (D) the defendant cannot be present because:

       (i) the country where the witness is located will not permit the defendant to attend the deposition;

(ii) for an in-custody defendant, secure transportation and continuing custody cannot be assured at the witness's location; or

(iii) for an out-of-custody defendant, no reasonable conditions will assure an appearance at the deposition or at trial or sentencing; and

(E) the defendant can meaningfully participate in the deposition through reasonable means.

(d) **Expenses.** If the deposition was requested by the government, the court may – or if the defendant is unable to bear the deposition expenses, the court must – order the government to pay:

(1) any reasonable travel and subsistence expenses of the defendant and the defendant's attorney to attend the deposition; and

(2) the costs of the deposition transcript.

(e) **Manner of Taking.** Unless these rules or a court order provides otherwise, a deposition must be taken and filed in the same manner as a deposition in a civil action, except that:

(1) A defendant may not be deposed without that defendant's consent.

(2) The scope and manner of the deposition examination and cross-examination must be the same as would be allowed during trial.

(3) The government must provide to the defendant or the defendant's attorney, for use at the deposition, any statement of the deponent in the government's possession to which the defendant would be entitled at trial.

(f) **Admissibility and Use as Evidence.** An order authorizing a deposition to be taken under this rule does not determine its admissibility. A party may use all or part of a deposition as provided by the Federal Rules of Evidence.

(g) **Objections.** A party objecting to deposition testimony or evidence must state the grounds for the objection during the deposition.

(h) **Depositions by Agreement Permitted.** The parties may by agreement take and use a deposition with the court's consent.

Rule 16. Discovery and Inspection

(a) **Government's Disclosure.**

(1) *Information Subject to Disclosure.*

(A) *Defendant's Oral Statement.* Upon a defendant's request, the government must disclose to the defendant the substance of any relevant oral statement made by the defendant, before or after arrest, in response to interrogation by a person the defendant knew was a government agent if the government intends to use the statement at trial.

(B) *Defendant's Written or Recorded Statement.* Upon a defendant's request, the government must disclose to the defendant, and make available for inspection, copying, or photographing, all of the following:

(i) any relevant written or recorded statement by the defendant if:

• the statement is within the government's possession, custody, or control; and

• the attorney for the government knows – or through due diligence could know – that the statement exists;

(ii) the portion of any written record containing the substance of any relevant oral statement made before or after arrest if the defendant made the statement in response to interrogation by a person the defendant knew was a government agent; and

(iii) the defendant's recorded testimony before a grand jury relating to the charged offense.

(C) *Organizational Defendant.* Upon a defendant's request, if the defendant is an organization, the government must disclose to the defendant any statement described in Rule 16(a)(1)(A) and (B) if the government contends that the person making the statement:

(i) was legally able to bind the defendant regarding the subject of the statement because of that person's position as the defendant's director, officer, employee, or agent; or

(ii) was personally involved in the alleged conduct constituting the offense and was legally able to bind the defendant regarding that conduct because of that person's position as the defendant's director, officer, employee, or agent.

(D) *Defendant's Prior Record.* Upon a defendant's request, the government must furnish the defendant with a copy of the defendant's prior criminal record that is within the government's possession, custody, or control if the attorney for the government knows – or through due diligence could know – that the record exists.

(E) *Documents and Objects.* Upon a defendant's request, the government must permit the defendant to inspect and to copy or photograph books, papers, documents, data, photographs, tangible objects, buildings or places, or copies or portions of any of these items, if the item is within the government's possession, custody, or control and:

(i) the item is material to preparing the defense;

(ii) the government intends to use the item in its case-in-chief at trial; or (iii) the item was obtained from or belongs to the defendant.

(F) *Reports of Examinations and Tests.* Upon a defendant's request, the government must permit a defendant to inspect and to copy or photograph the results or reports of any physical or mental examination and of any scientific test or experiment if:

(i) the item is within the government's possession, custody, or control;

(ii) the attorney for the government knows – or through due diligence could know – that the item exists; and

(iii) the item is material to prepare the defense or the government intends to use the item in its case-in chief at trial.

(G) *Expert Witnesses.* At the defendant's request, the government must give to the defendant a written summary of any testimony that the government intends to use under Rules 702, 703, or 705 of the Federal Rules of Evidence during its case-in-chief at trial. If the government requests discovery under subdivision (b)(1)(C)(ii) and the defendant complies, the government must, at the defendant's request, give to the defendant a written summary of testimony that the government intends to use under Rules 702, 703, or 705 of the Federal Rules of Evidence as evidence at trial on the issue of the defendant's mental condition. The summary provided under this subparagraph must describe the witness's opinions, the bases and reasons for those opinions, and the witness's qualifications.

(2) ***Information Not Subject to Disclosure.*** Except as permitted by Rule 16(a)(1)(A)–(D), (F), and (G), this rule does not authorize the discovery or inspection of reports, memoranda, or other internal

government documents made by an attorney for the government or other government agent in connection with investigating or prosecuting the case. Nor does this rule authorize the discovery or inspection of statements made by prospective government witnesses except as provided in 18 U.S.C. § 3500.

(3) ***Grand Jury Transcripts.*** This rule does not apply to the discovery or inspection of a grand jury's recorded proceedings, except as provided in Rules 6, 12(h), 16(a)(1), and 26.2.

(b) **Defendant's Disclosure.**

(1) ***Information Subject to Disclosure.***

(A) *Documents and Objects.* If a defendant requests disclosure under Rule 16(a)(1)(E) and the government complies, then the defendant must permit the government, upon request, to inspect and to copy or photograph books, papers, documents, data, photographs, tangible objects, buildings or places, or copies or portions of any of these items if:

(i) the item is within the defendant's possession, custody, or control; and

(ii) the defendant intends to use the item in the defendant's case-in-chief at trial.

(B) *Reports of Examinations and Tests.* If a defendant requests disclosure under Rule 16(a)(1)(F) and the government complies, the defendant must permit the government, upon request, to inspect and to copy or photograph the results or reports of any physical or mental examination and of any scientific test or experiment if:

(i) the item is within the defendant's possession, custody, or control; and

(ii) the defendant intends to use the item in the defendant's case-in-chief at trial or intends to call the witness who prepared the report, and the report relates to the witness's testimony.

(C) *Expert Witnesses.* The defendant must, at the government's request, give to the government a written summary of any testimony that the defendant intends to use under Rules 702, 703, or 705 of the Federal Rules of Evidence as evidence at trial, if –

(i) the defendant requests disclosure under subdivision (a)(1)(G) and the government complies; or

(ii) the defendant has given notice under Rule 12.2(b) of an intent to present expert testimony on the defendant's mental condition. This summary must describe the witness's opinions, the bases and reasons for those opinions, and the witness's qualifications[.]

(2) ***Information Not Subject to Disclosure.*** Except for scientific or medical reports, Rule 16(b)(1) does not authorize discovery or inspection of:

(A) reports, memoranda, or other documents made by the defendant, or the defendant's attorney or agent, during the case's investigation or defense; or

(B) a statement made to the defendant, or the defendant's attorney or agent, by:

(i) the defendant;

(ii) a government or defense witness; or

(iii) a prospective government or defense witness.

(c) **Continuing Duty to Disclose.** A party who discovers additional evidence or material before or during trial must promptly disclose its existence to the other party or the court if:

(1) the evidence or material is subject to discovery or inspection under this rule; and

(2) the other party previously requested, or the court ordered, its production.

(d) **Regulating Discovery.**

    (1) ***Protective and Modifying Orders.*** At any time, the court may, for good cause, deny, restrict, or defer discovery or inspection, or grant other appropriate relief. The court may permit a party to show good cause by a written statement that the court will inspect ex parte. If relief is granted, the court must preserve the entire text of the party's statement under seal.

    (2) ***Failure to Comply.*** If a party fails to comply with this rule, the court may:

        (A) order that party to permit the discovery or inspection; specify its time, place, and manner; and prescribe other just terms and conditions;

        (B) grant a continuance;

        (C) prohibit that party from introducing the undisclosed evidence; or

        (D) enter any other order that is just under the circumstances.

Rule 17. Subpoena

(a) **Content.** A subpoena must state the court's name and the title of the proceeding, include the seal of the court, and command the witness to attend and testify at the time and place the subpoena specifies. The clerk must issue a blank subpoena – signed and sealed – to the party requesting it, and that party must fill in the blanks before the subpoena is served.

(b) **Defendant Unable to Pay.** Upon a defendant's ex parte application, the court must order that a subpoena be issued for a named witness if the defendant shows an inability to pay the witness's fees and the necessity of the witness's presence for an adequate defense. If the court orders a subpoena to be issued, the process costs and witness fees will be paid in the same manner as those paid for witnesses the government subpoenas.

(c) **Producing Documents and Objects.**

    (1) ***In General.*** A subpoena may order the witness to produce any books, papers, documents, data, or other objects the subpoena designates. The court may direct the witness to produce the designated items in court before trial or before they are to be offered in evidence. When the items arrive, the court may permit the parties and their attorneys to inspect all or part of them.

    (2) ***Quashing or Modifying the Subpoena.*** On motion made promptly, the court may quash or modify the subpoena if compliance would be unreasonable or oppressive.

    (3) ***Subpoena for Personal or Confidential Information About a Victim.*** After a complaint, indictment, or information is filed, a subpoena requiring the production of personal or confidential information about a victim may be served on a third party only by court order. Before entering the order and unless there are exceptional circumstances, the court must require giving notice to the victim so that the victim can move to quash or modify the subpoena or otherwise object.

(d) **Service.** A marshal, a deputy marshal, or any nonparty who is at least 18 years old may serve a subpoena. The server must deliver a copy of the subpoena to the witness and must tender to the witness one day's witness-attendance fee and the legal mileage allowance. The server need not tender the attendance fee or mileage allowance when the United States, a federal officer, or a federal agency has requested the subpoena.

(e) **Place of Service.**

(1) *In the United States.* A subpoena requiring a witness to attend a hearing or trial may be served at any place within the United States.

(2) *In a Foreign Country.* If the witness is in a foreign country, 28 U.S.C. § 1783 governs the subpoena's service.

(f) **Issuing a Deposition Subpoena.**

(1) *Issuance.* A court order to take a deposition authorizes the clerk in the district where the deposition is to be taken to issue a subpoena for any witness named or described in the order.

(2) *Place.* After considering the convenience of the witness and the parties, the court may order – and the subpoena may require – the witness to appear anywhere the court designates.

(g) **Contempt.** The court (other than a magistrate judge) may hold in contempt a witness who, without adequate excuse, disobeys a subpoena issued by a federal court in that district. A magistrate judge may hold in contempt a witness who, without adequate excuse, disobeys a subpoena issued by that magistrate judge as provided in 28 U.S.C. § 636(e).

(h) **Information Not Subject to a Subpoena.** No party may subpoena a statement of a witness or of a prospective witness under this rule. Rule 26.2 governs the production of the statement.

Rule 17.1. Pretrial Conference

On its own, or on a party's motion, the court may hold one or more pretrial conferences to promote a fair and expeditious trial. When a conference ends, the court must prepare and file a memorandum of any matters agreed to during the conference. The government may not use any statement made during the conference by the defendant or the defendant's attorney unless it is in writing and is signed by the defendant and the defendant's attorney.

Rule 18. Place of Prosecution and Trial

Unless a statute or these rules permit otherwise, the government must prosecute an offense in a district where the offense was committed. The court must set the place of trial within the district with due regard for the convenience of the defendant, any victim, and the witnesses, and the prompt administration of justice.

Rule 19. [Reserved]
Rule 20. Transfer for Plea and Sentence

(a) **Consent to Transfer.** A prosecution may be transferred from the district where the indictment or information is pending, or from which a warrant on a complaint has been issued, to the district where the defendant is arrested, held, or present if:

(1) the defendant states in writing a wish to plead guilty or nolo contendere and to waive trial in the district where the indictment, information, or complaint is pending, consents in writing to the court's disposing of the case in the transferee district, and files the statement in the transferee district; and

(2) the United States attorneys in both districts approve the transfer in writing.

(b) **Clerk's Duties.** After receiving the defendant's statement and the required approvals, the clerk where the indictment, information, or complaint is pending must send the file, or a certified copy, to the clerk in the transferee district.

(c) **Effect of a Not Guilty Plea.** If the defendant pleads not guilty after the case has been transferred under Rule 20(a), the clerk must return the papers to the court where the prosecution began, and that court must restore the proceeding to its docket. The defendant's statement that the defendant wished to plead guilty or nolo contendere is not, in any civil or criminal proceeding, admissible against the defendant.

(d) **Juveniles.**

    (1) ***Consent to Transfer.*** A juvenile, as defined in 18 U.S.C. § 5031, may be proceeded against as a juvenile delinquent in the district where the juvenile is arrested, held, or present if:

        (A) the alleged offense that occurred in the other district is not punishable by death or life imprisonment;

        (B) an attorney has advised the juvenile;

        (C) the court has informed the juvenile of the juvenile's rights – including the right to be returned to the district where the offense allegedly occurred – and the consequences of waiving those rights;

        (D) the juvenile, after receiving the court's information about rights, consents in writing to be proceeded against in the transferee district, and files the consent in the transferee district;

        (E) the United States attorneys for both districts approve the transfer in writing; and

        (F) the transferee court approves the transfer.

    (2) ***Clerk's Duties.*** After receiving the juvenile's written consent and the required approvals, the clerk where the indictment, information, or complaint is pending or where the alleged offense occurred must send the file, or a certified copy, to the clerk in the transferee district.

Rule 21. Transfer for Trial

(a) **For Prejudice.** Upon the defendant's motion, the court must transfer the proceeding against that defendant to another district if the court is satisfied that so great a prejudice against the defendant exists in the transferring district that the defendant cannot obtain a fair and impartial trial there.

(b) **For Convenience.** Upon the defendant's motion, the court may transfer the proceeding, or one or more counts, against that defendant to another district for the convenience of the parties, any victim, and the witnesses, and in the interest of justice.

(c) **Proceedings on Transfer.** When the court orders a transfer, the clerk must send to the transferee district the file, or a certified copy, and any bail taken. The prosecution will then continue in the transferee district.

(d) **Time to File a Motion to Transfer.** A motion to transfer may be made at or before arraignment or at any other time the court or these rules prescribe.

Rule 22. [Transferred]

Rule 23. Jury or Nonjury Trial

(a) **Jury Trial.** If the defendant is entitled to a jury trial, the trial must be by jury unless:

    (1) the defendant waives a jury trial in writing;

    (2) the government consents; and

    (3) the court approves.

(b) **Jury Size.**

    (1) ***In General.*** A jury consists of 12 persons unless this rule provides otherwise.

    (2) ***Stipulation for a Smaller Jury.*** At any time before the verdict, the parties may, with the court's approval, stipulate in writing that:

        (A) the jury may consist of fewer than 12 persons; or

        (B) a jury of fewer than 12 persons may return a verdict if the court finds it necessary to excuse a juror for good cause after the trial begins.

(3) *Court Order for a Jury of 11.* After the jury has retired to deliberate, the court may permit a jury of 11 persons to return a verdict, even without a stipulation by the parties, if the court finds good cause to excuse a juror.

(c) **Nonjury Trial.** In a case tried without a jury, the court must find the defendant guilty or not guilty. If a party requests before the finding of guilty or not guilty, the court must state its specific findings of fact in open court or in a written decision or opinion.

Rule 24. Trial Jurors

(a) **Examination.**

(1) *In General.* The court may examine prospective jurors or may permit the attorneys for the parties to do so.

(2) *Court Examination.* If the court examines the jurors, it must permit the attorneys for the parties to:

(A) ask further questions that the court considers proper; or

(B) submit further questions that the court may ask if it considers them proper.

(b) **Peremptory Challenges.** Each side is entitled to the number of peremptory challenges to prospective jurors specified below. The court may allow additional peremptory challenges to multiple defendants and may allow the defendants to exercise those challenges separately or jointly.

(1) *Capital Case.* Each side has 20 peremptory challenges when the government seeks the death penalty.

(2) *Other Felony Case.* The government has 6 peremptory challenges, and the defendant or defendants jointly have 10 peremptory challenges when the defendant is charged with a crime punishable by imprisonment of more than one year.

(3) *Misdemeanor Case.* Each side has 3 peremptory challenges when the defendant is charged with a crime punishable by fine, imprisonment of one year or less, or both.

(c) **Alternate Jurors.**

(1) *In General.* The court may impanel up to 6 alternate jurors to replace any jurors who are unable to perform or who are disqualified from performing their duties.

(2) *Procedure.* (A) Alternate jurors must have the same qualifications and be selected and sworn in the same manner as any other juror. (B) Alternate jurors replace jurors in the same sequence in which the alternates were selected. An alternate juror who replaces a juror has the same authority as the other jurors.

(3) *Retaining Alternate Jurors.* The court may retain alternate jurors after the jury retires to deliberate. The court must ensure that a retained alternate does not discuss the case with anyone until that alternate replaces a juror or is discharged. If an alternate replaces a juror after deliberations have begun, the court must instruct the jury to begin its deliberations anew.

(4) *Peremptory Challenges.* Each side is entitled to the number of additional peremptory challenges to prospective alternate jurors specified below. These additional challenges may be used only to remove alternate jurors.

(A) *One or Two Alternates.* One additional peremptory challenge is permitted when one or two alternates are impaneled.

(B) *Three or Four Alternates.* Two additional peremptory challenges are permitted when three or four alternates are impaneled.

(C) *Five or Six Alternates.* Three additional peremptory challenges are permitted when five or six alternates are impaneled.

Rule 25. Judge's Disability

(a) **During Trial.** Any judge regularly sitting in or assigned to the court may complete a jury trial if:

   (1) the judge before whom the trial began cannot proceed because of death, sickness, or other disability; and

   (2) the judge completing the trial certifies familiarity with the trial record.

(b) **After a Verdict or Finding of Guilty.**

   (1) *In General.* After a verdict or finding of guilty, any judge regularly sitting in or assigned to a court may complete the court's duties if the judge who presided at trial cannot perform those duties because of absence, death, sickness, or other disability.

   (2) *Granting a New Trial.* The successor judge may grant a new trial if satisfied that:

      (A) a judge other than the one who presided at the trial cannot perform the post-trial duties; or

      (B) a new trial is necessary for some other reason.

Rule 26. Taking Testimony

In every trial the testimony of witnesses must be taken in open court, unless otherwise provided by a statute or by rules adopted under 28 U.S.C. §§ 2072–2077.

Rule 26.1. Foreign Law Determination

A party intending to raise an issue of foreign law must provide the court and all parties with reasonable written notice. Issues of foreign law are questions of law, but in deciding such issues a court may consider any relevant material or source – including testimony – without regard to the Federal Rules of Evidence.

Rule 26.2. Producing a Witness's Statement

(a) **Motion to Produce.** After a witness other than the defendant has testified on direct examination, the court, on motion of a party who did not call the witness, must order an attorney for the government or the defendant and the defendant's attorney to produce, for the examination and use of the moving party, any statement of the witness that is in their possession and that relates to the subject matter of the witness's testimony.

(b) **Producing the Entire Statement.** If the entire statement relates to the subject matter of the witness's testimony, the court must order that the statement be delivered to the moving party.

(c) **Producing a Redacted Statement.** If the party who called the witness claims that the statement contains information that is privileged or does not relate to the subject matter of the witness's testimony, the court must inspect the statement in camera. After excising any privileged or unrelated portions, the court must order delivery of the redacted statement to the moving party. If the defendant objects to an excision, the court must preserve the entire statement with the excised portion indicated, under seal, as part of the record.

(d) **Recess to Examine a Statement.** The court may recess the proceedings to allow time for a party to examine the statement and prepare for its use.

(e) **Sanction for Failure to Produce or Deliver a Statement.** If the party who called the witness disobeys an order to produce or deliver a statement, the court must strike the witness's testimony from the record. If an attorney for the government disobeys the order, the court must declare a mistrial if justice so requires.

(f) **"Statement" Defined.** As used in this rule, a witness's "statement" means:

    (1) a written statement that the witness makes and signs, or otherwise adopts or approves;

    (2) a substantially verbatim, contemporaneously recorded recital of the witness's oral statement that is contained in any recording or any transcription of a recording; or

    (3) the witness's statement to a grand jury, however taken or recorded, or a transcription of such a statement.

(g) **Scope.** This rule applies at trial, at a suppression hearing under Rule 12, and to the extent specified in the following rules: (1) Rule 5.1(h) (preliminary hearing); (2) Rule 32(i)(2) (sentencing); (3) Rule 32.1(e) (hearing to revoke or modify probation or supervised release); (4) Rule 46(j) (detention hearing); and (5) Rule 8 of the Rules Governing Proceedings under 28 U.S.C. § 2255.

Rule 26.3. Mistrial

Before ordering a mistrial, the court must give each defendant and the government an opportunity to comment on the propriety of the order, to state whether that party consents or objects, and to suggest alternatives.

Rule 27. Proving an Official Record

A party may prove an official record, an entry in such a record, or the lack of a record or entry in the same manner as in a civil action. (As amended Apr. 29, 2002, eff. Dec. 1, 2002.)

Rule 28. Interpreters

The court may select, appoint, and set the reasonable compensation for an interpreter, including an interpreter for the victim. The compensation must be paid from funds provided by law or by the government, as the court may direct.

Rule 29. Motion for a Judgment of Acquittal

(a) **Before Submission to the Jury.** After the government closes its evidence or after the close of all the evidence, the court on the defendant's motion must enter a judgment of acquittal of any offense for which the evidence is insufficient to sustain a conviction. The court may on its own consider whether the evidence is insufficient to sustain a conviction. If the court denies a motion for a judgment of acquittal at the close of the government's evidence, the defendant may offer evidence without having reserved the right to do so.

(b) **Reserving Decision.** The court may reserve decision on the motion, proceed with the trial (where the motion is made before the close of all the evidence), submit the case to the jury, and decide the motion either before the jury returns a verdict or after it returns a verdict of guilty or is discharged without having returned a verdict. If the court reserves decision, it must decide the motion on the basis of the evidence at the time the ruling was reserved.

(c) **After Jury Verdict or Discharge.**

    (1) *Time for a Motion.* A defendant may move for a judgment of acquittal, or renew such a motion, within 14 days after a guilty verdict or after the court discharges the jury, whichever is later.

    (2) *Ruling on the Motion.* If the jury has returned a guilty verdict, the court may set aside the verdict and enter an acquittal. If the jury has failed to return a verdict, the court may enter a judgment of acquittal.

    (3) *No Prior Motion Required.* A defendant is not required to move for a judgment of acquittal before the court submits the case to the jury as a prerequisite for making such a motion after jury discharge.

(d) **Conditional Ruling on a Motion for a New Trial.**

    (1) *Motion for a New Trial.* If the court enters a judgment of acquittal after a guilty verdict, the court must also conditionally determine whether any motion for a new trial should be granted if the judgment of acquittal is later vacated or reversed. The court must specify the reasons for that determination.

    (2) *Finality.* The court's order conditionally granting a motion for a new trial does not affect the finality of the judgment of acquittal.

    (3) *Appeal.*

        (A) *Grant of a Motion for a New Trial.* If the court conditionally grants a motion for a new trial and an appellate court later reverses the judgment of acquittal, the trial court must proceed with the new trial unless the appellate court orders otherwise.

        (B) *Denial of a Motion for a New Trial.* If the court conditionally denies a motion for a new trial, an appellee may assert that the denial was erroneous. If the appellate court later reverses the judgment of acquittal, the trial court must proceed as the appellate court directs.

Rule 29.1. Closing Argument

Closing arguments proceed in the following order:

(a) the government argues;

(b) the defense argues; and

(c) the government rebuts.

Rule 30. Jury Instructions

(a) **In General.** Any party may request in writing that the court instruct the jury on the law as specified in the request. The request must be made at the close of the evidence or at any earlier time that the court reasonably sets. When the request is made, the requesting party must furnish a copy to every other party.

(b) **Ruling on a Request.** The court must inform the parties before closing arguments how it intends to rule on the requested instructions.

(c) **Time for Giving Instructions.** The court may instruct the jury before or after the arguments are completed, or at both times.

(d) **Objections to Instructions.** A party who objects to any portion of the instructions or to a failure to give a requested instruction must inform the court of the specific objection and the grounds for the objection before the jury retires to deliberate. An opportunity must be given to object out of the jury's hearing and, on request, out of the jury's presence. Failure to object in accordance with this rule precludes appellate review, except as permitted under Rule 52(b).

Rule 31. Jury Verdict

(a) **Return.** The jury must return its verdict to a judge in open court. The verdict must be unanimous.

(b) **Partial Verdicts, Mistrial, and Retrial.**

    (1) *Multiple Defendants.* If there are multiple defendants, the jury may return a verdict at any time during its deliberations as to any defendant about whom it has agreed.

    (2) *Multiple Counts.* If the jury cannot agree on all counts as to any defendant, the jury may return a verdict on those counts on which it has agreed.

(3) **Mistrial and Retrial.** If the jury cannot agree on a verdict on one or more counts, the court may declare a mistrial on those counts. The government may retry any defendant on any count on which the jury could not agree.

(c) **Lesser Offense or Attempt.** A defendant may be found guilty of any of the following:

(1) an offense necessarily included in the offense charged;

(2) an attempt to commit the offense charged; or

(3) an attempt to commit an offense necessarily included in the offense charged, if the attempt is an offense in its own right.

(d) **Jury Poll.** After a verdict is returned but before the jury is discharged, the court must on a party's request, or may on its own, poll the jurors individually. If the poll reveals a lack of unanimity, the court may direct the jury to deliberate further or may declare a mistrial and discharge the jury.

Rule 32. Sentencing and Judgment

(a) **[Reserved.]**

(b) **Time of Sentencing.**

(1) **In General.** The court must impose sentence without unnecessary delay.

(2) **Changing Time Limits.** The court may, for good cause, change any time limits prescribed in this rule.

(c) **Presentence Investigation.**

(1) **Required Investigation.**

(A) *In General.* The probation officer must conduct a presentence investigation and submit a report to the court before it imposes sentence unless:

(i) 18 U.S.C. § 3593(c) or another statute requires otherwise; or

(ii) the court finds that the information in the record enables it to meaningfully exercise its sentencing authority under 18 U.S.C. § 3553, and the court explains its finding on the record.

(B) *Restitution.* If the law permits restitution, the probation officer must conduct an investigation and submit a report that contains sufficient information for the court to order restitution.

(2) **Interviewing the Defendant.** The probation officer who interviews a defendant as part of a presentence investigation must, on request, give the defendant's attorney notice and a reasonable opportunity to attend the interview.

(d) **Presentence Report.**

(1) **Applying the Advisory Sentencing Guidelines.** The presentence report must:

(A) identify all applicable guidelines and policy statements of the Sentencing Commission;

(B) calculate the defendant's offense level and criminal history category;

(C) state the resulting sentencing range and kinds of sentences available;

(D) identify any factor relevant to:

(i) the appropriate kind of sentence, or

(ii) the appropriate sentence within the applicable sentencing range; and

(E) identify any basis for departing from the applicable sentencing range.

(2) **Additional Information.** The presentence report must also contain the following:

(A) the defendant's history and characteristics, including:

    (i) any prior criminal record;

    (ii) the defendant's financial condition; and

    (iii) any circumstances affecting the defendant's behavior that may be helpful in imposing sentence or in correctional treatment;

(B) information that assesses any financial, social, psychological, and medical impact on any victim;

(C) when appropriate, the nature and extent of non-prison programs and resources available to the defendant;

(D) when the law provides for restitution, information sufficient for a restitution order;

(E) if the court orders a study under 18 U.S.C. § 3552(b), any resulting report and recommendation;

(F) a statement of whether the government seeks forfeiture under Rule 32.2 and any other law; and

(G) any other information that the court requires, including information relevant to the factors under 18 U.S.C. § 3553(a).

(3) *Exclusions.* The presentence report must exclude the following:

(A) any diagnoses that, if disclosed, might seriously disrupt a rehabilitation program;

(B) any sources of information obtained upon a promise of confidentiality; and

(C) any other information that, if disclosed, might result in physical or other harm to the defendant or others.

(e) **Disclosing the Report and Recommendation.**

(1) *Time to Disclose.* Unless the defendant has consented in writing, the probation officer must not submit a presentence report to the court or disclose its contents to anyone until the defendant has pleaded guilty or nolo contendere or has been found guilty.

(2) *Minimum Required Notice.* The probation officer must give the presentence report to the defendant, the defendant's attorney, and an attorney for the government at least 35 days before sentencing unless the defendant waives this minimum period.

(3) *Sentence Recommendation.* By local rule or by order in a case, the court may direct the probation officer not to disclose to anyone other than the court the officer's recommendation on the sentence.

(f) **Objecting to the Report.**

(1) *Time to Object.* Within 14 days after receiving the presentence report, the parties must state in writing any objections, including objections to material information, sentencing guideline ranges, and policy statements contained in or omitted from the report.

(2) *Serving Objections.* An objecting party must provide a copy of its objections to the opposing party and to the probation officer.

(3) *Action on Objections.* After receiving objections, the probation officer may meet with the parties to discuss the objections. The probation officer may then investigate further and revise the presentence report as appropriate.

(g) **Submitting the Report.** At least 7 days before sentencing, the probation officer must submit to the court and to the parties the presentence report and an addendum containing any unresolved objections, the grounds for those objections, and the probation officer's comments on them.

(h) **Notice of Possible Departure from Sentencing Guidelines.** Before the court may depart from the applicable sentencing range on a ground not identified for departure either in the presentence report or in a party's prehearing submission, the court must give the parties reasonable notice that it is contemplating such a departure. The notice must specify any ground on which the court is contemplating a departure.

(i) **Sentencing.**

    (1) ***In General.*** At sentencing, the court:

        (A) must verify that the defendant and the defendant's attorney have read and discussed the presentence report and any addendum to the report;

        (B) must give to the defendant and an attorney for the government a written summary of – or summarize in camera – any information excluded from the presentence report under Rule 32(d)(3) on which the court will rely in sentencing, and give them a reasonable opportunity to comment on that information;

        (C) must allow the parties' attorneys to comment on the probation officer's determinations and other matters relating to an appropriate sentence; and

        (D) may, for good cause, allow a party to make a new objection at any time before sentence is imposed.

    (2) ***Introducing Evidence; Producing a Statement.*** The court may permit the parties to introduce evidence on the objections. If a witness testifies at sentencing, Rule 26.2(a)–(d) and (f) applies. If a party fails to comply with a Rule 26.2 order to produce a witness's statement, the court must not consider that witness's testimony.

    (3) ***Court Determinations.*** At sentencing, the court:

        (A) may accept any undisputed portion of the presentence report as a finding of fact;

        (B) must – for any disputed portion of the presentence report or other controverted matter – rule on the dispute or determine that a ruling is unnecessary either because the matter will not affect sentencing, or because the court will not consider the matter in sentencing; and

        (C) must append a copy of the court's determinations under this rule to any copy of the presentence report made available to the Bureau of Prisons.

    (4) ***Opportunity to Speak.***

        (A) *By a Party*. Before imposing sentence, the court must:

            (i) provide the defendant's attorney an opportunity to speak on the defendant's behalf;

            (ii) address the defendant personally in order to permit the defendant to speak or present any information to mitigate the sentence; and

            (iii) provide an attorney for the government an opportunity to speak equivalent to that of the defendant's attorney.

        (B) *By a Victim*. Before imposing sentence, the court must address any victim of the crime who is present at sentencing and must permit the victim to be reasonably heard.

        (C) *In Camera Proceedings*. Upon a party's motion and for good cause, the court may hear in camera any statement made under Rule 32(i)(4).

(j) **Defendant's Right to Appeal.**

    (1) ***Advice of a Right to Appeal.***

(A) *Appealing a Conviction.* If the defendant pleaded not guilty and was convicted, after sentencing the court must advise the defendant of the right to appeal the conviction.

(B) *Appealing a Sentence.* After sentencing – regardless of the defendant's plea – the court must advise the defendant of any right to appeal the sentence.

(C) *Appeal Costs.* The court must advise a defendant who is unable to pay appeal costs of the right to ask for permission to appeal in forma pauperis.

(2) **Clerk's Filing of Notice.** If the defendant so requests, the clerk must immediately prepare and file a notice of appeal on the defendant's behalf.

(k) **Judgment.**

(1) **In General.** In the judgment of conviction, the court must set forth the plea, the jury verdict or the court's findings, the adjudication, and the sentence. If the defendant is found not guilty or is otherwise entitled to be discharged, the court must so order. The judge must sign the judgment, and the clerk must enter it.

(2) **Criminal Forfeiture.** Forfeiture procedures are governed by Rule 32.2.

Rule 32.1. Revoking or Modifying Probation or Supervised Release

(a) **Initial Appearance.**

(1) **Person in Custody.** A person held in custody for violating probation or supervised release must be taken without unnecessary delay before a magistrate judge.

(A) If the person is held in custody in the district where an alleged violation occurred, the initial appearance must be in that district.

(B) If the person is held in custody in a district other than where an alleged violation occurred, the initial appearance must be in that district, or in an adjacent district if the appearance can occur more promptly there.

(2) **Upon a Summons.** When a person appears in response to a summons for violating probation or supervised release, a magistrate judge must proceed under this rule.

(3) **Advice.** The judge must inform the person of the following:

(A) the alleged violation of probation or supervised release;

(B) the person's right to retain counsel or to request that counsel be appointed if the person cannot obtain counsel; and

(C) the person's right, if held in custody, to a preliminary hearing under Rule 32.1(b)(1).

(4) **Appearance in the District with Jurisdiction.** If the person is arrested or appears in the district that has jurisdiction to conduct a revocation hearing – either originally or by transfer of jurisdiction – the court must proceed under Rule 32.1(b)–(e).

(5) **Appearance in a District Lacking Jurisdiction.** If the person is arrested or appears in a district that does not have jurisdiction to conduct a revocation hearing, the magistrate judge must:

(A) if the alleged violation occurred in the district of arrest, conduct a preliminary hearing under Rule 32.1(b) and either:

(i) transfer the person to the district that has jurisdiction, if the judge finds probable cause to believe that a violation occurred; or

      (ii) dismiss the proceedings and so notify the court that has jurisdiction, if the judge finds no probable cause to believe that a violation occurred; or

   (B) if the alleged violation did not occur in the district of arrest, transfer the person to the district that has jurisdiction if:

      (i) the government produces certified copies of the judgment, warrant, and warrant application, or produces copies of those certified documents by reliable electronic means; and

      (ii) the judge finds that the person is the same person named in the warrant.

  (6) ***Release or Detention.*** The magistrate judge may release or detain the person under 18 U.S.C. § 3143(a)(1) pending further proceedings. The burden of establishing by clear and convincing evidence that the person will not flee or pose a danger to any other person or to the community rests with the person.

(b) Revocation.

  (1) ***Preliminary Hearing.***

   (A) *In General.* If a person is in custody for violating a condition of probation or supervised release, a magistrate judge must promptly conduct a hearing to determine whether there is probable cause to believe that a violation occurred. The person may waive the hearing.

   (B) *Requirements.* The hearing must be recorded by a court reporter or by a suitable recording device. The judge must give the person:

      (i) notice of the hearing and its purpose, the alleged violation, and the person's right to retain counsel or to request that counsel be appointed if the person cannot obtain counsel; (ii) an opportunity to appear at the hearing and present evidence; and

      (ii) upon request, an opportunity to question any adverse witness, unless the judge determines that the interest of justice does not require the witness to appear.

   (C) *Referral.* If the judge finds probable cause, the judge must conduct a revocation hearing. If the judge does not find probable cause, the judge must dismiss the proceeding.

  (2) ***Revocation Hearing.*** Unless waived by the person, the court must hold the revocation hearing within a reasonable time in the district having jurisdiction. The person is entitled to:

   (A) written notice of the alleged violation;

   (B) disclosure of the evidence against the person;

   (C) an opportunity to appear, present evidence, and question any adverse witness unless the court determines that the interest of justice does not require the witness to appear;

   (D) notice of the person's right to retain counsel or to request that counsel be appointed if the person cannot obtain counsel; and

   (E) an opportunity to make a statement and present any information in mitigation.

(c) Modification.

  (1) ***In General.*** Before modifying the conditions of probation or supervised release, the court must hold a hearing, at which the person has the right to counsel and an opportunity to make a statement and present any information in mitigation.

  (2) ***Exceptions.*** A hearing is not required if:

   (A) the person waives the hearing; or

    (B) the relief sought is favorable to the person and does not extend the term of probation or of supervised release; and

    (C) an attorney for the government has received notice of the relief sought, has had a reasonable opportunity to object, and has not done so.

(d) **Disposition of the Case.** The court's disposition of the case is governed by 18 U.S.C. § 3563 and § 3565 (probation) and § 3583 (supervised release).

(e) **Producing a Statement.** Rule 26.2(a)–(d) and (f) applies at a hearing under this rule. If a party fails to comply with a Rule 26.2 order to produce a witness's statement, the court must not consider that witness's testimony.

Rule 32.2. Criminal Forfeiture

(a) **Notice to the Defendant.** A court must not enter a judgment of forfeiture in a criminal proceeding unless the indictment or information contains notice to the defendant that the government will seek the forfeiture of property as part of any sentence in accordance with the applicable statute. The notice should not be designated as a count of the indictment or information. The indictment or information need not identify the property subject to forfeiture or specify the amount of any forfeiture money judgment that the government seeks.

(b) **Entering a Preliminary Order of Forfeiture.**

    (1) *Forfeiture Phase of the Trial.*

        (A) *Forfeiture Determinations.* As soon as practical after a verdict or finding of guilty, or after a plea of guilty or nolo contendere is accepted, on any count in an indictment or information regarding which criminal forfeiture is sought, the court must determine what property is subject to forfeiture under the applicable statute. If the government seeks forfeiture of specific property, the court must determine whether the government has established the requisite nexus between the property and the offense. If the government seeks a personal money judgment, the court must determine the amount of money that the defendant will be ordered to pay.

        (B) *Evidence and Hearing.* The court's determination may be based on evidence already in the record, including any written plea agreement, and on any additional evidence or information submitted by the parties and accepted by the court as relevant and reliable. If the forfeiture is contested, on either party's request the court must conduct a hearing after the verdict or finding of guilty.

    (2) *Preliminary Order.*

        (A) *Contents of a Specific Order.* If the court finds that property is subject to forfeiture, it must promptly enter a preliminary order of forfeiture setting forth the amount of any money judgment, directing the forfeiture of specific property, and directing the forfeiture of any substitute property if the government has met the statutory criteria. The court must enter the order without regard to any third party's interest in the property. Determining whether a third party has such an interest must be deferred until any third-party files a claim in an ancillary proceeding under Rule 32.2(c).

        (B) *Timing.* Unless doing so is impractical, the court must enter the preliminary order sufficiently in advance of sentencing to allow the parties to suggest revisions or modifications before the order becomes final as to the defendant under Rule 32.2(b)(4).

(C) *General Order.* If, before sentencing, the court cannot identify all the specific property subject to forfeiture or calculate the total amount of the money judgment, the court may enter a forfeiture order that:

    (i) lists any identified property;

    (ii) describes other property in general terms; and

    (iii) states that the order will be amended under Rule 32.2(e)(1) when additional specific property is identified, or the amount of the money judgment has been calculated.

(3) **Seizing Property.** The entry of a preliminary order of forfeiture authorizes the Attorney General (or a designee) to seize the specific property subject to forfeiture; to conduct any discovery the court considers proper in identifying, locating, or disposing of the property; and to commence proceedings that comply with any statutes governing third-party rights. The court may include in the order of forfeiture conditions reasonably necessary to preserve the property's value pending any appeal.

(4) **Sentence and Judgment.**

(A) *When Final.* At sentencing – or at any time before sentencing if the defendant consents – the preliminary forfeiture order becomes final as to the defendant. If the order directs the defendant to forfeit specific property, it remains preliminary as to third parties until the ancillary proceeding is concluded under Rule 32.2(c).

(B) *Notice and Inclusion in the Judgment.* The court must include the forfeiture when orally announcing the sentence or must otherwise ensure that the defendant knows of the forfeiture at sentencing. The court must also include the forfeiture order, directly or by reference, in the judgment, but the court's failure to do so may be corrected at any time under Rule 36.

(C) *Time to Appeal.* The time for the defendant or the government to file an appeal from the forfeiture order, or from the court's failure to enter an order, begins to run when judgment is entered. If the court later amends or declines to amend a forfeiture order to include additional property under Rule 32.2(e), the defendant or the government may file an appeal regarding that property under Federal Rule of Appellate Procedure 4(b). The time for that appeal runs from the date when the order granting or denying the amendment becomes final.

(5) **Jury Determination.**

(A) *Retaining the Jury.* In any case tried before a jury, if the indictment or information states that the government is seeking forfeiture, the court must determine before the jury begins deliberating whether either party requests that the jury be retained to determine the forfeitability of specific property if it returns a guilty verdict.

(B) *Special Verdict Form.* If a party timely requests to have the jury determine forfeiture, the government must submit a proposed Special Verdict Form listing each property subject to forfeiture and asking the jury to determine whether the government has established the requisite nexus between the property and the offense committed by the defendant.

(6) **Notice of the Forfeiture Order.**

(A) *Publishing and Sending Notice.* If the court orders the forfeiture of specific property, the government must publish notice of the order and send notice to any person who reasonably appears to be a potential claimant withstanding to contest the forfeiture in the ancillary proceeding.

    (B) *Content of the Notice.* The notice must describe the forfeited property, state the times under the applicable statute when a petition contesting the forfeiture must be filed, and state the name and contact information for the government attorney to be served with the petition.

    (C) *Means of Publication; Exceptions to Publication Requirement.* Publication must take place as described in Supplemental Rule G(4)(a)(iii) of the Federal Rules of Civil Procedure and may be by any means described in Supplemental Rule G(4)(a)(iv). Publication is unnecessary if any exception in Supplemental Rule G(4)(a)(i) applies.

    (D) *Means of Sending the Notice.* The notice may be sent in accordance with Supplemental Rules G(4)(b)(iii)–(v) of the Federal Rules of Civil Procedure.

(7) **Interlocutory Sale.** At any time before entry of a final forfeiture order, the court, in accordance with Supplemental Rule G(7) of the Federal Rules of Civil Procedure, may order the interlocutory sale of property alleged to be forfeitable.

(c) **Ancillary Proceeding; Entering a Final Order of Forfeiture.**

(1) **In General.** If, as prescribed by statute, a third-party files a petition asserting an interest in the property to be forfeited, the court must conduct an ancillary proceeding, but no ancillary proceeding is required to the extent that the forfeiture consists of a money judgment.

    (A) In the ancillary proceeding, the court may, on motion, dismiss the petition for lack of standing, for failure to state a claim, or for any other lawful reason. For purposes of the motion, the facts set forth in the petition are assumed to be true.

    (B) After disposing of any motion filed under Rule 32.2(c)(1)(A) and before conducting a hearing on the petition, the court may permit the parties to conduct discovery in accordance with the Federal Rules of Civil Procedure if the court determines that discovery is necessary or desirable to resolve factual issues. When discovery ends, a party may move for summary judgment under Federal Rule of Civil Procedure 56.

(2) **Entering a Final Order.** When the ancillary proceeding ends, the court must enter a final order of forfeiture by amending the preliminary order as necessary to account for any third-party rights. If no third party files a timely petition, the preliminary order becomes the final order of forfeiture if the court finds that the defendant (or any combination of defendants convicted in the case) had an interest in the property that is forfeitable under the applicable statute. The defendant may not object to the entry of the final order on the ground that the property belongs, in whole or in part, to a codefendant or third party; nor may a third party object to the final order on the ground that the third party had an interest in the property.

(3) **Multiple Petitions.** If multiple third-party petitions are filed in the same case, an order dismissing or granting one petition is not appealable until rulings are made on all the petitions, unless the court determines that there is no just reason for delay.

(4) **Ancillary Proceeding Not Part of Sentencing.** An ancillary proceeding is not part of sentencing.

(d) **Stay Pending Appeal.** If a defendant appeals from a conviction or an order of forfeiture, the court may stay the order of forfeiture on terms appropriate to ensure that the property remains available pending appellate review. A stay does not delay the ancillary proceeding or the determination of a third party's rights or interests. If the court rules in favor of any third party while an appeal is pending, the court may amend the order of forfeiture but must not transfer any property interest to a third party until the decision on appeal becomes final, unless the defendant consents in writing or on the record.

(e) **Subsequently Located Property; Substitute Property.**

(1) *In General.* On the government's motion, the court may at any time enter an order of forfeiture or amend an existing order of forfeiture to include property that: (A) is subject to forfeiture under an existing order of forfeiture but was located and identified after that order was entered; or (B) is substitute property that qualifies for forfeiture under an applicable statute.

(2) *Procedure.* If the government shows that the property is subject to forfeiture under Rule 32.2(e)(1), the court must: (A) enter an order forfeiting that property, or amend an existing preliminary or final order to include it; and (B) if a third party files a petition claiming an interest in the property, conduct an ancillary proceeding under Rule 32.2(c).

(3) *Jury Trial Limited.* There is no right to a jury trial under Rule 32.2(e).

Rule 33. New Trial

(a) **Defendant's Motion.** Upon the defendant's motion, the court may vacate any judgment and grant a new trial if the interest of justice so requires. If the case was tried without a jury, the court may take additional testimony and enter a new judgment.

(b) **Time to File.**

(1) *Newly Discovered Evidence.* Any motion for a new trial grounded on newly discovered evidence must be filed within 3 years after the verdict or finding of guilty. If an appeal is pending, the court may not grant a motion for a new trial until the appellate court remands the case.

(2) *Other Grounds.* Any motion for a new trial grounded on any reason other than newly discovered evidence must be filed within 14 days after the verdict or finding of guilty.

Rule 34. Arresting Judgment

(a) **In General.** Upon the defendant's motion or on its own, the court must arrest judgment if the court does not have jurisdiction of the charged offense.

(b) **Time to File.** The defendant must move to arrest judgment within 14 days after the court accepts a verdict or finding of guilty, or after a plea of guilty or nolo contendere.

Rule 35. Correcting or Reducing a Sentence

(a) **Correcting Clear Error.** Within 14 days after sentencing, the court may correct a sentence that resulted from arithmetical, technical, or other clear error.

(b) **Reducing a Sentence for Substantial Assistance.**

(1) *In General.* Upon the government's motion made within one year of sentencing, the court may reduce a sentence if the defendant, after sentencing, provided substantial assistance in investigating or prosecuting another person.

(2) *Later Motion.* Upon the government's motion made more than one year after sentencing, the court may reduce a sentence if the defendant's substantial assistance involved:

(A) information not known to the defendant until one year or more after sentencing;

(B) information provided by the defendant to the government within one year of sentencing, but which did not become useful to the government until more than one year after sentencing; or

(C) information the usefulness of which could not reasonably have been anticipated by the defendant until more than one year after sentencing and which was promptly provided to the government after its usefulness was reasonably apparent to the defendant.

(3) *Evaluating Substantial Assistance.* In evaluating whether the defendant has provided substantial assistance, the court may consider the defendant's presentence assistance.

(4) *Below Statutory Minimum.* When acting under Rule 35(b), the court may reduce the sentence to a level below the minimum sentence established by statute.

(c) **"Sentencing" Defined.** As used in this rule, "sentencing" means the oral announcement of the sentence.

Rule 36. Clerical Error

After giving any notice it considers appropriate, the court may at any time correct a clerical error in a judgment, order, or other part of the record, or correct an error in the record arising from oversight or omission.

Rule 37. Indicative Ruling on a Motion for Relief That Is Barred by a Pending Appeal

(a) **Relief Pending Appeal.** If a timely motion is made for relief that the court lacks authority to grant because of an appeal that has been docketed and is pending, the court may:

(1) defer considering the motion;

(2) deny the motion; or

(3) state either that it would grant the motion if the court of appeals remands for that purpose or that the motion raises a substantial issue.

(b) **Notice to the Court of Appeals.** The movant must promptly notify the circuit clerk under Federal Rule of Appellate Procedure 12.1 if the district court states that it would grant the motion or that the motion raises a substantial issue.

(c) **Remand.** The district court may decide the motion if the court of appeals remands for that purpose.

Rule 38. Staying a Sentence or a Disability

(a) **Death Sentence.** The court must stay a death sentence if the defendant appeals the conviction or sentence.

(b) **Imprisonment.**

(1) *Stay Granted.* If the defendant is released pending appeal, the court must stay a sentence of imprisonment.

(2) *Stay Denied; Place of Confinement.* If the defendant is not released pending appeal, the court may recommend to the Attorney General that the defendant be confined near the place of the trial or appeal for a period reasonably necessary to permit the defendant to assist in preparing the appeal.

(c) **Fine.** If the defendant appeals, the district court, or the court of appeals under Federal Rule of Appellate Procedure 8, may stay a sentence to pay a fine or a fine and costs. The court may stay the sentence on any terms considered appropriate and may require the defendant to:

(1) deposit all or part of the fine and costs into the district court's registry pending appeal;

(2) post a bond to pay the fine and costs; or

(3) submit to an examination concerning the defendant's assets and, if appropriate, order the defendant to refrain from dissipating assets.

(d) **Probation.** If the defendant appeals, the court may stay a sentence of probation. The court must set the terms of any stay.

(e) **Restitution and Notice to Victims.**

(1) *In General.* If the defendant appeals, the district court, or the court of appeals under Federal Rule of Appellate Procedure 8, may stay – on any terms considered appropriate – any sentence providing for restitution under 18 U.S.C. § 3556 or notice under 18 U.S.C. § 3555.

(2) ***Ensuring Compliance.*** The court may issue any order reasonably necessary to ensure compliance with a restitution order or a notice order after disposition of an appeal, including:

    (A) a restraining order;

    (B) an injunction;

    (C) an order requiring the defendant to deposit all or part of any monetary restitution into the district court's registry; or

    (D) an order requiring the defendant to post a bond.

(f) **Forfeiture.** A stay of a forfeiture order is governed by Rule 32.2(d).

(g) **Disability.** If the defendant's conviction or sentence creates a civil or employment disability under federal law, the district court, or the court of appeals under Federal Rule of Appellate Procedure 8, may stay the disability pending appeal on any terms considered appropriate. The court may issue any order reasonably necessary to protect the interest represented by the disability pending appeal, including a restraining order or an injunction.

Rule 39. [Reserved]

Rule 40. Arrest for Failing to Appear in Another District or for Violating Conditions of Release Set in Another District

(a) **In General.** A person must be taken without unnecessary delay before a magistrate judge in the district of arrest if the person has been arrested under a warrant issued in another district for: (i) failing to appear as required by the terms of that person's release under 18 U.S.C. §§ 3141–3156 or by a subpoena; or (ii) violating conditions of release set in another district.

(b) **Proceedings.** The judge must proceed under Rule 5(c)(3) as applicable.

(c) **Release or Detention Order.** The judge may modify any previous release or detention order issued in another district but must state in writing the reasons for doing so.

(d) **Video Teleconferencing.** Video teleconferencing may be used to conduct an appearance under this rule if the defendant consents.

Rule 41. Search and Seizure

(a) **Scope and Definitions.**

    (1) ***Scope.*** This rule does not modify any statute regulating search or seizure, or the issuance and execution of a search warrant in special circumstances.

    (2) ***Definitions.*** The following definitions apply under this rule:

        (A) "Property" includes documents, books, papers, any other tangible objects, and information.

        (B) "Daytime" means the hours between 6:00 a.m. and 10:00 p.m. according to local time.

        (C) "Federal law enforcement officer" means a government agent (other than an attorney for the government) who is engaged in enforcing the criminal laws and is within any category of officers authorized by the Attorney General to request a search warrant.

        (D) "Domestic terrorism" and "international terrorism" have the meanings set out in 18 U.S.C. § 2331.

        (E) "Tracking device" has the meaning set out in 18 U.S.C. § 3117(b).

(b) **Venue for a Warrant Application.** At the request of a federal law enforcement officer or an attorney for the government:

(1) a magistrate judge with authority in the district – or if none is reasonably available, a judge of a state court of record in the district – has authority to issue a warrant to search for and seize a person or property located within the district;

(2) a magistrate judge with authority in the district has authority to issue a warrant for a person or property outside the district if the person or property is located within the district when the warrant is issued but might move or be moved outside the district before the warrant is executed;

(3) a magistrate judge – in an investigation of domestic terrorism or international terrorism – with authority in any district in which activities related to the terrorism may have occurred has authority to issue a warrant for a person or property within or outside that district;

(4) a magistrate judge with authority in the district has authority to issue a warrant to install within the district a tracking device; the warrant may authorize use of the device to track the movement of a person or property located within the district, outside the district, or both; and

(5) a magistrate judge having authority in any district where activities related to the crime may have occurred, or in the District of Columbia, may issue a warrant for property that is located outside the jurisdiction of any state or district, but within any of the following:

(A) a United States territory, possession, or commonwealth;

(B) the premises – no matter who owns them – of a United States diplomatic or consular mission in a foreign state, including any appurtenant building, part of a building, or land used for the mission's purposes; or

(C) a residence and any appurtenant land owned or leased by the United States and used by United States personnel assigned to a United States diplomatic or consular mission in a foreign state.

(6) a magistrate judge with authority in any district where activities related to a crime may have occurred has authority to issue a warrant to use remote access to search electronic storage media and to seize or copy electronically stored information located within or outside that district if:

(A) the district where the media or information is located has been concealed through technological means; or

(B) in an investigation of a violation of 18 U.S.C. § 1030(a)(5), the media are protected computers that have been damaged without authorization and are located in five or more districts.

(c) **Persons or Property Subject to Search or Seizure.** A warrant may be issued for any of the following:

(1) evidence of a crime;

(2) contraband, fruits of crime, or other items illegally possessed;

(3) property designed for use, intended for use, or used in committing a crime; or

(4) a person to be arrested or a person who is unlawfully restrained.

(d) **Obtaining a Warrant.**

(1) *In General.* After receiving an affidavit or other information, a magistrate judge – or if authorized by Rule 41(b), a judge of a state court of record – must issue the warrant if there is probable cause to search for and seize a person or property or to install and use a tracking device.

(2) *Requesting a Warrant in the Presence of a Judge.*

(A) *Warrant on an Affidavit.* When a federal law enforcement officer or an attorney for the government presents an affidavit in support of a warrant, the judge may require the affiant to appear personally and may examine under oath the affiant and any witness the affiant produces.

> (B) *Warrant on Sworn Testimony.* The judge may wholly or partially dispense with a written affidavit and base a warrant on sworn testimony if doing so is reasonable under the circumstances.
>
> (C) *Recording Testimony.* Testimony taken in support of a warrant must be recorded by a court reporter or by a suitable recording device, and the judge must file the transcript or recording with the clerk, along with any affidavit.

(3) **Requesting a Warrant by Telephonic or Other Reliable Electronic Means.** In accordance with Rule 4.1, a magistrate judge may issue a warrant based on information communicated by telephone or other reliable electronic means.

(e) **Issuing the Warrant.**

(1) **In General.** The magistrate judge or a judge of a state court of record must issue the warrant to an officer authorized to execute it.

(2) **Contents of the Warrant.**

> (A) *Warrant to Search for and Seize a Person or Property.* Except for a tracking-device warrant, the warrant must identify the person or property to be searched, identify any person or property to be seized, and designate the magistrate judge to whom it must be returned. The warrant must command the officer to:
>
> > (i) execute the warrant within a specified time no longer than 14 days;
> >
> > (ii) execute the warrant during the daytime, unless the judge for good cause expressly authorizes execution at another time; and
> >
> > (iii) return the warrant to the magistrate judge designated in the warrant.
>
> (B) *Warrant Seeking Electronically Stored Information.* A warrant under Rule 41(e)(2)(A) may authorize the seizure of electronic storage media or the seizure or copying of electronically stored information. Unless otherwise specified, the warrant authorizes a later review of the media or information consistent with the warrant. The time for executing the warrant in Rule 41(e)(2)(A) and (f)(1)(A) refers to the seizure or on-site copying of the media or information, and not to any later off-site copying or review.
>
> (C) *Warrant for a Tracking Device.* A tracking-device warrant must identify the person or property to be tracked, designate the magistrate judge to whom it must be returned, and specify a reasonable length of time that the device may be used. The time must not exceed 45 days from the date the warrant was issued. The court may, for good cause, grant one or more extensions for a reasonable period not to exceed 45 days each. The warrant must command the officer to:
>
> > (i) complete any installation authorized by the warrant within a specified time no longer than 10 days;
> >
> > (ii) perform any installation authorized by the warrant during the daytime, unless the judge for good cause expressly authorizes installation at another time; and
> >
> > (iii) return the warrant to the judge designated in the warrant.

(f) **Executing and Returning the Warrant.**

(1) **Warrant to Search for and Seize a Person or Property.**

> (A) *Noting the Time.* The officer executing the warrant must enter on it the exact date and time it was executed.

(B) *Inventory.* An officer present during the execution of the warrant must prepare and verify an inventory of any property seized. The officer must do so in the presence of another officer and the person from whom, or from whose premises, the property was taken. If either one is not present, the officer must prepare and verify the inventory in the presence of at least one other credible person. In a case involving the seizure of electronic storage media or the seizure or copying of electronically stored information, the inventory may be limited to describing the physical storage media that were seized or copied. The officer may retain a copy of the electronically stored information that was seized or copied.

(C) *Receipt.* The officer executing the warrant must give a copy of the warrant and a receipt for the property taken to the person from whom, or from whose premises, the property was taken or leave a copy of the warrant and receipt at the place where the officer took the property. For a warrant to use remote access to search electronic storage media and seize or copy electronically stored information, the officer must make reasonable efforts to serve a copy of the warrant and receipt on the person whose property was searched or who possessed the information that was seized or copied. Service may be accomplished by any means, including electronic means, reasonably calculated to reach that person.

(D) *Return.* The officer executing the warrant must promptly return it – together with a copy of the inventory – to the magistrate judge designated on the warrant. The officer may do so by reliable electronic means. The judge must, on request, give a copy of the inventory to the person from whom, or from whose premises, the property was taken and to the applicant for the warrant.

(2) ***Warrant for a Tracking Device.***

(A) *Noting the Time.* The officer executing a tracking-device warrant must enter on it the exact date and time the device was installed and the period during which it was used.

(B) *Return.* Within 10 days after the use of the tracking device has ended, the officer executing the warrant must return it to the judge designated in the warrant. The officer may do so by reliable electronic means.

(C) *Service.* Within 10 days after the use of the tracking device has ended, the officer executing a tracking-device warrant must serve a copy of the warrant on the person who was tracked or whose property was tracked. Service may be accomplished by delivering a copy to the person who, or whose property, was tracked; or by leaving a copy at the person's residence or usual place of abode with an individual of suitable age and discretion who resides at that location and by mailing a copy to the person's last known address. Upon request of the government, the judge may delay notice as provided in Rule 41(f)(3).

(3) ***Delayed Notice.*** Upon the government's request, a magistrate judge – or if authorized by Rule 41(b), a judge of a state court of record – may delay any notice required by this rule if the delay is authorized by statute.

(g) **Motion to Return Property.** A person aggrieved by an unlawful search and seizure of property or by the deprivation of property may move for the property's return. The motion must be filed in the district where the property was seized. The court must receive evidence on any factual issue necessary to decide the motion. If it grants the motion, the court must return the property to the movant, but may impose reasonable conditions to protect access to the property and its use in later proceedings.

(h) **Motion to Suppress.** A defendant may move to suppress evidence in the court where the trial will occur, as Rule 12 provides.

(i) **Forwarding Papers to the Clerk.** The magistrate judge to whom the warrant is returned must attach to the warrant a copy of the return, of the inventory, and of all other related papers and must deliver them to the clerk in the district where the property was seized.

Rule 42. Criminal Contempt

(a) **Disposition After Notice.** Any person who commits criminal contempt may be punished for that contempt after prosecution on notice.

   (1) *Notice.* The court must give the person notice in open court, in an order to show cause, or in an arrest order. The notice must:

      (A) state the time and place of the trial;

      (B) allow the defendant a reasonable time to prepare a defense; and

      (C) state the essential facts constituting the charged criminal contempt and describe it as such.

   (2) *Appointing a Prosecutor.* The court must request that the contempt be prosecuted by an attorney for the government, unless the interest of justice requires the appointment of another attorney. If the government declines the request, the court must appoint another attorney to prosecute the contempt.

   (3) *Trial and Disposition.* A person being prosecuted for criminal contempt is entitled to a jury trial in any case in which federal law so provides and must be released or detained as Rule 46 provides. If the criminal contempt involves disrespect toward or criticism of a judge, that judge is disqualified from presiding at the contempt trial or hearing unless the defendant consents. Upon a finding or verdict of guilty, the court must impose the punishment.

(b) **Summary Disposition.** Notwithstanding any other provision of these rules, the court (other than a magistrate judge) may summarily punish a person who commits criminal contempt in its presence if the judge saw or heard the contemptuous conduct and so certifies; a magistrate judge may summarily punish a person as provided in 28 U.S.C. § 636(e). The contempt order must recite the facts, be signed by the judge, and be filed with the clerk.

Rule 43. Defendant's Presence

(a) **When Required.** Unless this rule, Rule 5, or Rule 10 provides otherwise, the defendant must be present at:

   (1) the initial appearance, the initial arraignment, and the plea;

   (2) every trial stage, including jury empanelment and the return of the verdict; and

   (3) sentencing.

(b) **When Not Required.** A defendant need not be present under any of the following circumstances:

   (1) *Organizational Defendant.* The defendant is an organization represented by counsel who is present.

   (2) *Misdemeanor Offense.* The offense is punishable by fine or by imprisonment for not more than one year, or both, and with the defendant's written consent, the court permits arraignment, plea, trial, and sentencing to occur by video teleconferencing or in the defendant's absence.

   (3) *Conference or Hearing on a Legal Question.* The proceeding involves only a conference or hearing on a question of law.

   (4) *Sentence Correction.* The proceeding involves the correction or reduction of sentence under Rule 35 or 18 U.S.C. § 3582(c).

(c) **Waiving Continued Presence.**

(1) *In General.* A defendant who was initially present at trial, or who had pleaded guilty or nolo contendere, waives the right to be present under the following circumstances:

    (A) when the defendant is voluntarily absent after the trial has begun, regardless of whether the court informed the defendant of an obligation to remain during trial;

    (B) in a noncapital case, when the defendant is voluntarily absent during sentencing; or

    (C) when the court warns the defendant that it will remove the defendant from the courtroom for disruptive behavior, but the defendant persists in conduct that justifies removal from the courtroom.

(2) *Waiver's Effect.* If the defendant waives the right to be present, the trial may proceed to completion, including the verdict's return and sentencing, during the defendant's absence.

Rule 44. Right to and Appointment of Counsel

(a) **Right to Appointed Counsel.** A defendant who is unable to obtain counsel is entitled to have counsel appointed to represent the defendant at every stage of the proceeding from initial appearance through appeal, unless the defendant waives this right.

(b) **Appointment Procedure.** Federal law and local court rules govern the procedure for implementing the right to counsel.

(c) **Inquiry into Joint Representation.**

    (1) *Joint Representation.* Joint representation occurs when:

        (A) two or more defendants have been charged jointly under Rule 8(b) or have been joined for trial under Rule 13; and

        (B) the defendants are represented by the same counsel, or counsel who are associated in law practice.

    (2) *Court's Responsibilities in Cases of Joint Representation.* The court must promptly inquire about the propriety of joint representation and must personally advise each defendant of the right to the effective assistance of counsel, including separate representation. Unless there is good cause to believe that no conflict of interest is likely to arise, the court must take appropriate measures to protect each defendant's right to counsel.

Rule 45. Computing and Extending Time

(a) **Computing Time.** The following rules apply in computing any time period specified in these rules, in any local rule or court order, or in any statute that does not specify a method of computing time.

    (1) *Period Stated in Days or a Longer Unit.* When the period is stated in days or a longer unit of time:

        (A) exclude the day of the event that triggers the period;

        (B) count every day, including intermediate Saturdays, Sundays, and legal holidays; and

        (C) include the last day of the period, but if the last day is a Saturday, Sunday, or legal holiday, the period continues to run until the end of the next day that is not a Saturday, Sunday, or legal holiday.

    (2) *Period Stated in Hours.* When the period is stated in hours:

        (A) begin counting immediately on the occurrence of the event that triggers the period;

        (B) count every hour, including hours during intermediate Saturdays, Sundays, and legal holidays; and

(C) if the period would end on a Saturday, Sunday, or legal holiday, the period continues to run until the same time on the next day that is not a Saturday, Sunday, or legal holiday.

(3) *Inaccessibility of the Clerk's Office.* Unless the court orders otherwise, if the clerk's office is inaccessible:

(A) on the last day for filing under Rule 45(a)(1), then the time for filing is extended to the first accessible day that is not a Saturday, Sunday, or legal holiday; or

(B) during the last hour for filing under Rule 45(a)(2), then the time for filing is extended to the same time on the first accessible day that is not a Saturday, Sunday, or legal holiday.

(4) *"Last Day" Defined.* Unless a different time is set by a statute, local rule, or court order, the last day ends:

(A) for electronic filing, at midnight in the court's time zone; and

(B) for filing by other means, when the clerk's office is scheduled to close.

(5) *"Next Day" Defined.* The "next day" is determined by continuing to count forward when the period is measured after an event and backward when measured before an event.

(6) *"Legal Holiday" Defined.* "Legal holiday" means:

(A) the day set aside by statute for observing New Year's Day, Martin Luther King Jr.'s Birthday, Washington's Birthday, Memorial Day, Independence Day, Labor Day, Columbus Day, Veterans' Day, Thanksgiving Day, or Christmas Day;

(B) any day declared a holiday by the President or Congress; and

(C) for periods that are measured after an event, any other day declared a holiday by the state where the district court is located.

(b) **Extending Time.**

(1) *In General.* When an act must or may be done within a specified period, the court on its own may extend the time, or for good cause may do so on a party's motion made:

(A) before the originally prescribed or previously extended time expires; or

(B) after the time expires if the party failed to act because of excusable neglect.

(2) *Exception.* The court may not extend the time to take any action under Rule 35, except as stated in that rule.

(c) **Additional Time After Certain Kinds of Service.** Whenever a party must or may act within a specified time after being served and service is made under Rule 49(a)(4)(C), (D), and (E), 3 days are added after the period would otherwise expire under subdivision (a).

Rule 46. Release from Custody; Supervising Detention

(a) **Before Trial.** The provisions of 18 U.S.C. §§ 3142 and 3144 govern pretrial release.

(b) **During Trial.** A person released before trial continues on release during trial under the same terms and conditions. But the court may order different terms and conditions or terminate the release if necessary, to ensure that the person will be present during trial or that the person's conduct will not obstruct the orderly and expeditious progress of the trial.

(c) **Pending Sentencing or Appeal.** The provisions of 18 U.S.C. § 3143 govern release pending sentencing or appeal. The burden of establishing that the defendant will not flee or pose a danger to any other person or to the community rests with the defendant.

(d) **Pending Hearing on a Violation of Probation or Supervised Release.** Rule 32.1(a)(6) governs release pending a hearing on a violation of probation or supervised release.

(e) **Surety.** The court must not approve a bond unless any surety appears to be qualified. Every surety, except a legally approved corporate surety, must demonstrate by affidavit that its assets are adequate. The court may require the affidavit to describe the following:

    (1) the property that the surety proposes to use as security;

    (2) any encumbrance on that property;

    (3) the number and amount of any other undischarged bonds and bail undertakings the surety has issued; and

    (4) any other liability of the surety.

(f) **Bail Forfeiture.**

    (1) *Declaration.* The court must declare the bail forfeited if a condition of the bond is breached.

    (2) *Setting Aside.* The court may set aside in whole or in part a bail forfeiture upon any condition the court may impose if:

        (A) the surety later surrenders into custody the person released on the surety's appearance bond; or

        (B) it appears that justice does not require bail forfeiture.

    (3) *Enforcement.*

        (A) *Default Judgment and Execution.* If it does not set aside a bail forfeiture, the court must, upon the government's motion, enter a default judgment.

        (B) *Jurisdiction and Service.* By entering into a bond, each surety submits to the district court's jurisdiction and irrevocably appoints the district clerk as its agent to receive service of any filings affecting its liability.

        (C) *Motion to Enforce.* The court may, upon the government's motion, enforce the surety's liability without an independent action. The government must serve any motion, and notice as the court prescribes, on the district clerk. If so served, the clerk must promptly mail a copy to the surety at its last known address.

    (4) *Remission.* After entering a judgment under Rule 46(f)(3), the court may remit in whole or in part the judgment under the same conditions specified in Rule 46(f)(2).

(g) **Exoneration.** The court must exonerate the surety and release any bail when a bond condition has been satisfied or when the court has set aside or remitted the forfeiture. The court must exonerate a surety who deposits cash in the amount of the bond or timely surrenders the defendant into custody.

(h) **Supervising Detention Pending Trial.**

    (1) *In General.* To eliminate unnecessary detention, the court must supervise the detention within the district of any defendants awaiting trial and of any persons held as material witnesses.

    (2) *Reports.* An attorney for the government must report biweekly to the court, listing each material witness held in custody for more than 10 days pending indictment, arraignment, or trial. For each material witness listed in the report, an attorney for the government must state why the witness should not be released with or without a deposition being taken under Rule 15(a).

(i) **Forfeiture of Property.** The court may dispose of a charged offense by ordering the forfeiture of 18 U.S.C. § 3142(c)(1)(B)(xi) property under 18 U.S.C. § 3146(d), if a fine in the amount of the property's value would be an appropriate sentence for the charged offense.

(j) **Producing a Statement.**

    (1) *In General.* Rule 26.2(a)–(d) and (f) applies at a detention hearing under 18 U.S.C. § 3142, unless the court for good cause rules otherwise.

    (2) *Sanctions for Not Producing a Statement.* If a party disobeys a Rule 26.2 order to produce a witness's statement, the court must not consider that witness's testimony at the detention hearing.

Rule 47. Motions and Supporting Affidavits

(a) **In General.** A party applying to the court for an order must do so by motion.

(b) **Form and Content of a Motion.** A motion – except when made during a trial or hearing – must be in writing, unless the court permits the party to make the motion by other means. A motion must state the grounds on which it is based, and the relief or order sought. A motion may be supported by affidavit.

(c) **Timing of a Motion.** A party must serve a written motion – other than one that the court may hear ex parte – and any hearing notice at least 7 days before the hearing date, unless a rule or court order sets a different period. For good cause, the court may set a different period upon ex parte application.

(d) **Affidavit Supporting a Motion.** The moving party must serve any supporting affidavit with the motion. A responding party must serve any opposing affidavit at least one day before the hearing, unless the court permits later service.

Rule 48. Dismissal

(a) **By the Government.** The government may, with leave of court, dismiss an indictment, information, or complaint. The government may not dismiss the prosecution during trial without the defendant's consent.

(b) **By the Court.** The court may dismiss an indictment, information, or complaint if unnecessary delay occurs in:

    (1) presenting a charge to a grand jury;

    (2) filing an information against a defendant; or

    (3) bringing a defendant to trial.

Rule 49. Serving and Filing Papers

(a) **Service on a Party.**

    (1) *What is Required.* Each of the following must be served on every party: any written motion (other than one to be heard ex parte), written notice, designation of the record on appeal, or similar paper.

    (2) *Serving a Party's Attorney.* Unless the court orders otherwise, when these rules or a court order requires or permits service on a party represented by an attorney, service must be made on the attorney instead of the party.

    (3) *Service by Electronic Means.*

        (A) *Using the Court's Electronic-Filing System.* A party represented by an attorney may serve a paper on a registered user by filing it with the court's electronic-filing system. A party not represented by an attorney may do so only if allowed by court order or local rule. Service is complete upon filing but is not effective if the serving party learns that it did not reach the person to be served.

        (B) *Using Other Electronic Means.* A paper may be served by any other electronic means that the person consented to in writing. Service is complete upon transmission but is not effective if the serving party learns that it did not reach the person to be served.

(4) *Service by Nonelectronic Means.* A paper may be served by:

    (A) handing it to the person;

    (B) leaving it:

        (i) at the person's office with a clerk or other person in charge or, if no one is in charge, in a conspicuous place in the office; or

        (ii) if the person has no office or the office is closed, at the person's dwelling or usual place of abode with someone of suitable age and discretion who resides there;

    (C) mailing it to the person's last known address – in which event service is complete upon mailing;

    (D) leaving it with the court clerk if the person has no known address; or

    (E) delivering it by any other means that the person consented to in writing – in which event service is complete when the person making service delivers it to the agency designated to make delivery.

(b) Filing.

  (1) *When Required; Certificate of Service.* Any paper that is required to be served must be filed no later than a reasonable time after service. No certificate of service is required when a paper is served by filing it with the court's electronic-filing system. When a paper is served by other means, a certificate of service must be filed with it or within a reasonable time after service or filing.

  (2) *Means of Filing.*

    (A) *Electronically.* A paper is filed electronically by filing it with the court's electronic-filing system. A filing made through a person's electronic-filing account and authorized by that person, together with the person's name on a signature block, constitutes the person's signature. A paper filed electronically is written or in writing under these rules.

    (B) *Nonelectronically.* A paper not filed electronically is filed by delivering it:

        (i) to the clerk; or

        (ii) to a judge who agrees to accept it for filing, and who must then note the filing date on the paper and promptly send it to the clerk.

  (3) *Means Used by Represented and Unrepresented Parties.*

    (A) *Represented Party.* A party represented by an attorney must file electronically, unless nonelectronic filing is allowed by the court for good cause or is allowed or required by local rule.

    (B) *Unrepresented Party.* A party not represented by an attorney must file nonelectronically, unless allowed to file electronically by court order or local rule.

  (4) *Signature.* Every written motion and other paper must be signed by at least one attorney of record in the attorney's name – or by a person filing a paper if the person is not represented by an attorney. The paper must state the signer's address, e-mail address, and telephone number. Unless a rule or statute specifically states otherwise, a pleading need not be verified or accompanied by an affidavit. The court must strike an unsigned paper unless the omission is promptly corrected after being called to the attorney's or person's attention.

  (5) *Acceptance by the Clerk.* The clerk must not refuse to file a paper solely because it is not in the form prescribed by these rules or by a local rule or practice.

(c) **Service and Filing by Nonparties.** A nonparty may serve and file a paper only if doing so is required or permitted by law. A nonparty must serve every party as required by Rule 49(a) but may use the court's electronic-filing system only if allowed by court order or local rule.

(d) **Notice of a Court Order.** When the court issues an order on any post-arraignment motion, the clerk must serve notice of the entry on each party as required by Rule 49(a). A party also may serve notice of entry by the same means. Except as Federal Rule of Appellate Procedure 4(b) provides otherwise, the clerk's failure to give notice does not affect the time to appeal or relieve – or authorize the court to relieve – a party's failure to appeal within the allowed time.

Rule 49.1. Privacy Protection for Filings Made with the Court

(a) **Redacted Filings.** Unless the court orders otherwise, in an electronic or paper filing with the court that contains an individual's social-security number, taxpayer-identification number, or birth date, the name of an individual known to be a minor, a financial-account number, or the home address of an individual, a party or nonparty making the filing may include only;

    (1) the last four digits of the social-security number and taxpayer- identification number;

    (2) the year of the individual's birth;

    (3) the minor's initials;

    (4) the last four digits of the financial-account number; and (5) the city and state of the home address.

(b) **Exemptions from the Redaction Requirement.** The redaction requirement does not apply to the following:

    (1) a financial-account number or real property address that identifies the property allegedly subject to forfeiture in a forfeiture proceeding;

    (2) the record of an administrative or agency proceeding;

    (3) the official record of a state-court proceeding;

    (4) the record of a court or tribunal, if that record was not subject to the redaction requirement when originally filed;

    (5) a filing covered by Rule 49.1(d);

    (6) a pro se filing in an action brought under 28 U.S.C. §§ 2241, 2254, or 2255;

    (7) a court filing that is related to a criminal matter or investigation and that is prepared before the filing of a criminal charge or is not filed as part of any docketed criminal case;

    (8) an arrest or search warrant; and

    (9) a charging document and an affidavit filed in support of any charging document.

(c) **Immigration Cases.** A filing in an action brought under 28 U.S.C. § 2241 that relates to the petitioner's immigration rights is governed by Federal Rule of Civil Procedure 5.2.

(d) **Filings Made Under Seal.** The court may order that a filing be made under seal without redaction. The court may later unseal the filing or order the person who made the filing to file a redacted version for the public record.

(e) **Protective Orders.** For good cause, the court may by order in a case:

    (1) require redaction of additional information; or

    (2) limit or prohibit a nonparty's remote electronic access to a document filed with the court.

(f) **Option for Additional Unredacted Filing Under Seal.** A person making a redacted filing may also file an unredacted copy under seal. The court must retain the unredacted copy as part of the record.

(g) **Option for Filing a Reference List.** A filing that contains redacted information may be filed together with a reference list that identifies each item of redacted information and specifies an appropriate identifier that uniquely corresponds to each item listed. The list must be filed under seal and may be amended as of right. Any reference in the case to a listed identifier will be construed to refer to the corresponding item of information.

(h) **Waiver of Protection of Identifiers.** A person waives the protection of Rule 49.1(a) as to the person's own information by filing it without redaction and not under seal.

Rule 50. Prompt Disposition

Scheduling preference must be given to criminal proceedings as far as practicable.

Rule 51. Preserving Claimed Error

(a) **Exceptions Unnecessary.** Exceptions to rulings or orders of the court are unnecessary.

(b) **Preserving a Claim of Error.** A party may preserve a claim of error by informing the court – when the court ruling or order is made or sought – of the action the party wishes the court to take, or the party's objection to the court's action and the grounds for that objection. If a party does not have an opportunity to object to a ruling or order, the absence of an objection does not later prejudice that party. A ruling or order that admits or excludes evidence is governed by Federal Rule of Evidence 103.

Rule 52. Harmless and Plain Error

(a) **Harmless Error.** Any error, defect, irregularity, or variance that does not affect substantial rights must be disregarded.

(b) **Plain Error.** A plain error that affects substantial rights may be considered even though it was not brought to the court's attention.

Rule 53. Courtroom Photographing and Broadcasting Prohibited

Except as otherwise provided by a statute or these rules, the court must not permit the taking of photographs in the courtroom during judicial proceedings or the broadcasting of judicial proceedings from the courtroom. (As amended Apr. 29, 2002, eff. Dec. 1, 2002.)

Rule 54. [Transferred]

Rule 55. Records

The clerk of the district court must keep records of criminal proceedings in the form prescribed by the Director of the Administrative Office of the United States Courts. The clerk must enter in the records every court order or judgment and the date of entry.

Rule 56. When Court Is Open

(a) **In General.** A district court is considered always open for any filing, and for issuing and returning process, making a motion, or entering an order.

(b) **Office Hours.** The clerk's office – with the clerk or a deputy in attendance – must be open during business hours on all days except Saturdays, Sundays, and legal holidays.

(c) **Special Hours.** A court may provide by local rule or order that its clerk's office will be open for specified hours on Saturdays or legal holidays other than those set aside by statute for observing New Year's Day, Martin Luther King, Jr.'s Birthday, Washington's Birthday, Memorial Day, Independence Day, Labor Day, Columbus Day, Veterans' Day, Thanksgiving Day, and Christmas Day.

Rule 57. District Court Rules

(a) **In General.**

    (1) *Adopting Local Rules.* Each district court acting by a majority of its district judges may, after giving appropriate public notice and an opportunity to comment, make and amend rules governing its practice. A local rule must be consistent with – but not duplicative of – federal statutes and rules adopted under 28 U.S.C. § 2072 and must conform to any uniform numbering system prescribed by the Judicial Conference of the United States.

    (2) *Limiting Enforcement.* A local rule imposing a requirement of form must not be enforced in a manner that causes a party to lose rights because of an unintentional failure to comply with the requirement.

(b) **Procedure When There Is No Controlling Law.** A judge may regulate practice in any manner consistent with federal law, these rules, and the local rules of the district. No sanction or other disadvantage may be imposed for noncompliance with any requirement not in federal law, federal rules, or the local district rules unless the alleged violator was furnished with actual notice of the requirement before the noncompliance.

(c) **Effective Date and Notice.** A local rule adopted under this rule takes effect on the date specified by the district court and remains in effect unless amended by the district court or abrogated by the judicial council of the circuit in which the district is located. Copies of local rules and their amendments, when promulgated, must be furnished to the judicial council and the Administrative Office of the United States Courts and must be made available to the public.

Rule 58. Petty Offenses and Other Misdemeanors

(a) **Scope.**

    (1) *In General.* These rules apply in petty offense and other misdemeanor cases and on appeal to a district judge in a case tried by a magistrate judge, unless this rule provides otherwise.

    (2) *Petty Offense Case Without Imprisonment.* In a case involving a petty offense for which no sentence of imprisonment will be imposed, the court may follow any provision of these rules that is not inconsistent with this rule and that the court considers appropriate.

    (3) *Definition.* As used in this rule, the term "petty offense for which no sentence of imprisonment will be imposed" means a petty offense for which the court determines that, in the event of conviction, no sentence of imprisonment will be imposed.

(b) **Pretrial Procedure.**

    (1) *Charging Document.* The trial of a misdemeanor may proceed on an indictment, information, or complaint. The trial of a petty offense may also proceed on a citation or violation notice.

    (2) *Initial Appearance.* At the defendant's initial appearance on a petty offense or other misdemeanor charge, the magistrate judge must inform the defendant of the following:

        (A) the charge, and the minimum and maximum penalties, including imprisonment, fines, any special assessment under 18 U.S.C. § 3013, and restitution under 18 U.S.C. § 3556;

        (B) the right to retain counsel;

        (C) the right to request the appointment of counsel if the defendant is unable to retain counsel – unless the charge is a petty offense for which the appointment of counsel is not required;

(D) the defendant's right not to make a statement, and that any statement made may be used against the defendant;

(E) the right to trial, judgment, and sentencing before a district judge – unless:

(i) the charge is a petty offense; or

(ii) the defendant consents to trial, judgment, and sentencing before a magistrate judge;

(F) the right to a jury trial before either a magistrate judge or a district judge – unless the charge is a petty offense;

(G) any right to a preliminary hearing under Rule 5.1, and the general circumstances, if any, under which the defendant may secure pretrial release; and

(H) that a defendant who is not a United States citizen may request that an attorney for the government or a federal law enforcement official notify a consular officer from the defendant's country of nationality that the defendant has been arrested – but that even without the defendant's request, a treaty or other international agreement may require consular notification.

(3) *Arraignment.*

(A) *Plea Before a Magistrate Judge.* A magistrate judge may take the defendant's plea in a petty offense case. In every other misdemeanor case, a magistrate judge may take the plea only if the defendant consents either in writing or on the record to be tried before a magistrate judge and specifically waives trial before a district judge. The defendant may plead not guilty, guilty, or (with the consent of the magistrate judge) nolo contendere.

(B) *Failure to Consent.* Except in a petty offense case, the magistrate judge must order a defendant who does not consent to trial before a magistrate judge to appear before a district judge for further proceedings.

(c) **Additional Procedures in Certain Petty Offense Cases.** The following procedures also apply in a case involving a petty offense for which no sentence of imprisonment will be imposed:

(1) **Guilty or Nolo Contendere Plea.** The court must not accept a guilty or nolo contendere plea unless satisfied that the defendant understands the nature of the charge and the maximum possible penalty.

(2) **Waiving Venue.**

(A) *Conditions of Waiving Venue.* If a defendant is arrested, held, or present in a district different from the one where the indictment, information, complaint, citation, or violation notice is pending, the defendant may state in writing a desire to plead guilty or nolo contendere; to waive venue and trial in the district where the proceeding is pending; and to consent to the court's disposing of the case in the district where the defendant was arrested, is held, or is present.

(B) *Effect of Waiving Venue.* Unless the defendant later pleads not guilty, the prosecution will proceed in the district where the defendant was arrested, is held, or is present. The district clerk must notify the clerk in the original district of the defendant's waiver of venue. The defendant's statement of a desire to plead guilty or nolo contendere is not admissible against the defendant.

(3) **Sentencing.** The court must give the defendant an opportunity to be heard in mitigation and then proceed immediately to sentencing. The court may, however, postpone sentencing to allow the probation service to investigate or to permit either party to submit additional information.

(4) **Notice of a Right to Appeal.** After imposing sentence in a case tried on a not-guilty plea, the court must advise the defendant of a right to appeal the conviction and of any right to appeal the sentence.

If the defendant was convicted on a plea of guilty or nolo contendere, the court must advise the defendant of any right to appeal the sentence.

(d) **Paying a Fixed Sum in Lieu of Appearance.**

   (1) *In General.* If the court has a local rule governing forfeiture of collateral, the court may accept a fixed-sum payment in lieu of the defendant's appearance and end the case, but the fixed sum may not exceed the maximum fine allowed by law.

   (2) *Notice to Appear.* If the defendant fails to pay a fixed sum, request a hearing, or appear in response to a citation or violation notice, the district clerk or a magistrate judge may issue a notice for the defendant to appear before the court on a date certain. The notice may give the defendant an additional opportunity to pay a fixed sum in lieu of appearance. The district clerk must serve the notice on the defendant by mailing a copy to the defendant's last known address.

   (3) *Summons or Warrant.* Upon an indictment, or upon a showing by one of the other charging documents specified in Rule 58(b)(1) of probable cause to believe that an offense has been committed and that the defendant has committed it, the court may issue an arrest warrant or, if no warrant is requested by an attorney for the government, a summons. The showing of probable cause must be made under oath or under penalty of perjury, but the affiant need not appear before the court. If the defendant fails to appear before the court in response to a summons, the court may summarily issue a warrant for the defendant's arrest.

(e) **Recording the Proceedings.** The court must record any proceedings under this rule by using a court reporter or a suitable recording device.

(f) **New Trial.** Rule 33 applies to a motion for a new trial.

(g) **Appeal.**

   (1) *From a District Judge's Order or Judgment.* The Federal Rules of Appellate Procedure govern an appeal from a district judge's order or a judgment of conviction or sentence.

   (2) *From a Magistrate Judge's Order or Judgment.*

      (A) *Interlocutory Appeal.* Either party may appeal an order of a magistrate judge to a district judge within 14 days of its entry if a district judge's order could similarly be appealed. The party appealing must file a notice with the clerk specifying the order being appealed and must serve a copy to the adverse party.

      (B) *Appeal from a Conviction or Sentence.* A defendant may appeal to a magistrate judge's judgment of conviction or sentence to a district judge within 14 days of its entry. To appeal, the defendant must file a notice with the clerk specifying the judgment being appealed and must serve a copy on an attorney for the government.

      (C) *Record.* The record consists of the original papers and exhibits in the case; any transcript, tape, or other recording of the proceedings; and a certified copy of the docket entries. For purposes of the appeal, a copy of the record of the proceedings must be made available to a defendant who establishes by affidavit an inability to pay or give security for the record. The Director of the Administrative Office of the United States Courts must pay for those copies.

      (D) *Scope of Appeal.* The defendant is not entitled to a trial de novo by a district judge. The scope of the appeal is the same as in an appeal to the court of appeals from a judgment entered by a district judge.

(3) ***Stay of Execution and Release Pending Appeal.*** Rule 38 applies to a stay of a judgment of conviction or sentence. The court may release the defendant pending appeal under the law relating to release pending appeal from a district court to a court of appeals.

Rule 59. Matters Before a Magistrate Judge

(a) **Nondispositive Matters.** A district judge may refer to a magistrate judge for determination any matter that does not dispose of a charge or defense. The magistrate judge must promptly conduct the required proceedings and, when appropriate, enter on the record an oral or written order stating the determination. A party may serve and file objections to the order within 14 days after being served with a copy of a written order or after the oral order is stated on the record, or at some other time the court sets. The district judge must consider timely objections and modify or set aside any part of the order that is contrary to law or clearly erroneous. Failure to object in accordance with this rule waives a party's right to review.

(b) **Dispositive Matters.**

(1) ***Referral to Magistrate Judge.*** A district judge may refer to a magistrate judge for recommendation a defendant's motion to dismiss or quash an indictment or information, a motion to suppress evidence, or any matter that may dispose of a charge or defense. The magistrate judge must promptly conduct the required proceedings. A record must be made of any evidentiary proceeding and of any other proceeding if the magistrate judge considers it necessary. The magistrate judge must enter on the record a recommendation for disposing of the matter, including any proposed findings of fact. The clerk must immediately serve copies on all parties.

(2) ***Objections to Findings and Recommendations.*** Within 14 days after being served with a copy of the recommended disposition, or at some other time the court sets, a party may serve and file specific written objections to the proposed findings and recommendations. Unless the district judge directs otherwise, the objecting party must promptly arrange for transcribing the record, or whatever portions of it the parties agree to or the magistrate judge considers sufficient. Failure to object in accordance with this rule waives a party's right to review.

(3) ***De Novo Review of Recommendations.*** The district judge must consider de novo any objection to the magistrate judge's recommendation. The district judge may accept, reject, or modify the recommendation, receive further evidence, or resubmit the matter to the magistrate judge with instructions.

Rule 60. Victim's Rights

(a) **In General.**

(1) ***Notice of a Proceeding.*** The government must use its best efforts to give the victim reasonable, accurate, and timely notice of any public court proceeding involving the crime.

(2) ***Attending the Proceeding.*** The court must not exclude a victim from a public court proceeding involving the crime, unless the court determines by clear and convincing evidence that the victim's testimony would be materially altered if the victim heard other testimony at that proceeding. In determining whether to exclude a victim, the court must make every effort to permit the fullest attendance possible by the victim and must consider reasonable alternatives to exclusion. The reasons for any exclusion must be clearly stated on the record.

(3) ***Right to Be Heard on Release, a Plea, or Sentencing.*** The court must permit a victim to be reasonably heard at any public proceeding in the district court concerning release, plea, or sentencing involving the crime.

(b) Enforcement and Limitations.

   (1) *Time for Deciding a Motion.* The court must promptly decide on any motion asserting a victim's rights described in these rules.

   (2) *Who May Assert the Rights.* A victim's rights described in these rules may be asserted by the victim, the victim's lawful representative, the attorney for the government, or any other person as authorized by 18 U.S.C. § 3771(d) and (e).

   (3) *Multiple Victims.* If the court finds that the number of victims makes it impracticable to accord all of them their rights described in these rules, the court must fashion a reasonable procedure that gives effect to these rights without unduly complicating or prolonging the proceedings.

   (4) *Where Rights May Be Asserted.* A victim's rights described in these rules must be asserted in the district where a defendant is being prosecuted for the crime.

   (5) *Limitations on Relief.* A victim may move to reopen a plea or sentence only if:

      (A) the victim asked to be heard before or during the proceeding at issue, and the request was denied;

      (B) the victim petitions the court of appeals for a writ of mandamus within 10 days after the denial, and the writ is granted; and

      (C) in the case of plea, the accused has not pleaded to the highest offense charged.

   (6) *No New Trial.* A failure to afford a victim any right described in these rules is not grounds for a new trial.

Rule 61. Title

These rules may be known and cited as the Federal Rules of Criminal Procedure.

PART FOUR
CHAPTER SEVENTEEN

FEDERAL POST-CONVICTION RELIEF INTRODUCTION

Post-conviction relief, is a loosely defined principle that, provides a process by which a defendant may be relieved of an illegal sentence and/or conviction. It is designed to be invoked after the trial process has failed to reach the ends of justice, as it so often does. The post-conviction process is governed by rule and law; just as any other court proceeding. In the Federal Criminal Justice System, post-conviction relief is authorized by 28 U.S.C. § 2255, and the proceedings are executed by following the rule that govern § 2255 proceedings in the United States District Court.

RULES GOVERNING SECTION 2255 PROCEEDINGS FOR THE UNITED STATES DISTRICT COURTS

Rule 1. Scope

These rules govern a motion filed in a United States district court under 28 U.S.C. § 2255 by:

(a) a person in custody under a judgment of that court who seeks a determination that:

    (1) the judgment violates the Constitution or laws of the United States;

    (2) the court lacked jurisdiction to enter the judgment;

    (3) the sentence exceeded the maximum allowed by law; or

    (4) the judgment or sentence is otherwise subject to collateral review; and

(b) a person in custody under a judgment of a state court or another federal court, and subject to future custody under a judgment of the district court, who seeks a determination that:

    (1) future custody under a judgment of the district court would violate the Constitution or laws of the United States;

    (2) the district court lacked jurisdiction to enter the judgment;

    (3) the district court's sentence exceeded the maximum allowed by law; or

    (4) the district court's judgment or sentence is otherwise subject to collateral review.

Rule 2. The Motion

(a) **Applying for Relief.** The application must be in the form of a motion to vacate, set aside, or correct the sentence.

(b) **Form.** The motion must:

    (1) specify all the grounds for relief available to the moving party;

    (2) state the facts supporting each ground;

    (3) state the relief requested;

    (4) be printed, typewritten, or legibly handwritten; and

    (5) be signed under penalty of perjury by the movant or by a person authorized to sign it for the movant.

(c) **Standard Form.** The motion must substantially follow either the form appended to these rules, or a form prescribed by a local district-court rule. The clerk must make forms available to moving parties without charge.

(d) **Separate Motions for Separate Judgments.** A moving party who seeks relief from more than one judgment must file a separate motion covering each judgment.

Rule 3. Filing the Motion; Inmate Filing

(a) **Where to File; Copies.** An original and two copies of the motion must be filed with the clerk.

(b) **Filing and Service.** The clerk must file the motion and enter it on the criminal docket of the case in which the challenged judgment was entered. The clerk must then deliver or serve a copy of the motion on the United States attorney in that district, together with a notice of its filing.

(c) **Time to File.** The time for filing a motion is governed by 28 U.S.C. § 2255 para. 6.

(d) **Inmate Filing.** A paper filed by an inmate confined in an institution is timely if deposited in the institution's internal mailing system on or before the last day for filing. If an institution has a system designed for legal mail, the inmate must use that system to receive the benefit of this rule. Timely filing may be shown by a declaration in compliance with 28 U.S.C. § 1746 or by a notarized statement, either of which must set forth the date of deposit and state that first-class postage has been prepaid.

Rule 4. Preliminary Review

(a) **Referral to a Judge.** The clerk must promptly forward the motion to the judge who conducted the trial and imposed sentence or, if the judge who imposed sentence was not the trial judge, to the judge who conducted the proceedings being challenged. If the appropriate judge is not available, the clerk must forward the motion to a judge under the court's assignment procedure.

(b) **Initial Consideration by the Judge.** The judge who receives the motion must promptly examine it. If it plainly appears from the motion, any attached exhibits, and the record of prior proceedings that the moving party is not entitled to relief, the judge must dismiss the motion and direct the clerk to notify the moving party. If the motion is not dismissed, the judge must order the United States attorney to file an answer, motion, or other response within a fixed time, or to take other action the judge may order.

Rule 5. The Answer and the Reply

(a) **When Required.** The respondent is not required to answer the motion unless a judge so orders.

(b) **Contents.** The answer must address the allegations in the motion. In addition, it must state whether the moving party has used any other federal remedies, including any prior post- conviction motions under these rules or any previous rules, and whether the moving party received an evidentiary hearing.

(c) **Records of Prior Proceedings.** If the answer refers to briefs or transcripts of the prior proceedings that are not available in the court's records, the judge must order the government to furnish them within a reasonable time that will not unduly delay the proceedings.

(d) **Reply.** The moving party may submit a reply to the respondent's answer or other pleading within a time fixed by the judge.

Rule 6. Discovery

(a) **Leave of Court Required.** A judge may, for good cause, authorize a party to conduct discovery under the Federal Rules of Criminal Procedure or Civil Procedure, or in accordance with the practices and principles of law. If necessary, for effective discovery, the judge must appoint an attorney for a moving party who qualifies to have counsel appointed under 18 U.S.C. § 3006A.

(b) **Requesting Discovery.** A party requesting discovery must provide reasons for the request. The request must also include any proposed interrogatories and requests for admission and must specify any requested documents.

(c) Deposition Expenses. If the government is granted leave to take a deposition, the judge may require the government to pay the travel expenses, subsistence expenses, and fees of the moving party's attorney to attend the deposition.

Rule 7. Expanding the Record

(a) **In General.** If the motion is not dismissed, the judge may direct the parties to expand the record by submitting additional materials relating to the motion. The judge may require that these materials be authenticated.

(b) **Types of Materials.** The materials that may be required include letters predating the filing of the motion, documents, exhibits, and answers under oath to written interrogatories propounded by the judge. Affidavits also may be submitted and considered as part of the record.

(c) **Review by the Opposing Party.** The judge must give the party against whom the additional materials are offered an opportunity to admit or deny their correctness.

Rule 8. Evidentiary Hearing

(a) **Determining Whether to Hold a Hearing.** If the motion is not dismissed, the judge must review the answer, any transcripts and records of prior proceedings, and any materials submitted under Rule 7 to determine whether an evidentiary hearing is warranted.

(b) **Reference to a Magistrate Judge.** A judge may, under 28 U.S.C. § 636(b), refer the motion to a magistrate judge to conduct hearings and to file proposed findings of fact and recommendations for disposition. When they are filed, the clerk must promptly serve copies of the proposed findings and recommendations on all parties. Within 14 days after being served, a party may file objections as provided by local court rule. The judge must determine de novo any proposed finding or recommendation to which objection is made. The judge may accept, reject, or modify any proposed finding or recommendation.

(c) **Appointing Counsel; Time of Hearing.** If an evidentiary hearing is warranted, the judge must appoint an attorney to represent a moving party who qualifies to have counsel appointed under 18 U.S.C. § 3006A. The judge must conduct the hearing as soon as practicable after giving the attorneys adequate time to investigate and prepare. These rules do not limit the appointment of counsel under Sec. 3006A at any stage of the proceedings.

(d) **Producing a Statement.** Federal Rule of Criminal Procedure 26.2(a)-(d) and (f) applies at a hearing under this rule. If a party does not comply with Rule 26.2(a) order to produce a witness's statement, the court must not consider that witness's testimony.

Rule 9. Second or Successive Motions

Before presenting a second or successive motion, the moving party must obtain an order from the appropriate court of appeals authorizing the district court to consider the motion, as required by 28 U.S.C. § 2255, para. 8.

Rule 10. Powers of a Magistrate Judge

A magistrate judge may perform the duties of a district judge under these rules, as authorized by 28 U.S.C. § 636.

Rule 11. Certificate of Appealability; Time to Appeal

(a) **Certificate of Appealability.** The district court must issue or deny a certificate of appealability when it enters a final order adverse to the applicant. Before entering the final order, the court may direct the parties to submit arguments on whether a certificate should be issued. If the court issues a certificate, the court must state the specific issue or issues that satisfy the showing required by 28 U.S.C. § 2253(c)(2). If the court denies a certificate, a party may not appeal the denial but may seek a certificate from the court of appeals under Federal Rule of Appellate Procedure 22. A motion to reconsider a denial does not extend the time to appeal.

(b) **Time to Appeal.** Federal Rule of Appellate Procedure 4(a) governs the time to appeal an order entered under these rules. A timely notice of appeal must be filed even if the district court issues a certificate of appealability. These rules do not extend the time to appeal the original judgment of conviction.

Rule 12. Applicability of the Federal Rules of Civil Procedure and the Federal Rules of Criminal Procedure

The Federal Rules of Civil Procedure and the Federal Rules of Criminal Procedure, to the extent that they are not inconsistent with any statutory provisions or these rules, may be applied to a proceeding under these rules.

PURPOSE OF 28 U.S.C. § 2255

The Seventy-ninth Congress in regard to 28 U.S.C. § 2255. "restates, clarifies, and simplifies the procedure in the nature of the ancient writ of *error coram nobis*. It provides an expeditious remedy for correcting erroneous sentences without resort to *habeas corpus*. It has the approval of the "Judicial Conference of the United States." Its principle provisions are incorporated in H.R. 4233.

Although the expressed intent of the Seventy-ninth Congress was to provide "an expeditious remedy," 28 U.S.C. § 2255 provides anything but "an expeditious remedy." In reading 28 U.S.C. § 2255(b) you will discover that in writing the statute, codifying it, the drafters left out the part about the "expeditious remedy." To the confusion of many, § 2255(b) provides for a "prompt hearing" but fails to provide any guidance as to what "prompt hearing" means under the law.

This failure, by the drafters of 28 U.S.C. § 2255, has been used over time to cause years of delay at the cost of billions of dollars to the American taxpayers. Remember that the goal of judges, lawyers, and politicians is to prolong a sentence, of even the innocent, as long as possible, and thus preserve and/or uphold the conviction without regard to guilt and innocence. 28 U.S.C. § 2255 states:

§ 2255. FEDERAL CUSTODY; REMEDIES ON MOTION ATTACKING SENTENCE

(a) A prisoner in custody under sentence of a court established by Act of Congress claiming the right to be released upon the ground that the sentence was imposed in violation of the Constitution or laws of the United States, or that the court was without jurisdiction to impose such sentence. or that the sentence was in excess of the maximum authorized by law, or is otherwise subject to collateral attack, may move the court which imposed the sentence to vacate, set aside or correct the sentence.

(b) Unless the motion and the files and records of the case conclusively show that the prisoner is entitled to no relief, the court shall cause notice thereof to be served upon the United States attorney, grant a prompt hearing thereon, determine the issues and make findings of fact and conclusion of law with respect thereto. If the court finds that the judgment was rendered without jurisdiction, or that the sentence imposed was not authorized by law or otherwise open to collateral attack, or that there has been such a denial or infringement of the constitutional rights of the prisoner as to render the judgment vulnerable to collateral attack· the court shall vacate and set the judgment aside and shall discharge the prisoner or resentence him or grant a new trial or correct the sentence as may appear appropriate.

(c) A court may entertain and determine such motion without requiring the production of the prisoner at the hearing.

(d) An appeal may be taken to the court of appeals from the order entered on the motion as from the final judgment on application for a writ of *habeas corpus*.

(e) An application for a writ of *habeas corpus* on behalf of a prisoner who is authorized to apply for relief by motion pursuant to this section, shall not be entertained if it appears that the applicant has failed to apply for relief, by motion, to the court which sentenced him, or that such court has denied him relief, unless it also appears that the remedy by motion is inadequate or ineffective to test the legality of his detention.

(f) A 1-year period of limitation shall apply to a motion under this section. The limitation period shall run from the latest of –

    (1) the date on which the judgment of conviction becomes final;

    (2) the date on which the impediment to making a motion created by governmental action in violation of the Constitution or laws of the United States is removed, if the movant was prevented from making a motion by such governmental action;

    (3) the date on which the right asserted was initially recognized by the Supreme Court, if that right has been newly recognized by the Supreme Court and made retroactively applicable to cases on collateral review; or

    (4) the date on which the facts supporting the claim or claims presented could have been discovered through the exercise of due diligence.

(g) Except as provided in section 408 of the Controlled Substances Act [21 USCS § 848], in all proceedings brought under this section, and any subsequent proceedings on review, the court may appoint counsel, except as provided by a rule promulgated by the Supreme Court pursuant to statutory authority. Appointment of counsel under this section shall be governed by section 3006A of title 18.

(h) A second or successive motion must be certified as provided in section 2244 [28 USCS § 2244] by a panel of the appropriate court of appeal to contain –

    (1) newly discovered evidence that, if proven and viewed in light of the evidence as a whole, would be sufficient to establish by clear and convincing evidence that no reasonable factfinder would have found the movant guilty of the offense; or

    (2) a new rule of constitutional law made retroactive to cases on collateral review by the Supreme Court, that was previously unavailable.

VAGUENESS OF § 2255

The word vague is defined as 1: not clear, definite, or distinct in expression or perception. 2: not clearly felt or analyzed. When considering a criminal statute that is unclear about what conduct it holds as unlawful, the Supreme Court invalidates the statute holding it to be unconstitutionally void-for-vagueness, see *Johnson v. United States*, 576 U.S. ,135 S. Ct. 2551.

28 U.S.C. § 2255 is not a Criminal Statute, but it is however, a statute that was enacted to end the incarceration of people who had been erroneously sentenced. The federal statute, 28 U.S.C. § 2255, was enacted and then codified with an ambiguity that allows lower courts to disregard the intentions of Congress. The statutes lack of clarity leaves the U.S. District Courts to decide what the law really means. The ambiguity, between Congress's intent in enacting 28 U.S.C. § 2255 and the text of 28 U.S.C. § 2255(b), leaves the courts, rather than Congress to decide what Congress really intended when they enacted § 2255 into law. The lack of particularity in § 2255(b) has cost the American Taxpayers billions of dollars, years of false incarceration that were later overturned, and thousands of hours wasted judicial resources over the last seventy-one years. This ambiguity is one of the many causes of prisons being overcrowded and has never before been addressed by the Supreme Court. Such a question represents an issue of national importance and very likely the answer would be a huge step in criminal justice reform. The Supreme Court, in giving a bright line definition of two words, could have the largest impact on mass-incarceration in history. The question that has been before all lower courts, producing a different answer in each, is "what does 'prompt hearing' really mean?"

A definition of this term, for all lower courts to follow, would almost immediately end all frivolous litigation in the lower courts. The largest number of frivolous filings is from *pro se* litigants trying to obtain a "prompt hearing." If the Supreme Court of the United States were to provide a definition similar to:

> *The term "prompt hearing," for the purpose of 28 U.S.C. §2255(b), is defined as a period of time not to exceed seventy (70) days following the final substantive pleading or order filed in the case.*

With such a definition in force, *pro se* litigants would end their filings to allow the seventy (70) days to elapse in hopes of a "prompt hearing," the courts of appeals would no longer receive petitions for writs of mandamus, and district courts would never again be burdened with deciding what constitutes unnecessary delay in a post-conviction proceeding.

> *Author's Note: I go into this subject early on because the reader will have to prepare for the inevitable delay. As this book guides you through the post-conviction relief process it will address unnecessary delay before it happens in an effort to avoid it. Remember the district courts ordinarily do not grant § 2255's to pro se litigants. They will either deny outright or they will delay a meaningful claim. Their goal is to find that the Movant (you) failed to prosecute the claim. Thus, we must prepare for relief in the court of appeals at the very start of the post-conviction relief process.*

§ 2255 IN ACTUAL PRACTICE

A defendant has most often been shipped to a prison, to serve his sentence, long before his appeal is denied. During his first few months in prison, most defendants are still in denial about how the American Criminal Justice System works. This misconception is no mistake; it is planted in the minds of all first-time offenders by those who operate the system. Lawyers have said, over and over again, "if you lose your appeal, you can just file your § 2255 and go home." Although this sounds good to a defendant, it is not even close to true.

In the average criminal case the judge and defense counsel advises the defendant that no matter what happens, he can always file a motion under section § 2255 to set his sentence aside. The theory is that the federal system is made up of thousands of rules and laws, and if one is broken, the defendant is set free. *This is not true*. The truth is that there exists a very narrow path in which a defendant may challenge his sentence under § 2255. In reality the "any error" theory is applicable only under the All Writs Act, 28 U.S.C. § 1651 not § 2255. The Supreme Court had previously determined that (a) Although § 2255 restates clarifies and simplifies the procedure in the common law writ of *error coram nobis*, § 2255 does not supersede the writ of *coram nobis*; (2) A § 2255 would never be allowed to do the same service as of a direct appeal; and (3) to determine what issues are reviewable on a motion under § 2255 a district or appellate court can refer to decisions that have narrowed the availability of the federal *habeas corpus* remedy in the past.

This third element is probably the most important to a defendant. The courts have been closing the doors to relief at every turn allowed for the last thirty years. It was only in the last five years that the Supreme Court has started to turn back to the Constitution of the United States.

In today's practice of § 2255, where a defendant must file in *pro se*, a defendant must make a Constitutional claim. That claim must go directly to due process of law as described in the Fifth, Thirteenth, and Fourteenth Amendments. Thus, a defendant must claim that he or she was denied a fair trial and the opportunity to present a defense. When the defendant takes a good look at all the other Constitutional rights, he or she will find that they are all related to the elements of a fair trial as opposed to the trial itself. That means that the violation of one element I of a fair trial does not necessarily mean that the defendant was denied a fair trial. A very good example of this is the *Strickland v. Washington,* 466 U.S. 668, two-prong test. The Supreme Court's holding in *Strickland* allows a defense lawyer to provide ineffective assistance of counsel – which is a violation of a sixth Amendment Constitutional right – as long as the courts can conclude that the ineffectiveness did not make any difference.

FOLLOW CURRENT CASE LAW

§ 2255 proceedings are one of the few proceedings where case law is more important than the statutes. That's because the statute does not specifically list a number of issues that qualify under the "otherwise subject to collateral attack" clause of § 2255(a). Thus, the courts in theory follow the lead of other Supreme Court decisions. Therefore, it is important to stay current on recent case law.

The next issue that a defendant will face, once committed to a prison, is the inadequacy of the prison's law library. What the new prisoner will find is an electronic law library that contains hundreds of useless volumes. Most of the volumes that refer to post-conviction relief and 28 U.S.C. § 2255 are thirty years outdated. One of the most informative volumes in the federal prison law library is "Annotations from Lawyers Edition, Second Series." This volume is categorized by subject, and on most subjects, it has been kept as current as possible. The subject listed as "Federal Post-Conviction Remedy, 143 L. Ed. 2d 1055," however, does not list any decisions later than the listed cases decided in 2012. Therefore, a defendant should not rely on what the government provides as the principles controlling federal post-conviction relief; he or she must study the latest Supreme Court decisions for themselves.

CHAPTER EIGHTEEN

COLLATERAL PROCESS

§ 2255 is often referred to as a further step in the movant's criminal case, and not a separate civil action (see notes of advisory committee, Rule 1 of § 2255). Although a true statement, also know that § 2255 is not an appeal process. It is a form of collateral relief that attacks the way the trial process was handled, rather than the subject-matter that was on trial. This means, in plain terms, that § 2255 does not serve as a process to determine the facts presented at trial. § 2255 is specifically practiced determining if the defendant had a fair trial and if he did not, why.

PRACTICAL APPLICATION OF § 2255

§ 2255 authorizes a defendant to raise the claim that he or she has the right to release, from an illegal sentence, based on the ground that he or she was deprived of due process. The right referred to here is established by the Fifth Amendment holding that: "no person shall ... be deprived of life, liberty, or property, without due process of law." Again, and it cannot be said enough, due process in a criminal setting is the process that allows a defendant to be heard in his own defense at a fair trial. Therefore, if the error a defendant raises did not deprive him of a fair trial, or deprived him of a trial altogether, the error did not violate his constitutional right to due process. § 2255 allows a defendant to claim that the sentence was imposed in violation of the constitution or the laws of the United States. Although this sounds like it covers a broad spectrum of claims, that simply is not the case. § 2255 and § 2254 were enacted to remedy a very specific claim. That claim is that you deserve to be released from custody based on the grounds that your trial process was defective. Yes, all claims boil down to one of two things: (1) the defendant was deprived of a fair trial: or (2) the defendant had no trial at all. All other perceived errors are only elements that caused the defendant to be deprived of a meaningful trial process.

AFTER A GUILTY PLEA

As to the wide variety of possible grounds for relief under § 2255, the Supreme Court has carved out a few very specific claims that may be raised after a defendant enters a guilty plea. The High Court had previously indicated that it will generally be very difficult for a defendant, who pleaded guilty in federal court, to successfully attack the validity of the plea under § 2255. The Supreme Court, however, has also stated that the lower federal courts may not adopt a per se rule that completely bars relief under § 2255 from an unconstitutionally obtained guilty plea. Some of the court's most recent decisions have involved some serious constitutional issues.

Constitutionality of a Statute – Any time the government seeks a grand jury indictment; it is claiming that the defendant, who has been indicted, has violated a federal criminal statute, see title 18 of the United States Code, Crimes. As known to all courts, and most lawyers, Congress has the authority to pass laws that limit the conduct of the people. Congress's authority, however, is strictly governed by the Constitution of the United States. Any time Congress passes a law that stands outside of its law-making authority, Congress has exceeded its law-making authority under the Constitution. Thus, the law is unconstitutional.

Ordinarily, no one has the authority to question an act of Congress. At least not until it affects someone negatively. This is where the "case and controversy" standard is invoked. Basically, common citizens don't have a right to complain about an issue that does not cause them any loss. Likewise, the Supreme Court of the United States does not have the authority to review the Constitutionality of an Act of Congress until it is properly raised within the court's limited jurisdiction, see the rules of the Supreme Court of the United States. A federal defendant who has been charged under a Grand Jury indictment or information has the absolute right to raise an issue with the Constitutionality of a federal criminal statute, see *Carol Anne Bond v. United*

States, 564 U.S. 211, 131 S. Ct. 2355 (2011), holding that: Bond has standing to challenge the federal statute on grounds that the measure interferes with the powers reserved to the states. Simply stated, Ms. Bond was incarcerated and was therefore affected by the federal criminal statute. In the ordinary case a defendant is "affected," and has legal "standing" to challenge the Constitutionality of any criminal statute upon arrest or first appearance.

Counsel's Erroneous Advice to Plead Guilty – needless to say, it is a rare case in which a defendant enters a guilty plea without first being advised by counsel to do so. Defense counsel has an obligation, under the law and the constitution, to give sound advice to a defendant before he enters a guilty plea. Counsel must make his client aware of the essential elements of the charged offense; all possible defenses to the charged conduct; the statutory and guideline maximum and minimum sentences; all other possible consequences of pleading guilty; and the defendant's right to appeal from any appeal waivers, and other issues. Plainly stated, a defendant has a right to a reasonable expectation of a specific outcome after entering a guilty plea. It is defense counsel's obligation to advise the defendant, In a way that provides that accurate expectation of a specific outcome.

In the case of *Jae Lee v. United States*, 582 U.S.___ , 137 S. Ct. 1958, 198 L. Ed. 2d (2017), the court held that: Lee had adequately demonstrated a reasonable probability that, but for counsel's erroneous advice, he would have rejected a guilty plea where his plea colloquy and surrounding circumstances showed deportation was the determinative issue in his decision to accept the plea, and it was not irrational to reject the plea deal when there was some chance of avoiding deportation, however remote.

One consequence of overturning any guilty plea, that a defendant must be aware of, is that the result of doing so is facing a trial. Therefore, if the defendant has had charges dismissed under a plea agreement, he should consider all possible consequences before overturning a guilty plea.

Failure to Give Appeal Advice – The right to advice concerning appeal is absolute. It is because a defendant has the right to appeal from an unfair or unclear appeal waiver; thus, has an absolute right to be advised concerning his right to appeal after a guilty plea. This, counsel's duty to give appeal advice, should not be confused with a judge's duty to give Rule 11 appeal advice. Just a hint: any § 2255 that raises a claim against the presiding judge is a loser in most cases. If a defendant has a claim against a judge, his best option is usually to form it as counsel's failure to object.

Preparing an appeal begins with recognizing a claim and filing a notice of appeal. The task of navigating the appellate process begins with identifying a sound claim and doing so without a lawyer's assistance is often a disastrous effort for a layperson. The appellate process is complicated and usually well beyond the competence of untrained individuals who have little education, learning disabilities, and mental impairments, see *Evitts v. Lucey*, 469 U.S. 387, 393, 83 L. Ed. 2d 821, 105 S. Ct. 830 (1985) ("The services of a lawyer will for virtually every layman be necessary to present an appeal in a form suitable for appellate consideration on the merits."); *Gideon v. Wainwright*, 372 U.S. 335, 345, 9 L. Ed. 2d 799, 83 S. Ct. 792 (1963) ("Even the intelligent and educated layman has small and sometimes no skill in the science of law." (quoting *Powell v. Alabama*, 287 U.S. 45, 69, 77 L. Ed. 158, 53 S. Ct. 55 (1932)). Appeals by defendants convicted on their pleas may involve "myriad and often complicated" substantive issues, *Kowalski v. Tesmer*, 543 U.S., at 145, 160 L. Ed. 2d 519, 125 S. Ct. 564, and may be "no less complex than other appeals," *id.*, at 141, 160 L. Ed. 2d 519, 125 S. ct. 564 (same). A defendant who pleads guilty may still raise on appeal "Constitutional defects that are irrelevant to his factual guilt, double jeopardy claims requiring no further factual record, jurisdictional defects, challenges to the sufficiency of the evidence at the preliminary examination, preserved entrapment claims, mental competency claims, factual basis claims, claims that the state had no right to proceed in the first place, including claims that a defendant was charged under an inapplicable statute, and claims of ineffective assistance of counsel." See *Halbert v. Michigan*, 545 U.S. 605, 162 L. Ed. 2d 552, 125 S. Ct. 2582 (2005), see also Garza v. Idaho, 586 U.S. , 139 S. ct. , 203 L. Ed. 2d 77 (2019).

GROUNDS FOR RELIEF, GENERALLY

In its first paragraph, § 2255(a), specifies four grounds that are reviewable if raised in a motion under the statute. The key phrase in § 2255(a) is that a defendant may make a claim based "upon the ground that the sentence was imposed in violation of the constitution or laws of the United States, or that the court was without jurisdiction to impose such sentence, or that the sentence was in excess of the maximum authorized by law, or is otherwise subject to collateral attack."

As previously illustrated, the Supreme Court has ruled that relief should be granted, under § 2255, upon the showing of a deprivation of a Constitutional right; that is reviewable under the statute. Additionally, when raising a claim under § 2255, the prisoner must make a showing that he meets both *Strickland* prongs, "cause and prejudice." This means that the prisoner must show why he did not raise the issue on direct appeal ("cause") and how the issue deprived him of a fair trial process ("prejudice"). Remember also that the trial process starts at arraignment and continues "on through appeal." 3006A(c). "Where federal prisoner, who is seeking post-conviction relief under 28 U.S.C. § 2255, failed properly to raise claim on direct appeal, then relief is available only if the prisoner establishes cause for waiver and shows actual prejudice resulting from alleged violation, see *Reed v. Farley*, 129 L. Ed. 2d 277, 114 S. Ct. 2291.

Validity of a Guilty Plea – In the past five years there have been literally thousands of claims attacking the validity of guilty pleas. This of course is a fertile field, in which to cultivate a claim, because the defendant has indeed been denied a trial. And, as illustrated earlier, there is no Constitutional or statutory basis for a plea agreement. The prejudice in a claim against a plea agreement is that the defendant was deprived of a trial and that is shown by his willingness to go to trial. The only thing left to do is show why the defendant did not raise the claim in direct appeal. As circular as this reasoning appears, the defendant must show: (1) That defense counsel's error caused the defendant to plead guilty, depriving him of a trial; (2) That counsel failed to raise the issue on direct appeal due to the obvious conflict of interest; and (3) That there was a reasonable probability that the defendant would have gone to trial absent counsel's errors. Once the defendant can show counsel's erroneous advice, or other error, an affidavit will support the last two prongs. Claims against the validity of plea agreements have become a wide open and endless supply of possible claims, so please be creative and think outside of the box.

Post-Conviction Changes in Law – Convictions and sentences for conduct which, as a result of a later change of law, was no longer criminal has been determined by the Supreme Court to justify relief under 28 U.S.C. § 2255.

In *Davis v. United States*, 417 U.S. 333, 41 L. Ed. 2d 109, 94 S. Ct. 2298 (1974), the Supreme Court decided that a petitioner's conviction and punishment for an act which, as a result of a judicial decision, the law no longer made criminal justifies relief under § 2255. The petitioner, who had been convicted of violating the Selective Service laws, sought relief on the grounds that by a change in the law of the federal judicial circuit in which he was convicted, following his conviction, the military induction order he was convicted of violating was illegal. The test, according to the court, was whether the error of law was a fundamental defect which inherently resulted in a complete miscarriage of justice or which presented exceptional circumstances in which the need for a "*habeas corpus*" remedy was apparent.

In *Johnson v. United States*, 576 U.S. __, 135 S. Ct. 2551, 192 L. Ed. 2d 569 (2015), the Supreme Court decided that the residual clause of 18 U.S.C. § 924(e) was unconstitutionally void-for-vagueness. The court invalidated the statutes residual clause, under which Mr. Johnson was sentenced, and granted him *certiorari* ordering the lower courts to grant him post-conviction relief under 28 U.S.C. § 2255. Also see *Sessions v. Dimaya*, 584 U.S. __, 138 S. ct. 1204, 200 1. Ed. 2d 549 (2018).

CHAPTER NINETEEN

REQUIREMENTS FOR FILING § 2255 MOTION

The filing of a motion under 28 U.S.C. § 2255 is governed by the text of the statute (§ 2255), the Rules governing Section 2255 proceedings, and the discretion of the court involved. This chapter is written for the purpose of making clear what Congress intended when it enacted 28 U.S.C. § 2255. This illustration will be referencing that statute, paragraph by paragraph, and comparing its text to that of the corresponding rules and the courts authority to rule.

JURISDICTION

In § 2255(a) the statute begins with defining who and for what reasons a prisoner may obtain post-conviction relief. Paragraph (a) defines the authority to grant relief under the statute, i.e., its jurisdiction. Custody- "A prisoner in custody," is a specific statement that requires that the person filing for relief be deprived of his liberty. This requirement is established in the words of the Supreme Court of the United States, "It is clear … that the essence of *habeas corpus* is an attack by a person in custody upon the legality of that custody, and that the traditional function of the writ is to secure release from illegal custody," *Preiser v. Rodriguez*, (1973).

Initially the Supreme Court held that *habeas corpus* was appropriate only in those situations in which the petitioner's claim would result in an immediate release from a present custody, as in *McNally v. Hill*, 293 U.S. 131 (1934). This was later changed in *Payton v. Rowe*, 391 U.S. 54 (1968), in which the court held that *habeas corpus* was a proper way to attack a consecutive sentence to be served in the future, expressing the view that consecutive sentences resulted in present custody under both judgments, not merely the one imposing the first sentence. This view was expanded in *Carafas v. LaVallee*, 391 U.S. 234 (1968), to recognize the propriety of *habeas corpus* in a case in which the petitioner was in custody when the petition was originally filed but had since been unconditionally released from custody, see the notes of the advisory committee that follow Rule 1 of Rules Governing Section 2254 cases.

Sentence – Additionally, the prisoner must be "under sentence of a court established by Act of Congress." This statement in plain terms means a federal district court. The reason that the statute states "by Act of Congress" is because that is how the court was established. In looking at Article one, Section one of the Constitution of the United States, you will find that, "all legislative (law making) powers herein granted shall be vested in a Congress of the United States." You will also find that Article one, Section eight lists a number of offences that Congress has the authority to punish, see Art. I, Sec. 8, clause 10. With the power provided it, by the Constitution, the U.S. Congress passed legislation that established the U.S. District Courts, in each of the United States, see 28 U.S.C. §§81-131.

Claim – This part of § 2255, which references "claiming the right to be released," has led to a mountain of frivolous filings over the years because prisoners have a habit of confusing this with the elements required to establish their "ground." This is very simple; a prisoner is required to be claiming that he or she has "the right to be released."

Ground – The next step is to decipher what "upon the ground that" means. Your ground is the foundation or basis on which your "claim to be released" rests. Although, there are thousands of possible grounds to base your claim upon; you will find that § 2255 requires that your ground fit into one of four specific categories: (1) the sentence was imposed in violation of the Constitution or laws of the United States; (2) that the court was without jurisdiction to impose such sentence; (3) that the sentence was in excess of the maximum authorized by law; or (4) is otherwise subject to collateral attack.

Author's Note: The most important aspect of filing a motion under 28 U.S.C. § 2255 is basing your claim on a solid ground. Because of recent court decisions, that ground must include a denial of trial, fair trial, appeal advice, or fair sentencing after a trial, for those of you filing based solely on your criminal case. The next most important issue is your consideration of the Strickland two-part test, as you formulate your grounds. In all grounds that I raise, under this context, I start out with the ineffective assistance of counsel. I then move on to what critical stage of the trial process that the client was deprived of. By doing this I go straight to the heart of the Strickland test: Cause – ineffective assistance of counsel; and Prejudice – deprived of Constitutional due process right to a fair trial, etc.

If you consider the test long before you begin to write, you won't have to start over later.

If the defendant makes a claim based on a ground formulated as previously described the defendant, then, "may move the court which imposed the sentence to vacate, set aside or correct the sentence."

ENTITLED TO RELIEF

§ 2255(b) governs the courts evaluation of the grounds that the prisoner presented in accordance with § 2255(a). Paragraph (b) also grants the court a great deal of decision-making power. When a prisoner is preparing his or her grounds, it is a good idea to compare its elements to this paragraph just as it should be compared to the *Strickland* two-part test.

Preliminary Review – "Unless the motion and the files and records of the case conclusively show that the prisoner is entitled to no relief" … although this statement seems to be clear, it can be confusing. What it means is that the court is going to review the grounds the prisoner has raised and compare them to the record of the criminal case to see if together they prove that the prisoner is entitled to no relief. Such as if a prisoner were to claim the right to be released on the ground of actual innocence, after admitting on the record to have "owned guns and kept them in his home, sold drugs in his home, and at times, his customers may have seen his guns in his home," *Latorre v. United States*, 193 F. 3d 1035 (8th Cir. 1999).

CHAPTER TWENTY

OTHER CONSIDERATIONS

Once a prisoner is transferred to a facility, his mind often begins its attempt to determine what went wrong. It does not matter if he is wrongfully convicted or just over-sentenced; the mind's natural instinct drives him to find the answer. This chapter is added to help the average prisoner save time, by going over the limited set of circumstances in which a prisoner can raise a meaningful claim under 28 U.S.C. § 2255.

ONE YEAR LIMITATION

Generally, there is a one-year limitation in which a prisoner may raise a claim under § 2255. Although there are some exceptions, most claims must be raised within that time period, see 28 U.S.C. § 2255(f). Just as a reminder, all grounds for relief should include three elements: (1) a denial of the due process right to a fair trial; (2) the prisoner's failure to appeal was caused by ineffective assistance of counsel; and (3) that the prisoner suffered some prejudice, even if it's only the denial of the trial he was entitled to. The following grounds must be raised within the one-year limitation:

- Invalid guilty plea
- Invalid appeal waiver
- Statute is void-for-vagueness
- Invalid search and seizure
- Sentence enhancements
- Deprived of counsel
- Jury instructions
- Failure to give appeal advice

For purposes of § 2255's one-year limitation, the period, for federal prisoners to raise a claim seeking post-conviction relief, begins when the criminal judgment becomes final. The judgment becomes final when:

(1) the Supreme Court;

    (A) affirms the conviction on the merits of direct appeal, or

    (B) denies *Certiorari* petition; or

(2) if the petitioner does not seek *certiorari*, when time for filing *certiorari* petition expires. Argument that if a petitioner declines to seek *certiorari*, then limitations period starts to run when court of appeals issues mandate, has been rejected.

Direct review process for purposes of § 2255(f)(1) either "concludes" or "expires," depending on whether the petitioner pursues or forgoes direct appeal to Supreme Court, see *Gonzalez v. Thaler*, 181 L. Ed. 2d 619, 132 S. Ct. 641 (2012). In the federal context the time limit will be determined to have started on the day the district judge files the judgment and conviction order if no direct appeal in the Circuit Court is taken.

OUTSIDE THE ONE-YEAR LIMITATION

As with all rules and laws, there are always some exceptions. In terms of § 2255 considerations, there are three recognized exceptions:

Change in Constitutional Law – A change in Constitutional law that is made retroactive by the Supreme Court, or a change in the law that excludes a certain conduct or a specific group of people, is actionable from the date of the change. Even those prisoners who have filed a § 2255 motion before may file for a leave to file a second § 2255 motion, see 28 U.S.C. § 2255(h); § 2244(a); and rules governing section § 2255 proceedings, Rule 9. For guidance, review the case that follows:

WELCH V. UNITED STATES
578 U.S. __, 136 S. CT. 1257 (2016)

DECISION

Holding in *Johnson v. United States* (2015, US) 135 S. Ct. 2551, 192 L. Ed. 2d 569, 2015 U.S. LEXIS 4251that increased sentence under 18 U.S.C.S. § 924(e)(2)(B)'s residual clause violated due process under Federal Constitution's Fifth Amendment – announced new substantive rule that applied retroactively.

CASE SUMMARY

Johnson v. United States, which held that the residual clause of the Armed Career Criminal Act, U.S.C.S. § 924(e)(2)(B), was void for vagueness, was a substantive decision that applied retroactively to a prisoner's case on collateral review; it affected the reach of the Act rather than the judicial procedures by which the Act was applied.

OVERVIEW

Issue: Whether *Johnson v. United States*, which held that the residual clause of the Armed Career Criminal Act of 1984, 18 U.S.C.S. § 924(e) (2) (B) (H), was void for vagueness, was a substantive decision that applied retroactively to a prisoner's case on collateral review.

Holdings: [1] Johnson changed the substantive reach of the Act and was therefore a substantive decision. It was not a procedural decision, as it affected the reach of the underlying statute rather than the judicial procedures by which the statute was applied; [2] The Teague balance did not depend on whether the underlying constitutional guarantee was procedural or substantive, but instead on whether the new rule itself had a procedural or substantive function; [3] It was not necessary for the new rule to limit Congress's power in order to be substantive.

OUTCOME

Judgment vacated and case remanded; 7-1 Decision; 1 Dissent

SYLLABUS

Federal law makes the possession of a firearm by a felon a crime punishable by a prison term of up to 10 years, 18 U.S.C. §§ 922(g), 924(a)(2), but the Armed Career Criminal Act of 1984 increases that sentence to a mandatory 15 years to life if the offender has three or more prior convictions for a "serious drug offense" or a "violent felony," § 924(e)(1). The definition of "violent felony" includes the so-called residual clause, covering any felony that "otherwise involves conduct that presents a serious potential risk of physical injury to another." § 924(e)(2)(B)(ii). In *Johnson v. United States*, 576 U.S.___ , 135 S. Ct. 2551, 192 L. Ed. 2d 569, this Court held that clause unconstitutional under the void-for-vagueness doctrine.

Petitioner Welch was sentenced under the Armed Career Criminal Act before *Johnson* was decided. On direct review, the Eleventh Circuit affirmed his sentence, holding that Welch's prior Florida conviction for robbery qualified as a "violent felony" under the residual clause. After his conviction became final, Welch sought collateral relief under 28 U.S.C. § 2255, which the District Court denied. The Eleventh Circuit then denied Welch a certificate of appealability. Three weeks later, the Court decided *Johnson*. Welch now seeks the retroactive application of *Johnson* to his case.

Held: *Johnson* announced a new substantive rule that has retroactive effect in cases on collateral review. Pp. ___-___ , 194 L. Ed. 20, at 398-404.

(a) An applicant seeking a certificate of appealability in a § 2255 proceeding must make "a substantial showing of the denial of a constitutional right" § 2253(c)(2). That standard is met when "reasonable jurists could debate whether … the petition should have been resolved in a different manner," see *Slack v. McDaniel*, 529 U.S. 473, 484, 120 S. Ct. 1595, 146 L. Ed. 2d 542. The question of whether Welch met that standard implicates a broader legal issue: whether *Johnson* is a substantive decision with retroactive effect in cases on collateral review. If so, then on the present record reasonable jurists could at least debate whether Welch should obtain relief in his collateral challenge to his sentence. Pp. ___-___ , 194 L. Ed. 2d, at 398-399.

(b) New constitutional rules of criminal procedure generally do not apply retroactively to cases on collateral review, but new substantive rules do apply retroactively, as in *Teague v. Lane*, 489 U.S. 288, 310, 109 S. Ct. 1060, 103 L. Ed. 2d 334; *Schriro v. Summerlin*, 542 U.S. 348, 351, 124 S. Ct. 2519, 159 L. Ed. 2d 442. Substantive rules alter the range of conduct or the class of persons that the law punishes," *id.*, at 353, 124 S. Ct. 2519, 159 L. Ed. 2d 442. Procedural rules, by contrast, "regulate only the *manner of determining* the defendant's culpability." *ibid.* Under this framework, *Johnson* is substantive. Before *Johnson*, the residual clause could cause an offender to face a prison sentence of at least 15 years instead of at most 10. Since *Johnson* made the clause invalid, it can no longer mandate or authorize any sentence. By the same logic, *Johnson* is not procedural, since it had nothing to do with the range of permissible methods a court might use to determine whether a defendant should be sentenced under the Act, see *Schriro*, supra, at 353, 124 S. Ct. 2519, 159 L. Ed. 2d 442. Pp. ___-___ , 194 L. Ed. 2d, at 399-400.

(c) The counter arguments made by Court-appointed *amicus* are unpersuasive. She contends that *Johnson* is a procedural decision because the void-for- vagueness doctrine is based on procedural due process. But the *Teague* framework turns on whether the function of the rule is substantive or procedural, not on the rule's underlying constitutional source. *Amicus*'s approach would lead to results that cannot be squared with prior precedent. Precedent also does not support *amicus*'s claim that a rule must limit Congress's power to be substantive only because they implement the intent of Congress. The separation-of-powers argument raised by *amicus* is also misplaced, for regardless of whether a decision involves statutory interpretation or statutory invalidation, a court lacks the power to exact a penalty that has not been authorized, by any valid criminal statute, Pp. ___-___ , 194 L. Ed. 2d, at 400-404.

Vacated and remanded

Denied Counsel in Collateral Review – In the federal context, the § 2255 proceeding is the first tier-review in which a prisoner may raise a claim of ineffective assistance of trial counsel. The prisoner has no right to counsel in collateral proceedings; thus, he is deprived of counsel and/or direct review from a claim that trial counsel was ineffective. This circumvents Congress's intent in 18 U.S.C. § 3006A(c). All federal inmates must make this claim a paramount issue in their collateral proceedings. This claim has been held reviewable after one year. For guidance review the case that follows:

RAMIREZ V. UNITED STATES
799 F. 3D 845 (7TH CIR. 2015),
U.S. DISTRICT COURT SO. DIST. ILLINOIS
CIVIL CASE NO.: 11-CV-719-JPG

OPINION

Memorandum and Order – This matter comes before the Court on petitioner Israel C. Ramirez's Motion to Vacate, Set aside or Correct Sentence pursuant to 28 U.S.C. § 2255 (Doc. 2). Per the Order of United States court of Appeals for the Seventh Circuit (Doc. 42), this matter under 28 U.S.C. § 2255 was reopened on

September 28, 2015. Respondent filed a Response (Doc. 46) and Petitioner filed a Reply (Doc. 53). For the following reasons, the Court grants Petitioner's Motion.

1. BACKGROUND

On December 2, 2008, Ramirez entered an open plea of guilty to possessing over two tons of marijuana with intent to distribute in violation of 21 U.S.C. § 841(a)(1). On March 26, 2009, this Court sentenced Ramirez as a career offender to 300 months' incarceration, five years supervised release, a $500 fine, and a $100 special assessment. Attorney John D. Stobbs ("Stobbs") represented Ramirez throughout these proceedings. At sentencing, Stobbs failed to object to Ramirez's career offender classification, see *USA v. Ramirez*, 08-cr-30182.

On direct appeal, Stobbs initially filed a motion to withdraw and an *Anders* brief contending that he could not make a non-frivolous argument. The Seventh Circuit, however, denied Stobbs's motion to withdraw, concluding that a non-frivolous argument could be made with regard to Ramirez's career offender classification. Stobbs then made the following arguments on appeal: (1) Ramirez's Texas domestic assault convictions were not divisible and should not have impacted his career offender status; and (2) if those convictions were divisible, the Court committed plain error when it sentenced Ramirez as a career offender absent a sufficient record to conclude the nature of the Texas convictions.

Ramirez's career offender classification depended on whether his two Texas domestic assault convictions were crimes of violence. The Texas statute under which Ramirez was convicted made it a felony to "intentionally, knowingly, or recklessly" cause bodily injury to a family member, Tex. Penal Code § 22.01(a)(1), (b)(2) (1999). For purposes of the career offender guideline, a conviction under the "intentional" or "knowing" prongs of the statute is a crime of violence; however, a conviction under the "reckless" prong: is not a crime of violence, see *Begay v. United States*, 553 U.S. 137, 128 S. Ct. 1581, 170 L. Ed. 2d 490 (2008); *United States v. Woods*, 576 F.3d 400 (7th Cir. 2009).

Accordingly, the Seventh Circuit concluded that the Texas statute under which Ramirez was convicted is divisible, meaning the court can consider certain underlying documents to determine under which prong Ramirez was convicted, see *United States v. Ramirez*, 606 F. 3d 396,397-98 (7th Cir. 2010) (citing *Taylor v. United States*, 495 U.S. 575, 111 S. Ct. 2143, 109 L. Ed. 2d 607 (1990); *Shepard v. United States*, 544 U.S. 13, 125 S. Ct. 1254, 161 L. Ed. 2d 205 (2005)). The record, however, included only the Texas indictments and judgments which did not shed light on the nature of the conviction. Thus, Ramirez argued the Court committed plain error when it applied the career offender enhancement absent the appropriate record, and he was entitled to be resentenced.

After briefing the matter, the Government confessed error and agreed that Ramirez should be resentenced. The Seventh Circuit, however, concluded that the record did not support a plain error finding and thus affirmed Ramirez's sentence. Specifically, the Seventh Circuit found Ramirez (1) failed to demonstrate that the presentence investigation report, which stated his Texas convictions appeared to consist of deliberate behavior, was incorrect; and (2) that he did not argue that he was deceived or mislead into not protesting in the district court. Accordingly, the Seventh Circuit held that Ramirez failed to meet his burden of proving error.

The Petitioner, through attorney Erin Griebel, then filed the instant § 2255 motion on August 18, 2011. He raised two grounds for relief. Ground one which alleged ineffective assistance of counsel during the sentencing phase for counsel's failure to object to his career offender classification and ground two which alleged ineffective assistance of counsel during the appellate phase for Stobbs' failure to obtain the appropriate underlying documents from his Texas convictions.

However, Ramirez again failed to attach the underlying records and without such documentation, the Court was unable to determine whether Ramirez's Texas convictions fell under the reckless prong and/or established prejudice. The Court denied Petitioner's § 2255 motion and certificate of appealability on January 30, 2013. (Doc. 9). Petitioner appealed (Doc. 11) and also filed a Federal Rule of Civil Procedure 60(b)(6) motion (Doc. 16). On November 19, 2013, the Court denied Petitioner's Rule 60(b)(6) motion on the basis that the Petitioner once again failed to establish prejudice and that there was no right to claim ineffective assistance of counsel on collateral review. (Doc. 17). Petitioner then appealed the denial of the Rule 60(b)(6) motion (Doc. 20).

The United States Court of Appeals for the Seventh Circuit dismissed Petitioner's appeal (Doc. 31) of the denial of § 2255 motion for lack of jurisdiction. The appellate court stated that the denial was entered on January 30, 2013, and the appeal was not filed until November 7, 2013. As such, it was over seven months late and the district court did not grant an extension of the appeal period, see *Ramirez v. USA*, 799 F. 3d 845 (7th Cir. 2014).

However, with regard to the appeal of the Rule 60(b)(6), the Seventh Circuit vacated the denial of the Rule 60(b)(6) motion and remanded with instructions to grant the Rule 60(b)(6) motion and reopen the proceedings under § 2255. The Court found that district court's reliance on *Coleman v. Thompson*, 501 U.S. 722, 752, 111 S. Ct. 2546, 115 L. Ed. 2d 640 (1991) was incorrect and that the District court should have made its determination based on *Trevino v. Thaler*, 133 S.Ct. 1911, 185 L. Ed. 2d 1044 (2013), and *Martinez v. Ryan*, 132 S. Ct. 1309, 182 L. Ed. 2d 272 (2012). Those two cases changed the "approach to claims of ineffective assistance of counsel at initial-review collateral proceedings."

The Court further stated that the, "record was insufficient to determine if Ramirez has other qualifying convictions that might support affirmance of the sentence on other grounds" (Doc. 42-1) see also *Ramirez v. USA*, 799 F.3d 845 (7th Cir. 2015).

As directed, this Court vacated its order denying Petitioner's Rule 60(b)(6) and granted the motion. The Court further reopened this matter and Petitioner's Motion to Vacate, Set Aside or Correct Sentence pursuant to 28 U.S.C. § 2255 is once again before the Court.

2. STANDARD

The Court must grant a § 2255 motion when a defendant's "sentence was imposed in violation of the Constitution or laws of the United States." 28 U.S.C. § 2255. However, "[h]abeas corpus relief under 28 U.S.C. § 2255 is reserved for extraordinary situations." *Prewitt v. United States*, 83 F.3d 812, 816 (7th Cir. 1996). "Relief under § 2255 is available only for errors of constitutional or jurisdictional magnitude, or where the error represents a fundamental defect which inherently results in a complete miscarriage of justice." *Kelly v. United States*, 29 F.3d 1107, 1112 (7th Cir. 1994) (quotations omitted).

The Sixth Amendment to the Constitution provides that "[i]n all criminal prosecutions, the accused shall enjoy the right…to have the Assistance of Counsel for his defense." U.S. Const. amend. VI. This right to assistance of counsel encompasses the right to *effective* assistance of counsel, see *McMann v. Richardson*, 397 U.S. 759, 771, n. 14, 90 S. Ct. 1441, 25 L. Ed. 2d 763 (1970); and *Watson v. Anglin*, 560 F. 3d 687, 690 (7th Cir. 2009). A party claiming ineffective assistance of counsel bears the burden of showing (1) that counsel's performance fell below objective standards for reasonably effective representation and (2) that this deficiency prejudiced the defense. *Strickland v. Washington*, 466 U.S. 668, 688-94, 104 S. Ct. 2052, 80 L. Ed. 2d 674 (1984); *United States v. Jones*, 635 F.3d 909, 915 (7th Cir. 2011); Wyatt v. United States, 574 F.3d 455, 457 (7th Cir. 2009), cert. denied, 559 U.S. 1117, 130 S. Ct. 2431, 176 L. Ed. 2d 945 (2010); *Fountain v. United States*, 211 F.3d 429, 434 (7th Cir. 2000).

To satisfy the first prong of the *Strickland* test, the petitioner must direct the Court to specific acts or omissions of his counsel. Wyatt, 574 F.3d at 458. The Court must then consider whether in light of all oI the circumstances counsel's performance was outside the wide range of professionally competent assistance, *id.* The Court's review of counsel's performance must be "highly deferential [,] … indulg[ing] a strong presumption that counsel's conduct falls within the wide range of reasonable professional assistance." *Strickland*, 466 U.S. at 689; accord *Wyatt*, 574 F.3d at 458. Counsel's performance must be evaluated keeping in mind that an attorney's trial strategies are a matter of professional judgment and often turn on facts not contained in the trial record, as in *Strickland*, 466 U.S. at 689. The Court cannot become a "Monday morning quarterback." Harris v. Reed, 894 F.2d 871, 877 (7th Cir. 1990).

To satisfy the second prong of the *Strickland* test, the plaintiff must show that there is a reasonable probability that, but for counsel's unprofessional errors, the result of the proceedings would have been different, such that the proceedings were fundamentally unfair or unreliable, see *United States v. Jones*, 635 F.3d 909, 915 (7th Cir. 2011); *Fountain*, 211 F.3d at 434; *Adams v. Bertrand*, 453 F.3d 428, 435 (7th Cir. 2006). "A reasonable probability is defined as one that is sufficient to undermine the confidence in an outcome." *Adams*, 453 F.3d at 435 (citing *Strickland*, 466 U.S. at 694).

3. ANALYSIS.

The Petitioner alleges ineffective assistance of counsel during the sentencing phase for counsel's failure to object to Petitioner's career offender classification and alleged ineffective assistance of counsel during the appellate phase for counsel's failure to obtain the appropriate underlying documents from Petitioner's Texas convictions (Doc. 2).

The Seventh Circuit has stated that Petitioner's "trial counsel's performance was deficient. An attorney's failure to object to an error in the court's guidelines calculation that results in a longer sentence for the defendant can demonstrate constitutionally ineffective performance." The Court further held that the counsel's deficiencies prejudiced the Petitioner as it was the government's burden to show that Ramirez's prior convictions, "were knowing or intentional conduct, not reckless actions." (Doc. 42-1, pg. 16). As the government has conceded, it could not meet that burden with regard to the two Texas convictions. The Seventh Circuit, however, stated that the record was "insufficient to determine if Ramirez has other qualifying convictions that might support an affirmance of the sentences on other grounds." The Seventh Circuit also found that, "Counsel's abandonment deprived Ramirez of the ability to press his ineffective assistance argument on appeal," *id.*

The Seventh Circuit found that Petitioner met the first prongs of the *Strickland* test by determining that Petitioner's trial counsel's performance was deficient by failing to object to the Petitioner's career offender status. The Seventh Circuit stated that the Petitioner need only to show that his sentence, "would have been different had counsel objected to his characterization as a career offender" in order to demonstrate prejudice. The advisory guidelines, which the Court considered, strongly suggest that the Petitioner's sentence may have been lower. However, as the Seventh Circuit noted, there may be other qualifying convictions which would have still placed the Petitioner in a career offender status.

In the Government's response, it states that, "[w]ith respect to the two convictions utilized by the District Court in sentencing Ramirez as a Career Offender – the two vicious assaults on his wife in Texas Case Nos. CR-0335-01 and CR-0984-01-E - the Government has no further documents to support its claims that these should be considered crimes of violence under the Career Offender provision. The Government also indicates that it has no additional records that would establish the Petitioner as a career offender.

The only provision:hat the Government puts forth is that "if this Court should find that it would have sentenced the violence-pronged Ramirez to the same 300-months sentence even without relying on the Career

Offender provision; then it cannot be said that counsel's deficient performance prejudiced Ramirez," (Doc. 46, pg. 4).

Petitioner's reply indicates that, regardless of whether the guidelines are advisory, the government provides no authority that an error in the guidelines range does not affect a defendant's sentence - especially since this court in sentencing the Petitioner stated it considered the "guideline computations." Petitioner also contends that a 300-month sentence "would be substantively unreasonable without the career-offender enhancement," (Doc. 53).

Petitioner's initial advisory guideline range was 151 - 188 months and with the career offender enhancement, his advisory guideline range became 262 - 327 months. The Court takes all factors into consideration and although some factors may weigh more heavily that others, each affects the final decision of the Court. As such, the Court cannot state that it would have sentenced Mr. Ramirez to the same sentence without consideration of the guideline computations.

The Petitioner has met both prongs of the *Strickland* test. He directed the Court to the specific act or omission (failing to object to his career offender status) of his trial counsel and that there is a reasonable probability based on the advisory guideline that, but for counsel's unprofessional errors, the result of the proceedings would have been different as the Texas convictions should not have been used and there were no other convictions that would have placed the Petitioner in a career offender status. As such, the proceedings were fundamentally unfair or unreliable. Petitioner's alleged ineffective assistance of counsel during the appellate phase for counsel's failure to obtain the appropriate underlying documents from Petitioner's Texas convictions is moot upon the Court's finding the Petitioner's trial counsel was ineffective.

4. CONCLUSION.

Based on the above, the Court:

Grants: Israel C. Ramirez's § 2255 motion (Doc. 2);

Vacates: the sentence imposed on March 26, 2009, in Ramirez's criminal case as reflected in the judgment entered on April 2, 2009. (Doc. 47 in Case No. 08-cr-30182-JPG); and

Directs: the Clerk of Court to enter judgment accordingly.

It Is So Ordered.

Dated: 3/17/2016

Actual Innocence – The claim of actual innocence is the primary purpose of the constitutional right to *habeas corpus*. It is also reviewable after the one-year statute of limitations. For guidance, review the following case.

McQUIGGIN V. PERKINS
569 U.S. 383, 133 S. CT. 1924 (2013)

Disposition: 670 F.3d 665, vacated and remanded

DECISION

Actual innocence, if proved, held to be gateway through which state prisoner petitioning for federal *habeas corpus* relief might pass, regardless of whether impeded by procedural bar or expiration of 28 U.S.C.S. § 2244(d)(1)'s limitations period.

CASE SUMMARY

Procedural Posture: Respondent state inmate filed a petition for a writ of *habeas corpus*, seeking federal district court review of his conviction for first-degree murder. The district court dismissed the petition; however, the U.S. Court of Appeals for the Sixth Circuit reversed and remanded. The U.S. Supreme Court granted *certiorari* to resolve a conflict among the circuits on whether 28 U. S.C.S. § 2244(d)(1) could be overcome by a showing of actual innocence. Although state inmate who sought habeas relief in federal court six years after he obtained the last of three affidavits which supported his claim that he did not commit murder was not barred by 28 U.S.C.S. § 2244(d)(I) from seeking review, court of appeals erred to extent it eliminated timing as a factor relevant to evaluating Inmate's affidavits.

Overview: The inmate filed a petition for a writ of *habeas corpus* in 2008, more than eleven years after his conviction for first-degree murder became final, claiming that he was innocent and receive ineffective assistance of counsel during his trial, and he submitted three affidavits signed by witnesses that supported his claim. The district court found that even if the affidavits could be characterized as newly discovered evidence, the inmate was not entitled to relief because he obtained the last affidavit in 2002 but did not file his petition until 2008. Although the Sixth Circuit found that the inmate's petition was untimely under 28 U.S.C.S. § 2244(d)(I), it held that his claim of actual innocence allowed him to pursue his habeas petition as if it had been filed on time. The Supreme Court vacated the Sixth Circuit's decision and remanded the case. While the Court rejected the State's argument that habeas petitioners who asserted convincing actual-innocence claims had to prove diligence to cross a federal court's threshold, it found that the Sixth Circuit erred to the extent that it eliminated timing as a factor relevant in evaluating the reliability of the affidavits.

Outcome: The Supreme Court vacated the Sixth Circuit's decision and remanded the case.

5-4 Decision; 1 dissent

SYLLABUS

Rodney Henderson was found stabbed to death after leaving a party in Flint, Michigan, with respondent Floyd Perkins and Damarr Jones. Perkins was charged with murder. Jones, the key prosecution witness testified that Perkins alone committed the murder while Jones looked on. Perkins, however, testified that Jones and Henderson left him during the evening, and that he later saw Jones with blood on his clothing. Perkins was convicted of first-degree murder and sentenced to life in prison without the possibility of parole. His conviction became final in 1997.

The Antiterrorism and Effective Death Penalty Act of 1996 (AEDPA) gives a state prisoner one year to file a federal habeas petition, starting from "the date on which the judgment became final." 28 U.S.C. § 2244(d)(l)(A). But if the petition alleges newly discovered evidence, the filing deadline is one year from "the date on which the factual predicate of the claim … could have been discovered through … due diligence." § 2244(1)(D).

More than 11 years after his conviction became final, Perkins filed his federal habeas petition, alleging, inter alia, ineffective assistance of trial counsel. To overcome AEDPA's time limitations, he asserted newly discovered evidence of actual innocence, relying on three affidavits, the most recent dated July 16, 2002, each pointing to Jones as the murderer. The District Court found that, even if the affidavits could be characterized as evidence newly discovered, Perkins had failed to show diligence entitling him to equitable tolling of AEDPA's limitation period. Alternatively, the court found, Perkins had not shown that, taking account of all the evidence, no reasonable juror would have convicted him. The Sixth Circuit reversed. Acknowledging that Perkins' petition was untimely and that he had not diligently pursued his rights, the court held that Perkins' actual innocence claim allowed him to present his ineffective-assistance-of-counsel claim as if it had been filed on time. In so ruling, the court apparently considered Perkins' delay irrelevant to appraisal of his actual-innocence claim.

Held:

(1) Actual innocence, if proved, serves as a gateway through which a petitioner may pass whether the impediment is a procedural bar, as it was in *Schlup v. Delo*, 513 U.S. 298, 115 S. Ct. 851, 130 L. Ed. 2d 808, and *House v. Bell*, 547 U.S. 518, 126 S. Ct. 2064, 165 L. Ed. 2d or expiration of the AEDPA statute of limitations as in this case. Pp. 391-398, 185 L. Ed. 2d, at 1030-1034

(A) Perkins, who waited nearly six years from the date of the 2002 affidavit to file his petition, maintains that an actual-innocence plea can overcome AEDPA's one-year limitations period. This Court's decisions support his view. The Court has not resolved whether a prisoner may be entitled to habeas relief based on a freestanding actual-innocence claim, *Herrera v. Collins*, 506 U.S. 390, 404-405, 113 S. Ct. 853, 122 L. Ed. 2d 203, but it has recognized that a prisoner "otherwise subject to defenses of abusive or successive use of the writ may have his federal constitutional claim considered on the merits if he makes a proper showing of actual innocence," *id.*, at 404, 113 S. Ct. 853, 122 L. Ed. 2d 203.

The Court has applied this "fundamental miscarriage of justice exception" to overcome various procedural defaults, including, as most relevant here, failure to observe state procedural rules, such as filing deadlines, see Coleman v. Thompson, 501 U.S. 722, 750, 111 S. Ct. 2546, 115 L. Ed. 2d 640. The exception, the Court's decisions bear out, survived AEDPA's passage, see e.g., Calderon v. Thompson, 523 U.S. 538, 558, 118 S. Ct. 1489, 140 L. Ed. 2d 728; House, 547 U.S., at 537-538, 126 S. Ct. 2064, 165 L. Ed. 2d 1. These decisions "see[k] to balance the societal interests in finality, comity, and conservation of scarce judicial resources with the individual interest in justice that arises in the extraordinary case," *Schlup*, 513 U.S., at 324, 115 S. Ct. 851, 130 L. Ed. 2d 808. Sensitivity to the injustice of incarcerating an innocent individual should not abate when the impediment is AEDPA's statute of limitations, Pp. 391-394, 185 L. Ed. 2d, at 1030- 1031.

(B) The State urges that recognition of a miscarriage of justice exception would render § 2244(1)(D) superfluous. That is not so, for AEDPA's time limitations apply to the typical case in which no actual-innocence claim is made, while the exception applies to a severely confined category: cases in which new evidence shows "it is more likely than not that 'no reasonable juror' would have convicted [the petitioner]," *Schlup*, 513 U. S., at 329, 115 S. Ct. 851, 130 L. Ed. 2d 808. Many petitions that could not pass through the actual-innocence gateway will be timely or not measured by § 2244(d)(1)(D) is triggering provision. Nor does Congress inclusion of a miscarriage of justice exception in § 2244(b)(2)(B) and 2254(e)(2) indicate an intent to preclude courts from applying the exception in § 2244(d)(1)(D) cases. Congress did not simply incorporate the miscarriage of justice exception's application with respect to second-or-successive petitions and the holding of evidentiary hearings in federal court. The more rational inference to draw from the incorporation of a modified version of the exception into other provisions of AEDPA's is that, in a case not governed by those provisions, the exception survived AEDPA's passage intact and unrestricted. Pp. 394-398, 185 L. Ed. 2d, at 1032-1034.

(2) A federal habeas court, faced with an actual-innocence gateway claim, should count unjustifiable delay on a habeas petitioner's part, not as an absolute barrier to relief, but as a factor in determining whether actual innocence has been reliably shown. A petitioner invoking the miscarriage of justice exception "must show that it is more likely than not that no reasonable juror would have convicted him in the light of the new evidence," *Schlup*, 513 U.S., at 327, 115 S. Ct. 851, 130 L. Ed. 2d 808. Unexplained delay in presenting new evidence bears on the determination whether the petitioner has made the requisite showing. Taking account of the delay in the context of the merits of a petitioner's actual-innocence claim, rather than treating timeliness as a threshold inquiry, is tuned to the exception's underlying rationale of ensuring "that

federal constitutional errors do not result in the incarceration of innocent persons." Herrera, 506 U.S., at 404, 113 S. Ct. 853, 122 L. Ed. 2d 203. Pp. 398-400, 185 L. Ed. 2d, at 1034-135.

(3) Here, the District Court's appraisal of Perkins' petition as insufficient to meet *Schlup*'s actual-innocence standard should be dispositive, absent cause, which this Court does not currently see, for the Sixth Circuit to upset that evaluation. Under *Schlup*'s demanding standard, the gateway should open only when a petition presents "evidence of innocence so strong that a court cannot have confidence in the outcome of the trial unless the court is also satisfied that the trial was free of non-harmless constitutional error." 513 U.S., at 316, 115 S. Ct. 851, 130 L. Ed. 2d 808. Pp. 400- 401, 185 L. Ed. 2d, at 1035-1036. 670 F.3d 665, vacated and remanded.

RODELLA V. UNITED STATES
U.S. DISTRICT COURT, NEW MEXICO
CASE NO.: 1:19-CV-275-JB-CG (2019)

Example Motion – Many publications provide cases, laws, and thoughts. But here you will see the working motion that was filed as an actual innocence claim. The motion was several months overdue and was otherwise dismissible. What you can review is every filing between the prisoner and the judge in a case that proceeded in an out of time § 2255.

- § 2255 motion, notice that the motion is constructed in a custom format, yet in compliance with the Rules governing Section 2255 proceedings, Rule 2(c). I suggest this format for someone filing his very first motion because it's less confusing to use. A blank copy is added in the back of this book.

- Document two is an order of reference relating to prisoner cases. As I have said, many prisoner cases are treated much differently than other cases. Almost all prisoner cases, and all *pro se* prisoner cases, will be denied in the long run regardless of its merit. These cases serve as nothing more than practice for magistrate judges.

- Document three is an order to show cause. This step is, in most cases a simple formality, a dare to the prisoner to offer evidence of his innocence. This step is critical to any *pro se* litigant, so be prepared to prove your innocence with new and reliable evidence. An affidavit will not work. It is for this purpose that the government spends millions of dollars a year demonizing criminal in the media. The public must be convinced that all prisoners are untrustworthy to maintain its own illusion of an honorable slave trade.

- Document four, is a filing that the reader should pay special attention to. In "Mr. Rodella's Response Showing Cause Why His § 2255 Motion Should Not Be Dismissed As Untimely," a narrative of the proof offered was summarized. The self-authenticating proof of actual innocence (evidence) was attached. Notice that the response was a direct answer to what the magistrate judge requested and assumed was not available I might add. The evidence is summarized to save the judge time. Please note that unnecessary pages were omitted to save space, this case is available on Pacer.gov.

- Document five is the action that all late filers are hoping for, it is the judge's order to the government to answer Mr. Rodella's § 2255. This means that his response was accepted because he provided "new reliable evidence" that shows Mr. Rodella's actual innocence.

  Also note that Mr. Rodella's § 2255 challenged the constitutionality of 18 U.S.C. § 924(c)(3)(B), which as of June 24, 2019, was invalidated by the Supreme Court as unconstitutionally void-for-vagueness. Mr. Riggs has been a strong proponent for the statutes invalidation since the invalidation of 18 U.S.C. § 924(e)'s residual clause. He has filed over 30 cases that should now be granted relief. Although unavailable at the time this book was written it should be in the Supreme Court updates or the latest digest in LEXIS NEXUS, or any other prison law library, see *United States v. Davis, et. al.* Case No.: 18-431, *certiorari* to the United States Court of Appeals for the Fifth Circuit. The Sixth filing in this case is the "Entry of Appearance," by the government. This means that the government has assigned an attorney to argue the case. But know that with the Davis ruling in the Supreme Court, the government has already lost.

MOTION UNDER 28 U.S.C. § 2255
TO VACATE, SET ASIDE, OR CORRECT SENTENCE BY A PERSON IN FEDERAL CUSTODY

United States District Court	District

Name *(under which you were convicted)*: Thomas R. Rodella	Docket or Case No.: 1:19-cv-275-JB

Place of Confinement: Seagoville, Texas	Prisoner No.: 784480-051

UNITED STATES OF AMERICA	Movant *(include name under which convicted)*
V.	Thomas R. Rodella

MOTION

1. (a) Name and location of court which entered the judgment of conviction you are challenging:

    United States District Court for the District of New Mexico, Albuquerque, N.M.

    (b) Criminal docket or case number (if you know): 1: 14CR02783-00IJB / 14-2783-JB

2. (a) Date of the judgment of conviction (if you know): 9/26/2014

    (b) Date of sentencing: 1/21/2015

3. Length of sentence: 121 months

4. Nature of crime (all counts):

    1) Deprivation of Rights, 18 U.S.C. § 242

    2) Brandishing a Firearm, 18 U.S.C. § 924(c)(1)(A)(ii)

5. (a) What was your plea? (Check one)

    (1) Not guilty [✓]   (2) Guilty [ ]   (3) Nolo contendere (no contest) [ ]

6. (b) If you entered a guilty plea to one count or indictment, and a not guilty plea to another count or indictment, what did you plead guilty to and what did you plead not guilty to?

    N/A

6. If you went to trial, what kind of trial did you have? (Check one)   Jury [✓]   Judge only [ ]

234

8. Did you appeal from the judgment of conviction?   Yes ☑   No ☐

9. If you did appeal, answer the following:

    (a) Name of court: United States Court of Appeals

    (b) Docket or case number (if you know): 15-2023

    (c) Result: Affirm district court's judgment

    (d) Date of result (if you know): 11/4/2015

    (e) Citation to the case (if you know): Unknown

    (f) Grounds raised:

Sufficiency of the evidence
Failure to instruct or deminimize injury requirement
Admission of evidence of other incidence involving Rodella
Admission of evidence of training materials
Cumulative errors

    (g) Did you file a petition for certiorari in the United States Supreme Court?   Yes ☑   No ☐

        If "Yes," answer the following:

        (1) Docket or case number (if you know): 15-1158

        (2) Result: Denied

        (3) Date of result (if you know): 10/3/2016

        (4) Citation to the case (if you know): Unknown

        (5) Grounds raised:

More than Deminimis injury
Probable cause and provocation

10. Other than the direct appeals listed above, have you previously filed any other motions, petitions, or applications, concerning this judgment of conviction in any court?
    Yes ☐   No ☑

11. If your answer to Question 10 was "Yes," give the following information:

    (a) (1) Name of court: N/A

        (2) Docket or case number (if you know): N/A

        (3) Date of filing (if you know): N/A

        (4) Nature of the proceeding: N/A

        (5) Grounds raised:

    N/A

        (4) Nature of the proceeding: N/A

        (5) Grounds raised:

    N/A

(6) Did you receive a hearing where evidence was given on your motion, petition, or application?

    Yes ☐   No ☐ N/A

(7) Result: N/A

(8) Date of result (if you know): N/A

(c) Did you appeal to a federal appellate court having jurisdiction over the action taken on your motion, petition, or application?

  (1) First petition: Yes ☐   No ☐ N/A

  (2) Second petition: Yes ☐   No ☐ N/A

(d) If you did not appeal from the action on any motion, petition, or application, explain briefly why you did not:

Deprived effective assistance of counsel

12.   For this motion, state every ground on which you claim that you are being held in violation of the Constitution, laws, or treaties of the United States. Attach additional pages if you have more than four grounds. State the facts supporting each ground. Any legal arguments must be submitted in a separate memorandum.

GROUND ONE:

Mr. Thomas Robert Rodella was deprived of the effective assistance of counsel when Mr. Robert Gorence failed to call Mr. Rodella as the first defense witness. Thus, Mr. Rodella was deprived of his fundamental due process right to present his case and/or the basic right to be heard in his defense at a fair trial.

(a) Supporting facts: Mr. Gorence provided advice that effectively deprived Mr. Rodella of an opportunity to give his testimony at trial. No other witness could have given the recollection that Mr. Rodella could provide of the events in question. Mr. Rodella adamantly fought to testify as the first defense witness. Mr. Gorence's advice for Mr. Rodella not to testify resulted in the testimony of the government's witness going unrebutted. The jury never had an opportunity to hear Mr. Rodella's testimony, which included a number of events that were critical to the jury's ability to formulate a clear picture from the· facts of the case. Mr. Gorence's assistance was ineffective and did deprive Mr. Rodella of an opportunity to be heard. Thus, Mr. Gorence's ineffectiveness resulted in a miscarriage of justice, where his advice facilitated the jury's verdict convicting Mr. Rodella, who is actually innocent.

    Mr. Rodella states that:

(1) On March 11, 2014, Sheriff Rodella was returning home from serving an official function to continue serving as County Sheriff. Sheriff Rodella and his son, Thomas Robert Rodella Jr. were travelling westbound on State Road 399. They were driving a four-door Jeep Wrangler with Mr. Rodella Jr. a t the steering wheel.

(2) At approximately 6:10 pm, Mr. Rodella Jr. having entered onto S.R. 399, noticed a blue Mazda approaching S.R. 399 from a private drive that intersected with S.R. 399. The blue Mazda was travelling too fast to yield to oncoming traffic.

(3) Sheriff Rodella realized, given the speed of the blue Mazda, and the distance to the intersection, the blue Mazda would be unable to stop. Recognizing the dangerous situation created by the driver of the Mazda, sheriff Rodella made Mr. Rodella Jr. aware of the situation.

(4) As the blue Mazda entered onto S.R. 399 without stopping at the intersection or yielding to oncoming traffic, Mr. Rodella Jr. braked and swerved, avoiding collision with the blue Mazda.

(5) Immediately, the Mazda accelerated to a high rate of speed. S.R. 399 was not designed for aggressive driving or high speed. As the Mazda continued to accelerate, it was obvious the driver of the blue

Mazda had no intention of stopping for a white sedan that was stopped in the westbound lane of S.R. 399, signaling its intention to turn left. As the blue Mazda approached the white sedan, it crossed into the eastbound lane, in a no passing zone, clearly with the intention of passing the white sedan. At the same time a gray colored pick-up came into view in the eastbound lane.

(6) Sheriff Rodella observed the blue Mazda sharply cut back into the westbound lane, when he observed the gray pickup, clearly recognizing a head-on collision would have occurred had the driver of the blue Mazda not returned to his proper lane. As soon as the blue Mazda entered the westbound lane, it went off onto the north shoulder. Sheriff Rodella recognized that the driver of the blue Mazda realized he would be unable to avoid colliding with the stopped white sedan, thus took evasive action by going off onto the shoulder in a side-slide. As the blue Mazda came to rest on the shoulder, the gray pick-up passed, the white sedan completed its left-hand turn, and Mr. Rodella Jr. came upon the blue Mazda as the driver remained behind the wheel, staring straight ahead with both hands tightly gripping the steering wheel.

(7) As Mr. Rodella Jr. continued west on S.R. 399, Sheriff Rodella instructed him to remain on the road and stop approximately 15 feet ahead of the blue Mazda. The Sheriff, by state statute, was on duty 24/7, and had a responsibility to find out why the driver of the Mazda was operating the vehicle with such disregard for the law. He set about to investigate the situation and the condition of the driver. As Sheriff, Rodella recognized that he was on duty whether in uniform or not, according to the state law.

(8) After the Sheriff's son stopped, the Sheriff exited the Jeep and approached the Mazda with his sheriff's badge above and in front of him. The driver seemed dazed as he waved for Sheriff Rodella to come closer. The Sheriff was concerned that the driver might be in need of medical assistance, and he approached the car.

(9) When the Sheriff was approximately two feet from the Mazda, he heard what he believed to be gravel striking the undercarriage of the car and the front tires spinning. He instinctively jumped out of the way when he realized that the driver was trying to drive away, almost striking him with the Mazda.

(10) Sheriff Rodella regained his composure as the Mazda accelerated back onto S.R. 399, continuing in the original direction. The Sheriff returned to his seat on the passenger's side, and he instructed his son to follow the Mazda at a safe distance.

(11) Again on S.R. 399 heading west, the Rodellas followed the Mazda at times as far back as one thousand yards. Sheriff Rodella placed a phone call to a uniformed Deputy, Vince Crespin, from his cellphone. The sheriff shared the details of the evolving incident with Deputy Crespin and requested assistance in the apprehension and arrest of the Mazda's driver. At that point, the Mazda's driver had driven recklessly and nearly struck the Sheriff with his motor vehicle.

(12) The Rodellas realized that the Mazda's driver had trapped himself in an area of the county that provided him no other exit other than to return past the Rodellas. Notwithstanding the Mazda's high speed, the Sheriff was confident that the driver of the Mazda could not evade him. Sheriff Rodella then allowed the Mazda to proceed, observing him from a distance. Sheriff Rodella was determined to minimize the threat to the community by waiting until additional deputies were available.

(13) Due to the distance between the Mazda and the Jeep, Sheriff Rodella lost visual contact as the Mazda entered a low-lying area of the roadway. Seconds later, Sheriff Rodella saw that the Mazda was stopped in the low-lying area, possibly hoping to evade detection by the county Sheriff. The lengths the Mazda driver had gone to so far to avoid contact with the Sheriff were concerning. The Sheriff's thoughts included what possible scenarios would lead the Mazda driver to nearly hit the Sheriff with his vehicle, and to nearly collide with 3 other vehicles.

(14) Directly in front of the Mazda was a stop sign where County Road 126 split off into 3 branches marked as County Road 126A, 126B, and 126C.

(15) Upon seeing the Sheriff's vehicle, the Mazda driver left his hiding spot, speeding through the stop sign and failing to yield to any traffic. The Mazda's driver maneuvered onto County Road 126B. He was then heading into an inhabited rural area that contained homes and the potential of residents moving about on foot.

(16) As the Mazda continued, it encountered speed bumps in the roadway, forcing it to slow down. The difference in ground clearance and capability between the Mazda and the Jeep allowed Mr. Rodella Jr. to close the gap between the vehicles to about ten (10) car lengths as the Mazda at times slowed below the speed limit.

(17) Nearing the end of County Road 126B, the Mazda turned onto a dirt road, where he first encountered pedestrians. Sheriff Rodella observed a male jogger who ran off the road and onto higher ground. Sheriff Rodella observed the Mazda pause near the jogger, then continue on.

(18) The Sheriff stopped when he neared the jogger. As the jogger stepped closer to the Jeep, Sheriff Rodella displayed his badge to him and verbally identified himself. Realizing the Mazda may have entered the jogger's property, the Sheriff explained to the jogger that he was after the Mazda driver. The jogger directed Sheriff Rodella to proceed. The Sheriff proceeded towards the Mazda.

(19) As the Mazda driver continued onto the property where the house was located, he continued to drive erratically, entering the cul-de-sac and stopping halfway through it.

(20) Sheriff Rodella saw the Mazda driver's apparent disregard for human life during the time he attempted to evade arrest. This, coupled with the fact they had entered a private drive, dictated to the Sheriff that the driver of the Mazda had to be apprehended quickly, as the danger was increasing.

(21) The Sheriff advised his son to block ingress and egress on the cul-de-sac, protecting any passing motorist from having contact with the Mazda.

(22) The Sheriff exited the Jeep, holding his badge in his left hand with his arm extended in front of him. As he approached the stopped Mazda, Sheriff Rodella continued to identify himself as the Sheriff in a loud voice and ordering the Mazda driver out of the vehicle.

(23) When the Sheriff was close enough to see the driver, he could see the driver turning the steering wheel to the left and shifting the car into reverse. In one sudden motion, the front end of the Mazda swung out to the right, in reverse and the Mazda driver headed directly toward the Sheriff. The Sheriff realized that he was in immediate danger and could possibly lose his life. To avoid being hit or run over by the Mazda, Sheriff Rodella began to run backwards.

(24) As the Mazda struck the Sheriff, he was able to absorb much of the impact with his hands.

(25) Before the Mazda came to a sudden stop, Sheriff Rodella had been pushed approximately fifteen (15) feet from the Mazda. The Sheriff circled around the passenger's side of the Mazda and ordered the driver to exit the vehicle. It was then that the Sheriff realized that the Mazda's rear bumper had become lodged on a large metal pipe that protruded about two (2) feet out of the ground.

(26) Sheriff Rodella observed the driver quickly shifting in and out of gear and depressing the Mazda's accelerator. This was all in an effort to dislodge the car from the pipe. The front tires spun in place, filling the air with dust.

(27) The Sheriff realized that the Mazda driver was determined to flee at any cost, again placing people in harm. The Sheriff realized that if he acted to take control of the Mazda immediately, less than lethal

force might accomplish the task. Given the Sheriff's proximity to the Mazda, the Sheriff drew his .38 revolver and held it at the "down and ready" position, in the event an already extremely dangerous situation escalated. The Sheriff ordered the driver to surrender and exit the vehicle as he slowly approached the Mazda.

(28) Having closed the distance to the Mazda, the Sheriff could see by the Mazda driver's actions that he would not surrender and the aggressiveness by which the driver manipulated the transmission and the accelerator clearly signaled to the Sheriff how the danger of the situation increased with the passage of time.

(29) Knowing that time was of the essence, Sheriff Rodella seized the moment, and having no time to struggle with the Mazda's locked door, he jumped into the car through the passenger-side window. Sheriff Rodella's upper body landed on the legs of the driver, allowing him to pin the driver against the seat with his left forearm. Sheriff Rodella further de-escalated the situation by shifting the Mazda's transmission into the "park" position. He then reached for the Mazda's ignition switch, trying to turn the engine off.

(30) When the Sheriff reached for the key in the ignition, the Mazda driver grabbed the barrel of the Sheriff's .38 revolver with both hands. Sheriff Rodella had a firm grip on the revolver handle, but he feared the Mazda driver was attempting to strip him of his revolver. Sheriff Rodella was forced to strike the driver three (3) times before the driver surrendered control of the revolver.

It is beyond any reasonable doubt that had the jury heard the facts that would only be available in Mr. Rodella's testimony, the outcome of the trial would more than likely have been quite different. Mr. Gorence's failure to call Mr. Rodella as the first defense witness likely deprived Mr. Rodella of acquittal in the case. It is beyond doubt that Mr. Gorence's assistance fell far below reasonable professional norms. There is no doubt that Mr. Rodella has been prejudiced by his incarceration. He had to study federal law at the prison to learn the legal issues that Mr. Gorence deprived him of.

Mr. Rodella's sentence should be vacated, and the case be remanded for a new trial.

(b) **Direct Appeal of Ground One:**

    (1) If you appealed from the judgment of conviction, did you raise this issue?

        Yes ☐   No ☑

    (2) If you did not raise this issue in your direct appeal, explain why:

    Deprived of effective Counsel

(c) **Post-Conviction Proceedings:**

    (1) Did you raise this issue in any post-conviction motion, petition, or application?

        Yes ☐   No ☑

    (2) If you answer to Question (c)(1) is "Yes," state:

    Type of motion or petition: N/A

    Name and location of the court where the motion or petition was filed:

Docket or case number (if you know):   N/A

Date of the court's decision: N/A

Result (attach a copy of the court's opinion or order, if available):

(3) Did you receive a hearing on your motion, petition, or application?

Yes ☐   No ☐   N/A

(4) Did you appeal from the denial of your motion, petition, or application?

Yes ☐   No ☐   N/A

(5) If your answer to Question (c)(4) is "Yes," did you raise the issue in the appeal?

Yes ☐   No ☐

(6) If your answer to Question (c)(4) is "Yes," state: N/A

Name and location of the court where the appeal was filed: N/A

Docket or case number (if you know): N/A

Date of the court's decision: N/A

Result (attach a copy of the court's opinion or order, if available):

(7) If your answer to Question (c)(4) or Question (c)(5) is "No," explain why you did not appeal or raise this issue:

Deprived of effective counsel

GROUND TWO

Mr. Rodella was deprived of the effective assistance of counsel during the trial preparation stage of his criminal proceedings. His attorney, Mr. Gorence, failed to investigate critical issues in the case. Counsel's failures rendered Mr. Rodella's trial fundamentally unreliable, because counsel's conduct deprived Mr. Rodella of his due process right to present critical defense evidence at trial.

(a) Supporting Facts:

Mr. Rodella adopts, by reference, the facts contained in ground one here in ground two. He further explains that Mr. Gorence provided less than adequate representation (ineffective assistance of counsel) when he failed to retrieve the available evidence contained in the public record or in the possession of the government. This additional evidence would have had a profound impact on Mr. Rodella's trial. Mr. Gorence failed to review many pieces of evidence to ascertain their veracity. Moreover, Mr. Gorence advised Mr. Rodella that the government would provide Mr. Gorence with their investigative findings, which did not include the listed items. Thus, Mr. Gorence violated Mr. Rodella's trust, depriving him of his attorney's honest service. In support, Mr. Rodella shows:

(1) On May 2, 2014, Mr. Tafoya, the driver of the blue Mazda, made false statements to the Federal Bureau of Investigation Agents at the behest of U.S. Attorney Damon Martinez. Mr. Tafoya claimed he had been beaten up by Mr. Rodella, Mr. Rodella Jr., and the Rio Arriba Sheriff's deputies in the course of his arrest.

Just four (4) hours after his arrest, Mr. Tafoya was photographed at the jail. The booking photo of Mr. Tafoya was a part of his arrest record, which is available at the Rio Arriba County detention facility upon request. Mr. Rodella made Mr. Gorence aware of the fact the photo was available and would show that Mr. Tafoya had not suffered any facial injuries, as Mr. Tafoya claimed several days after the incident.

240

(2) Mr. Rodella shared with Mr. Gorence that Mr. Tafoya had a history of making false statements concerning law enforcement. During the trial preparation, Mr. Rodella made Mr. Gorence aware of information he had that Mr. Tafoya had been arrested in California for impersonating a police officer and had in his possession a badge he had stolen from a New Mexico State police officer.

Mr. Tafoya had also conspired with petty theft criminal Renee Dominguez, to prepare a false statement, which was given to federal authorities in order to minimize his culpability in the state criminal court.

Confronted with the existence of evidence of Mr. Tafoya's perjured testimony, Mr. Gorence claimed to have spoken to the Federal Bureau of Investigation. Mr. Gorence alleges that the Federal Bureau of Investigation investigated and found that the badge evidence was about a different Michael Tafoya, who had been a dispatcher for the New Mexico State Police, stolen the badge, and been arrested in California for impersonating an officer. Although Mr. Rodella continued to ask Mr. Gorence to inquire about the matter, Mr. Gorence never retrieved the evidence to ascertain its veracity for himself.

(3) When Mr. Rodella attempted to neutralize the threat, Mr. Tafoya posed to the public, Mr. Tafoya attempted to strip Mr. Rodella's revolver by force. When Mr. Rodella tried to turn the Mazda engine off, Mr. Tafoya grabbed the barrel of Mr. Rodella's revolver. In Mr. Tafoya's effort to strip Mr. Rodella of his revolver, Mr. Tafoya left his fingerprints on the barrel of the revolver in Mr. Rodella's possession.

Mr. Rodella's weapon was confiscated during the F.B.I.'s search, but not once did Mr. Gorence request that the revolver be analyzed for fingerprints. Had Mr. Gorence requested the government's fingerprint evidence from Mr. Rodella's revolver, he could have shown that Mr. Tafoya had, for the third (3rd) time, used aggressive behavior which could have led to the injury or death of Mr. Rodella, all in the line of duty.

(4) Mr. Gorence failed to interview or depose available witnesses in preparation for Mr. Rodella's trial. The 911 dispatch logs reflected that two (2) 911 calls were made concerning Mr. Tafoya's arrest.

This belied Mr. Tafoya's claims that he was unaware that Mr. Rodella was the Sheriff. Thus, causing him to fight and resist arrest. However, in reviewing the 911 record, it is easily discovered that an adolescent male had called 911, and within seconds of calling 911, the adolescent had identified Mr. Rodella as a law enforcement officer trying to subdue a dangerous person.

Mr. Gorence failed to review the dispatch logs, therefore failing to identify the eyewitness that would have discredited Mr. Tafoya's false testimony. This court should vacate Mr. Rodella's sentence and conviction without prejudice so that he may exercise his due process right to a fair trial.

(b) **Direct Appeal of Ground Two:**

    (1) If you appealed from the judgment of conviction, did you raise this issue?

        Yes ☐   No ☑

    (2) If you did not raise this issue in your direct appeal, explain why:

    Deprived of effective counsel

(c) **Post-Conviction Proceedings:**

    (1) Did you raise this issue in any post-conviction motion, petition, or application?

        Yes ☐   No ☑

(2)   If you answer to Question (c)(1) is "Yes," state:

Type of motion or petition: N/A

Name and location of the court where the motion or petition was filed:
N/A

Docket or case number (if you know): N/A

Date of the court's decision: N/A

Result (attach a copy of the court's opinion or order, if available):

N/A

(3)   Did you receive a hearing on your motion, petition, or application?
      Yes ☐   No ☐   N/A

(4)   Did you appeal from the denial of your motion, petition, or application?
      Yes ☐   No ☐   N/A

(5)   If your answer to Question (c)(4) is "Yes," did you raise the issue in the appeal?
      Yes ☐   No ☐   N/A

(6)   If your answer to Question (c)(4) is "Yes," state:

Name and location of the court where the appeal was filed:

Docket or case number (if you know): N/A

Date of the court's decision: N/A

Result (attach a copy of the court's opinion or order, if available):

  N/A

(7)   If your answer to Question (c)(4) or Question (c)(5) is "No," explain why you did not appeal or raise this issue:

  Deprived of effective counsel

GROUND THREE:

Mr. Gorence provided ineffective assistance of counsel at trial when he failed to object to plain errors at the trial that affected Mr. Radella's substantial rights.

(b) Supporting Facts:

Mr. Rodella adopts by reference the facts in grounds one and two here in ground three. Mr. Rodella explains that during his trial, two (2) related, yet distinctly different plain errors occurred. Either of the two (2) errors, by itself, would have provided the jury with the fact that more than likely would have resulted in an acquittal. Mr. Gorence failed to recognize or object to the errors. Regardless of whether Mr. Gorence's conduct was malicious or incompetent, it rendered his assistance to Mr. Rodella ineffective. Mr. Rodella was subjected to prejudice not only because he was deprived of a fair trial, but also because he is now forced to present his claim in the post-conviction phase rather than on direct appeal. Mr. Rodella also is not afforded counsel for post-conviction proceedings and must overcome a more stringent standard of review.

(1) The first plain error was when the court determined by a preponderance of the evidence that Mr. Rodella's conduct of protecting the public from a man who had committed acts that could have injured or killed Mr. Rodella was a violent act of the Sheriff. The duty of fact determination belongs to the jury in a criminal trial. The court's use of the preponderance standard was a plain error, and Mr. Gorence failed to object.

(2) Mr. Rodella was found guilty of depriving Mr. Tafoya of his civil rights and brandishing a firearm in the furtherance of a crime of violence, a violation of 18 U.S.C. §924(c). The predicate for the §924(c) violation was depriving Mr. Tafoya of his civil rights. However, deprivation of civil rights is not a proper predicate under §924(c) because the crime of deprivation of rights does not have "as an element the use, attempted use, or threatened use of physical force against the person or property of another," 18 U.S.C. §924(c)(3)(A). Thus, for the deprivation of civil rights to qualify as a proper predicate, the crime must constitute a residual clause offense under §924(c)(3)(B), but §924(c)(3)(B) is now unconstitutional. Accordingly, Mr. Rodella is entitled to vacatur of his §924(c) conviction.

(b) Direct Appeal of Ground Three:

(1) If you appealed from the judgment of conviction, did you raise this issue?

Yes ☐   No ☑

(2) If you did not raise this issue in your direct appeal, explain why:

Deprived of effective counsel

(c) Post-Conviction Proceedings:

(1) Did you raise this issue in any post-conviction motion, petition, or application?

Yes ☐   No ☑

(2) If you answer to Question (c)(1) is "Yes," state:

Type of motion or petition: N/A

Name and location of the court where the motion or petition was filed:

Docket or case number (if you know): N/A

Date of the court's decision: N/A

Result (attach a copy of the court's opinion or order, if available):

(3) Did you receive a hearing on your motion, petition, or application?

Yes ☐   No ☐   N/A

(4) Did you appeal from the denial of your motion, petition, or application?

Yes ☐   No ☐   N/A

(5) If your answer to Question (c)(4) is "Yes," did you raise the issue in the appeal?

Yes ☐   No ☐   N/A

(6) If your answer to Question (c)(4) is "Yes," state:

Name and location of the court where the appeal was filed:

Docket or case number (if you know): N/A

Date of the court's decision: N/A

Result (attach a copy of the court's opinion or order, if available):

(7) If your answer to Question (c)(4) or Question (c)(5) is "No," explain why you did not appeal or raise this issue:

Deprived of effective counsel

GROUND FOUR:

The District Court imposed Mr. Rodella's sentence without jurisdiction to enter a judgement. Moreover, Mr. Gorence's failure to object constituted ineffective assistance of counsel.

(a) Supporting Facts:

Mr. Rodella adopts by reference facts contained in grounds one (1), two (2), and three (3) here in ground four (4). He further explains that Mr. Gorence provided ineffective assistance of counsel by failing to recognize and object to the court committing a structural error. Mr. Rodella further shows that:

(1) The court instructed the jury in a manner that deprived them of their authority to make findings of fact concerning guilt. Specifically, instruction number seven (7) requires the jury to assume that Mr. Rodella had "road rage" by stating:

(i) "Mr. Rodella's motive and intent for pursuing Michael Tafoya was to express his road rage ..."

This statement instructs the jury to find that Mr. Rodella was overcome by "road rage."

(2) The court, having decided the fact that Mr. Rodella suffered from "road rage," implied a pre-determination of guilt, regarding the §924(c) count of the indictment, depriving the jury of its authority.

(3) Following the court's instructions, the jury was left to deliberate. The jury was also given a verdict form with four (4) questions, one (1) of which specifically states, "if your answers to either question three (3), or four (4) is yes, then proceed to question five (5).

(4) In reading the verdict form, you discover that question five (5) is actually a jury determination: "5. We the jury, find the defendant, Thomas R. Rodella, guilty or not-guilty as charged in count (1) of the indictment."

Without a presentation of question five (5), it is structurally impossible to make a finding of guilt as to count one (1) of the indictment; based on the facts. The jury was not instructed as to the relationship of fact as well as law, thus believed that answering yes to either question three (3), or four (4) constituted automatic guilt because of the court's earlier implication that Mr. Rodella had "road rage," an inherently violent act.

Without a valid finding of guilt by the jury, the court is without jurisdiction to impose a sentence. Mr. Rodella's sentence should be vacated because the court was without jurisdiction to impose the sentence.

(b) **Direct Appeal of Ground Four:**

(1) If you appealed from the judgment of conviction, did you raise this issue?

Yes ☐   No ☑

(2) If you did not raise this issue in your direct appeal, explain why:

Deprived of effective counsel

(c) **Post-Conviction Proceedings:**

(1) Did you raise this issue in any post-conviction motion, petition, or application?

Yes ☐   No ☑

(2) If you answer to Question (c)(1) is "Yes," state:

Type of motion or petition: N/A

Name and location of the court where the motion or petition was filed:

Docket or case number (if you know): N/A

Date of the court's decision: N/A

Result (attach a copy of the court's opinion or order, if available):

N/A

(3) Did you receive a hearing on your motion, petition, or application?

Yes ☐   No ☐   N/A

(4) Did you appeal from the denial of your motion, petition, or application?

Yes ☐   No ☐   N/A

(5) If your answer to Question (c)(4) is "Yes," did you raise the issue in the appeal?

Yes ☐   No ☐   N/A

(6) If your answer to Question (c)(4) is "Yes," state:

Name and location of the court where the appeal was filed:

Docket or case number (if you know): N/A

Date of the court's decision: N/A

Result (attach a copy of the court's opinion or order, if available):

(7) If your answer to Question (c)(4) or Question (c)(5) is "No," explain why you did not appeal or raise this issue:

Deprived of effective counsel

GROUND FIVE:

Mr. Rodella received ineffective assistance of counsel at the appellate stage of the proceeding, when counsel failed to raise certain plain errors on direct appeal.

(a) Supporting Facts:

Mr. Rodella adopts the facts raised in grounds one (1), through four (4) here in ground five (5) and further explicates that his appellate counsel provided ineffective assistance of counsel by failing to raise plain errors that are in the record. After trial, Mr. Rodella was represented by Mr. John D. Cline for the direct appeal stage of his criminal proceedings. Mr. Cline failed to consult the entire trial record; thus he could not raise the obvious plain errors that are in the record. Mr. Rodella now suffers the prejudice of a stricter standard of review.

Had Mr. Cline raised the plain errors at direct appeal, Mr. Rodella would have enjoyed his sixth amendment right to counsel on a plain error standard of review on direct appeal. But, because of counsel's errors, Mr. Rodella must now rely on a "jailhouse lawyer" to present his case of ineffective assistance of counsel in a post-conviction proceeding under the cause and prejudice standards of review.

(b) **Direct Appeal of Ground Five:**

    (1) If you appealed from the judgment of conviction, did you raise this issue?

        Yes ☐   No ☑

    (2) If you did not raise this issue in your direct appeal, explain why:

Deprived of effective counsel

(c) **Post-Conviction Proceedings:**

    (1) Did you raise this issue in any post-conviction motion, petition, or application?

        Yes ☐   No ☑

    (2) If you answer to Question (c)(1) is "Yes," state:

Type of motion or petition: N/A

Name and location of the court where the motion or petition was filed:

Docket or case number (if you know): N/A

Date of the court's decision: N/A

Result (attach a copy of the court's opinion or order, if available):

N/A

    (3) Did you receive a hearing on your motion, petition, or application?

        Yes ☐   No ☐ N/A

    (4) Did you appeal from the denial of your motion, petition, or application?

        Yes ☐   No ☐ N/A

    (5) If your answer to Question (c)(4) is "Yes," did you raise the issue in the appeal?

        Yes ☐   No ☐ N/A

    (6) If your answer to Question (c)(4) is "Yes," state:

Name and location of the court where the appeal was filed:

Docket or case number (if you know): N/A

Date of the court's decision: N/A

Result (attach a copy of the court's opinion or order, if available):

(7) If your answer to Question (c)(4) or Question (c)(5) is "No," explain why you did not appeal or raise this issue:

Deprived of effective counsel

GROUND SIX:

Mr. Rodella's incarceration represents a weaponization of the federal criminal justice system that has resulted in a violation of the thirteenth amendment.

(a) Supporting Facts:

Mr. Rodella's federal prosecution is an extension of a civil dispute between the United States Forest Rangers and the Rio Arriba County Sheriff's office over control of state law enforcement within the county's boundaries.

(1) In 1985, Mr. Rodella had been an officer with the New Mexico State Police for approximately three (3) years. During one of his days off, he visited his family at their home. His father was a deputy with the Rio Arriba County Sheriff's office. During their visit, Mr. Rodella's father responded to a request for additional patrol. He was to investigate a possible incident in an area only accessible by traveling across forest lands. Mr. Rodella's father responded to the call and Mr. Rodella volunteered to accompany him to provide assistance if necessary.

(2) The alleged incident was reported to have occurred in Archuleta Canyon, in northern Rio Arriba County. After making their presence known in the area, they began their return trip. As they drove through forest land, they observed a forest ranger vehicle approximately half a mile off the road. The ranger appeared to be alone and to have stopped a brown pickup, and there were two (2) men standing nearby. Because the area was so I isolated, and backup for the ranger would be minimally one (1) hour away, Mr. Rodella and his father decided to check on the ranger. Mr. Rodella's father drove the marked sheriff's vehicle to where the ranger was. After inquiring into his welfare, Mr. Rodella and his father stood by until the ranger finished issuing citations to the two (2) individuals in the brown pickup. Knowing that the two (2) male subjects in the pickup may be harboring ill-feelings towards the ranger, Mr. Rodella and his father chose to continue providing visibility by patrolling the forest roads. Believing there would be no further incident resulting from the interaction between the ranger and the two (2) male subjects, Mr. Rodella and his father began to make their way home. Minutes later the ranger executed a traffic stop on Mr. Rodella's father and cited him for driving off road. The alleged incident, for which Mr. Rodella's father was cited, was that he drove off road to where the ranger was citing the two (2) subjects, while doing his welfare check on the ranger himself.

At the hearing before the U.S. Magistrate judge, the judge asked the ranger if the Sheriff and the Ranger's reciprocity agreements were still valid. When the Ranger answered, "yes," the judge then proceeded to dismiss the matter before him.

(3) In Mr. Rodella's early years, he came to realize that many of the people in Rio Arriba County depended on wood for their stoves and fireplaces. For many of the elderly, it was their only source of heat, their only means of cooking a meal. Because many of the elderly in the rural communities of Rio Arriba County were on fixed income, modernizing their homes was not an option. There is something to be said about a meal cooked over a fire.

(4) Years later Mr. Rodella observed forest rangers stopping the citizens of the county, outside of forest land, in county jurisdiction. Some of these citizens who were stopped by the rangers would be offered the opportunity to forfeit their wood, their chainsaws, and their pickups, in lieu of being charged with

a crime, even though the wood had been obtained legally. The authority to stop and harass county citizens on county land by forest rangers was typically granted by the elected sheriff who commissioned, or deputized, the rangers. This vested the rangers with the authority to enforce state laws outside of forest lands, but within the county.

(5) As a candidate for Sheriff of Rio Arriba County, Mr. Rodella committed to not commissioning the rangers. After winning office in a landslide, Mr. Rodella met with the rangers. In this meeting, Mr. Rodella made it clear he supported the rangers. However, before he would consider commissioning the rangers, Mr. Rodella requested they attend culture sensitivity courses. The rangers refused his offer and again, Mr. Rodella reiterated his commitment to support the rangers in their endeavors yet stood strong on not commissioning the rangers until they became culturally sensitive.

(6) Shortly thereafter, Aban Lucero, a forest ranger supervisor, along with a forest service administrator, visited with Mr. Rodella. They offered him additional grants for the sheriff's office if Mr. Rodella commissioned the rangers. Mr. Rodella, dismayed by this offer, maintained his position not to commission the forest rangers until they became culturally sensitive, and again reiterated his willingness to support the rangers in any matter that was done legally.

(7) In April 2014, shortly after Mr. Rodella's refusal to accept "grants" in lieu of commissioning the rangers, he attended a public meeting with forest administration personnel from Washington, D.C. Hundreds of forest land users were also in attendance. In the closing minutes of the meeting, Mr. Rodella was asked to share a few words with the attendees. He thanked everyone for attending and implored the forest service representatives to be respectful of the people who depended on the roadways around the forest lands for travel and gaining access to life-supporting resources. He continued his plea that the Forest Rangers be sensitive to the needs of the county's elderly citizens. Mr. Rodella's words were part of his continued effort to overcome the bad feelings that had led to hostilities and the takeover of forest lands and the Rio Arriba County Courthouse. The courthouse raid was in June of 1967, in Tierra Amarilla, N.M.

(8) On May 07, 2014, Mr. Rodella attended a meeting at the U.S. Attorney's office in Albuquerque, N.M. and was accompanied by Jake Arnold, Public Information Officer for the Rio Arriba Sherriff's office; Debbie Rodella, State Representative; and Felipe Martinez, Rio Arriba County Commissioner. Also attending the meeting telephonically for the Rio Arriba County delegation were Ted Trujillo, County Attorney and Moises Morales, former County Commissioner. Ironically, Mr. Morales had been a leader in the 1967 courthouse raid, in which a New Mexico State Police officer and a Rio Arriba County jailer were seriously wounded by gunfire. Two (2) persons were taken hostage by the raiders. One of the hostages was a Rio Arriba Sheriff's deputy, and the other was a newspaper reporter.

During the Tierra Amarilla Courthouse raid, the Governor of the State of New Mexico ordered the New Mexico National Guard be activated. Tanks and other heavy military vehicles, along with air support were dispatched into Rio Arriba County with orders to bring peace and restore order.

(9) These events were the very matters that Mr. Rodella reminded the attendees about when pleading with the Forest Service Administrators. Mr. Rodella pleaded that they be a part of any solution that would prevent a repeat of the raid that caused blood shed on American soil. Sometime later, the jailer who had been shot in the courthouse raid was found dead and his body mutilated. His death has never been solved. Many citizens of the county believe that the killer(s) of the jailer came from within the ranks of the Courthouse raiders.

(10) During a second and private meeting, Mr. Rodella made clear his duties under state law and questioned the sincerity of U.S. Attorney Damon Martinez, in wanting to find a working solution. Mr.

Martinez, obviously angered by Mr. Rodella's assertion, asked if anyone was recording the meeting. After receiving confirmation that no one was recording the meeting, Mr. Martinez moved to the edge of his chair, leaned across the table and looked directly at Mr. Rodella and stated, "If you arrest any forest rangers, I will have you prosecuted." Mr. Rodella recognized that U.S. Attorney Martinez was attempting to hijack Sheriff Rodella's authority, in order to ensure that the forest rangers were able to enforce state laws while on state territory outside of forest lands, and still within the County of Rio Arriba. Mr. Rodella continuously expressed his concern that forest rangers were violating the Constitutional rights of the citizenry. The rangers were executing traffic stops outside of forest land boundaries without cause and then illegally seizing the citizens' property.

(11) Mr. Rodella remained cordial and thanked everyone for inviting him and for their attendance. He quietly gathered his belongings and, accompanied by the Rio Arriba delegation, left the meeting. Nine (9) days later, Damon Martinez, U.S. Attorney for New Mexico, launched a full-scale federal investigation against Mr. Rodella. One hundred thirty-nine (139) days later, Mr. Rodella was convicted for protecting the county of Rio Arriba.

(b) **Direct Appeal of Ground Six**

    (1) If you appealed from the judgment of conviction, did you raise this issue?

        Yes ☐   No ☑

    (2) If you did not raise this issue in your direct appeal, explain why:

    Deprived of effective counsel

(c) **Post-Conviction Proceedings:**

    (1) Did you raise this issue in any post-conviction motion, petition, or application?

        Yes ☐   No ☑

    (2) If you answer to Question (c)(1) is "Yes," state:

    Type of motion or petition: N/A

    Name and location of the court where the motion or petition was filed:

    Docket or case number (if you know): N/A

    Date of the court's decision: N/A

    Result (attach a copy of the court's opinion or order, if available):

    N/A

    (3) Did you receive a hearing on your motion, petition, or application?

        Yes ☐   No ☐ N/A

    (4) Did you appeal from the denial of your motion, petition, or application?

        Yes ☐   No ☐ N/A

    (5) If your answer to Question (c)(4) is "Yes," did you raise the issue in the appeal?

        Yes ☐   No ☐ N/A

    (6) If your answer to Question (c)(4) is "Yes," state:

Name and location of the court where the appeal was filed:

_____

Docket or case number (if you know): N/A

Date of the court's decision: N/A

Result (attach a copy of the court's opinion or order, if available):

_____

(7) If your answer to Question (c)(4) or Question (c)(5) is "No," explain why you did not appeal or raise this issue:

Deprived of effective counsel

_____

13. Is there any ground in this motion that you have <u>not</u> previously presented in some federal court? If so, which ground or grounds have not been presented, and state your reasons for not presenting them:

This is the first round collateral motion

14. Do you have any motion, petition, or appeal <u>now pending</u> (filed and not decided yet) in any court for the you are challenging?   Yes ☐   No ☑

If "Yes," state the name and location of the court, the docket or case number, the type of proceeding, and the issues raised.

15. Give the name and address, if known, of each attorney who represented you in the following stages of the judgment you are challenging:

(a) At the preliminary hearing:
Robert Gorence

(b) At the arraignment and plea:
Robert Gorence

(c) At the trial:
Robert Gorence

(d) At sentencing:
Robert Gorence

(e) On appeal:
John D. Clien

(f) In any post-conviction proceeding:
Pro Se

(g) On appeal from any ruling against you in a post-conviction proceeding:

Pro Se

16. Were you sentenced on more than one court of an indictment, or on more than one indictment, in the same court and at the same time?　　Yes ☑　　No ☐

17. Do you have any future sentence to serve after you complete the sentence for the judgment that you are challenging?　　Yes ☐　　No ☑

(a) If so, give name and location of court that imposed the other sentence you will serve in the future:

N/A

(b) Give the date the other sentence was imposed:

(c) Give the length of the other sentence:

(d) Have you filed, or do you plan to file, any motion, petition, or application that challenges the judgment or sentence to be served in the future?　　Yes ☐　　No ☐

18. TIMELINESS OF MOTION: If your judgment of conviction became final over one year ago, you must explain why the one-year statute of limitations as contained in 28 U.S.C. § 2255 does not bar your motion.*

---

* The Antiterrorism and Effective Death Penalty Act of 1996 ("AEDPA") as contained in 28 U.S.C. § 2255, paragraph 6, provides in part that:

A one-year period of limitation shall apply to a motion under this section. The limitation period shall run from the latest of –

(1) the date on which the judgment of conviction became final;

(2) the date on which the impediment to making a motion created by governmental action in violation of the Constitution or laws of the United States is removed, if the movant was prevented from making such a motion by such governmental action;

(3) the date on which the right asserted was initially recognized by the Supreme Court, if that right has been newly recognized by the Supreme Court and made retroactively applicable to cases on collateral review; or

(4) the date on which the facts supporting the claim or claims presented could have been discovered through the exercise of due diligence.

Therefore, movant asks that the Court grant the following relief:

Issue a writ of habeas corpus and vacate his sentence

or any other relief to which movant may be entitled.

Filed Pro Se
Signature of Attorney (if any)

I declare (or certify, verify, or state) under penalty of perjury that the foregoing is true and correct and that this Motion under 28 U.S.C. § 2255 was placed in the prison mailing system on _____.

(month, date, year)

Executed (signed) on _____　　(date)

_____
Signature of Movant

If the person signing is not movant, state relationship to movant and explain why movant is not signing this motion.

KELLY PATRICK RIGGS

IN THE UNITED STATES DISTRICT COURT
FOR THE DISTRICT OF NEW MEXICO

THOMAS R RODELLA,

        Plaintiff,

                                                   CIV 19-275 JB/CG

USA.

        Defendant.

ORDER OF REFERENCE RELATING TO
PRISONER CASES

In accordance with the provisions of 28 U.S.C. §§ 636(b)(1)(8), (b)(3), and *Va. Beach Fed. Sav. & Loan Ass'n v. Wood*, 901 F.2d 849 (10th Cir. 1990), this case is referred to Magistrate Judge Carmen E. Garza to conduct hearings, if warranted, including evidentiary hearings, and to perform any legal analysis required to recommend to the Court an ultimate disposition of the case. The Magistrate Judge will submit an analysis, including findings of fact, if necessary, and recommended disposition, to the District Judge assigned to the case, with copies provided to the parties. The parties will be given the opportunity to object to the proposed findings, analysis, and disposition as described in 28 U.S.C. § 636(b)(1). Objections must be filed within fourteen (14) days after being served with a copy of the proposed disposition.

                                          _____
                                          JAMES O. BROWNING
                                          UNITED STATES DISTRICT JUDGE

IN THE UNITED STATES DISTRICT COURT
FOR THE DISTRICT OF NEW MEXICO

THOMAS R. RODELLA,

      Movant,

No. CV 19-275 JB/CG

No. CR 14-2783 JB

v.

UNITED STATES OF AMERICA,

      Respondent.

ORDER TO SHOW CAUSE

THIS MATTER is before the Court on Movant Thomas R. Rodella's Motion Under 28 U. S. C. § 2255 to Vacate, Set Aside, or Correct Sentence by a Person in Federal Custody (the "Motion"), (CV Doc. 1; CR Doc. 242), filed March 25, 2019, and Rule 4 of the Rules Governing Section 2255 Proceedings in the United States District Courts. It appears on the face of the Motion that it was not filed within one year as required by 28 U.S.C. § 2255(f). Therefore, the Court will order Movant to show cause why the Motion should not be dismissed as untimely.

Section 2255(f) states:
A 1-year period of limitation shall apply to a motion under this section. The limitation period shall run from the latest of –
(1) the date on which the judgment of conviction becomes final;
(2) the date on which the impediment to making a motion created by governmental action in violation of the Constitution or laws of the United States is removed, if the movant was prevented from making a motion by such governmental action; (3) the date on which the right asserted was initially recognized by the Supreme Court, if that right has been newly recognized by the Supreme Court and made retroactively applicable to cases on collateral review; or (4) the date on which the facts supporting the claim or claims presented could have been discovered through the exercise of due diligence.

Movant was sentenced and judgment was entered on February 6, 2015. (CR Doc. 192). An Amended Judgment and a Second Amended Judgment were entered on February 9 and February 18, 2015. (CR Doc. 198, 206). Movant filed a Notice of Appeal on February 6, 2015. (CR Doc. 194). The United States Court of Appeals for the Tenth Circuit affirmed the conviction and sentence in an Opinion entered November 4, 2015. (CR Doc. 232-1 and 232-2). The Tenth Circuit's Mandate issued December 22, 2015. (CR Doc. 232). Movant petitioned the U.S. Supreme Court for a writ of *certiorari* and his Petition was denied by the Supreme Court on October 3, 2016. (CR Doc. 239). Therefore, Movant's judgment of conviction became final on October 3, 2016, and his Motion filed March 25, 2019, appears to be untimely. *Clay v. United States*, 537 U.S. 522, 524 (2003).

Movant's Motion under 28 U.S.C. § 2255 was not filed until March 25, 2019, more than two years after the judgment became final. Unless there is a basis for the limitations period to run from a different date or for tolling of the time period, Movant's Motion is untimely under 28 U.S.C. § 2255(f)(1). Therefore, the Court will order Movant to show cause why his Motion should not be dismissed as untimely. In his response to this Order, Movant shall identify any basis he claims for timeliness of his Motion under § 2255(f), including any basis for equitable tolling, and shall set out the facts supporting such a basis. To be entitled to equitable tolling, a movant must show (1) that he has been pursuing his rights diligently, and (2) that some extraordinary circumstance stood in his way and prevented timely filing. *Lawrence v. Florida*, 549 U.S. 327, 336 (2007); *Yang. v. Archuleta*, 525 F.3d 925, 928 (10th Cir. 2008). If Movant contends the statute of limitations should be tolled based on actual innocence, he must support his claim with "new reliable evidence-whether it be exculpatory scientific evidence, trustworthy eyewitness accounts, or critical physical evidence-that was not presented at trial," and show "that it is more likely than not that no reasonable juror would have convicted him in the light of the new evidence." *Schlup v. Delo*, 513 U.S. 298, 324 and 327

(1995). If Movant fails to show cause **by May 22, 2019**, the Court may dismiss his Motion as untimely without further notice.

IT IS THEREFORE ORDERED that, **by May 22, 2019**, Movant shall show cause why his Motion Under 28 U.S.C. § 2255 to Vacate, Set Aside, or Correct Sentence by a Person in Federal Custody, (CV Doc. 1; CR Doc. 242), should not be dismissed as untimely under 28 U.S.C. § 2255(f).

_____
THE HONORABLE CARMEN E. GARZA
CHIEF UNITED STATES MAGISTRATE JUDGE

UNITED STATES DISTRICT COURT

DISTRICT OF NEW MEXICO

Thomas R. Rodella

v.

United States

Case No.: 1:19-cv-275-JB-CG

MR. RODELLA'S RESPONSE SHOWING CAUSE WHY HIS §2255 MOTION SHOULD NOT BE DISMISSED AS UNTIMELY

Mr. Rodella has recently filed his 28 U.S.C. §2255 motion without the assistance of counsel. The court questions "Why the motion should not be dismissed as untimely." Thus, Mr. Rodella files this "Response showing cause …" particularizing two clear and convincing issues showing why his motion should not be dismissed. Mr. Rodella shows that:

A)   New reliable evidence exists that was not presented at trial, and that it is more likely than not that no reasonable juror would have convicted Mr. Rodella in light of the new evidence. See *Schlup v. Delo*, 513 U.S. 298, 324 and 327 (1995).

B) The timeliness standard of 28 U.S.C. §2255(f), cannot be applied as controlling concerning claims of ineffective assistance of counsel.

Mr. Rodella provides a clarifying explanation for each claim in turn.

A) New reliable evidence exists that was not presented at trial, and that it is more likely than not that, no reasonable juror would have convicted Mr. Rodella in light of the new evidence. *See Schlup v. Delo*, 315 U.S. 298, 324 and 327.

1) On October 3, 2016, the Supreme Court denied Mr. Rodella's petition for a writ of *certiorari*. Since the day that he received a copy of the court's order, Mr. Rodella had been diligent in learning a new federal procedure (Rules governing §2255) and obtaining evidence of his innocence.

2) On February 6, 2019, Raquel Pina-Baca transcribed the recording of a 911 call. The call was placed by witness David Thompson, on March 11, 2014. Mr. Rodella came to possess the certified transcript days later. The transcript having been made on February 6, 2019, was not available for presentation at Mr. Rodella's

256

INEFFECTIVE ASSISTANCE OF COUNSEL: OVERCOMING THE INEVITABLE

trial, which had concluded September 26, 2014. Thus, the certified transcript constitutes "New reliable evidence that was not presented at trial." *Schlup v. Delo*, 513 U.S., at 324 (1995).

3) Mr. Rodella's case represents the threat of incarceration that every law enforcement officer faces when performing his duty. When an officer makes an arrest, the bright line between his official duty and depriving someone of his civil rights, is marked by probable cause.

4) In Mr. Rodella's case he was duty bound to stop and offer assistance, as the Sheriff of Rio Arriba County and/or a civilian passerby, when Mr. Tafoya's car left the right of way "in-aside-slide" (DE-1 pg. 5, ¶ 6) or in any other traffic emergency.

5) When Mr. Rodella approached Mr. Tafoya's car on foot, he presented his badge to identify himself as he was offering assistance. Upon seeing Mr. Rodella's badge, Mr. Tafoya sped away, nearly striking Mr. Rodella in the process. Probable cause to arrest attached the moment that Mr. Tafoya assaulted Mr. Rodella with a deadly weapon, his car. (DE- 7, pg. 6, ¶ 9).

6) Mr. Rodella's duty was invoked when he witnessed the felony assault committed by Mr. Tafoya. Mr. Rodella's duty as Sheriff required him to be on duty twenty-four hours a day, requiring him to apprehend Mr. Tafoya.

7) On the date of the incident, March 11, 2014, Mr. Rodella was unaware that Mr. Tafoya was fleeing from him because he had an illegal gun in his car (911 manuscript pages 2, 3, 6, and 7).

8) Because the 911 transcript was not present at trial, the defense was unaware that a gun was involved in the incident as well.

9) The transcript of the 911 call shows that on March 11, 2014, a young man named David Thompson made a call to a 911 emergency operator. The call was handled by 911-operator Veronica Quintana, of the Espanola 911 dispatch center in Rio Arriba County, New Mexico.

10) Mr. Thompson reported to the 911 operator that, "There's a guy over here ..." Mr. Thompson continues by stating, "I don't know if that's a cop right behind his car, but he's ..." identifying that there are two men involved, one that is Mr. Thompson's subject of concern, prompting the 911 call, and a second man behind the first man's car that Mr. Thompson believes is a cop (police officer).

11) Mr. Thompson's second statement was interrupted by the 911 operator who, following emergency protocol, pursued her duty in establishing the location of the ongoing incident. "Where are you at?" the 911 operator asked.

12) Mr. Thompson did not answer the 911 operator's question. Instead, he continued to report, "This guy has a gun," identifying that the subject is armed. Mr. Thompson again identifies a second man at the scene, "I don't know if that's a cop right there but …" again Mr. Thompson is interrupted by the 911 operator who asks, "Okay. Where are you at?" Mr. Thompson answers, "I'm here in Serpent Ranch. I don't know the exact location."

13) While Mr. Thompson and the 911 operator are exchanging words about the location of the ongoing incident, Mr. Thompson confirms that the second man is indeed a law enforcement officer, "oh, there's a cop here. It's Okay," Mr. Thompson stated. Mr. Thompson and the 911 operator continue a short dialogue concerning who the "cop" is and Mr. Thompson's location.

14) As the exchange between Mr. Thompson and the 911 operator continues, Mr. Thompson again identifies the second man, saying, "Yeah. But there's a cop already here. He got the guy already." Indicating that the second man, whom Mr. Thompson believes is a law enforcement officer, has taken the man with the gun into custody.

15) The 911 operator, in an attempt to be thorough asks Mr. Thompson, "Is it a Santa Clara cop?" Mr. Thompson then states, "I think so." The 911 operator continues by identifying Mr. Thompson by name, then informs him that she intends to make a positive identification of the second man who Mr. Thompson believes to be a "cop." "Oh, okay David. We'll – we'll go ahead and call Santa Clara to make sure that's an officer there at your house," the 911 operator said.

16) The 911 operator calls the Santa Clara Police department dispatch office to positively identify that the second man is indeed an officer. The 911 operator informs Santa Clara dispatch that, "I just got a 911 transfer from – with David Thompson." The operator continues, "He said he was at the Serpent Ranch and there was someone outside with a gun. Do you guys have an officer there? Because he [David Thompson] said there was a Santa Clara officer there now, and they just caught the guy." Santa Clara dispatch replied that, "No. I only have one on, and he's here at the office."

17) After some additional conversation the two dispatch operators decide that the second man is not a Santa Clara police officer. The 911 operator then contacts the County's central dispatch, becoming involved in an ongoing conversation between the central dispatch operator and a Rio Arriba Deputy Sheriff. The Deputy reports that, "Central, we've got a – a 911 call RA1 is involved in a foot pursuit in La Mesilla off of County Road 126, I believe, Charles. 126 Charles. Myself and RA14 are en route." The deputy finished. After some discussion between the three operators, they decide that the call from the Serpent Ranch and the call from La Mesilla are the same incident. The 911 operator goes on to say, "Oh, okay. We'll go ahead and – well, can

you guys send an officer out there because I think this call's going to be related to another call. One of our deputies just got a call in [sic] out a foot pursuit. If you guys can get your officer going out there, as well."

18) Within approximately nine minutes of dialogue between the 911 operator, Santa Clara Dispatch, and Central Dispatch, they concluded that the second man was Rio Arriba County Sheriff, Thomas Rodella, when the Central dispatcher reported, "Yeah. We just got a call now that RA1, the Sheriff – is out there and that he's requesting assistance. So, we have two deputies on the way." Additionally, sheriff's deputy Randy Sanches, advised Central dispatch, "Central, RA6. Dispatch, RA units en route, be advised just before he called in out to La Mesilla, I received a 911 reference to a subject and a gun at Serpent Ranch which is, I believe, there in La Mesilla."

Sanches continues, "During the call, caller advised to cancel, there was a cop there that was with the subject with a gun. I did call Santa Clara to get their unit going out there, as well."

19) Upon arrival at the Serpent Ranch, the Rio Arriba Sheriff's deputies did identify the second man as Thomas R. Rodella, the sheriff of Rio Arriba County. Additionally, the sheriff had been confirmed to have placed in custody the man with the gun, Michael Tefoya.

20) Mr. Rodella's §2255 should be heard, and relief granted, or in the alternative, this court will have declared open season on all law enforcement officers nationwide who perform their duty.

B) The timeliness standard of 28 U.S.C. §2255(f) cannot be applied as controlling concerning claims of ineffective assistance of counsel.

21) Because of the lower court's interpretation of *Massaro v. United States*, 538 U.S. 500 (2003), a §2255 motion serves as a federal defendant's direct appeal from an illegal sentence caused by the ineffective assistance of defense counsel. Therefore, a procedural bar that denies review, where counsel was not appointed, is unconstitutional. The failure to appoint counsel side-stepped congress's intent in 18 U.S.C. §3006A, which demands that an indigent defendant be appointed counsel in all appeals, see 18 U.S.C. §3006A(c).

22) Moreover, depriving Mr. Rodella of review because of a procedural default would result in an unconstitutional deprivation of his due process right to direct appeal with the benefit of counsel, which is guaranteed by the constitution's Sixth Amendment. The Supreme Court of the United States in *Buck v. Davis*, 137 S. Ct. 759 (2017), upheld its decision in *Martinez v. Ryan*, 566 U.S. I, at 9, holding: "that when a state formally limits the adjudication of claims of ineffective assistance of trial counsel to collateral review, a prisoner may establish cause for procedural default if (1) 'the State Courts did not appoint counsel in the

initial review collateral proceeding', or 'appointed counsel in [that] proceeding ... was ineffective under the standards of *Strickland v. Washington*, 466 U.S. 668, 104 S. Ct. 2052, 80 L. Ed. 2d 674 (1984)'; and (2) 'the underlying ... claim is a substantial one, which is to say that ... the claim has some merit.' *id.*, at 14, 132 S. Ct. 1309, 182 L. Ed. 2d 272."

23) The merit in Mr. Rodella's §2255 is self-evident. He presented the claim that he was deprived of his due process right to be heard at a fair trial, because of the ineffectiveness of his defense counsel. Counsel's failure not only violated Mr. Rodella's right to counsel, but also his due process right to a fair trial where he could have been heard in his own defense.

24) Mr. Rodella shows that under the procedural default doctrine, if a prisoner "defaulted his federal claims in state court pursuant to an independent and adequate state procedural rule, federal habeas review of the claims is barred unless the prisoner can demonstrate cause for the default and 'actual prejudice as a result of the alleged violation of federal law ..." *Coleman v. Thompson*, 501 U.S. 722, 750 (1991). In general, lack of an attorney and attorney error in state post-conviction proceedings do not establish cause to excuse a procedural default, *id.* at 757, III St. Ct. at 2568.

25) In *Martinez*, The supreme Court announced a narrow, equitable, and non- constitutional exception to Coleman's holding (that ineffective assistance of collateral counsel cannot serve as cause to excuse a procedural default) in the limited circumstances where (1) a state requires a prisoner to raise ineffective-trial-counsel claims at an initial-review collateral proceeding; (2) the prisoner failed properly to raise ineffective-trial-counsel claims in his state initial-review collateral proceeding; (3) the prisoner did not have collateral counselor his counsel was ineffective; and (4) failing to excuse the prisoner's procedural default would cause the prisoner to lose a "substantial" ineffective-trial-counsel claim. In such a case, the Supreme Court explained that there may be "cause" to excuse the procedural default of the ineffective-trial counsel claim. *Martinez*, 132 S. Ct., at 1319. Subsequently, the Supreme Court extended Martinez's rule to cases where state law technically permits ineffective-trial-counsel claims on direct appeal but state procedure make it "virtually impossible" to actually raise ineffective-trial-counsel claims on direct appeal, see *Trevino v. Thaler*, 133 S. Ct., at 1915, 1918-21.

26) There can be no question that the federal criminal court system requires that Ineffective Assistance of Counsel claims should be brought in collateral proceedings, not on direct appeal. Such claims brought on direct appeal are presumptively dismissible, and virtually all will be dismissed. The reasons for this rule are also self-evident. A factual record must be developed in and addressed by the district court in the first instance

for ineffective review. Even if evidence is not necessary, at the very least counsel accused of deficient performance can explain their reasonings and actions, and the district court can render its opinion on the merits of the claim. An opinion by a district court is a valuable aid to appellate review for many reasons, not the least of which is that in most cases the district court is familiar with the proceedings and has observed counsel's performance, in context, firsthand. Thus, even if the record appears to need no further development, the claim will still be presented first to the district court in collateral proceedings, which should be instituted without delay, so the reviewing court can have the benefit of the district court's views. Therefore, the statutory right to appeal, that is a part of today's due process in the federal system, has been reduced to a right that no longer includes a right to appeal from a Sixth Amendment claim of ineffective assistance of trial counsel.

27) Mr. Rodella claims that it is because he had no counsel during the preparation period in his First-Tier collateral (§2255) proceeding that serves a cause for his procedural default.

Wherefore, based on the foregoing, Mr. Rodella respectfully moves this court to find that cause "why the motion should not be dismissed as untimely" exists, and to order the government to show cause why Mr. Rodella's requested relief should not be granted.

Respectfully submitted on May 9, 2019, by:

x _____
Thomas R. Rodella, Pro Se
Reg. #78448-051
Federal Correctional Institution
P.O. Box 9000
Seagoville, TX 75159

CERTIFICATE OF SERVICE

I do hereby certify that I have served a copy of this response on the clerk of court properly addressed, first-class postage pre-paid, and placed in the institution's mailing system as available to inmates, on May 9, 2019. Respectfully submitted by:

x _____
Thomas R. Rodella, Pro Se
Reg. #78448-051
Federal Correctional Institution
P.O. Box 9000
Seagoville, TX 75159

1   Rio Arriba County

2   Incident Details for RASO 2014002463

3

4

5

6

7

8

9   TRANSCRIPT OF

10   ESPANOLA 911 DISPATCH

11   MARCH 11, 2014

12   20:59:25

13

14

15

16

17

18

19   TRANSCRIBED BY: Raquel Pina-Baca,

20   Certified Steno transcriptionist

21

22

23

24

25

1   DISPATCH: Espanola 911, where is your

2   emergency?

3   MR. THOMPSON: Yes, there's a guy over

4   here. I don't know if that's a cop right behind his

5   car, but he's --

6   DISPATCH: Where are you at?

7   MR. THOMPSON: This guy has a gun. I don't

8   know if that's a cop right there but -

9   DISPATCH: Okay. Where are you at? MR.

10 THOMPSON: I'm here in Serpent Ranch.

11 I don't know the exact location.

12 DISPATCH: In front of which ranch?

13 MR. THOMPSON: Serpent Ranch.

14 DISPATCH: Where's that at?

15 MR. THOMPSON: Oh, there's a cop here.

16 It's okay.

17 DISPATCH: Okay. Well, where -- where are

18 you at? What -- what ranch is that? What ranch is

19 that at? Where is -- what county is that?

20 MR. THOMPSON: It's like in Santa Clara

21 here in Rio Arriba County.

22 DISPATCH: It's in Santa Clara, and you

23 said a cop that's there?

24 MR. THOMPSON: Yeah. It's Serpent Ranch.

25 DISPATCH: Serpent Ranch?

1   MR. THOMPSON: Yeah. But there's a cop

2 already here. He got the guy already.

3   DISPATCH: Is it a Santa Clara cop?

4   MR. THOMPSON: I think so.

5   DISPATCH: Oh, okay. What's your name?

6   MR. THOMPSON: David Thompson.

7   DISPATCH: Oh, okay, David. Well -- we'll

8 go ahead and call Santa Clara to make sure that that's

9 an officer there at your house. What's your address?

10   MR. THOMPSON: I don't really know this

11 address.

12   DISPATCH: Okay. We'll go ahead and

13 call -- we'll go ahead --

14   [Note: Telephone dialing.]

15   SC DISPATCH: Santa Clara office, how may

16 I help you?

17   DISPATCH: Yeah. This is (inaudible) here

18 in Espanola.

19   SC DISPATCH: Uh-huh.

20   DISPATCH: I just got a 911 transfer

21 from -- with David Thompson. He said he was at the

22 Serpent Ranch and there was someone outside with a gun.

23 Do you guys have an officer there? Because he said

24 there was a Santa Clara officer there now, and they

25 just caught the guy.

1   SC DISPATCH: No. I only have one on, and
2 he's here at the office.
3   DISPATCH: Okay. And -- because he said he
4 was at Serpent Ranch, and he said it was inside the
5 Santa Clara.
6   SC DISPATCH: Okay. Let me -- I don't
7 think he'd be there. Hold on.
8   [Note: Talking on radio.]
9   Santa Clara base AC-1. You're not in La
10 Mesilla, right?
11   No. Like I said, I only have one.
12 Wouldn't it be state police?
13   DISPATCH: No. I asked if it was a Santa
14 Clara cop, and he said it was Santa Clara.
15   SC DISPATCH: Huh, okay.
16   DISPATCH: He didn't know -- he didn't have
17 an address at all. Where -- where is the Serpent Ranch
18 at?
19   SC DISPATCH: It's, oh, jeez, I don't
20 remember the exact location. I can go ahead and send
21 my guy out there.
22   DISPATCH: Okay. Are you guys familiar
23 with David Thompson?
24   SC DISPATCH: Yeah.
25   DISPATCH: Okay. That was the guy who

1 called us.

2   SC DISPATCH: Okay.

3   DISPATCH: What -- what's his address?

4   SC DISPATCH: Let me get it for you. Hold

5 on one second.

6   DISPATCH: All righty.

7   OFFICER: All right. Get central.

8   CENTRAL DISPATCH: Go ahead, RA6.

9   OFFICER: Central, we've got a -- a 911

10 call RA1 is involved in a foot pursuit in La Mesilla

11 off of County Road 126, I believe, Charles. 126

12 Charles. Myself and RA14 are en route.

13   CENTRAL DISPATCH: (In audible).

14   SC DISPATCH: Okay. We don't have an

15 address, but we have him listed under Serpent Ranch.

16   DISPATCH: Oh, okay. (Inaudible)?

17   SC DISPATCH: Yeah.

18   DISPATCH: Oh, okay. We'll go ahead and --

19 well, can you guys send an officer out there because I

20 think this call's going to be related to another call.

21 One of our deputies just got a call in out a foot

22 pursuit. If you guys can get your officer going out

23 there, as well.

24   SC DISPATCH: Okay.

25   DISPATCH: Okay.

```
 1              SC DISPATCH:  Bye.
 2              DISPATCH:  Bye.
 3              CENTRAL DISPATCH:  Central dispatch, can I
 4   help you?
 5              SC DISPATCH: This is Nadine here at -- not
 6   Central -- at Santa Clara.
 7              CENTRAL DISPATCH:  Uh-huh.
 8              SC DISPATCH:  I guess RASO is the one
 9   that's out there at Serpent Ranch.
10              CENTRAL DISPATCH:  Yeah.  We just got a
11   call now that RA1, the sheriff --
12              SC DISPATCH:  Oh, okay.
13              CENTRAL DISPATCH:  -- is out there and that
14   he's requesting assistance.  So, we have two deputies
15   on the way.
16              SC DISPATCH:  Okay.  I have one headed out
17   there, too.
18              CENTRAL DISPATCH:  Okay.
19              SC DISPATCH:  All right, thanks.
20              CENTRAL DISPATCH:  All right, bye-bye.
21              OFFICER:  Central, RA6. Dispatch, RA units
22   en route, be advised just before he called in out to La
23   Mesilla, I received a 911 reference to a subject and a
24   gun at Serpent Ranch which is, I believe, there in La
25   Mesilla.
```

1   During the call, caller advised to cancel,
2 there was a cop there that was with the subject with a
3 gun. I did call Santa Clara to get their unit going
4 out there, as well.
5   All right, Two Central, where are those
6 units at in La Mesilla?
7   DISPATCH: They haven't called up anywhere
8 yet. Break central RA6, what's your location?
9   OFFICER: (Inaudible). We are (inaudible)
10 the other side of County Road 126 (inaudible). We're
11 on the -- on the back side.
12   OFFICER: Direct RA6, RA2 direct.
13   OFFICER: RA6, RA2, go ahead. (Inaudible).
14   OFFICER: (Inaudible).
15   DISPATCH: Central is direct.
16   OFFICER: RA6 central (inaudible).
17   DISPATCH: Central RA6, (inaudible) OLN.
18   OFFICER: (Inaudible) 502-95-9794, repeat
19 502-95-9794 (inaudible).
20   DISPATCH: Central, RA 6, be advised I got
21 the OLN, everything else after that came in very 10-1 a
22 lot of staticky. Michael Tafoya a valid (inaudible),
23 negative on two line.
24   OFFICER: RA6, Central, did you get a clear
25 OLN?

1 DISPATCH: Affirmative. I got the OLN for

2 Michael Tafoya, 502-959-794. He was negative on 2-9.

3 OFFICER: 10-4, 1-10, 50.

4 DISPATCH: And for any advised, guys had to

5 be detained and you came in 10-1 when you're advising

6 (inaudible). And I wasn't sure if you advised that he

7 was tazed or negative on the taze?

8 OFFICER: Negative on the taze. Negative

9 on the taze. Sheriff RA1 had him detained when we

10 arrived.

11 DISPATCH: Direct 6. Also, you guys direct

12 on that earlier for -- about that 911 in that same

13 area?

14 OFFICER: Affirmative. That was RA1.

15 DISPATCH: Yeah, before, I did advise Santa

16 Clara to get a PD unit or one of their units going out

17 there just call them 22 or negative?

18 OFFICER: I think it's 110-97.

19 DISPATCH: 10-4.

20 OFFICER: Hey, Randy, after the bridge, do

21 I go left or right? Just outside.

22 OFFICER: Go left and it'll be the middle

23 of -- it'll be 126 Boy, 126 Boy.

24 OFFICER: How far down are you?

25 OFFICER: Go all the way to the end and

1 then it turns to a dirt road, and we're at the dirt

2 road.

3   OFFICER: RA14, Central.

4   CENTRAL DISPATCH: Go ahead.

5   OFFICER: Can you clear on a VIN and also

6 the year, make, and model and VIN.

7   CENTRAL DISPATCH: Go ahead.

8   OFFICER: 2007, Mazda, then as follows:

9 John, Mary, 1, boy, team, 143171729075.

10   10-4, standby.

11   OFFICER: RA6, Central.

12   CENTRAL DISPATCH: Go ahead.

13   OFFICER: RA6, Central.

14   CENTRAL DISPATCH: RA6, go ahead.

15   OFFICER: On that same Mazda, go ahead and

16 start me a 1046.

17   CENTRAL DISPATCH: 10-4.

18   OFFICER: RA14, Central. I got one 15 en

19 route to the 81.

20   CENTRAL DISPATCH: 10-4. On the Mazda,

21 returned to a blue 2007 Mazda to Michael Tafoya out of

22 Fairview, expires March of 2015, negative 2-9.

23   OFFICER: 10-4. Can you mark and hold that

24 also on the OLN that (inaudible) so I can go pick him

25 up from your 81.

1   CENTRAL DISPATCH: Affirmative.

2   TOWING OPERATOR: Towing service.

3   CENTRAL DISPATCH: Hi. I'm calling for the

4 SO.

5   TOWING OPERATOR: Yeah, go ahead.

6   CENTRAL DISPATCH: We have one for Robert.

7 That's going to be County Road 126C as in Charles.

8   CENTRAL DISPATCH: There in La Mesilla, all

9 the way to the end.

10   TOWING OPERATOR: Yeah, 126C as in Charlie

11 all the way to the end?

12   CENTRAL DISPATCH: Yeah.

13   TOWING OPERATOR: Okay.

14   CENTRAL DISPATCH: Okay. All right,

15 bye-bye.

16   OFFICER: Central unit be advised your

17 (inaudible) guy is en-route to the 81.

18   OFFICER: (Inaudible) 21.

19   OFFICER: Standby directing for -- or

20 standby for 21.

21   OFFICER: RA14, Central, be at your back

22 door.

23   OFFICER: 10-4, 1-4.

24   OFFICER: RA14, Central, at the 81 with the

25 50.

1   OFFICER: 10-4,1-4.

2   OFFICER: I'm sorry. I forgot to ask you.

3 Can you draw me a case number for aggravated assault on

4 a peace officer.

5   OFFICER: 10-4, standby.

6   OFFICER: RA6, Central, do we know who the

7 46 who is coming out here?

8   DISPATCH: 10-4, standby. I'll get you

9 that in just a sec. I think it was -- I think it was

10 Roberts, I'm not too sure. I'll go back and check now.

11   OFFICER: RA14, Central. If you can just

12 give me a call with that case number when -- whenever

13 you have a chance?

14   DISPATCH: 10-4, will do.

15   OFFICER: Hello.

16   DISPATCH: Hey, Andy?

17   OFFICER: Hey.

18   DISPATCH: Your case number is -- I just

19 assigned you a case number.

20   Where is it at? Oh, okay. Your case

21 number is going to be 310.

22   OFFICER: 310. Thanks, brother.

23   DISPATCH: No problem.

24   OFFICER: Okay, bye.

25   DISPATCH: Okay. And do we have an address

1   at that house where he was in front of?

2   OFFICER: It is -- hold on real quick. Let

3   me get it for you. Okay.

4   It's 100C, County Road 126, Las Mesilla.

5   DISPATCH: Okay. County Road 126?

6   OFFICER: Yeah.

7   DISPATCH: Okay. And you ran --

8   officer: Okay.

9   DISPATCH: And you ran that 126B, then,

10   right?

11   OFFICER: Yeah.

12   DISPATCH: Okay. Sounds good.

13   OFFICER: Okay. Thanks.

14   DISPATCH: Okay. Bye.

15   OFFICER Bye.

16   Officer: Central dispatch, RA 6.

17   DISPATCH: RA6. I was,46 that's going out

18   there for the vehicle is going to be Robert.

19   OFFICER: 10-4, thank you.

20   DISPATCH: No problem.

21   OFFICER: RA6 Central.

22   CENTRAL DISPATCH: (Inaudible)

23   OFFICER: RA6. Is a 10-46, Robert's

24   coming, has the vehicle.

25   I'll be 10-98 (inaudible) be en-route 1081.

1   CENTRAL DISPATCH: RA-6 (inaudible)

2   [The recording concludes.]

3

4   In re:

5   Incident Details for RASO 2014002463

6   ---

7   **CERTIFICATE**

8   I, Raquel Piña-Baca, Certified
     Transcriptionist, DO HEREBY CERTIFY that on February 6,

9   2019, the above-captioned transcription was prepared by
     me; that the RECORDING was reduced to typewritten

10   transcript by me; that I listened to the entire
     RECORDING; that the foregoing transcript is a complete

11   record of all material included thereon, and that the
     foregoing pages are a true and correct transcription of

12   the recorded proceedings, to the best of my knowledge
     and hearing ability. The recording was of GOOD

13   quality.

14
     I FURTHER CERTIFY that I am neither employed

15   by nor related to nor contracted with any of the
     parties or attorneys in this matter, and that I have no

16   interest whatsoever in the final disposition of this
     matter.

17

18

19   Raquel Piña-Baca
                          Certified Transcriptionist

20   AAERT CET-822

21

22

23

24

25

**IN THE UNITED STATES DISTRICT COURT
FOR THE DISTRICT OF NEW MEXICO**

THOMAS R. RODELLA,

      Movant,

No. CV 19-275 JB/CG

No. CR 14-2783 JB

v.

UNITED STATES OF AMERICA,

      Respondent.

<u>ORDER TO ANSWER</u>

THIS MATTER is before the Court, *sua sponte* under Rule 4(b) of the Rules Governing Section 2255 Cases, on Movant's Motion Under 28 U.S.C. § 2255 to Vacate, Set Aside, or Correct Sentence (CV Doc. 1; CR Doc. 242). The Court will direct the United States to answer Movant's Motion. The Court requests that, in addition to any other response to Movant's Motion, the United States address any statute of limitations issue under 28 U.S.C. § 2255(f) in its answer.

IT IS HEREBY ORDERED that the Clerk is directed to forward to the United States of America a copy of Movant's Motion Under 28 U.S.C. § 2255 to Vacate, Set Aside, or Correct Sentence (CV Doc. 1; CR Doc. 242) and supporting papers and exhibits, if any, together with a copy of this Order;

IT IS FURTHER ORDERED that, by July 8, 2019, the United States answer Movant's § 2255 motion.

_____
THE HONORABLE CARMEN E. GARZA
CHIEF UNITED STATES MAGISTRATE JUDGE

IN THE UNITED STATES DISTRICT COURT
FOR THE DISTRICT OF NEW MEXICO

THOMAS R. RODELLA,   )
)
          Movant,   )
)
vs.   )   No. CV 19-275 JB/CG
)
UNITED STATES OF AMERICA,   )
)
          Respondent.   )

ENTRY OF APPEARANCE

The United States of America, by and through Jeremy Pena, Assistant United States Attorney, for said district

notifies the Court that he hereby enters his appearance as counsel on behalf of the United States.

The United States requests that all future notices, pleadings and correspondence be delivered to the attention

of Jeremy Peña.

                                     Respectfully submitted,

                                     JOHN C. ANDERSON
                                     United States Attorney

                                     /s/ Electronically filed on June 12. 2019
                                     JEREMY PEÑA
                                     Assistant United States Attorney
                                     P.O. Box 607
                                     Albuquerque, NM 87103
                                     (505) 346-7274

I HEREBY CERTIFY that on the 12th day
of June, 2019, I filed the foregoing
pleading electronically through the
CM/ECF system, which caused counsel
of record for defendant to be served
by electronic means.

/s/ Electronically filed on June 12. 2019
JEREMY PENA
Assistant United States Attorney

PART FIVE
CHAPTER TWENTY-ONE

MOVING FOR POST-CONVICTION RELIEF

A lesson I learned years ago is that the best books reach out to touch their readers on a very personal level. In this section you will notice that I am writing from a different perspective, as if for only one person. My intention in this section is reaching out to touch only you.

If you read the foreword and Chapter Nineteen you will have discovered some of the effort that I put into Thomas Rodella's case. In this section I won't be talking about what I have done for others. Instead, I'm going to show you what we are going to do for you in your case. If you follow along closely, we will be able to walk you all the way through a post-conviction relief process.

PERSONAL CLAIM DEVELOPMENT

Evaluating Potential Claims – First things first: stop complaining to everyone who will listen. I already know that you got screwed, and I already know that your lawyer was ineffective, that's why the sub-title of this book is 'overcoming the inevitable.'

What you have to do now is get your head together so you can evaluate your claims realistically. First off, you need to figure out in your own heart if you are actually innocent, if you are over-sentenced, or the court was without jurisdiction to sentence you in the first place. Once you have those issues in proper perspective, it's time to move on to how guilt was determined. Did you enter a plea of guilty or were you found guilty by a jury?

Taking Notes – Once you have decided what you will be claiming, you need to write it down. From here on out you must write everything down. The most important aspect of your note taking process is the truthfulness of the notes. Keep in mind that the federal criminal justice system is based on telling lies. It begins at arraignment when a defendant is asked to plea "not guilty," and then directed later to plead "guilty." One of these two statements is a lie, it can't be both. In the event the defendant went to trial, then the government and its witnesses are more than willing to do the lying for you. Then at sentencing, the judge is willing to get started lying as well, when he or she starts adding enhancements. Ask any defendant in a drug case about "ghost dope."

The entire goal of the lie is to maintain the status quo. The Federal Bureau of Prisons must maintain near 200,000 prisoners to avoid laying-off its staff. Yes, the federal prison scheme is a lot like a modern-day slave trade.

With all this lying going on, I cannot stress you enough to be honest in your note taking. If you tell one lie in this process you will have to support that lie in everything you do, until you are painted into a corner by your own words.

Personal Narrative – Writing your narrative starts with bullet points. Bullet points are nothing more than a line or two, just reminders of certain events. For example:

"– On June 19, 2019, my lawyer said he had filed a notice of appeal." Notice, one simple statement that reminds you of an event and gives the date that it occurred. As I previously said, the lawyer's failure to file the notice of appeal is ineffectiveness. So, your bullet points should point to that one issue alone. This means that you do not need to include bullet points about what your wife and children did at that time period because it is simply unrelated. Now, write all your bullet points as they relate to your case without regard to specific grounds.

Your Paragraphs – Once you have your bullet points complete, you will start to write your paragraphs. In your paragraphs you are providing the rest of the details for each bullet point. What you are doing is painting a clear picture for your reader with words. I know that this can seem intimidating, but just take it one bullet point at a time and – it will be finished before you know it. *Example*:

"On June 19, 2019, my attorney, John D. Lloyd, visited me at Jefferson County jail in Birmingham, Alabama. He explained to me that I had 14 days to file a notice of appeal from the date of my final sentencing. In addition, he said that he found my argument for appeal did have merit, because the residual clause of 18 U.S.C. § 2422(b) was indeed unconstitutionally void-for-vagueness.

"I asked him if I should file a notice of appeal myself. He explained that I should not file my own because his duty was to file the notice of appeal on my behalf, and that he already had filed the notice."

Notice that I did not say anything about his failure to file the notice. That's because his failure to file is a distinct and separate event, which did not occur until the final day for filing the notice had passed.

Now write your story out from all your bullet points. When you do this, I recommend using a wireless notebook or a binder. Write one paragraph per page and write only on one side of the paper. I do this so I can add details to the page as necessary.

Your paragraphs make up your factual basis. It is additional information that the court has not seen before. It is very important that the new information be accurate. One of the biggest claim-killers is exaggeration. I have witnessed prisoners exaggerate so the latest winning decision will fit around their own personal case. This is a fatal mistake. Prisoners have been known to work hundreds of hours learning the facts of a case, only to discover that the new case decision almost fits. All he has to do is leave out a couple of small details so it will sound good, and he'll be done. Don't try this. A diligent prosecutor will not only catch it but will monopolize on the attempt to deceive the court, and nothing else you say will be taken seriously.

Individualize Your Claims – At this point, you should have paragraphs that explain your entire criminal case, from the moment the alleged conduct began all the way to the moment your conviction became final. If, for some reason, yours does not cover the entire span I just described, now is the time to add more paragraphs. What you have done so far is lay all the facts out on paper so you may begin making your claims. Know also, that more than one claim can be derived from the same set of operative facts. For example, a claim of being deprived of a process to obtain witnesses because of ineffective assistance of counsel; is a different claim than being deprived of appeal advice based on the same error. The difference in these two claims is the ending point. In the first, the facts will end at trial where the witnesses were not called. In the second, the facts will end fourteen days after sentencing. The facts of both claims begin at establishing the availability of the witnesses. Therefore, you should be able to see that both claims will share a large number of the same facts.

Short and Simple – Next, your grounds should be short but informative. It is very important to use only the paragraphs needed to make your point. Any paragraph that seems extra or not necessary, take it out. Having already established that you believe events have transpired that warrant your release, you can move forward to preparing your grounds. Your right to trial, and the effective assistance of counsel in that trial, has been set out in previous chapters; now you can move forward and prepare the grounds for your motion. To do this I always start with the end result in my mind. Again, keep it short and simple. Use only the paragraphs that show how you were deprived of a trial, appeal, or fair sentencing where applicable. Next, show how the ineffectiveness of your trial counsel deprived you of a direct appeal on your issue. And last, describe what would have been different and what its benefit was to you, i.e. "I was deprived of a trial where my alibi witnesses would have testified to my actual innocence."

Once you have separated your grounds from one another, you should begin to show support for each of them. You will be using the facts or the events from your case, to show the court that a path different than the due process of law was followed; and that it deprived you of the fair trial guaranteed by the Constitution of the United States. Once you have supported your grounds with your facts or your paragraphs, read them backward and forward, remove any unnecessary information and fill in any necessary gaps. This also means that you should abandon any grounds that are repetitions of other grounds stated differently.

Author's Note: When preparing a § 2255 motion, be sure not to quote the law or any cases, and definitely don't tell the court about your rights. They already know about your rights and how they were trampled. Although, a brief in support of a § 2255 motion can be helpful to a court in understanding a pro se litigants' motion; a memorandum of law is a waste of time for you and the court. The court already knows the law for the most part, and nothing in your memorandum becomes a part of the record. This is the time to build the record, so add affidavits of witnesses and other tangible evidence the court doesn't have, such as letters and notes. This is not the time to re-litigate your criminal case, it's the time to prove it wasn't conducted properly.

CHAPTER TWENTY-TWO

THE § 2255 MOTION – RULE TWO

The form of a 28 U.S.C. § 2255 motion to vacate, set aside, or correct the sentence must substantially follow either the form appended to the Rules Governing § 2255; or a form prescribed by a local district court rule. Also, the clerks of the district courts must make forms available to moving parties without charge, see Rule 2, Rules governing Section 2255 Proceedings.

You will find a wide variety of good ideas that pertain to the filing for post-conviction relief. One of the most common prison tactics is to file a "memorandum of law" in the place of a § 2255 motion. This is a very bad idea. In the average case, the district court is looking to deny your motion or delay relief until your sentence is finished. Don't help them. The filing of your initial motion should be constructed in one of three ways. Two of which can be filed by uncounseled prisoners proceeding in *pro se* and the other is reserved for prisoners who are represented by counsel.

Pro se Filing – For those of you who are filing in *pro se*, meaning you are filing on your own behalf, your job is to provide additional information to the court. Either way, you should use a form that follows the forms provided by the court. Forms are provided at all federal prisons that I have had the misfortune to visit. The forms that I have seen in the past have been one of many types, but they all contain the same information. I strongly recommend that you use a form that follows what the courts routinely accept. When using one of the stock forms, you will always find that there is never enough room to write everything out. That is when you will add clearly marked "continuation pages." The most common practice is the one where the ground is stated on the form and is then followed by the first few lines of supporting facts. Then in the last but separate line it states, "See Continuation Pages of Ground One." Then following the signature page of the form motion, you find the continuation pages clearly marked "Continuation of Ground One." The continuation pages are a complete and independent copy of the ground. It begins by listing the ground in its entirety and then lists all the supporting facts without any interruptions. Remember also that you will not be quoting or arguing cases or laws, this is not the time for that.

The second, and my favorite, form of a *pro se* § 2255 motion is my custom form. If you remember back to the Rodella filing in Chapter 20, you will remember that it contained no continuation pages. My custom motion was designed to aid both the court and the prisoner, by reducing the need of the writer to produce; or the need of the court to follow, broken dialogue from the standard form to the many pages of addenda and back to the form. Again, the Rodella filing is a good example of the form's use, and you will find a blank copy of this at the end of this book.

Attorney Filing – Know in advance that neither the court nor the United States Congress intended for § 2255 motions to be filed with the assistance of counsel. But, for those of you who can afford counsel, know also that very few lawyers know how to do it right. In the event that you find one who is capable, you will discover that his or her filing is quite different from the *pro se* filings that are authorized by law and Rule. You will discover that counsel, as opposed to a prisoner, is authorized to argue both laws as well as previous case decisions. They are authorized to do so because attorneys, in theory, are trained to assist the court in arriving at a just end. *Please do not attempt to do this as a pro se filer.*

This is an example of a lawyer's filing. Although the names and places have been changed, this motion was filed in a real federal case.

WARNING

The following example should not be copied or relied on in any way. This memorandum is an example of a filing that will be accepted from an attorney but *will not* be accepted from an indigent *pro se* litigant. In plain terms, filing one will get you denied. Take your time in reading this memorandum and you will notice some serious errors that will ultimately affect the outcome of the case. Again, as seen in this memorandum, the attorney is quoting and arguing the meaning of both law and court rulings (cases) a *pro se* litigant is not authorized to do either of these.

WARNING

Do not use attorney filings if you are a pro se litigant!

GROUND ONE: Counsel Was Ineffective for Failing to Seek Suppression of Mr. Doe's Confession. Had Mr. Doe's Confession Been Suppressed, There Is a Reasonable Probability Mr. Doe Would Have Gone to Trial.

FBI agents interviewed Doe twice after the bank robbery in this case occurred. After the first interview, FBI agents approached Doe and arrested him. Doe told the agent that he wanted to speak with a lawyer after he was arrested. The agent told Doe that they merely needed another follow-up statement about what happened during the robbery, and that Doe would be free to go after he provided the statement. Doe again reiterated his desire for an attorney. One of the agents responded that "innocent people don't need lawyers." Doe then proceeded to provide a confession to his involvement with the robbery after being told by the agents what to say.

Doe and Ken Young Esq. discussed the circumstances surrounding Doe's confession. At no time did Mr. Young advise Doe that moving for suppression of his confession was an option. When Doe attempted to discuss with Young the advantages and disadvantages of going to trial, Young advised Doe not to go to trial because of the confession Doe made. Young was ineffective for failing to seek suppression of Doe's coerced confession. There is a reasonable probability the Court would have suppressed Doe's confession, and with the confession suppressed, there is a further reasonable probability Doe would have gone to trial instead of. pleading guilty, see Memorandum of Law and Facts in Support.

GROUND TWO: Doe's Guilty Plea Was Unknowing and Involuntary Because Doe Did Not Understand the True Nature of the 924(c) Charge.

Doe pleaded guilty to aiding and abetting a violation of 18 U.S.C. §924(c). The predicate for the §924(c) charge was the bank robbery, to which Doe also pleaded guilty under a theory of aiding and abetting. In light of *Sessions v. Dimaya*, 138 S.Ct. 1204 (2018), Doe argues that aiding and abetting armed bank robbery no longer constitutes a proper predicate for a §924(c) violation. This is because aiding and abetting armed robbery does not fall within §924(c)(3)(A), and thus can only remain a qualifying predicate under §924(c)(3)(B). However, §924(c)(3)(B) is unconstitutionally vague under the reasoning of *Dimaya* because there is no functional difference between 18 U.S.C. §16(b), the statutory provision at issue in *Dimaya*, and §924(c)(3)(B).

In *Bousley v. United States*, 523 U.S. 614 (1998), the Court held that a defendant may challenge the voluntary character of a plea, notwithstanding procedural default considerations, if the plea "has probably resulted in the conviction of one who is actually innocent." *id.* at 623, Doe is legally and factually innocent of the §924(c) charge as Doe did not aid or abet the robbery nor have any advance knowledge that Wells, the bank robber, would in fact rob the bank – much less use a firearm in doing so. Moreover, based on

Dimaya, Doe cannot knowingly and voluntarily plead guilty to something that is not a crime, see Memo of Law for More Support.

GROUND THREE: Doe's 924(c) Conviction Is Unconstitutional In Light of *Dimaya*.

Doe pleaded guilty to aiding and abetting a violation of 18 U.S.C. §924(c). The predicate for the §924(c) violation was aiding and abetting armed bank robbery. However, aiding and abetting armed bank robbery is not a proper predicate under §924(c)(3)(A) because the crime of aiding and abetting does not have "an element the use, attempted use, or threatened use of physical force against the person or property of another" 18 U.S.C. 924(c)(3)(A). Thus, for aiding and abetting armed bank robbery to qualify as a proper predicate, the crime must constitute a residual clause offense under 924(c)(3)(B). There is no principled distinction between the residual clause struck down in *Dimaya*, 18 U.S.C. §16(b), and §924(c)(3)(B). Accordingly, Doe is entitled to a vacatur of his §924(c) conviction in light of *Dimaya*, see Memo of Law for more support.

UNITED STATES DISTRICT COURT
NORTHER DISTRICT OF ALABAMA
SOUTHERN DIVISION

BRANDON DOE	)	
	)	
V.	)	CASE NO: 6:17-cv-9083-KOB
	)	
UNITED STATES OF AMERICA	)	
	)	

MEMORANDUM OF LAW IN SUPPORT OF
AMENDED 28 U.S.C. §2255 MOTION

I. INTRODUCTION

Police obtained a confession from Brandon Doe ("Doe") about his involvement in the bank robbery in this case. But that confession was involuntary because Doe twice asked for an attorney. The first request for counsel occurred when Doe was arrested. The next request for counsel happened during Doe's interrogation. Rather than honor Doe's request for counsel during the interrogation, police told Doe that "innocent people

don't need lawyers." Doe then "confessed" after he was told "we just need one more follow-up statement and you'll be free to go.

Notwithstanding the obvious involuntariness of Doe's confession, Doe's counsel failed to seek suppression of Doe's confession. This was ineffective assistance as there is a reasonable probability the Court would have suppressed Doe's confession if suppression had been sought. Further, there is a reasonable probability that Doe would have gone to trial had his confession been suppressed. Accordingly, for these and

the other reasons argued herein, the Court should grant Doe 28 U.S.C § 2255 relief.

II. BACKGROUND

Doe was charged in a two-count indictment with (count one) aiding and abetting armed bank robbery in violation of 18 U.S.C. §§ 2113(a) and (d) and 2; and (Count Two) aiding and abetting the brandishing of a firearm during and in relation to the bank robbery, a violation of 18 U.S.C. §§ 924(c)(l)(A)(ii) and 2. (ECF CR 16 at 1-2).

The charges stemmed from an armed bank robbery of the Region Bank In Birmingham, Alabama on November 8, 2016 (ECF CR 16 at 1). Donny Wells, Doe's co-defendant was quickly apprehended by police after the robbery. (ECF CR 1 at ¶7). Detective Anthony Fuller and the FBI agent Kevin Brown interviewed Wells. (ECF CR 1 at ~ 8). Wells purportedly agreed to speak with Fuller and Brown voluntarily, and then proceeded to confess to his involvement in the bank robbery. (ECF CR 1 at ¶¶ 13-15). According to Brown, Wells also identified Doe as being a participant in the crime, *id.*

However, new information cast significant doubt about the voluntariness of Wells' confession. In a statement recently obtained by Doe, Wells declares under penalty of perjury that he asked for a lawyer immediately after he was arrested, but police ignored his request, see, Exhibit 1 at 1. Wells was later interrogated by Fuller and Brown, *id.* at 2. Per Wells, Brown was dissatisfied with Wells' confession and "directed [him] to change [his] statement to implicate two other people, which included [his] sister Sienna Wells and [his] childhood friend Brandon Doe. [He] did not voluntarily include either of these people in [his] statement." *id.* (alterations added). Further, Wells states that he "changed [his] statement to suite Agent Brown's facts so he would not act so aggressive to [him], *id.*

According to Brown, he and Fuller directed Doe's arrest after Wells' confession. (ECF CR 1 at ~ 16). The arrest was effectuated by Birmingham police officer "Crawford," *id.* At the time of Doe's arrest, Doe told police that he wanted an attorney (Doe Decl. ¶ 1). Doe was subsequently transported to the Birmingham Police Department and interrogated by Brown and Fuller. (ECR CR 1 ¶¶ 17-21). During the interrogation, Doe purportedly "confessed" to his involvement in the bank robbery, *id.*

Doe asserts, however, that he renewed his request for a lawyer during the interrogation, (ECR CR 2 ¶ 15). In response to Doe's request for a lawyer, Brown became agitated and aggressive and then "began yelling "Innocent people don't need lawyers," *id.* According to Doe:

> Feeling physically threatened, I panicked and asked them what they wanted me to say. Once they briefed me on what I should say, they turned on a small recorder and recorded me saying what I was instructed to say.

(ECF CR 2 ¶ 15). Further, Brown and Fuller told Doe that they "just need[ed] one more follow-up statement and you'll be free to go." (Doe Decl. 3). Doe then "confessed."

Doe was represented by Ken Young. (ECR CR 25). Prior to entering a guilty plea in the case, Young met with Doe only two times. (Doe Decl. ¶ 4). The first meeting occurred in January 2017 while Doe was in county jail. (Doe Decl. ¶ 5). Doe discussed with Young the possibility of Doe proceeding to trial, but Young told Doe that he was "going to lose because of that confession." (Doe Decl. 5). Doe explained to Young what happened during his arrest and his interrogation. (Doe Decl. ¶ 6). Specifically, Doe advised

Young that he had twice asked for counsel: first when he was arrested, and again when he was being interrogated. (Doe Decl. ¶ 7). Doe also told Young about how he told Brown and Fuller what they wanted to hear after feeling threatened by Brown and being assured that he would be "free to go" after Doe gave the statement Brown and Fuller wanted him to say. (Doe Decl. ¶ 8). In response, Young told Doe that he was going to look into some things and get back to him (Doe Decl. ¶ 9).

Sometime after meeting with Young, Doe talked with his father about whether he should proceed to trial. In response, Doe's father told him "I don't know what to tell you. Take the advice of your lawyer," (Doe Decl. ¶ 10). The only other time Doe saw Young was the day before pleading guilty and the day before sentencing. (Doe Decl. ¶ 10).

Doe agreed to plead guilty pursuant to a plea agreement, (ECF CR 49). The terms of the plea required Doe to plead to both counts of the indictment, *id.* ¶ 1. In return for Doe's plea, the Government agreed to recommend that Doe receive a three-level downward adjustment for acceptance of responsibility and to recommend the low end of the advisory Guideline range. (*Id.* ¶¶ 7-8). The Court subsequently sentenced Doe to 36 months on Count One and 84 months on Count Two for a total term of imprisonment of 120 months, (ECF CR 63).

Doe timely sought 28 U.S.C. 2255 relief, and without opposition from the Government, subsequently amended his § 2255 motion (ECF 1, 10).

III. STANDARD OF REVIEW

Guilty plea ineffectiveness is demonstrated upon a showing of (1) deficient performance by counsel; and (2) a reasonable probability that, but for counsel's deficient performance, the defendant would have insisted on going to trial. *Hill v. Lockhart*, 474 U.S. 52, 59 (1985); *Strickland v. Washington*, 466 U.S. 668 (1984). A "reasonable probability" is a "probability sufficient to undermine confidence in the outcome." *Id.* at 694. When a defendant faults his attorney for failing to seek suppression of evidence:

> *both the deficient performance and prejudice prongs of Strickland*
> *turn on the viability of the motion to suppress. This is because a lawyer's performance only fails*
> *outside the range of competence demanded of counsel if she did not pursue a motion to suppress*
> *that would have affected the outcome of the case had the defendant rejected the plea and proceeded to*
> *trial.*

Arvelo v. Secretary, Florida Dept. of Corrections, 788 F.3d 1345, 1348 (11th Cir. 2015).

286

IV. ARGUMENT

Ground One: Counsel Was Ineffective for Failing to Seek Suppression of Doe's Confession. There Is a Reasonable Probability Doe Would Have Proceeded to Trial if His Confession Had Been Suppressed

The Supreme Court's decisions in *Edward v. Arizona*, 451 U.S. 477 (1981), and *Arizona v. Roberson*, 486 U.S. 675 (1988) dictate that "after a person in custody has expressed his desire to deal with the police only through counsel, he 'is not subject to further interrogation by authorities until counsel has been made available to him, unless the accused himself initiates further communication, exchanges, or conversations with the police,'" *Roberson*, 486 U.S. at 682, and that this rule applies "[w]hether a contemplated reinterrogation concerns the same or different offense, or whether the same or different law enforcement authorities are involved in the second interrogation," ide at 687.

In addition, the Eleventh Circuit has recognized that:

> In *Bram v. United States*, 168 U.S. 532, 18 S.Ct. 183, 183 L.Ed. 568 (1897), the Supreme Court observed that "a confession, in order to be admissible, must be free and voluntary; that is, must not be extracted by any sort of threats or violence, nor obtained by any direct or implied promises, however slight." *id*. at 542, 18 S.Ct. 183 (internal quotations omitted). In *Brady v. United States*, 397 U.S. 742, 90 S.Ct. 1463, 25 L.Ed.2d 747 (1970), the Supreme Court explained that *Bram* suggested that "even a mild promise of leniency," though not "an illegal act as such," undermines the voluntariness of a confession "because defendants at such times are too sensitive to inducement and the possible impact on them too great to ignore and too difficult to assess," *id*. at 754, 90 S.Ct. 1463. Nevertheless, *Bram*'s suggestion of a per se rule that would render a confession involuntary if it was preceded by "any direct or implied promises, however slight," has been rejected by the Supreme Court, see *Fulminante*, 499 U.S. at 284-85, 111 S.Ct. 1246. Instead, the issue of voluntariness must be determined by examining the totality of the circumstances, *id*. The burden is on the prosecution to establish, by a preponderance of the evidence, that a challenged confession was voluntary, *Lego v. Twomey*, 404 U.S. 477, 489, 92 S.Ct. 619, 30 L.Ed.2d 618 (1972).

United States v. Lall, 607 F.3d 1277, 1285-86 (11th Circ. 2010). Further, Lall cited approvingly of the Fifth Circuit's decision in *Streetman v. Lynaugh*, which held that "certain promises, if not kept, are so attractive that they render a resulting confession involuntary … A promise of immediate release or that any statement will not be used against the accused is such a promise," *Streetman v. Lynaugh*, 812 F.2d 950, 957 (5th Cir. 1987); Lall, 607 F.3d 1286 (emphasis added).

Doe was initially taken into custody by Birmingham Police officer "Crawford." (ECF CR 1 ¶ 16). Doe asserts that he told Officer Crawford that he wants to speak with a lawyer. (Doe Decl. ¶ 1). Dow was then taken to the Birmingham Police Department and interrogated by Fuller and Brown. While Fuller and Brown asserted that Doe voluntarily agreed to speak with them, Doe asserts that he again reiterated his request for counsel and was, for all intents and purposes coerced into confessing based on Brown's "agitated and aggressive" behavior, which made Doe feel "physically threatened." (ECF at 2 ¶ 15). Additionally, Doe asserts that he told Brown and Fuller what they asked him to say because of their promise that he would "be free to go" afterwards. (Doe Decl. ¶ 3).

Doe's allegations demonstrate three constitutional violations. First, Doe asked for an attorney when he was initially arrested by Officer Crawford. Even if Officer Crawford never told Brown and fuller about Doe's request for counsel, Roberson requires suppression of Doe's confession. Second, Doe's rights were again violated when he asked for a lawyer while being interrogated by Fuller and Brown. Finally, Doe's confession was involuntarily obtained when Fuller and Brown promised Doe he would be "free to go" after he provided the statement they were seeking, *Streetman*, 812 F.2d. at 957.

Further, as already recounted in the Background above, Doe explained the facts surrounding his arrest and interrogation to Young. Young recognized the importance of Doe's confession. Indeed, as Doe asserts, that is the reason Young told Doe he should not go to trial. (Doe Decl. ¶ 5). But under the circumstances, it was deficient performance for Young not to have pursued suppression of Doe's confession. The plea agreement the Government offered was nothing more than a plea to what was already charged in the indictment, plus a recommendation that Doe receive a three-level downward adjustment for acceptance of responsibility.

There was no downside to seeking suppression of Doe's confession under the circumstances. And more importantly, the above shows that the Court would have been compelled to grant suppression of Doe's confession had Young so moved. Finally, without the confession, it is clear that there is a reasonable probability Doe would have insisted on going to trial. (Doe Decl. ¶ 12). Accordingly, the Court should hold that Young was ineffective for failing to seek suppression of Doe's confession and vacate Doe's guilty plea.

Grounds Two & Three: Doe's Guilty Plea Was Unknowing and Involuntary Because He Did Not Understand the True Nature Of the § 924(c) Charge. Additionally, Doe's § 924(c) Conviction is Unconstitutional

Doe pleaded guilty to aiding and abetting a violation of 18 U.S.C. § 924(c). The predicate for the § 924(c) charge was the bank robbery, to which Doe also pleaded guilty under a theory of aiding and abetting. In light of *Sessions v. Dimaya*, 138 S.Ct. 1204 (2018), Doe argues that aiding and abetting armed bank robbery no longer constitutes a proper predicate for a § 924(c) violation. This is because aiding and abetting armed bank robbery does not fall within § 924(c)(3)(A), and thus can only remain a qualifying predicate under § 924(c)(3)(B). However, § 924 (c)(3)(B) is unconstitutionally vague under the reasoning of *Dimaya* because there is no functional difference between 18 U.S.C. § 16(b), the statutory provision at issue in *Dimaya* and § 924(c)(3)(B). In addition, Doe argues that his § 924(c) conviction is unconstitutional based on *Dimaya*.

In *Bousley v. United States*, 523 U.S. 614 (1998), the Court held that a defendant may challenge the voluntary character of a plea, notwithstanding procedural default considerations, if the plea "has probably resulted in the conviction of one who is actually innocent," *id.* at 623, Doe is legally and factually innocent of the § 924(c) charge as Doe did not aid nor abet the robbery nor have any advance knowledge that Wells, the bank robber, would in fact rob the bank – much less use a firearm in doing so. Moreover, based on *Dimaya*, Doe cannot knowingly and voluntarily plead guilty to something that is not a crime.

The Eleventh Circuit recently agreed to rehear *Ovalles v. United States*, No. 17-10172 (11th Cir.) *en banc*. At issue in *Ovalles* is whether *Dimaya* applies to 18 U.S.C. § 924(c)(3)(B). Because the outcome of *Ovalles* is likely dispositive of Doe's claim in Counts Two and Three, the Court should defer ruling on these ground until *Ovalles* is decided. In the interim, the Court has plenty to consider with respect to Ground One, to and including the necessity of an evidentiary hearing given Doe's allegations.

V. AN EVIDENTIARY HEARING IS NEEDED

The Court should schedule an evidentiary hearing on Ground One of Doe's motion. It is well settled that an evidentiary hearing required unless the files and records of the case "conclusively" refute the allegations presented, 28 U.S.C. 2255. Much of Doe's argument is based on facts outside the record. As such, this claim cannot be properly resolved without a hearing.

VI. CONCLUSION

Based on the foregoing, the Court should grant Doe 28 U.S.C. 2255 relief.

CHAPTER TWENTY-THREE

FILING THE MOTION – RULE THREE

Although a proceeding under 28 U.S.C. § 2255 is filed under a new civil docket number, you will discover a few differences. For example, there is no filing fee required of a movant (defendant in the criminal case) under the Rules Governing Section 2255 Proceedings. This is a change from the practice of charging $15.00 and is done to recognize the specific nature of a § 2255 motion as being a continuation of a criminal case whose judgment is under attack.

Also notice that § 2255 is intended to provide a remedy similar to a writ of *habeas corpus* to federal prisoners. A § 2255 request for relief is called a motion instead of a petition; thus, it is not specifically engineered to begin a new action, but to broaden the scope of an existing action.

In reading Rule Three, you will also discover a number of additional differences:

First, in a § 2255 proceeding, the movant (formerly the defendant) must file two copies plus the original motion with the clerk of court. The clerk then files the motion in the criminal docket as opposed to opening the new civil action pending an initial review. The original motion is what the court posts on the CM/ECF system. I recommend that it not be stapled for the court clerk's convenience. The other two copies I routinely staple because one goes to the district judge who presided over the criminal case, and the other is served upon the government after the district court's initial review. Although, you will find many prisoners who will tell you to file only one copy of a § 2255 motion; I would suggest that you follow the court's rules to the strictest detail.

The time for filing your motion is governed by 28 U.S.C. § 2255(f), and Rules governing Section 2255 Proceedings, Rule 3(d). The rule holds that, "A paper filed by an inmate confined in an institution is timely if deposited in the institution's internal mailing system on or before the last day for filing."

Anyone who has filed for relief knows that the rule is not followed by most federal courts. The rule that the courts follow is an unspoken rule, but experience will show that all motions that can be denied will be considered timely and then summarily denied. All claims that have merit, however, will be scrutinized from every angle. The mailbox rule is one of those angles.

In the event that your filing is within two weeks of your filing deadline, timely filing will become the first defense for both the court and the government. Be aware that neither the prison mail system nor a declaration under 28 U.S.C. § 1746 will be honored. The prison mailing system does not provide a prisoner with proof that the prisoner did in-fact deposit any specific filing in the system.

My first suggestion to any prisoner is to file your motion sixty days before the deadline. If this is not possible, use the prison legal mail system, but also take a cop-out with you requesting that your specific piece of mail be entered into the system. At the mailroom, ask the mail clerk to stamp your cop-out as well, this will serve as a receipt from the mail clerk verifying the date of mailing.

Your second option is to send your filing through certified mail. When the little green slip gets back to you, it will be date stamped by the post office providing you with a receipt for filing. Additionally, you can have a loved one track your mailing, including the date the clerk received it, by going to USPS.gov.

CHAPTER TWENTY-FOUR

PRELIMINARY REVIEW – RULE FOUR

Comparing Rule Four to the §2255 statute, you will discover that this rule gives the court instructions on how to apply §2255(b). Rule four specifies the court's options and responsibilities once the motion is properly filed with the court. Once received, the §2255 motion *must* be presented to the assigned judge promptly. The judge must then examine the motion, and all its attachments, in comparison to "the files and records." If it appears to the judge, based on this comparison, that the prisoner is entitled to no relief; the judge must enter an order that summarily dismisses the motion and causes the prisoner to be notified.

Show Cause Order – If you have filed your §2255 motion within the one- year limitation of §2255(f), the court will send a copy of the motion to the government along with a show cause order. The rule requires that the judge must order the government to file a response within a time period that is specified by the order to show cause. Also, realize that a show cause order for a motion that was timely filed is nothing to get excited about. Most courts treat the §2255 rules only as a formality. The courts don't read timely filed motion, because they already intend to deny relief anyway. The court will, at its first opportunity, deny your motion based upon the government's opinion. Thus, your reply is the most important filing that you can provide.

Out of Time §2255 Motions – Also require a show cause order to proceed. But once the prisoner has failed to file his § 2255 motion on time, it is the prisoner who must show cause. As discussed in earlier chapters, it is important to know where you're heading before taking the first step. Thus, if you know you are late in filing your §2255 motion; make sure you have refined your argument that justifies your late filing before you are ordered to show cause.

Magistrate Judge – Although the authority of a Magistrate judge is particularized in Rule Ten of the Rules Governing Section 2255 Proceedings; it is here in the rule four preliminary review stage that the case will be assigned to a magistrate. Much like the reason new prosecutors are assigned to the post-conviction section of the U.S. Attorney's office; magistrate judges are assigned to §2255 proceedings to learn how important it is to place the finality of conviction over a prisoner's constitutional rights to due process.

In §2255 proceedings, a magistrate will make all the non-dispositive (not final) decisions in the case and will prepare a report and recommendation for the district judge. The report and recommendation will almost always favor a denial. It's the very rare case that a district judge rejects the magistrate's recommendation before the §2255 is denied. Most commonly the report and recommendation are accepted no matter how inconceivable its theories may be.

In the magistrate's report and recommendation, you will find instructions directing you on how to file an objection to the magistrate's recommendations. You *must object*. If you fail to file a timely objection to the magistrate's report and recommendation, you won't be able to apply for a certificate of appealability. Again, you must object.

CHAPTER TWENTY-FIVE

THE ANSWER AND REPLY – RULE FIVE

When you file a properly prepared, and timely, §2255 motion and the court issues an order to the government, to show cause; the government must explain why the court should not grant the relief you requested. Although this sounds fair, don't get your hopes up. In the ordinary case, the court will give the government instructions as to what is needed to deny the motion. In referring back to Tommy Rodella's case, in Chapter Twenty, you will find in the magistrate's order to show cause includes instructions to the government, to "address any statute of limitations issue under 28 U.S.C. §2255(f) in its answer."

I tell you this in hopes that you will not forget that the court and the government are two of three adversaries who are working together to keep you in prison. When you are appointed counsel for your evidentiary hearing, you will meet your third adversary, who wants you to remain in prison.

Government's Answer – The government's answer will likely be filed on its due date, usually right before midnight via the CM/ECF court filing system. They will also mail out a hard copy to you the next day. In the "answer" the government's attorney will give "cause" by ignoring all the meaningful claims that are raised; only then to chase his or her legal tail for an average of about twenty-five pages. The use of many words often seems impressive in its first read, but it's not. They are trying to "baffle you will bullshit."

Your Reply – The key to a good "reply" is keeping it short and simple. Stay focused on the grounds that you have raised, rather than the version offered by the government. The government's answer is most often designed to distract a prisoner, you, from the meaningful issues. I always compare my original grounds for relief to the government's answer. I'm most often looking for two things: what did the government reword or re-characterize into a different ground, and what did the government fail to answer. The reply that follows is an example of an effective reply. It is also the reply that currently holds my own personal post-conviction case in litigation.

**UNITED STATES DISTRICT COURT
NORTHERN DISTRICT OF ALABAMA
SOUTHERN DIVISION**

KELLY PATRICK RIGGS

Case No.

v.

2:15-CV-8043-KOB

UNITED STATES OF AMERICA

_____/

MR. RIGGS'S REPLY TO "UNITED STATES' RESPONSE"

Mr. Riggs has recently filed his amended 28 U.S.C. §2255 motion. The government opposes the motion, notwithstanding the fact that the A.U.S.A conceded several critical issues. Moreover, the government's response merely places some of Mr. Riggs's allegations into contest. Consequently, governing authorities require this court to conduct an evidentiary hearing to determine the facts. 28 U.S.C. §2255(b). Alternatively, this court should predicate its decision on Mr. Riggs's facts and events as they are presented in his amended §2255.

Mr. Riggs addresses the government's response in three parts:

1) Mr. Riggs demonstrates that on the existing record he was deprived of counsel at critical stages of the criminal proceedings. This claim is conceded by the government.

2) Mr. Riggs demonstrates that on the existing record he has a judicially noticed alibi defense establishing his actual innocence. This claim is conceded by the government.

3) Mr. Riggs demonstrates that on the existing record he was deprived of the effective assistance of counsel where Glennon F. Threatt, Jr. provided false information to his client, Mr. Riggs, and the district court. This claim is conceded by the government.

Mr. Riggs provides a clarifying explanation for each claim in turn.

1) Mr. Riggs demonstrates that on the existing record he was deprived of counsel at critical stage of the criminal proceeding. This claim is conceded by the government.

First, Mr. Riggs points out that ground Two of his amended §2255 raises a *Cronic* error that the government conceded by failing to address the issue. Mr. Riggs stands firmly on all points raised in his original and amended §2255 motions. This reply will address only the points raised in the government's response that require a reply and reiterate claims the government conceded. The crux of the government's response is hinged on an erroneous belief that the Eleventh Circuit Court of Appeals' decision serves as a bar, and that "Riggs cannot relitigate his ineffective assistance claims because the Eleventh Circuit already adjudicated that matter against him." The government's contention that "The court should deny Riggs's motion without a hearing. Riggs is barred from litigating his section §2255 claims because the Eleventh Circuit has already adjudicated those claims against him" is clearly wrong.

In Mr. Riggs's Ground Two he claimed that he "was deprived of the effective assistance of counsel …" Due to Mr. Riggs being abandoned by counsel at direct appeal, coupled with his ignorance of law, this claim – that he was without counsel – was never raised on direct appeal. Thus, the court of appeals was unable to adjudicate the claim.

Moreover, the court could easily find what the higher courts have previously held, that it's a constitutional right to have the assistance of counsel at trial, but yet a violation that is ordinarily unreviewable on direct appeal. The Eleventh Circuit Court of Appeals holds that "A claim of ineffective assistance of counsel may not be raised on direct appeal where the claim has not been heard by the district court nor a factual record developed," *United States v. Khoury*, 901 F. 2d 948, 969 (11th Cir. 1990); "The preferred method of raising the issue of ineffective assistance of counsel is not on direct appeal, but instead in a 28 U.S.C. §2255 motion to vacate," *Massaro v. United States*, 538 U.S. 500 (2003); "only when the record is sufficiently developed will we consider an ineffective assistance claim on direct appeal," *United States v. Bender*, 290 F.3d 1279, 1284 (11th Cir. 2002).

In Mr. Riggs's claim Two he showed in pertinent part that,

> Mr. Riggs was taken into a hearing to determine if a conflict of interest existed. The court, failing to appoint unconflicted counsel, conducted the hearing with Mr. Threatt as Mr. Riggs's counsel. On the day of the hearing Mr. Riggs's interests were to prove a conflict of interest existed. Mr. Threatt's interest was to prove that a conflict did not exist. The interests of Mr. Riggs and Mr. Threatt were in conflict on September 5, 2013. On that day Mr. Riggs was either represented by conflicted counselor he had no counsel at all."

In either scenario, Mr. Riggs suffered a Sixth Amendment violation because the primary concern of a conflict of interest could not have been determined at a hearing where Mr. Riggs had no counsel; see *Strickland* and *Cronic* both supra.

The conflict-of-interest hearing in Mr. Riggs's case was a critical stage in his trial proceedings that was rendered unconstitutional because the court failed to appoint un-conflicted counsel. In *United States v. Roy*, 855 F.3d 1133 (11th Cir. 2017) (*en banc*), the court of appeals asked, "What, then is a 'critical stage' of a trial?" In the case of *Roy*, counsel's seven-minute absence did not rise to a *Cronic* error because counsel only missed a small portion of the trial itself and not "an entire 'stage of the trial.'" See *Cronic*, 466 U.S. at 659. As noted by the Eleventh Circuit Court of Appeals sitting *en banc*, "The Supreme Court has instructed us that it has used the term 'critical stage' 'to denote a step of a crminal proceeding, such as arraignment, that held significant consequences for the accused,' Bell v. Cone 535, U.S. at 695-96, 122 S. Ct at 1851." And decision after decision shows that what the court means when it does use the term 'stage' for *Cronic* purposes is a qualitatively distinct, discrete, and separate phase or step of a criminal proceeding where the defendant has a right to counsel, such as an arraignment, a post-indictment line-up, a preliminary hearing, a plea hearing, closing arguments as a whole, or a sentence proceeding as a whole, see *Montejo v. Louisiana*, 556 U.S. 778 (2009)(describing post indictment interrogation as a critical stage); *Iowa v. Tovar*, 541 U.S. 77 (2004)('A plea hearing qualifies as a "critical stage."'); *Gardner v. Florida*, 430 U.S. 349, (1977) ("Sentencing is a critical stage of the criminal proceeding at which the defendant is entitled to the effective assistance of counsel."); *Gilbert v. California*, 388 U.S. 263, (1967)("A post-indictment pretrial lineup ... is a critical stage of the criminal prosecution ..."); *White*, 373 U.S. at 59-60, 83 S. Ct. at 1051 ("Whatever may be the normal function of the 'preliminary hearing' under Maryland law, it was in this case as 'Critical' a stage as arraignment ..."); *Hamilton*, 368 U.S. at 53, (describing arraignment as "a critical stage in a criminal proceeding"); See also *Harrington v. Gillis*, 456 F.3d 118, 132 (3rd Cir. 2006)(noting that "an appeal is a critical stage of a criminal proceeding"); *United States v. Sanchez-Barreto*, 93 F.3d 17, 20 (1st Cir. 1996)(Noting that a "plea withdrawal hearing" is a critical stage).

Mr. Riggs's primary contention is that his counsel's conflict caused damage to his defense. When the district court failed to appoint un-conflicted counsel at a conflict-of-interest hearing, Mr. Riggs was outright denied counsel at a critical stage of his criminal proceedings. Thus, Mr. Riggs, acting alone against his own counsel, failed to present his claim adequately. Ultimately, Mr. Riggs was deprived of a public speedy trial by conflicted counsel who encouraged him to forgo trial, his alibi defense, and enter into a defunct plea agreement with the expectation of protection for him and his family.

Mr. Riggs contends that he has met both prongs of the *Strickland* test, see *Jae Lee v. United States*, 582 U.S. ___, 137 S. Ct. ___ , holding that "when a defendant alleges his counsel's deficient performance led him to accept a guilty plea rather than go to trial, courts consider whether the defendant was prejudiced by the denial of the entire judicial proceeding to which he had a right. When a defendant claims that his counsel's deficient performance deprived him of a trial by causing him to accept a plea, the defendant can show prejudice by demonstrating a reasonable probability that, but; for counsel's errors, he would not have pleaded guilty and would have insisted on going to trial."

Notwithstanding the government conceding to the foregoing claim, Mr. Riggs reminds that the Eleventh Circuit said in *Roy* that "The *Cronic* decision limited the presumption of prejudice to cases where defense counsel 'entirely fails to subject the prosecution's case to meaningful adversarial testing in the trial or where there is the complete denial of counsel' at a 'critical stage of [the] trial.' *Cronic* 466 U.S. at 659, 104 S. Ct. at 2047 (emphasis added)"

This claim alone presents a claim of constitutional magnitude that is not only untenable, but also the government concedes in its response. This court should return Mr. Riggs to the pre-plea stage of the criminal proceedings. In the alternative, this court could require Mr. Riggs's presence at an evidentiary hearing.

2) Mr. Riggs demonstrates that on the existing record he has a judicially noticed alibi defense establishing his actual innocence. This claim is conceded by the government.

In all of the claims in Mr. Riggs amended §2255 he showed that an alibi existed. The government in its reply conceded the fact, and went on to say that "Riggs's claims that these attorneys failed to investigate the case, or interview or subpoena witnesses, lies in square conflict with Mr. Threatt's testimony concerning the assistance the federal public defender's office provided Riggs." The government goes on to make note of "Mr. Threatt explaining his advice not to assert an alibi defense inconsistent with Riggs's videotaped confession," makes known that an alibi did in fact exist where the government raised no contest to the claim.

What is most interesting is that Mr. Threatt, on December 20, 2013, testified that he gave notice of alibi and that ten subpoenas were issued. Mr. Threatt's testimony is in clear conflict with the record because the docket reflects neither a notice of alibi nor a witness list for the defense.

Moreover, on December 20, 2013, in a conversation Mr. Riggs was having with Judge Bowdre, she testified that she did not issue a subpoena. Thus, even Mr. Threatt's own testimony is contradicted by the record, where he made false statements to the court.

Alibi is defined as, "a defense based on the physical impossibility of a defendant's guilt by placing the defendant in a location other than the scene of the crime at the relevant time. Fed. R. Crim. P. 12.1. Blacks Law Dictionary, third pocket edition.

Mr. Riggs has shown that he was elsewhere and with many alibi witnesses when the alleged offense occurred and electronically recorded. Glennon F. Threatt, Jr. claimed in court record that he filed a notice of alibi and subpoenaed ten witnesses. The district court took judicial notice that Mr. Threatt's testimony was accurate.

In Mr. Riggs case, either Mr. Threatt was ineffective for making false claims to the court concerning Mr. Riggs and the court was in error for taking judicial notice, or Mr. Riggs is actually innocent supported by a judicially noticed alibi defense. In either scenario Mr. Riggs is due an evidentiary hearing. Thus, the government's argument that "the court should deny Riggs's motion without a hearing" is misplaced, see: *McQuiggin v. Perkins*, 569 U.S. ___ (2013), where even "a prisoner otherwise subject to defense of abuse or successive use of the writ [of *habeas corpus*] may have his federal constitutional claim considered on the merits if he makes a proper showing of actual innocence."

In Mr. Riggs's case he has made a proper showing of actual innocence. Thus, this court should at a minimum hold an evidentiary hearing.

3) Mr. Riggs demonstrates that on the existing record he was deprived of the effective assistance of counsel where Glennon F. Threatt, Jr. provided false information to his client, Mr. Riggs, and the district court. This claim is conceded by the government.

In Mr. Riggs's amended §2255 motion he raised issue with Glennon F. Threatt, who provided false testimony to the court, which is established by the record; who presented an edited version of the videotaped interview that the government now relies on; and who provided information to a colleague who represented cartel members Mr. Riggs provided information against. These claims were unaddressed in the government's response, thus conceded.

Under such circumstances the prosecutor, even when new to a case, has an obligation to seek justice. The A.B.A. Model Rules of Professional Conduct, Rule 3.8: Special Responsibilities of a Prosecutor, 3.8(g) and (h). Mr. Riggs has shown and goes unaddressed that he has been, since 2001, an informant for several law enforcement agencies. He presented facts and claims that if true would constitute grounds for relief. The government, however, in violation of A.B.A. standards has shirked its duty to seek justice and asks this court to preserve a miscarriage of justice.

INEFFECTIVE ASSISTANCE OF COUNSEL: OVERCOMING THE INEVITABLE

Mr. Riggs has shown in his amended §2255 that Glennon F. Threatt, Jr. has obstructed justice in several investigations by presenting false information to Mr. Riggs and the court. The actions of Glennon Threatt constitute a criminal act where he actually aided and abetted Alvin Ray Johnson, Jr., Lakendrick Dunn, and Ronny Davis in the concealment of Mr. DeAndrea Washington's murder. Mr. Threatt and Sabra Barnett took an active role in aiding and abetting uncharged persons in facilitating the murder of Sambo Hazelrig and his girlfriend. A minimum level of investigation would reveal that Mr. Riggs is in fact a witness in multiple cases; that Mr. Riggs's testimony proved harmful to Alabama State officials; that state officials including, but not limited to, Hoover Police Dept. have effectively weaponized a United States government effort; and that Glennon F. Threatt, Jr. concealed evidence, made false statements, and manipulated Mr. Riggs's case in an effort to obstruct justice.

This claim has gone unanswered by the government and is therefore conceded. The court should at a minimum require Mr. Riggs's presence in court and hold an evidentiary hearing where he may present his case.

Wherefore, Mr. Riggs shows that his claims are not procedurally barred, and this court is established for the purpose of addressing the merits of constitutional claims, just like these, among other things. Mr. Riggs moves this court to vacate his sentence and/or set the court's judgment aside in an effort to seek justice in this case.

Respectfully submitted this 23 day of April, 2018

_____

Kelly Patrick Riggs, *pro se*
Reg. No.
Address

KELLY PATRICK RIGGS

CERTIFICATE OF SERVICE

Mr. Riggs certifies that he has served all parties as required by rule and law to include and not limited to the clerk of this court and the United States at 1801 4th Ave. N; Birmingham, AL 35203

Respectfully submitted this 23 day of April, 2018

_____

Kelly Patrick Riggs, *pro se*
Reg. No.
Address

USPS TRACKING # **9114 9012 3080 1329 5933 72**
& CUSTOMER   For Tracking or inquiries go to USPS.com
RECEIPT   or call 1-800-222-1811.

CHAPTER TWENTY-SIX

EVIDENTIARY HEARINGS

Getting ready for an evidentiary hearing should be considered before you file your §2255 motion. Although, this subject is governed by three different rules; the court will only allow the use of one.

Rule 6. Discovery – A U.S. District Court has never, that I know of, authorized a prisoner, filing in *pro se*, to conduct any kind of discovery. The view of the court is simple; if the prisoner filed a motion, he or she should already have the evidence necessary to support it. The district court's job in any post-conviction proceeding is to secure the finality of the conviction. Thus, authorizing you to conduct discovery would be counterproductive to the court's efforts.

Rule 7. Expanding the Record – Rule 7 serves the government only. I have been witnessed to courts summarily deciding that affidavits supplied by prisoners are untrue, and all evidence questionable. Another issue is that in a §2255 proceeding the action is before the convicting judge. Thus, the court will feel no need to expand the record because the trial judge is the one presiding, and as such, should have the complete record at their disposal. The last thing that the court will do is grant you leave to search for new evidence to vacate the conviction that the court is trying to preserve.

Rule 8. Evidentiary Hearing – "Unless the motion and files and records of the case conclusively show that the prisoner is entitled to no relief, the court shall grant a prompt hearing thereon ..." 28 U.S.C. §2255(b). Don't be distracted, you have no need to ask for an evidentiary hearing. To do so causes a court to realize that you are unsure about the facts. When your facts are correct making your sentence open to collateral attack, "the court shall vacate and set the judgment aside and shall discharge the prisoner or resentence him or grant a new trial or correct the sentence as may appear appropriate," 28 U.S.C. §2255(b). Therefore, you must decide what you want the court to do:

- vacate and set the judgment aside, discharging the prisoner;
- resentence him or grant a new trial; or
- correct the sentence as may appear appropriate.

When a hearing is required, either the court or government will ask for one.

When a hearing is ordered, its purpose is to discredit your facts and evidence. Therefore, you don't particularly want a hearing.

Appointment of Counsel – "If an evidentiary hearing is warranted, the judge must appoint an attorney to represent a moving party who qualifies to have counsel appointed under 18 U.S.C. §3006A." Rule 8(c) of the Rules Governing Section 2255 Proceedings. The most important thing to understand is that a §2255 is not a criminal case. Thus, you *do not* have a Sixth Amendment right to counsel in a §2255 proceeding. The appointment of counsel at the hearing is for the benefit of the court and the government; he is not on your side. The sole purpose of the appointment of counsel in most cases is to threaten the prisoner, advising him to withdraw the motion that got him to court. Again, know the facts of your case along with all the possible outcomes. The first enemy you will have to overcome is your own appointed attorney.

At the Hearing – Once you have convinced your appointed lawyer that you are not going to withdraw, he will switch gears. The second favored tactic is to talk a good game about how the lawyer is just doing his job. He or she will talk about how hard he will fight and all the things he will prove on your behalf. But, once he gets you to court, he will remain silent and wait for the government to explain why you shouldn't get relief. Your lawyer will then give a brief recap leading your claims for relief to a quick denial.

In the very beginning, you must understand that you, and you alone, are responsible for prosecuting your §2255 hearing. If you are brought to court, you must make your claims for relief known on the record. You are the first to speak unless directed otherwise. Your lawyer should do all the talking, but when he or she fails you must stand and advise the court that, (1) your appointed §2255 lawyer is failing to provide the effective assistance of counsel; and (2) speak your grounds for relief in open court for the court reporter to enter into the official record. In the event this does not get done by you or your lawyer, your chances of winning a certificate of appealability from the court of appeals is dramatically reduced.

In the very beginning you should obtain a copy of your §2255, from either your lawyer or simply ask the court for a copy before the hearing. And of course, make your request on the record. Give your lawyer a chance to voice your claim, if he does not you interrupt and read your grounds aloud. Remember, read the grounds only and advise the court that the supporting facts speak for themselves.

Remember also that the first hearing is only a formality, almost all §2255 will lose no matter what. §2255 motions are routinely denied by the district court no matter what the truth is. The §2255 motions that are granted are ordered to be granted by a court of appeals or the Supreme Court of the United States. Your job here is simply to make your grounds heard on the record in preparation for appeal.

Notice of Appeal – No matter what happens, regardless of if the district court issues a certificate of appealability, you must file a notice of appeal, see Federal Rules of Appellate procedure, Rule 4(a). The notice of appeal must be filed with the district court clerk within 30 days after entry of the judgment or order appealed from. Federal Rules of Appellate Procedure, Rule 4(a)(1)(A).

Denial of Certificate of Appealability – You don't have to appeal from the district court's denial of a certificate of appealability. All you have to do is apply to the Circuit Court asking that they issue the certificate, see 28 U.S.C. §2253(c)(2). And remember the constitutional claim is the lack of trial or a fair trial process. The following documents were filed in a real federal case in the Eleventh Circuit.

UNITED STATES DISTRICT COURT
NORTHERN DISTRICT OF ALABAMA
SOUTHERN DIVISION

KELLY PATRICK RIGGS

V.

UNITED STATES OF AMERICA

Case No.: 2:15-CV-8043-KOB

NOTICE OF APPEAL

Mr. Riggs gives notice of appeal from this Courts final judgment to deny him a certificate of appealability and/or denial of evidentiary hearing to settle contested factual issues.

Mr. Riggs shows that the district judge's ruling is in direct contradiction with *Clisby v. Jones*, 960 F.2d. 925 (11th Cir. 1992) (*en banc*). The order handed down by the Court addresses only three of Mr. Riggs's four claims and the three it did address are incomplete. In Mr. Riggs's petition, to request a certificate of appealability will particularize that the district court left unanswered the following:

1) his claim of Conflict of Interest with the Federal Public Defenders office as a whole.

2) his claim of outright denial of counsel at a critical stage of the criminal proceedings. (Ground Three)

3) his claim that Glennon F. Threatt and Sabra Barnett conspired to murder Mr. Riggs in a jail cell by discussing his case with cartel associate Lois Rodriguez.

4) his claim that Brett Bloomston provided ineffective assistance of trial counsel by failing to refine and/or clarify Mr. Riggs's claims in his motion to withdraw his plea agreement.

5) his claim that Glennon Threatt failed to provide effective assistance of counsel by presenting a version of a police video, edited to appear to be a confession, rather than challenging the government's evidence.

6) that Glennon Threatts representation was in fact a constructive denial of counsel where he "testified that he felt an alibi defense would be inconsistent with Mr. Riggs confession." Thus, failing to provide adversarial testing of government's evidence.

7) Mr. Riggs expressly moved for the appointment of conflict free counsel, yet the Court dispatched Glennon Threatt to counsel Mr. Riggs concerning the conflict of interest. Thus, Mr. Riggs did not know, "of

305

the right to obtain other counsel" where the Court failed to advise him and failed to appoint un-conflicted counsel. Moreover, Mr. Threatt counseled, likely at the behest of the Court, that Mr. Riggs wouldn't get new counsel because he was getting time served for his assistance anyway.

8) The claim that Brett Bloomston abandoned Mr. Riggs at appeal, making it highly unlikely that Mr. Riggs could articulate meaningful appeal claims on his own, an inability the Court now relies on to deny Mr. Riggs his right to an evidentiary hearing. §2255(b).

9) In this action it's the Court itself that obstructs justice by concealing the contested video confession, the alibi witnesses, and the presiding judge's personal and church relationship with Brad Taylor and the Hazelrig family. Researching the murder of Sambo Hazelrig and the attempted murder of Mr. Riggs in 2011.

10) The district court commits fraud on the American people of the Northern District of Alabama by falsifying established Court record in her memorandum. The record reflects that on December 20, 2013, *id* at 74, states "we actually filed a Notice of Alibi" and "we subpoenaed at least ten people in the case," *id* at 55.

11) That Mr. Riggs claims that the ineffectiveness of counsel has facilitated the conviction of someone who is actually innocent. The facts of the criminal case show that Mr. Riggs was in a pool with his wife and children at the time the Court testified that Mr. Riggs answered the agents' messages.

12) Mr. Riggs will show that neither the government nor the Court has provided a single affidavit from anyone on anything the Court currently is testifying to.

13) Mr. Riggs's claim that he was not appointed un-conflicted counsel at a conflict-of-interest hearing. The Court tries to dismiss the claim by not addressing Mr. Riggs's Ground Three and addressing the claim, in part, in a foot note on page eight of the Court's memorandum. The facts are:

A) Mr. Riggs has filed no briefs and set his claim out clearly in Ground Three of his amended § 2255 Motion.

B) The Court refuses to "re-evaluate the underlying finding that Mr. Threatt had no conflict, because Mr. Riggs had the opportunity to challenge that finding and failed to do so." But the Court fails to state that Mr. Riggs's only opportunity to challenge the finding was while he was deprived of counsel.

C) Mr. Riggs challenged Mr. Threatt's loyalties in a *pro se* motion.

D) The Court dispatched Mr. Threatt, to address Mr. Riggs's motion with Mr. Riggs, rather than un-conflicted counsel.

E) The Court failed to advise Mr. Riggs of his right to un-conflicted counsel at the conflict hearing and failed to appoint un-conflicted counsel to advise Mr. Riggs concerning his right to conflict free counsel at the conflict hearing.

F) At the hearing Mr. Riggs's interest was to prove that counsel was conflicted, Glennon Threatts' interest was to prove there was no conflict. This represents a second independent conflict of interest where Mr. Riggs was without counsel.

G) The Court did not advise Mr. Riggs of his right to un-conflicted counsel to assist him in deciding to waive the conflict of counsel. Nor did the Court conduct a *Ferretta* hearing to decide if Mr. Riggs could represent his own interests or understand the impact of his decision to represent himself in waiving his right to conflict free counsel.

14) Finally, the Court has rushed Mr. Riggs to judgment where the Court issued an "order regarding summary disposition," in which it "gives Mr. Riggs until May 15, 2018 … to supply any additional evidentiary materials or legal arguments …" but yet issued a "Final Order to deny Mr. Riggs' § 2255 on May 2, 2018. Mr. Riggs moves this Court to designate the record for appeal. Submitted on May 14, 2018, By:

_____
Kelly Patrick Riggs
Register No.:
Address

KELLY PATRICK RIGGS

CERTIFICATE OF SERVICE

I have served a copy of this notice on the clerk of this Court, the United States of America, the 11th Circuit Court Clerk, and the Release of Innocent Prisoners Effort, Inc. All in the interest of justice and publication on social media. "What we do in the dark will come to the light."

Submitted on May 14, 2018, By:

_____

Kelly Patrick Riggs
Register No.:
Address

UNITED STATES COURT OF APPEALS
FOR THE ELEVENTH CIRCUIT
APPEAL NO.: 18-12111-F

KELLY PATRICK RIGGS

VS.

UNITED STATES OF AMERICA

On appeal from the US District Court
for the Northern District of Alabama

Civil No.: 2:15-CV-8043-KOB
Criminal No.: 2:12-CR-297-KOB-JEO

Judge Karen Owen Bowdre

MOTION FOR ISSUANCE OF A CERTIFICATE OF APPEALABILITY

KELLY PATRICK RIGGS
REGISTER NO.:
ADDRESS

IN THE

UNITED STATES COURT OF APPEALS

FOR THE ELEVENTH CIRCUIT

KELLY PATRICK RIGGS,	:	Appeal No.: 18-12111-F
Appellant,	:	(Appealed from the
V.	:	UNITED STATES DISTRICT COURT
	:	NORTHERN DISTRICT OF ALABAMA
UNITED STATES OF AMERICA,	:	Crim. No.: 2:12-cr-297-KOB-JEO-l)
Appellee,	:	Civil No.: 2:15-cv-8043-KOB

CERTIFICATE OF INTERESTED PERSONS

AND CORPORATE DISCLOSURE STATEMENT

Pursuant to the Eleventh Circuit Rule 26.1, the Appellant, KELLY PATRICK RIGGS, certifies that the following persons may have an interest in the outcome of this case:

1) Manu K. Balachandran, A.U.S.A.

2) Brett Bloomston, Former Appellate Counsel

3) Karen Owen Bowdre, Chief District Judge

4) Jeffrey D. Braemer, Former Defense Counsel

5) Kevin L. Butler, Former Defense Counsel

6) Allison Case, Former Defense Counsel

7) Staci Cornelius, Former A.U.S.A.

8) Daniel Fortune, A.U.S.A.

9) John D. Lloyd, Conspirator with Defense Counsel

10) Davis S. Luker, Former Defense Counsel

11) John E. Ott, Magistrate Judge

12) Robert Posey, Acting US Attorney

13) Kelly Patrick Riggs, Appellant

14) Jennifer Murnaham Smith, A.U.S.A.

15) Michael B. Billingsley, A.U.S.A.

16) Glennon F. Threatt, Jr., Former Defense Counsel

17) Jay E. Town, US Attorney

KELLY PATRICK RIGGS

UNITED STATES COURT OF APPEALS
FOR THE ELEVENTH CIRCUIT
APPEAL NO.: 18-12111-F

KELLY PATRICK RIGGS

VS.

UNITED STATES OF AMERICA

On appeal from the US District Court
for the Northern District of Alabama

Civil No.: 2:15-CV-8043-KOB
Criminal No.: 2:12-CR-297-KOB-JEO

Judge Karen Owen Bowdre

MOTION FOR ISSUANCE OF A CERTIFICATE OF APPEALABILITY

Mr. Riggs moves this Court to issue a certificate of appealability (C.O.A. hereafter). He seeks the issuance of a C.O.A. pursuant to 28 USC § 2253(c) (2) authorizing him (Mr. Riggs) to appeal the denial of his 28 USC § 2255 Motion to Vacate, set aside or correct sentence, see *Buck v. Davis*, 137 S.Ct. 759 (2017); *Slack v. McDaniel*, 529 US 473 (2000); *Miller-El v. Cockrell*, 537 US 322; *Prozer v. US*, 696 Fed. Appx. 977(11th Cir 2017); *Termitus v. Secretary, Florida Dept. of Corr.*, 667 Fed. Appx. 303 (11th Cir. 2016); and *Mitchell v. US*, 612 Fed. Appx. 542 (11th Cir. 2015).

I.

STATEMENT OF JURISDICTION

Jurisdiction to issue a C.O.A. is given to this Court of Appeals pursuant to 28 USC §§§ 1291; 2253(c) (2); and 2255.

II.

STATEMENT OF THE CASE

Following Mr. Riggs's criminal case he filed an instant motion pursuant to 28 USC § 2255, in which he raised several contested factual issues that go unresolved, see *Clisby v. Jones*, 960 F.2d 925 (11th Cir 1992) (*en banc*).

1) On or about November 16, 2015, the Clerk of the District Court received Mr. Riggs's 28 USC § 2255 Motion.

2) On or about December 11, 2015, the United States Attorney's Office filed its response.

3) On or about December 22, 2015, Mr. Riggs concluded the substantive pleading by filing his reply. After which Mr. Riggs filed a number of poorly drafted Motions that served to hinder the district Court.

4) On or about March 17, 2016 the district Court issued its "ORDER REGARDING SUMMARY DISPOSITION."

5) On or about March 30, 2016, Mr. Riggs filed his opposition to the Courts intentions.

6) On or about June 13, 2017, Mr. Riggs filed his "Motion for Leave to Amend."

7) On or about January 2, 2018, Mr. Riggs filed his "PETITION FOR A WRIT OF MANDAMUS," with the Eleventh Circuit Court of Appeals and serving a copy on Judge Karen Owen Bowdre.

8) On or about January 12, 2018, the district Court issued its order granting Mr. Riggs's Motion for Leave to Amend. The order providing that, "Mr. Riggs may file his amended § 2255 Motion on or by February 17, 2018."

9) On or about February 14, 2018, the District Court Clerk received for filing Mr. Riggs's amended § 2255 Motion, USPS Tracking Number, 9114-9012-3080-1329- 5910-88.

10) On or about March 2, 2018, the Court issued an "ORDER TO SHOW CAUSE."

11) On or about March 9, 2018, Mr. Riggs filed a Motion to Appoint Counsel.

12) On or about March 20, 2018, the government filed its response but failed to provide Mr. Riggs with service.

13) On or about April 2, 2018, Mr. Riggs filed a Motion seeking an order requiring the government to provide service.

14) On or about April 23, 2018, Mr. Riggs filed his "Reply To 'United States'" belated response.

15) On or about April 24, 2018, the district Court issued its "ORDER REGARDING SUMMARY DISPOSITION." In the Courts order it provides, "Mr. Riggs until May 15, 2018, twenty days after the date

of this order, to supply any additional evidentiary materials or legal arguments he may wish to offer regarding whether the motion is subject to summary disposition."

16) On or about May 2, 2018, the Court issued its "FINAL ORDER" in which the Court "Denies Mr. Riggs's § 2255 Motion," Identifying a 'Rush to Judgment.'

17) On or about May 3, 2018, Mr. Riggs filed his "objection and opposition to the Courts order Regarding summary disposition" in good faith. Additionally, Mr. Riggs filed a motion for judicial notice on that same day.

18) On or about May 14, 2018, after Mr. Riggs received the Courts order to deny and before the date in which the Court set for Mr. Riggs's filing additional materials, Mr. Riggs filed his Notice of Appeal.

19) On or about May 17, 2018, the Court "Denied as Moot" Mr. Riggs additional evidentiary materials.

III.

STATEMENT OF THE FACTS

Due in large part to Mr. Riggs ignorance of complex *habeas corpus* law and his legal disability; he files his motion, for issuance of Certificate of Appealability, with an abundance of caution. He files this motion for C.O.A. believing that the Court, more likely, should vacate the district Courts denial and remand for consideration of all Constitutional claims raised.

The Eleventh Circuit has long held that a district Court must resolve all claims for relief raised in a § 2255 Motion. Regardless of whether habeas relief is granted or denied, see *Clisby*, 960 F.2d at 936. A claim for relief is "any allegation of a Constitutional violation." *Clisby*, 960 F.2d 936. The Court of Appeals cannot consider claims not resolved by the district Court in the first instance, see *id.*at 935. Instead, when a district Court fails to address all claims in a Motion to Vacate, the Eleventh Circuit "Will vacate the district Courts judgment without prejudice and remand the case for consideration of all remaining claims," *id.* at 938. Ineffective assistance of counsel is a violation of a defendant's Sixth Amendment rights and, as a result, is a claim of a constitutional violation. *Strickland v. Washington*, 466 US 668, 685-86, 104 S.Ct. 2052, 2063-64, 80 L.Ed. 2d 674 (1984), see *Prozer v. United States*, 696 Fed. Appx. 977 (11th Cir. 2017).

In Mr. Riggs's Amended § 2255 Motion he raised four grounds for relief (Appended hereto). In the district Courts "Memorandum opinion," however, it only addressed three of the four grounds. Page 1 of 18 DE-76- 1. (Appended hereto). In addition, Mr. Riggs raised a detailed claim of ineffective assistance of counsel against Brett M. Bloomston, appointed counsel, see § 2255 Ground One, at ¶32; and Ground Three, at ¶10. The district Court in its memorandum opinion makes no mention of the claim against Mr. Brett Bloomston.

IV.

UNADDRESSED CLAIMS

1) Mr. Riggs was deprived of his sixth Amendment right to counsel at a critical stage of the criminal proceedings. Ground Three.

2) Brett Bloomston was ineffective for failing to refine or clarify Mr. Riggs Motion to Withdraw his plea agreement.

3) Brett Bloomston abandoned Mr. Riggs at appeal, leaving an alibi defense unexplored.

4) Glennon Threatt and Sabra Barnett conspired together to intimidate and/or attempt to murder Mr. Riggs by discussing details concerning Mr. Riggs with Mexican National Lois Rodriguez, see attached letter to the Alabama Bar Association.

5) Denial of Mr. Riggs's right to an evidentiary hearing, pursuant to 28 USC § 2255 (b), leaves open the contested factual issue of whether an edited version of a police interview serves as proof of Glennon Threatt's ineffectiveness.

CONCLUSION

Wherefore, Mr. Riggs moves this Court to vacate the district Courts denial of his § 2255 Motion in compliance withstanding Eleventh Circuit precedent. In the alternative this Court could grant Mr. Riggs request for C.O.A. and remand for further proceedings.

Submitted on June 6, 2018, By:

_____

Kelly Patrick Riggs, Pro se
Register No.:
Address

KELLY PATRICK RIGGS

<u>CERTIFICATE OF SERVICE</u>

I have served a copy of this petition on the US Attorney's Office, mailing it to:

1801 4th Avenue N.
Birmingham, AL 35203

Submitted on June 6, 2018, By:

_____

Kelly Patrick Riggs, Pro se
Register No.:
Address

CHAPTER 27

MARTINEZ EXCEPTION

The Martinez exception is a fairly new non-constitutional exception that can provide cause for procedural default of an ineffective assistance of *Trial* counsel claim. Note that I highlighted the word, *Trial*. That's because the exception is reserved for the trial process as opposed to the appellate process. Remembering, that Due Process means a right to a fair trial; it stands to reason that the exception would be limited to the trial process.

> *Author's Note: I personally believe that the Martinez exception is the Supreme Court's way of bringing about criminal justice reform in the wake of Congress's repeated failure to do so. This exception is also a new trend in criminal justice. It targets the failure of the process to provide any meaningful opportunity for federal prisoners to appeal from convictions that are facilitated by the ineffectiveness of trial counsel.*

In Today's practice, lawyers have become so comfortable that they don't even read the convicting statutes they are defending people from. Most often the prosecutors and CJA lawyers trade one defendant for another over a phone call. They both know that the defendant won't win at trial without meaningful counsel. They also know that the U.S. District Courts encourage defense lawyers to be ineffective to maintain a high conviction average. Also be aware that in this atmosphere §2255 motions are not granted at the district court unless ordered by the Court of Appeals to do so. First, no judge wants to admit to their own corruption in the criminal justice scheme. Nor do they want to admit to the scheme being financially motivated.

This trend in practice is quickly evolving in the federal context; therefore, I suggest that everyone become acquainted with the *Martinez* exception. Notice that I used the Martinez exception to overcome the procedural default in the Rodella case, see my "Response Showing Cause Why …" Rodella's §2255 motion should not be dismissed. Indeed, his §2255 was almost two years late, but the Martinez exception provided Rodella with cause for his procedural default.

Please take some time to understand the three Supreme Court cases that follow:

MARTINEZ V. RYAN
566 U.S. 1: 132 S. CT. 1309 (2012)

DECISION

State prisoner's failure to raise ineffective-assistance-of-trial-counsel claims in only proceeding-initial-review collateral proceeding-in which state allowed such claims held not to bar federal *habeas corpus* court from hearing claims; if prisoner had no, or ineffective, counsel in proceeding.

SUMMARY

Procedural Posture: A district court denied petitioner inmate's habeas claim of ineffective assistance of trial counsel, ruling that Ariz. Rule Crim. P. 32.2(a)(3) was an adequate and independent state-law ground to bar federal review and no case was shown to excuse the procedural default since post-conviction counsel's errors did not qualify as cause for a default. The U.S. Court of Appeals for the Ninth Circuit affirmed. *Certiorari* was granted.

Overview: Where, under state law, claims of ineffective assistance (IA) of trial counsel had to be raised in an initial-review collateral proceeding (IRCP), a procedural default would not bar a federal habeas court from hearing a substantial claim of IA at trial if, in the IRCP, there was no counsel or counsel in that proceeding was ineffective. The inmate's attorney in the IRCP filed a notice akin to an *Anders* brief, in effect conceding a lack of any meritorious claim, including a claim of IA at trial, which the inmate argued was IA. The Ninth Circuit did not decide if it was. Rather, it held that because he did not have a right to an attorney in the IRCP, the attorney's errors in the IRCP could not establish cause for the failure to comply with the State's rules. Thus, the Ninth Circuit did not determine if the attorney in the IRCP was ineffective or whether the claim of IA of trail counsel was substantial. Nor was prejudice addressed. Those issues remained open for a decision on remand. While 28 U.S.C.S. §2254(i) precluded relying on IA of a post-conviction attorney as a "ground for relief" it did not stop its use to establish "cause" to excuse procedural default.

Outcome: The judgment upholding the denial of habeas relief was reversed, and the case was remanded for further proceedings.

7-2 decision; 1 opinion, 1 dissent

SYLLABUS

Arizona prisoners may raise claims of ineffective assistance of trial counsel only in state collateral proceedings, not on direct review. In petitioner Martinez's first state collateral proceeding, his counsel did not raise such a claim. On federal habeas review with new counsel, Martinez argued that he received ineffective assistance both at trial and in his first state collateral proceeding. He also claimed that he had a constitutional right to an effective attorney in the collateral proceeding because it was the first place to raise his claim of ineffective assistance at trial. The district Court denied the petition, finding that Arizona's preclusion rule was an adequate and independent state-law ground barring federal review, and that under *Coleman v. Thompson*, 501 U.S. 722, 111 S. Ct 2546, 115 L. Ed. 2d 640, the attorney's errors in the post-conviction proceeding did not qualify as cause to excuse the procedural default. The Court of Appeals for the Ninth Circuit affirmed.

Held:

1) Where, under state law, ineffective-assistance-of-trial-counsel claims must be raised in an initial-review collateral proceeding, a procedural default will not bar a federal habeas court from hearing those claims if, in the initial-review collateral proceeding, there was no counselor counsel in that proceeding was ineffective. Pp. ___-___ , 182 1. Ed. 2d, at 282-288.

(a) Given that the precise question here is whether ineffective assistance in an initial-review collateral proceeding on an ineffective-assistance-at-trial claim may provide cause for a procedural default in a federal habeas proceeding, this is not the case to resolve the question left open in Coleman: whether a prisoner has a constitutional right to effective counsel in initial-review collateral proceedings. However, to protect prisoners with potentially legitimate ineffective-assistance claims, it is necessary to recognize a narrow exception to Coleman's unqualified statement that an attorney's ignorance or inadvertence in a post-conviction proceeding does not qualify as cause to excuse a procedural default, namely, that inadequate assistance of counsel at initial-review collateral proceedings may establish cause. Pp. ___-___ , 182 L. Ed. 2d, at 282.

(b) A federal court can hear Martinez's ineffective assistance claim only if he can establish cause to excuse the procedural default and prejudice from a violation of federal law. Coleman held that a post-conviction attorney's negligence "does not qualify as cause," because "the attorney is the prisoner's agent," and "the principal bears the risk of" his agent's negligent conduct, *Maples v. Thomas*, ante, at 132 S. Ct. 912, 181 L. Ed. 2d 807. However, in Coleman, counsel's alleged error was on appeal from an initial-review collateral proceeding. Thus, his claims were addressed by the state habeas trial court. This marks a key difference between initial-review collateral proceedings and other collateral proceedings. Here, where the initial-review collateral proceeding is the first designated proceeding for a prisoner to raise the ineffective-assistance claim, the collateral proceeding is the equivalent of a prisoner's direct appeal as to that claim because the state habeas court decides the claim's merits, no other court has address the claim, and defendants "are generally ill equipped to represent themselves" where they have no brief from counsel and no court opinion addressing their claim. *Halbert v. Michigan*, 545 U.S. 605, 617, 125 S. Ct. 2582, 162 L. Ed. 2d 552. An attorney's errors during an appeal on direct review may provide cause to excuse a procedural default; for if the attorney appointed by the State is ineffective, the prisoner has been denied fair process and the opportunity to comply with the State's procedures and obtain adjudication on the merits of his claim. Without adequate representation in an initial-review collateral proceeding, a prisoner will have similar difficulties vindicating a substantial ineffective-assistance- at trial claim. The same would be true if the State did not appoint an attorney for the initial-review collateral proceeding. A prisoner's inability to present an ineffective-assistance claim is of particular concern because the right to effective trial counsel is a bedrock principle in this Nation's justice system.

Allowing a federal habeas court to hear a claim of ineffective assistance at trial when an attorney's errors (or attorney's absence) cause a procedural default in an initial-review collateral proceeding acknowledges, as an equitable matter, that a collateral proceeding, if undertaken with no counselor ineffective counsel, may not have been sufficient to ensure that proper consideration was given to a substantial claim. It thus follows that, when a State requires a prisoner to raise a claim of ineffective assistance at trial in a collateral proceeding, a prisoner may establish cause for a procedural default of such claim in two circumstances: where the state courts did not appoint counsel in the initial-review collateral proceeding for an ineffective-assistance-at-trial claim; and where appointed counsel in the initial-review collateral proceeding, where that claim would have been raised, was ineffective under *Strickland v. Washington*, 466 U.S. 668, 104 S. Ct. 2052, 80 L. Ed. 2d 674. To overcome the default, a prisoner must also demonstrate that the underlying ineffective- assistance-at-trial claim is substantial. Most jurisdictions have procedures to ensure counsel is appointed for substantial ineffective-assistance claims. It is likely that such attorneys are qualified to perform, and do perform, according to prevailing professional norms. And where that is so, States may enforce a procedural default in federal habeas proceedings. Pp. ___, ___ 182 L. Ed. 2d, at 282-286.

(c) This limited qualification of *Coleman* does not implicate state decisis concerns. *Coleman*'s holding remains true except as to initial-review collateral proceedings for claims of ineffective assistance at trial. The holding in this case should not put a significant strain on state resources. A State facing the question of cause for an apparent default may answer that the ineffective-assistance-of-trial-counsel claim is insubstantial. The limited circumstances recognized here also reflect the importance of the right to effective assistance at trial. Other claims may not imply the same fundamentals of the adversary system. The Antiterrorism and Effective Death Penalty Act of 1996 does not speak to the question presented here, and thus does not bar Martinez from asserting attorney error as cause for a procedural default. P. , 182 L. Ed. 2d, at 286-288.

2) Whether Martinez's attorney in his first collateral proceeding was ineffective and whether his ineffective-assistance-at-trial claim is substantial, as well as the question of prejudice, are questions that remain open for a decision on remand. P.___,182 L. Ed. 2d, at 288.

623 F.3d 731, reversed and remanded

TREVINO V. THALER
569 U.S. 413: 133 S. CT. 1911 (2013)
DECISION

Procedural default held not to bar federal *habeas corpus* court from hearing substantial claim of ineffective assistance of counsel at trial, where state procedural framework typically made meaningful opportunity to raise ineffective assistance claim on direct appeal highly unlikely.

CASE SUMMARY

Procedural Posture: A Texas court found petitioner death row inmate's ineffective assistance of trial counsel (IATC) claim was procedurally defaulted for failure to raise it in initial state post-conviction proceedings. On the inmate's federal habeas petition, the district court held the procedural default was an independent and adequate state ground barring federal review. The U.S. Court of Appeals for the Fifth Circuit affirmed. *Certiorari* was granted. Because in Texas it was highly unlikely an inmate had a meaningful opportunity to raise an ineffective assistance of trial counsel claim on direct appeal, procedural default did not bar a federal habeas court from hearing it if, in initial-review collateral proceedings, there was no counsel or counsel in that proceeding was ineffective.

Overview: Texas did not expressly require IATC claims be raised on initial collateral review. Texas law on its face appear to permit (but not require) that the claim be raised on direct appeal. But Texas procedure made it virtually impossible for appellate counsel to adequately present an IATC claim on direct review, as the trial record often failed to contain the necessary substantiating information. A motion-for-new-trial was often inadequate because of time constraints and the lack of the trial record being transcribed at that point. In Texas, a writ of *habeas corpus* issued in state collateral proceedings ordinarily was essential to gathering the facts necessary to evaluate IATC claims. As a systematic matter, Texas did not afford meaningful review of an IATC claim. Where a state procedural framework, by reason of its design and operation, made it highly unlikely in a typical case that a defendant would have a meaningful opportunity to raise and IATC claim on direct appeal, a procedural default would not bar a federal habeas court from hearing a substantial IATC claim if, in the initial-review collateral proceeding, there was no counsel or counsel in that proceeding was ineffective.

Outcome: The Fifth Circuit's judgment finding that procedural default of the ineffective assistance of trial counsel claim was an independent adequate state ground barring the federal review was vacated and the case was remanded for further proceedings,

5-4 Decision; 2 Dissents

SYLLABUS

In *Martinez v. Ryan*, 566 U.S. 1, 17, 566 U.S. 1 132 S. Ct. 1309, 182 L. Ed. 2d 272, 278, 288 this Court held that "a procedural default will not bar a federal habeas court from hearing a substantial claim of ineffective assistance at trial if, in the [State's] initial-review collateral proceeding, there was no counselor counsel in that proceeding was ineffective." Martinez regarded a prisoner from Arizona, where state procedural law required the prisoner to raise the claim during his first state collateral review proceeding, *ibid.* This case regards a prisoner from Texas, where state procedural law does not require a defendant to raise his ineffective-assistance-of-trial-counsel claim on collateral review. Rather, Texas law appears to permit a prisoner to raise such a claim on direct review, but the structure and design of the Texas system make it virtually impossible for a prisoner to do so. The question presented in this case is whether, despite this difference, the rule set out in Martinez applies in Texas.

Petitioner Trevino was convicted of capital murder in Texas state court and sentenced to death after the jury found insufficient mitigating circumstances to warrant a life sentence. Neither new counsel appointed for his direct appeal nor new counsel appointed for state collateral review raised the claim that Trevino's trial counsel provided ineffective assistance during the penalty phase by failing to adequately investigate and present mitigating circumstances. When that claim was finally raised in state court, the state court found the claim procedurally defaulted because of Trevin's failure to raise it in his initial state prost-conviction proceedings, and the federal court then concluded that this failure was an independent and adequate state ground barring the federal courts from considering the claim. The Fifth Circuit affirmed. Its decision predated *Martinez*, but that court has since concluded that *Martinez* does not apply in Texas because *Martinez*'s good-cause exception applied only where state law says that a defendant must initially raise his ineffective-assistance-of-trial-counsel claim in initial state collateral review proceedings, while Texas law appears to permit a defendant to raise that claim on direct appeal.

Held: Where, as here, a State's procedural framework, by reason of its design and operation, makes it highly unlikely in a typical case that a defendant will have a meaningful opportunity to raise an ineffective-assist of-trial-counsel claim on direct appeal, the exception recognized in Martinez applies. Pp. 421-429, 185 L. Ed. 2d, at 1051-1057.

(a) A finding that a defendant's state law "procedural default" rests on "an independent and adequate state ground" ordinarily prevents a federal habeas court from considering the defendant's federal constitutional claim, *Coleman v. Thompson*, 501 U.S. 722, 729-730, 111 S. Ct. 2546, 115 L. Ed. 2d 640. However, a "prisoner may obtain federal review of a defaulted claim by showing cause for the default and prejudice from a violation of federal law." Martinez, supra, at 10, 132 S.Ct. 1309, 182 L. Ed. 2d 272, 283. In Martinez, the Court recognized a "narrow exception" to Coleman's statement "that an attorney's ignorance or inadvertence in a post-conviction proceeding does not qualify as cause to excuse a procedural default." 566 U.S., at 9, 132, S. Ct. 1309, 182 L. Ed. 2d 272, 278, 282. That exception allows a federal habeas court to find "cause" to excuse such default where (1) the ineffective-assistance-of-trial-counsel claim was a "substantial" claim; the "cause" consisted of there being "no counsel" or only "ineffective" counsel during the state collateral review proceeding; (3) the state collateral review proceeding was the "initial" review proceeding in respect to the "ineffective-assistance-of-trial-counsel claim"; and (4) state law requires that the claim "be raised in an initial-review collateral proceeding." *Id.*, at 14, 17, 132, S. Ct. 1309, 182 L. Ed. 2d 272, 288. Pp. 421-423, 185 L. Ed. 2d, at 1051-1053.

(b) The difference between the Texas law – which in theory grants permission to bring an ineffective-assistance-of-trial-counsel claim on direct appeal but in practice denies a meaningful opportunity to do so – and the Arizona law at issue in *Martinez* – which required the claim to be raised in an initial collateral review proceeding – does not matter in respect to the application of *Martinez*. Pp. 423-429, 185 L. Ed. 2d, at 1053-1057.

(1) This conclusion is supported by two characteristics of Texas's procedures. First, Texas procedures make it nearly impossible for an ineffective-assistance-of-trial-counsel claim to be presented on direct review. The nature of an ineffective-assistance claim means that the trial record is likely to be insufficient to support the claim. And a motion for a new trial to develop the record is usually inadequate because of Texas rules regarding time limits on the filing, and the disposal, of such motions and the availability of trial transcripts. Thus, a writ of *habeas corpus* is normally needed to gather the facts necessary for evaluating these claims in Texas. Second, were *Martinez* not to apply, the Texas procedural system would create significant unfairness because Texas courts in effect have directed defendants to raise ineffective-assistance-of-trial-counsel claims on collateral, rather than

on direct, review. Texas can point to only a few cases in which a defendant has used the motion-for-a-new-trial mechanism to expand the record on appeal. Texas suggests that there are other mechanisms by which a prisoner can expand the record on appeal, but these mechanisms seem special and limited in their application, and cannot overcome the Texas courts' own well-supported determination that collateral review normally is the preferred procedural route for raising an ineffective-assistance-of-trial-counsel claim. Respondent also argues that there is no equitable problem here, where appellate counsel's failure to bring a substantial ineffective-assistance claim on direct appeal may constitute cause to excuse the procedural default, but respondent points to no case in which such a failure by appellate counsel has been deemed constitutionally ineffective. Pp. 423-428, 185 L. Ed. 2d, at 1053-1056.

(2) The very factors that led this Court to create a narrow exception to Coleman in *Martinez* similarly argue for applying that exception here. The right involved adequate assistance of trial counsel – is similarly and critically important. In both instances practical considerations – the need for a new lawyer, the need to expand the trial court record, and the need for sufficient time to develop the claim – argue strongly for initial consideration of the claim during collateral, not on direct, review, see *Martinez*, 566 U.S., at 13, 132 S. Ct. 1309, 182 L. Ed. 2d 272-277. In both instances failure to consider a lawyer's "ineffectiveness" during an initial-review collateral proceeding as potential. "cause" for excusing a procedural default will deprive the defendant of any opportunity for review of an ineffective-assistance-of-trial-counsel claim, see *id.*, at 11, 132, S. Ct. 1309, 182 L. Ed. 2d 272. Thus, for present purposes, a distinction between (1) a State that denies permission to raise the claim on direct appeal and (2) a State that grants permission but denies a fair, meaningful opportunity to develop the claim is a distinction without a difference. Pp. 428-429, 185 L. Ed. 2d, at 1056-1057. 449 Fed. Appx. 415, vacated and remanded.

BUCK V. DAVIS
580 U.S.; 137 S. CT. 759 (2017)
DECISION

Where Federal Court of Appeals denied certificate of appealability (COA) for review of claim of ineffective assistance of trial counsel, (1) Court of Appeals exceeded scope of COA analysis; (2) accused demonstrated ineffective assistance; and (3) Federal District Court abused discretion by denying motion for relief under Rule 60(b)(6) of Federal Rules of Civil Procedure.

Case Summary: It was error to deny a prisoner a COA to pursue his Sixth Amendment claims on appeal where he demonstrated ineffective assistance when his attorney called an expert who testified about a connection between his race and the likelihood of violence, and that error entitled him to relief under Fed. R. Civ. P. 60(b)(6).

Overview; Holdings: [1] – Because a reviewing court inverted the statutory order of operations by deciding the merits of an appeal and then denying the COA based on adjudication of the actual merits, it placed too heavy a burden on the prisoner at the COA stage; [2] – For Sixth Amendment purposes, the prisoner demonstrated prejudice during the sentencing phase where his attorney called an expert who testified about a connection between his race and the likelihood of violence, and it was reasonably probable that the death sentence would not have been imposed otherwise; [3] – Denying a Fed. R. Civ. P. 60(b)(6) motion was error where it was clear that the prisoner may have been sentenced to death due to his race, the State had admitted that sentencing based on race considerations was error in other cases, and it was inappropriate to consider race no matter how it was injected into the proceeding.

Outcome: Judgment reversed; case remanded.

6-2 Decision; 1 Dissent

SYLLABUS

Petitioner Duane Buck was convicted of capital murder in a Texas court. Under state law, the jury was permitted to impose a death sentence only if it found unanimously and beyond a reasonable doubt that Buck was likely to commit acts of violence in the future. Buck's attorney called a psychologist, Dr. Walter Quijano, to offer his opinion on that issue. Dr. Quijano had been appointed to evaluate Buck by the presiding judge and had prepared a report setting out his conclusion. To determine the likelihood that Buck would act violently in the future. Dr. Quijano concluded that Buck was unlikely to be a future danger. His report also stated that Buck was statistically more likely to act violently because he is black. The report read, in relevant part: "Race. Black: Increased probability." App. 19a. Despite knowing the contents of the report, Buck's counsel called Dr. Quijano to the stand, where he testified that race is a factor "known to predict future dangerousness." *id.*, at 146. Dr. Quijano's report was admitted into evidence at the close of his testimony. The prosecution questioned Dr. Quijano about his conclusions on race and violence during cross-examination, and it relied on his testimony in summation. During deliberations, the jury requested and received the expert reports admitted into evidence, including Dr. Quijano's. The jury returned a sentence of death.

Buck contends that his attorney's introduction of this evidence violated his Sixth Amendment right to the effective assistance of counsel. Buck failed to raise this claim in his first state post-conviction proceeding. While that proceeding was pending, this Court received a petition for *certiorari* in *Saldano v. Texas*, 530 U.S. 1212, 120 S. Ct. 2214, 147 L. Ed. 2d 246, a case in which Dr. Quijano had testified that the petitioner's Hispanic heritage weighed in favor of a finding of future dangerousness. Texas confessed error on that ground, and this Court vacated the judgment below. Soon afterward, the Texas Attorney General issued a public statement identifying six similar cases in which Dr. Quijano had testified. Buck's was one of them. In the other five cases, the Attorney General confessed error and consented to resentencing. But when Buck filed a second state habeas petition alleging that his attorney had been ineffective in introducing Dr. Quijano's testimony, the State did not confess error, and the court dismissed the petition as an abuse of the writ on the ground that Buck had failed to raise the claim in his first petition.

Buck then sought federal habeas relief under 28 U.S.C. §2254. The State again declined to confess error, and Buck's ineffective assistance claim was held procedurally defaulted and unreviewable under *Coleman v. Thompson*, 501, U.S. 722, 111 S. Ct. 2546, 115 L. Ed. 2d 640. This Court's later decisions in *Martinez v. Ryan*, 566 U.S. 1, 132 S. Ct. 1309, 182 L. Ed. 2d 272, and *Trevino v. Thaler*, 569 U.S.___ , 133 S. Ct. 1911, 185 L. Ed. 2d 1044, modified the rule of *Coleman*. Had they been decided before Buck filed his federal habeas petition, Buck's claim could have been heard on the merits provided he had demonstrated that (1) state post-conviction counsel had been constitutionally ineffective in failing to raise the claim, and (2) the claim had some merit. Following the decision in *Trevino*, Buck sought to reopen his §2254 case under Federal Rule of Civil Procedure 60(b)(6). To demonstrate the "extraordinary circumstances" required for relief, *Gonzalez v. Crosby*, 545 U.S. 524, 535, 125 S. Ct. 2641, 162 L. Ed. 2d 480, Buck cited the change in law affected by *Martinez* and *Trevino*, as well as ten other factors including the introduction of expert testimony linking Buck's race to violence and the State's confession of error in similar cases. The District Court denied relief. Reasoning that "the introduction of any mention of race" during Buck's sentencing was "deminimis," the court concluded, first, that Buck had failed to demonstrate extraordinary circumstances and second, that even if the circumstances were extraordinary, Buck had failed to demonstrate ineffective assistance under *Strickland v. Washington*, 466 U.S. 668, 104 S. Ct. 2052, 80 L. Ed. 2d 674. Buck sought a certificate of appealability (COA) from the Fifth circuit to appeal the denial of his Rule 60(b)(6) motion. The Fifth Circuit denied his application, concluding that he had not shown extraordinary circumstances justifying relief from the District Court's judgment.

Held:

(1) The Fifth Circuit exceeded the limited scope of the COA analysis. The COA statute sets forth a two-step process: an initial determination whether a claim is reasonably debatable, and, if so, an appeal in the normal course. 28 U.S.C. §2253. At the first stage, the only question is whether the applicant has shown that "jurists of reason could disagree with the district court's resolution of his constitutional claims or … could conclude the issues presented are adequate to deserve encouragement to proceed further." *Miller-El v. Cockrell*, 537 U.S. 322, 327, 123 S. Ct. 1029, 154 L. Ed. 2d 931. Here, the Fifth Circuit phrased its determination in proper terms. But it reached its conclusion only after essentially deciding the case on the merits, repeatedly faulting Buck for having failed to demonstrate extraordinary circumstances. The question for the Court of Appeals was not whether Buck had shown that his case is extraordinary, it was whether jurists of reason could debate that issue. The State points to the Fifth Circuit's thorough consideration of the merits to defend that court's approach, but this hurts rather than helps its case. Pp.___-___ , 197 L. Ed. 2d, at 16-18.

(2) Buck has demonstrated ineffective assistance of counsel under *Strickland*, Pp. ___-___ , 197 L. Ed. 2d, at 18-20.

    (A) To satisfy *Strickland*, a defendant must first show that counsel performed deficiently. 466 U.S., at 687, 104 S. Ct. 2052, 80 L. Ed. 2d 674. Buck's trial counsel knew that Dr. Quijano's report reflected the view that Buck's race predisposed him to violent conduct and that the principal point of dispute during the penalty phase was Buck's future dangerousness. Counsel nevertheless called Dr. Quijano to the stand, specifically elicited testimony about the connection between race and violence and put Dr. Quijano's report into evidence. No competent defense attorney would introduce evidence that his client is liable to be a future danger because of his race. Pp. ___-___ , 197 L. Ed. 2d, at 18-19.

    (B) *Strickland* further requires a defendant to demonstrate prejudice – "a reasonable probability that, but for counsel's unprofessional errors, the result of the proceeding would have been different," 466 U.S., at 694, 104 S. Ct. 2052, 80 L. Ed. 2d at 674. It is reasonably probable that without Dr. Quijano's testimony on race and violence, at least one juror would have harbored a reasonable doubt on the question of Buck's future dangerousness. This issue required the jury to make a predictive judgment inevitably entailing a degree of speculation. But Buck's race was not subject to speculation, according to Dr. Quijano, that immutable characteristic carried with it an increased probability of future violence. Dr. Quijano's testimony appealed to a powerful racial stereotype and might well have been valued by jurors as the opinion of a medical expert bearing the court's imprimatur. For these reasons, the district court's conclusion that any mention of race during the penalty phase was *de minimis* is rejected. So is the State's argument that Buck was not prejudiced by Dr. Quijano's testimony because it was introduced by his own counsel, rather than the prosecution. Jurors understand that prosecutors seek convictions and may reasonably be expected to evaluate the government's evidence in light of its motivation. When damaging evidence is introduced by a defendant's own lawyer, it is in the nature of an admission against interest, more likely to be taken at face value. Pp. ___-___ , 197 L. Ed. 2d, at 19-20.

(3) The District Court's denial of Buck's Rule 60(b)(6) motion was an abuse of discretion, Pp. ___-___ , 197 L. Ed. 2d, at 21-24.

(A) Relief under Rule 60(b)(6) is available only in "extraordinary circumstances." Gonzalez, 545 U.S., at 535, 125 S. Ct. 2641, 162 L. Ed. 2d 480. Determining whether such circumstances are present may include consideration of a wide range of factors, including "the risk of injustice to the parties" and "the risk of undermining the public's confidence in the judicial process." *Lijeberg v. Health Services Acquisition Corp.*, 486 U.S. 847, 863-864, 108 S. Ct. 2194, 100 L. Ed. 2d 855. The District Court's denial of Buck's motion rested largely on its determination that race played only a *de minimis* role in his sentencing. But there is a reasonable probability that Buck was sentenced to death in part because of his race. This is a disturbing departure from the basic premise that our criminal law punishes people for what they do, no who they are. That it concerned race amplifies the problem. Relying on race to impose a criminal sanction "poisons public confidence" in the judicial process, Davis v. Ayala, 576 U.S. ___ , ___ 135 S. Ct. 2187, 192 L. Ed. 2d 323, a concern that supports Rule 60(b)(6) relief. The extraordinary nature of this case is confirmed by the remarkable steps the State itself took in response to Dr. Quijano's testimony in other cases. Although the State attempts to justify its decision to treat Buck differently from the other five defendants identified in the Attorney General's public statement, its explanations for distinguishing Buck's case from *Saldano* have nothing to do with the Attorney General's stated reasons for confessing error in that case, Pp. ___ - ___ , 197 L. Ed. 2d, at 21-23.

(B) Unless *Martinez* and *Trevino*, rather than *Coleman*, would govern Buck's case were it reopened, his claim would remain unreviewable, and Rule 60(b)(6) relief would be inappropriate. The State argues that *Martinez* and *Trevino* would not govern Buck's case because they announced a new rule under *Teague v. Lane*, 489 U.S. 288, 109 S. Ct. 1060, 103 L. Ed. 2d 334, that does not apply retroactively to cases (like Buck's) on collateral review. This argument, however, has been waived: the State failed to advance it in District Court, before the Fifth Circuit, or in its brief in opposition to Buck's petition for *certiorari*. Pp.___-___ , 197 L. Ed. 2d, at 23-24.

623 Fed. Appx. 668, reversed and remanded.

MOTION UNDER 28 U.S.C. § TO VACATE, SET ASIDE, OR CORRECT SENTENCE BY A PERSON IN FEDERAL CUSTODY

United States District Court	District	
Name *(under which you were convicted)*:		Docket or Case No.:
Place of Confinement:		Prisoner No.:
UNITED STATES OF AMERICA V.	Movant *(include name under which convicted)*	

MOTION

1. (a) Name and location of court which entered the judgment of conviction you are challenging:

   (b) Criminal docket or case number (if you know): _____

2. (a) Date of the judgment of conviction (if you know): _____

   (b) Date of sentencing: _____

3. Length of sentence: _____

4. Nature of crime (all counts):

5. (a) What was your plea? (Check one)

   (1) Not guilty ☐   (2) Guilty ☐   (3) Nolo contendere (no contest) ☐

6. (b) If you entered a guilty plea to one count or indictment, and a not guilty plea to another count or indictment, what did you plead guilty to and what did you plead not guilty to?

6. If you went to trial, what kind of trial did you have? (Check one)   Jury ☐   Judge only ☐

7. Did you testify at a pretrial hearing, trial, or post-trial hearing?   Yes ☐   No ☐

8. Did you appeal from the judgment of conviction?   Yes ☐   No ☐

9. If you did appeal, answer the following:
   (a) Name of court: _____
   (b) Docket or case number (if you know): _____
   (c) Result: _____
   (d) Date of result (if you know): _____
   (e) Citation to the case (if you know): _____
   (f) Grounds raised:

   (g) Did you file a petition for certiorari in the United States Supreme Court?   Yes ☐   No ☐
       If "Yes," answer the following:
       (1) Docket or case number (if you know): _____
       (2) Result: _____

       (3) Date of result (if you know): _____
       (4) Citation to the case (if you know): _____
       (5) Grounds raised:

10. Other than the direct appeals listed above, have you previously filed any other motions, petitions, or applications, concerning this judgment of conviction in any court?
    Yes ☐   No ☐

11. If your answer to Question 10 was "Yes," give the following information:
    (a) (1) Name of court: _____
        (2) Docket or case number (if you know): _____
        (3) Date of filing (if you know): _____
        (4) Nature of the proceeding: _____
        (5) Grounds raised:

(6) Did you receive a hearing where evidence was given on your motion, petition, or application?

Yes ☐   No ☐

(7) Result:

(8) Date of result (if you know):

(b) If you filed any second motion, petition, or application, give the same information:

(1) Name of court:

(2) Docket of case number (if you know):

(3) Date of filing (if you know):

(4) Nature of the proceeding:

(5) Grounds raised:

(6) Did you receive a hearing where evidence was given on your motion, petition, or application?

Yes ☐   No ☐

(7) Result:

(8) Date of result (if you know):

(c) Did you appeal to a federal appellate court having jurisdiction over the action taken on your motion, petition, or application?

(1) First petition: Yes ☐   No ☐

(2) Second petition: Yes ☐   No ☐

(d) If you did not appeal from the action on any motion, petition, or application, explain briefly why you did not:

12. For this motion, state every ground on which you claim that you are being held in violation of the Constitution, laws, or treaties of the United States. Attach additional pages if you have more than four grounds. State the facts supporting each ground. Any legal arguments must be submitted in a separate memorandum.

GROUND ONE:

(a) Supporting facts (Do not argue or cite law. Just state the specific facts that support your claim.):

(b) **Direct Appeal of Ground One:**

    (1) If you appealed from the judgment of conviction, did you raise this issue?

        Yes ☐   No ☐

    (2) If you did not raise this issue in your direct appeal, explain why:

(c) **Post-Conviction Proceedings:**

    (1) Did you raise this issue in any post-conviction motion, petition, or application?

        Yes ☐   No ☐

    (2) If you answer to Question (c)(1) is "Yes," state:

Type of motion or petition:

Name and location of the court where the motion or petition was filed:

Docket or case number (if you know):

Date of the court's decision:

Result (attach a copy of the court's opinion or order, if available):

    (3) Did you receive a hearing on your motion, petition, or application?

        Yes ☐   No ☐

    (4) Did you appeal from the denial of your motion, petition, or application?

        Yes ☐   No ☐

    (5) If your answer to Question (c)(4) is "Yes," did you raise the issue in the appeal?

        Yes ☐   No ☐

    (6) If your answer to Question (c)(4) is "Yes," state:

Name and location of the court where the appeal was filed:

Docket or case number (if you know):

Date of the court's decision:

Result (attach a copy of the court's opinion or order, if available):

    (7) If your answer to Question (c)(4) or Question (c)(5) is "No," explain why you did not appeal or raise this issue:

GROUND TWO:

(a) Supporting facts (Do not argue or cite law. Just state the specific facts that support your claim.):

(b) **Direct Appeal of Ground Two:**

    (1) If you appealed from the judgment of conviction, did you raise this issue?

        Yes ☐   No ☐

    (2) If you did not raise this issue in your direct appeal, explain why:

(c) **Post-Conviction Proceedings:**

    (1) Did you raise this issue in any post-conviction motion, petition, or application?

        Yes ☐   No ☐

    (2) If you answer to Question (c)(1) is "Yes," state:

Type of motion or petition:

Name and location of the court where the motion or petition was filed:

Docket or case number (if you know):

Date of the court's decision:

Result (attach a copy of the court's opinion or order, if available):

    (3) Did you receive a hearing on your motion, petition, or application?

        Yes ☐   No ☐

    (4) Did you appeal from the denial of your motion, petition, or application?

        Yes ☐   No ☐

    (5) If your answer to Question (c)(4) is "Yes," did you raise the issue in the appeal?

        Yes ☐   No ☐

    (6) If your answer to Question (c)(4) is "Yes," state:

Name and location of the court where the appeal was filed:

Docket or case number (if you know):

Date of the court's decision:

Result (attach a copy of the court's opinion or order, if available):

    (7) If your answer to Question (c)(4) or Question (c)(5) is "No," explain why you did not appeal or raise this issue:

GROUND THREE:

(a) Supporting facts (Do not argue or cite law. Just state the specific facts that support your claim.):

(b) **Direct Appeal of Ground Three:**

    (1) If you appealed from the judgment of conviction, did you raise this issue?

        Yes ☐   No ☐

    (2) If you did not raise this issue in your direct appeal, explain why:

(c) **Post-Conviction Proceedings:**

    (1) Did you raise this issue in any post-conviction motion, petition, or application?

        Yes ☐   No ☐

    (2) If you answer to Question (c)(1) is "Yes," state:

Type of motion or petition:

Name and location of the court where the motion or petition was filed:

Docket or case number (if you know):

Date of the court's decision:

Result (attach a copy of the court's opinion or order, if available):

    (3) Did you receive a hearing on your motion, petition, or application?

        Yes ☐   No ☐

    (4) Did you appeal from the denial of your motion, petition, or application?

        Yes ☐   No ☐

    (5) If your answer to Question (c)(4) is "Yes," did you raise the issue in the appeal?

        Yes ☐   No ☐

    (6) If your answer to Question (c)(4) is "Yes," state:

Name and location of the court where the appeal was filed:

Docket or case number (if you know):

Date of the court's decision:

Result (attach a copy of the court's opinion or order, if available):

    (7) If your answer to Question (c)(4) or Question (c)(5) is "No," explain why you did not appeal or raise this issue:

GROUND FOUR:

(a) Supporting facts (Do not argue or cite law. Just state the specific facts that support your claim.):

(b) **Direct Appeal of Ground Four:**

    (1) If you appealed from the judgment of conviction, did you raise this issue?

        Yes ☐   No ☐

    (2) If you did not raise this issue in your direct appeal, explain why:

(c) **Post-Conviction Proceedings:**

    (1) Did you raise this issue in any post-conviction motion, petition, or application?

        Yes ☐   No ☐

    (2) If you answer to Question (c)(1) is "Yes," state:

Type of motion or petition:

Name and location of the court where the motion or petition was filed:

Docket or case number (if you know):

Date of the court's decision:

Result (attach a copy of the court's opinion or order, if available):

    (3) Did you receive a hearing on your motion, petition, or application?

        Yes ☐   No ☐

    (4) Did you appeal from the denial of your motion, petition, or application?

        Yes ☐   No ☐

    (5) If your answer to Question (c)(4) is "Yes," did you raise the issue in the appeal?

        Yes ☐   No ☐

    (6) If your answer to Question (c)(4) is "Yes," state:

Name and location of the court where the appeal was filed:

Docket or case number (if you know):

Date of the court's decision:

Result (attach a copy of the court's opinion or order, if available):

    (7) If your answer to Question (c)(4) or Question (c)(5) is "No," explain why you did not appeal or raise this issue:

GROUND

_____

(a) Supporting facts (Do not argue or cite law. Just state the specific facts that support your claim.):

(b) **Direct Appeal of Ground**

    (1) If you appealed from the judgment of conviction, did you raise this issue?

        Yes ☐   No ☐

    (2) If you did not raise this issue in your direct appeal, explain why:

(c) **Post-Conviction Proceedings:**

    (1) Did you raise this issue in any post-conviction motion, petition, or application?

        Yes ☐   No ☐

    (2) If you answer to Question (c)(1) is "Yes," state:

Type of motion or petition:

Name and location of the court where the motion or petition was filed:

Docket or case number (if you know):

Date of the court's decision:

Result (attach a copy of the court's opinion or order, if available):

    (3) Did you receive a hearing on your motion, petition, or application?

        Yes ☐   No ☐

    (4) Did you appeal from the denial of your motion, petition, or application?

        Yes ☐   No ☐

    (5) If your answer to Question (c)(4) is "Yes," did you raise the issue in the appeal?

        Yes ☐   No ☐

    (6) If your answer to Question (c)(4) is "Yes," state:

Name and location of the court where the appeal was filed:

Docket or case number (if you know):

Date of the court's decision:

Result (attach a copy of the court's opinion or order, if available):

    (7) If your answer to Question (c)(4) or Question (c)(5) is "No," explain why you did not appeal or raise this issue:

13. Is there any ground in this motion that you have <u>not</u> previously presented in some federal court? If so, which ground or grounds have not been presented, and state your reasons for not presenting them:

14. Do you have any motion, petition, or appeal <u>now pending</u> (filed and not decided yet) in any court for the you are challenging?   Yes ☐   No ☐
    If "Yes," state the name and location of the court, the docket or case number, the type of proceeding, and the issues raised.

15. Give the name and address, if known, of each attorney who represented you in the following stages of the judgment you are challenging:
    (a) At the preliminary hearing:

    (b) At the arraignment and plea:

    (c) At the trial:

    (d) At sentencing:

    (e) On appeal:

    (f) In any post-conviction proceeding:

    (g) On appeal from any ruling against you in a post-conviction proceeding:

16. Were you sentenced on more than one court of an indictment, or on more than one indictment, in the same court and at the same time?   Yes ☐   No ☐

17. Do you have any future sentence to serve after you complete the sentence for the judgment that you are challenging?   Yes ☐   No ☐
    (a) If so, give name and location of court that imposed the other sentence you will serve in the future:

(b) Give the date the other sentence was imposed: _____

(c) Give the length of the other sentence: _____

(d) Have you filed, or do you plan to file, any motion, petition, or application that challenges the judgment or sentence to be served in the future?   Yes ☐   No ☐

18.   TIMELINESS OF MOTION: If your judgment of conviction became final over one year ago, you must explain why the one-year statute of limitations as contained in 28 U.S.C. § 2255 does not bar your motion.*

---

* The Antiterrorism and Effective Death Penalty Act of 1996 ("AEDPA") as contained in 28 U.S.C. § 2255, paragraph 6, provides in part that:

A one-year period of limitation shall apply to a motion under this section. The limitation period shall run from the latest of –

(1) the date on which the judgment of conviction became final;

(2) the date on which the impediment to making a motion created by governmental action in violation of the Constitution or laws of the United States is removed, if the movant was prevented from making such a motion by such governmental action;

(3) the date on which the right asserted was initially recognized by the Supreme Court, if that right has been newly recognized by the Supreme Court and made retroactively applicable to cases on collateral review; or

(4) the date on which the facts supporting the claim or claims presented could have been discovered through the exercise of due diligence.

Therefore, movant asks that the Court grant the following relief:

_____

or any other relief to which movant may be entitled.

_____

Signature of Attorney (if any)

I declare (or certify, verify, or state) under penalty of perjury that the foregoing is true and correct and that this Motion under 28 U.S.C. § 2255 was placed in the prison mailing system on _____ .

(month, date, year)

Executed (signed) on _____ (date)

_____

Signature of Movant

If the person signing is not movant, state relationship to movant and explain why movant is not signing this motion.

ABOUT THE AUTHOR

Kelly Patrick Riggs is a legal author and an advocate for criminal justice reform. He is also a freelance writer, a living kidney donor, and is the founder of a prison writers' program. He served as a Jailhouse Lawyer for over seven years- resulting in the early release of hundreds of federal prisoners.

Mr. Riggs is best known for writing his Post-Conviction Relief series, published by Freebird Publishers. He has also emerged in the mainstream market as a novelist. He is currently conducting research for his next book from inside a federal prison- his children patiently await his return.

FREEBIRD PUBLISHERS

Thanks for your interest in Freebird Publishers!

We value our customers and would love to hear from you! Reviews are an important part in bringing you quality publications. We love hearing from our readers-rather it's good or bad (though we strive for the best)!

If you could take the time to review/rate any publication you've purchased with Freebird Publishers we would appreciate it!

If your loved one uses Amazon, have them post your review on the books you've read. This will help us tremendously, in providing future publications that are even more useful to our readers and growing our business.

Amazon works off of a 5 star rating system. When having your loved one rate us be sure to give them your chosen star number as well as a written review. Though written reviews aren't required, we truly appreciate hearing from you.

Sample Review Received on Inmate Shopper

 poeticsunshine

★★★★★ **Truly a guide**

Reviewed in the United States on June 29, 2023

Verified Purchase

This book is a powerhouse of information. My son had to calm/ground himself to prioritize where to start.

Freebird Publishers
Post-Conviction Relief Series

Ineffective Assistance of Counsel: Overcoming the Inevitable

This book is endorsed by the former magistrate judge who wrote its foreword. And its material is used by thousands of legal professionals nationwide. It is also the first comprehensive layman's guide written to explain the duty of counsel, from initial appearance all the way through to direct appeal, and it is explained in plain English.

This ineffective assistance of counsel book is written from the perspective of someone who has fought his own personal fight. He litigated for himself, as his own "Jailhouse Lawyer" proceeding in pro se, all the way through the process. He finally won an order from the Eleventh Circuit Court of Appeals- remanding his case back to the district court. This book is a summary of the seven-year study he conducted as an established "Jailhouse Lawyer". His work is responsible for hundreds of sentence reductions granted, by the U.S. District and Appellate courts.

With this book the reader will be armed with the wisdom of hundreds of years of legal development. It contains the rules that the federal courts are supposed to follow in criminal cases and provides the laws and rules that govern the Post-Conviction procedures.

The book is made public for the purpose of fighting Mass-Incarceration one case at a time. Be a part of the movement by learning the laws and rules of the American criminal justice system- yours could be the next big win.

INEFFECTIVE ASSISTANCE OF COUNSEL
Overcoming the Inevitable

Kelly Patrick Riggs

Only $27.99
plus $7 S/h with tracking
SOFTCOVER, 8" x 10", 360+ pages

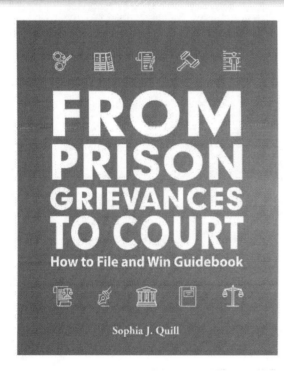

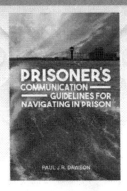

FREEBIRD PUBLISHERS

Pro Se Collection by Raymond E. Lumsden

This legal collection is the no-nonsense, easy to understand, and effective work by one of Freebird Publisher's Best Selling Legal Authors, Raymond E. Lumsden. Specifically written by an inmate with extensive legal training and education, for inmates seeking relief in the twisting and confusing legal system of America.

★ Easy to follow instructions;
★ Dozens of sample motions and pleadings;
★ Up to date case citings and writings;
★ **5** Star Amazon Ratings;
★ Numerous success stories of relief being obtained, etc.

A MUST HAVE COLLECTION FOR ANY PRO SE USER!!!

We accept all forms of payment!

★ COMING SOON ★
- *The Pro Se Guide to Parole*
- *"DNA": Proving Your Innocence*

PayPal
MasterCard VISA DISCOVER BANK
venmo @FreebirdPublishers   **Cash App** $FreebirdPublishers

For more info on each book, order our catalog!

CATALOG ONLY $5 - SHIPS BY FIRST CLASS MAIL
We have created four different versions of our new catalog A: Complete B:No Pen Pal Content C:No Sexy Photo Content D:No Pen Pal and Sexy Content. Available in full Color or B&W (please specify) please make sure you order the correct catalog based on your prison mail room regulations. We are not responsible for rejected or lost in the mail catalogs. Send SASE for payment by stamp options.
ADDITIONAL OPTION: add $5 for Shipping with Tracking

NO ORDER FORM NEEDED CLEARLY WRITE ON PAPER & SEND PAYMENT TO:
FREEBIRD PUBLSIHERS 221 Pearl St., Ste. 541, North Dighton, MA 02764
www.Freebird Publishers.com Diane@FreebirdPublishers.com Text/Phone: 774-406-8682

Made in the USA
Columbia, SC
10 July 2024